Paul Belloni Du Chaillu

A Journey To Ashango-Land

Paul Belloni Du Chaillu

A Journey To Ashango-Land

ISBN/EAN: 9783741127663

Manufactured in Europe, USA, Canada, Australia, Japa

Cover: Foto ©Andreas Hilbeck / pixelio.de

Manufactured and distributed by brebook publishing software
(www.brebook.com)

Paul Belloni Du Chaillu

A Journey To Ashango-Land

A JOURNEY

TO

ASHANGO-LAND

AND FURTHER PENETRATION INTO EQUATORIAL AFRICA.

By PAUL B. DU CHAILLU,

AUTHOR OF 'EXPLORATIONS IN EQUATORIAL AFRICA.'

Potamogale velox. *Mythomys of Gray.*

WITH MAP AND ILLUSTRATIONS.

LONDON:

JOHN MURRAY, ALBEMARLE STREET.

1867

BY THE SAME AUTHOR.

Tenth Thousand, with Map and Illustrations, 8vo.

EXPLORATIONS AND ADVENTURES IN EQUATORIAL AFRICA, 1856–9; with Accounts of the Manners and Customs of the People, and the Chase of the Gorilla, Crocodile, Leopard, Elephant, Hippopotamus, Nest-building Ape, Chimpanzee, and other Animals.

"M. Du Chaillu has fairly earned the distinction of being the most successful zoological traveller of the present time."—*Philadelphia Academy of Natural Sciences.*

"M. Du Chaillu has not only added greatly to the pre-existing acquaintance with the fauna of South Africa, but has by his clear and animated descriptions, convinced us that he has been as close an eye-witness of the habits of the gorilla and his associates as he has proved himself to be their successful assailant."—*Sir Roderick Murchison.*

"M. Du Chaillu's Collection is the most interesting illustration of the lower creation that has ever reached Europe, and has added considerably, and in very important respects, to our knowledge."—*Professor Owen.*

"M. Du Chaillu has struck into the very spine of Africa, and has lifted the veil of the torrid zone from its western rivers, swamps, and forests. He has found therein a variety of new types of living creatures, and others which were only partially and imperfectly known."—*The Times.*

PREFACE.

The position of an explorer of unknown countries in England is peculiar, and very difficult. If he returns home with nothing new or striking to relate he is voted a bore, and his book has no chance of being read; if he has some wonders to unfold, connected with Geography, the Natives, or Natural History, the fate of Abyssinian Bruce too often awaits him: his narrative being held up to scorn and ridicule, as a tissue of figments.

It was my lot, on the publication of my first volume of travels in Equatorial Africa, to meet with a reception of that sort from many persons in England and Germany. In fact I had visited a country previously unexplored by Europeans—the wooded region bordering the Equator, in the interior of Western Africa—and thus it was my good fortune to observe the habits of several remarkable species of animals found nowhere else. Hence my narrative describing unknown animals was condemned. The novelty of the subject was too striking for some of my critics; and not only were the accounts I gave of the animals and native tribes stigmatized as false, but my journey into the interior itself was pronounced a fiction.

Although hurt to the quick by these unfair and ungenerous criticisms, I cherished no malice towards my detractors, for I knew the time would come when the truth of all that was essential in the statements which had been disputed would be made clear; I was consoled, besides, by the support of many eminent men, who refused to believe that my narrative and observations were deliberate falsehoods. Making no pretensions to infallibility, any more than other travellers, I was ready to acknowledge any mistake that I might have fallen into, in the course of compiling my book from my rough notes. The only revenge I cherished was that of better preparing myself for another journey into the same region, providing myself with instruments and apparatus which I did not possess on my first exploration, and thus being enabled to vindicate my former accounts by facts not to be controverted.

It is necessary, however, to inform my English readers that most of the principal statements in my former book which were sneered at by my critics, have been already amply confirmed by other travellers in the same part of Africa, or by evidence which has reached England.

I may first mention the geographical part of my work. No portion of my book was more discredited than the journeys into the interior, and it will be recollected by many persons that the learned geographer, Dr. Barth, a man whose great attainments and services as an African traveller I esteemed most highly, published his disbelief in these interior explorations altogether. A map is in existence, showing the probable extent of my journeys according to Dr. Barth, and it marks my various excursions as not being in any case more than a few miles from the coast. My visit to Ashira-land, and discovery of the Ngouyai River, were thus considered pure inventions. Dr. Petermann, the well-known geographer, in constructing his map of my journeys, published in the 'Geographische Mittheilungen' in 1862, took into consideration the doubts of Dr. Barth and others, and though not so extreme a sceptic himself, believed it necessary to move all the positions I had given of places visited, much nearer the coast, so as to reduce greatly the length of my routes.

It must be recollected that I made no pretension to close accuracy in my own map. I had no instruments, and projected my route only by an estimate, necessarily rough, of the distances travelled. The circumstance of having been the first to explore the region was, besides, a disadvantage to me, for I had no previous map, however rough, to guide me; and in travelling with negroes day after day, under the shade of forests, often by circuitous routes, I was misled as to the length of the marches I made towards the east. I was therefore inclined to accept the corrections of Dr. Petermann, who had studied well the subject, and adopted his map in the French edition of my 'Equatorial Africa.' It was not long, however, before fresh evidence arrived, which proved that Dr. Petermann had gone too far in his corrections. In 1862 a French Government expedition, under Messrs. Serval and Griffon Du Bellay, explored the Ogobai river, and not only proved the general truth of my account of that great stream, but showed that the country of the Ashira, visited by me, had not been placed far wrong. Dr. Petermann, on the receipt of the French map, published in the 'Revue Maritime et Coloniale,' reconstructed his own map, and again moved my principal positions nearly to the same longitude in which I had originally placed them. The text accompanying the map ('Geographische Mittheilungen,' 1863, p. 446 et seq.), contains an explanation, couched in terms which I cannot but consider as highly flattering to me.

Similar confirmation of the accounts I gave of the cannibal Fans have been published by Captain Burton, the distinguished African traveller, and by others. The fact of the native harp possessing strings made of vegetable fibre—my statement of which roused a violent outburst of animosity against me—has been satisfactorily confirmed by the arrival of several such harps in England, and the examination of their strings. Other disputed facts I have discussed in the body of the present volume; such for instance as the structure and affinities of that curious animal the *Potamogale velox*, concerning which an eminent zoologist, Professor Allman, has published a memoir, in which he shows that my critic was wrong, and I was right. With regard to the accounts I gave of the existence of several distinct varieties, if not species, of chimpanzee, in the present absence amongst naturalists of a definite criterion of what constitutes a species, I must content myself by repeating that the negroes always distinguish these different kinds, and zoologists have published scientific descriptions of more than one species, considered distinct, from other parts of Western Tropical Africa.

Concerning the gorilla, the greatest of all the wonders of Western Equatorial Africa, I must refer my readers to the body of the present volume for the additional information I have been able to gather, during my last journey, concerning this formidable ape. It was not my object on the present journey to slaughter unnecessarily these animals, as the principal museums in civilized countries were already well supplied with skins and skeletons, but I devoted myself, when in the district inhabited by the gorilla, to the further study of its habits, and the effort to obtain the animal alive and send it to England; hoping that the observation of its actions in life would enable persons in England to judge of the accuracy of the description I gave of its disposition and habits; at least to some extent, as the actions of most animals differ much in confinement from what they are in the wild state. I had the good fortune again to see the gorilla several times in its native wilds, and obtained several living specimens through the natives. Some of the statements relating to its habits, such as its association only in very small bands, I have found reason, on further observation, to modify; but with regard to its beating its breast when enraged, and the savage nature of the young animals, as compared with young chimpanzees, fresh observations have confirmed my former statements. I succeeded in shipping one live gorilla for London, but, to my regret, it died during the passage.

The principal object I had in view in my last journey, was to make known with more accuracy than I had been able to do in my former one, the geographical features of the country, believing this to be the first duty of a traveller in exploring new regions. To enable me to do this I went through a course of instruction in the use of instruments, to enable me to fix positions by astronomical observations and compass bearings, and to ascertain the altitudes of places. I learnt also how to compute my observations, and test myself their correctness. It is for others to judge of the results of my endeavours in this important department of a traveller's work; I can only say that I laboured hard to make my work as accurate as possible, and although I was compelled, much to my sorrow, to abandon photography and meteorological observations, through the loss of my apparatus and instruments, I was fortunately able to continue astronomical observations nearly to the end of my route.

In camp at night, after my work with the sextant was done, I spent the still hours in noting down the observations, making three copies in as many different books, entrusted to different negro porters, so as to lessen the risk of loss of the whole. In our disastrous retreat from Ashango-land one only of these copies escaped being thrown into the bush, and this was the original one in my journal, where the entries were made from day to day; but it is not quite complete, as one volume out of five of my journal was lost with nearly all the rest of my outfit. On my return to England, the whole of these observations were submitted by the Council of the Royal Geographical Society to Mr. Edwin Dunkin, the Superintendent of the Altazimuth Department at Greenwich Observatory, who computed them, and furnished the results which are printed at the end of this volume, and which form the basis of the map of my routes now given to the public. I have thought it best to print also, without alteration, the original observations for latitude, longitude, and heights in the order in which they occur in my journal, and including a few that were incorrect. By this means cartographers will be able to see on how many separate observations a result for latitude or longitude is founded, and judge what degree of reliance may be placed upon them. I think it would be better if all travellers in new countries published in the same way, at the end of their narratives, their original observations, instead of the computed results solely, as is generally done. Adopted positions are generally the mean of the results of two or more observations, and unless the original data are published, geographers and future travellers are unable to judge to what degree the separate observations differed, or what reliance is to be placed on the observing powers of the earlier traveller.

In giving to the public a much-improved map of the field of my African explorations south of the Equator, I am glad to have been able to correct the errors of my former one. Most of the principal positions were there placed much too far to the east and north; and even those given by Dr. Petermann in his second map, already mentioned, prove to be a few miles too far in the same direction. Mr. Dunkin has stated, at a meeting of the Royal Geographical Society, that he considers the position of Máyolo as perfectly well determined by my observations: this may therefore be considered a fixed point by cartographers in reviewing my geographical work. But I must mention that two places, to the west of Máyolo, namely, Niembai and Obindji, have been placed on my map according to a calculation of distances travelled, as I had taken only one observation at each place. By the position of Máyolo, and that of the Samba Nagoshi Falls, visited by me in the last journey, I have been able to correct greatly the course given in my former map, and adopted by Dr. Petermann, of the great River Ngouyai. Unfortunately, my longitudes of these places render it difficult to connect my map with that given by Lieutenant Serval, of the Ogobai between Lake Anengue and the junction of the

Okanda. It would appear that M. Serval has extended the Ogobai much too far east. The second French expedition under Messrs. Labigot and Touchard, which carried the exploration of the Ogobai as far as the junction of the Ngouyai and Okanda, has probably made observations which would enable us to settle this doubtful part of the geography of the region; but I have been informed by my friend M. Malte-Brun, that the results of the expedition are not yet published.

Next to geography, I paid most attention, during my last expedition, to the study of the natives. My long experience amongst the tribes of the Fernand Vaz, and knowledge of the Commi and Ashira languages, gave me some facilities in investigating the political state of the tribes, and comprehending their customs, the meaning of their legends, and so forth. There is no part of Africa hitherto visited by travellers where the negro exists in a more primitive condition; for in the regions of the Niger and the Nile he has been much modified by the influences of Mahommedanism, in the interior of South Africa by the incursions of the Boers, and in Eastern Africa by contact with Arab traders. The descriptions I have given in the present volume ought therefore to be of some interest, as representing the negro as he is, undisturbed by the slave-dealing practices, the proselytism or the trading enterprise of other races.

The irreparable loss of the collection of photographs which I made myself on the earlier part of the journey, as related in the narrative, compelled me to have recourse to some rough pen-and-ink sketches in my journal, which have served as guides for the engravings in this volume, a few of which have been drawn under my own direction.

The pleasing duty now remains of thanking those gentlemen who have encouraged me by their sympathy and aid throughout my African explorations, or assisted me in the preparation of the present volume. To the Council of the Royal Geographical Society my first thanks are due, who have adhered to me in spite of adverse criticism from other quarters, and who were pleased to express their satisfaction with the geographical work I have performed, by presenting me with a testimonial at the last Annual Meeting of the Society. But I feel that I ought especially to thank the noble-hearted President of the Society, Sir Roderick Murchison, who sped me on my mission with hopeful words, and wrote frequently to me whilst I was in Africa, encouraging me when I stood sorely in need of it. To my honoured friend, Professor Owen, I am also indebted, for his steadfast support, and for the valuable essay on my collection of African skulls which enriches this volume. Other friends who have assisted me I have mentioned in the course of my narrative, amongst them Commander George, my kind instructor in the use of astronomical and surveying instruments, and M. Claudet, my master in photography. I ought also to express my thanks to Mr. Dunkin, for the great labour and care he has shown in personally computing my observations, and to Mr. J. R. Hind, the distinguished astronomer, for many acts of kindness. To Mr. Glaisher I am indebted for the benefit of his great experience in the testing of my aneroids. It was my good fortune, when preparing for my last expedition, to receive tokens of good-will from many persons, some of whom were personally unknown to me. I have mentioned in the body of the work the names of some of these friends; and I must not omit to add to the list those of Messrs. Howard and Co., who presented me with an ample stock of quinine, which proved of great service to me.

Lastly, I have to acknowledge my great obligation to my friend Mr. H. W. Bates, the well-known author of the 'Naturalist on the River Amazons,' who has given me his advice and assistance in the preparation of my journals for publication; and to another valued friend, Mr. George Bishop, under whose hospitable roof, on the banks of the Thames at Twickenham, the greater part of the present volume has been prepared for the press.

CONTENTS.

CHAPTER I.

THE VOYAGE.

Objects of the Journey—Preparatory studies—Difficulties in obtaining a passage—Departure from England—Arrival off the Coast—Miss the mouth of the Fernand Vaz—Return up the Coast—Excitement of the Natives—Old acquaintances—Changes in the bar of the River—Choice of a settlement near Djombouai's Village—Bonfires and rejoicings on the river banks—Commencement of disembarkation—Dangerous state of the shore—The boat upset in the breakers—Saved by the Negroes—Loss of instruments and stores .. .. Page 1

CHAPTER II.

THE FERNAND VAZ.

Outlines of the Coast region—The Ogobai—Prairies of the Fernand Vaz—The Commi nation—Distribution of the Clans—Chief Ranpano and his Spells—News of arrival sent to Quengueza, King of the Rembo—Arrival of Quengueza—His alarm at the great wealth I had brought him—A pet Chimpanzee, and his departure for England—Visit to Elindé and the mouth of the river—My illness—Tenderness of Ranpano—King Olenga-Yombi—Grand palaver of Commi chiefs—Permission granted me to ascend the river into the interior—Visit to my old place and to Rinkimongani's grave—Superstition of the natives—The *Bola Ivoga*—Ilabolo's fetich—Departure of the *Mentor* for England 13

CHAPTER III.

EXCURSIONS IN SEARCH OF THE GORILLA AND THE IPI.

Visit to King Olenga-Yombi—Storm on the Fernand Vaz—Land journey to Aniambié—First traces of Gorilla—Form of its tracks—Drunken orgies of the King—Magic island of Nengué Ncoma—Village of Nkongon Mbounba—Search of the Ipi, or great Pangolin—Its habits—

Village of Mburu Shara—Nkengo Nschiego variety of Chimpanzee—Bowers of the Chimpanzee—Group of Gorillas in a plantain-grove—Their mode of walking—Horrid form of monomania—Akondogo brings a live Gorilla—Return to the Fernand Vaz—Three more live Gorillas—Account of their capture—Modification of opinions concerning the Gorilla .. .. Page 37

CHAPTER IV.

START FOR THE INTERIOR.

Arrival of a fresh supply of Scientific Instruments—The first Steamer on the Fernand Vaz—Preliminary trip to Goumbi—Astonishment of the Natives at the fire-vessel—Despatch Collections to England—Live Gorilla embarked for London—His habits in confinement—Narrow escape of drowning when embarked—Preparations completed—Last look at the sea—Outfit—Body-guard of Commi men—Affecting parting scenes—I am deceived by Olenga-Yombi—The renowned doctor, Ouwe-ikou-e-niare—Arrival at Goumbi—Observations to fix latitude and altitude of Goumbi—Quengueza's Invocation of his Forefathers—Disobedient Wives—Excessive Drought—Obindji—Opposition of Bakalai—Arrival of Ashira Porters—Passage of the hills to Olenda 60

CHAPTER V.

VISIT TO THE SAMBA NAGOSHI FALLS.

King Olenda, his great age—Preparations for the journey to the Falls—We cross the Ovigui—Orangano Prairie—Ndgewho Mountains—Bakalai Village—A flock of Gorillas in the Forest—The Louvendji River—Dihaou and the Ashira Kambas—Navigate the Ngouyai River—The Avia Tribe—Village of Mandji—River Scenery—Nkoumou Nabouali Mountains—Nami Gemba—Village of Luba—The Spirit of the Falls—Village Deity—Arrival at Fougamou, the principal Fall—Legend of Fougamou—Night Encampment—Return to Dihaou—We step on a poisonous serpent—Forced March through flooded forest to Olenda 88

CHAPTER VI.

ASHIRA-LAND.

Grand Palaver to discuss the route into the interior—I am forbidden to pass through the Apingi country—Messengers sent to the Chief of Otando—Changes in Ashira Customs—Decrease of Population—The *Potamogale*

velox—Its habits—My former description of this Animal—Visit to Angouka—Immense Plantation of Plantain-trees—Quarrel with Mpoto, nephew of Olenda—Difficulties and anxieties—First rumours of the Small-pox .. .. Page 114

CHAPTER VII.

THE PLAGUE IN ASHIRA-LAND.

Breaking out of the Small-pox Epidemic—Noble Conduct of Quengueza—Departure of Quengueza's People—Illness of the Porters—My Commi Body-guard refuse to leave me—Departure of part of the baggage to Otando-land—Quengueza returns to Goumbi—Letters from Europe—Death of Mpoto—Death of King Olenda—His burial—Cemetery of the Ademba Chiefs—Wailing for the Dead—Death of Retonda—Arrival of Messengers from Máyolo—Distrust of the Natives—Trickery of Arangui—I am robbed by the Ashira People—Diminution of the Pestilence—Quengueza's message to the people of Olenda 124

CHAPTER VIII.

FROM OLENDA TO MÁYOLO.

Departure from Ashira-land—Passage of the Ovigui—Slave Village of King Olenda—A Slave Chief—Difficulties with the Porters—More Robberies—Illness of Macondai—Leave him behind—The Otando Range of Hills—Picturesque Cascade in the Forest—Cross the Louvendji—More difficulties with the Porters—Hunger in the Forest—Men sent to Máyolo for Relief—A Night in the Forest—Myth of Atungulu Shimba—Koola Nut-trees—Search for Food—Meet with a Gorilla—A Hungry Night—Unselfish act of the Ashira—Help arrives from Máyolo—Mpegui Nuts—Arrival in Otando-land 139

CHAPTER IX.

MÁYOLO.

Arrival at Máyolo—Reception by the Chief—Discovery of more Losses—I accuse the Ashira—Their Flight—Seizure of a Hostage—Gathering of the Head men of Otando—Máyolo falls ill—I am attacked by Fever—Great Heat and Thunderstorm—Arrival of Macondai and Igalo—Their Ill-treatment by the Ashira—Loss of Photographic Camera and Chemicals—Surgical Practice of the Otando—A Female Doctor—Matrimonial Squabbles—Máyolo's health improves—Witchcraft Ordeal

—My Speech to the People—Speech of Máyolo—Curiosity of the Otando—A Female Duel—The Bashikouay Ants—A Precocious Thief—Máyolo again falls ill—Good news from the Apono country—Astonishment of the Natives at the Musical-box and Magnets—Climate of Máyolo—Deposit of Dew—The Molimwas—Recovery of Macondai—The Alumbi Fetich—Departure from Máyolo .. .. .. Page 156

CHAPTER X.

THE OTANDO AND APONO REGION.

Geographical Position of Máyolo—Splendour of the Constellations as seen from the Equatorial Regions—The Zodiacal Light—Twinkling of the Stars—Meteoric Showers—The Otando and Apono Plains, or Prairies—The Otando People a branch of the Ashira Nation—Their Customs—Filing the Teeth—Tattooing—Native Dogs 203

CHAPTER XI.

ANTS.

The White Ants of the Prairies—The Mushroom-hived Termes—Interior of their Hives—Three classes in each Community: Soldiers, Workers, and Chiefs—Their mode of building—The Tree Ants—Curious structure of their Hives—Their process of constructing them—The Bark Ants—Curious tunnels formed by them—The Forest Ants—Large size of their Shelters or Hives—The stinging Black Ant 218

CHAPTER XII.

MÁYOLO TO APONO-LAND.

Leave Máyolo—Cross the Nomba Obana Hill—River Dooya—Arrival at Mouendi—Timidity of the Inhabitants—The Chief Nchiengain—Arrival of Ashangi Men—Loss and Recovery of a Thermometer—Nocturnal Reflections—African Story of the Sun and Moon—Smelling the White Man's Presents—Passage of the Ngouyai—Hippopotami and Crocodiles; reasons of their scarcity and abundance—Arrival at Dilolo—Opposition of the Inhabitants to our entering the Village—Pluck of my Commi Boys—Arrival at Mokaba—My system of a Medicine Parade for my Men 230

CHAPTER XIII.

THE MARCH THROUGH APONO-LAND.

Mokaba—Curiosity of the People—Renewed Illness of Máyolo—His return to Otando—Nchiengain's Speech—The Apono agree to take me to the Ishogo country—Description of the Apono Tribe—Their sprightly character—Arts—Weapons—Population—Description of Mokaba—Palm wine—Drunkenness—Ocuya Performances—Leave Mokaba—River Dougounda—Arrival at Igoumbié—Invitation from the elders of the village to remain there—Manners of the Ishogos—Description of Igoumbié—The Ishogo huts—Arrival at Yengué, in Ishogo-land Page 250

CHAPTER XIV.

JOURNEY THROUGH ISHOGO-LAND.

Village of the Obongos or Dwarf Negroes—Their Dwellings—Absence of the Inhabitants—The Elders and People of Yengué—Arrival of the Chief of Yengué—War Dance of the Aponos—Ceremony of the Mpazo—An uproarious Night—Good conduct of the Apono Porters—The River Ogoulou—Geographical Position and Altitude of Yengué—Passage of the Ogoulou—March to the Plateau of Mokenga—Eastern Limits of Ishogo-land—Quembila, King of Mokenga—Palavers—Contention between Chiefs for the possession of the "Ibamba"—Panic in Mokenga—Re-adjustment of Baggage—Ishogo Porters 269

CHAPTER XV.

FROM ISHOGO TO ASHANGO-LAND.

The Ishogos—Their Modes of dressing the Hair—Ishogo Villages—Picturesque Scenery—Granitic Boulders—Grooved Rocks—Leave Mokenga—Cross the Dongon—Continued Ascent—Mount Migoma—The River Odiganga—Boundaries of Ishogo and Ashango-lands—Arrival at Magonga—Plateau of Madombo—Mutiny of Ishogo Porters—An unfriendly Village—Elevated Country—Arrival and friendly Reception at Niembouai—The King's Wives—Prejudices of the Commi Men—Hear of a large River towards the East—The Ashangui Tribe—The Obongos 285

CHAPTER XVI.

ASHANGO-LAND.

Cloudy Skies of Ashango-land—Grand Palaver—Ishogo Porters dismissed—The Village Idol—Religious Rites—Visit to an Obongo Village—Abodes and Habits of the Dwarf Race—Measurements of their Height—River Ouano—Singular Ferry—Mount Mogiama—Its Altitude—Village of Mongon, its Latitude, Longitude, and Height above the Sea-level—Village of Niembouai Olomba—Its picturesque Site—Bashikouay Ants—Ascend Mount Birogou Bouanga—Its Altitude—More Troubles—Robbed by the Ashango Porters—Summary Measures—Resume our March—Arrive at Mobana—Departure of a Bride—Arrival at Mouaou Kombo .. .. Page 311

CHAPTER XVII.

FATAL DISASTERS AT MOUAOU KOMBO.

Unpromising state of affairs on arriving at Mouaou Kombo—Rakombo is threatened—Obstacles raised by the Villagers—Fair promises of the Chief—A Secret Meeting of the Villagers—Demands of the People—We leave the Village—Night Encampment in the Forest—Threats and Promises from the next Village—Invited to return to Mouaou—Reconciliation—Arrival of a hostile Deputation from the next Village—A Man accidentally Shot 344

CHAPTER XVIII.

RETREAT FROM ASHANGO-LAND.

A Palaver proposed to settle the Death of the Man—A Woman killed—The War Cry!—Retreat commenced—Igala and myself wounded with Poisoned Arrows—Narrow Escape of Macondai and Rebouka—We are closely pursued by the Natives—Collections and Note-books thrown into the Bush—We make a Stand—Two Men Shot—Pursuit continued—I am wounded a second time—Igala shoots the Bowman—We make another Stand—Cross the Bembo—Pass Mobana—Still pursued—Make a final Stand—The Pursuers driven off at last—A Halt—The Party all collected together—Sleep in the Forest—Night-March through Niembouai—Friendly conduct of the Head Chief—We are well received at a Plantation—Arrival of Magonga—We continue the March to Ishogo-land 354

CHAPTER XIX.

JOURNEY TO THE COAST.

Arrival at Mongon—Magouga recounts the Story of our Adventures to the Villagers—Reach Niembouai—Mistrust of the People—Restitution of Stolen Property—Magouga consents to guide us to Mokenga—Reach the last of the Ashango Villages—Passage into Ishogo-land, and out of danger of Pursuit—Magouga's Diplomacy—Arrival at Mokenga—Friendly Reception—Magouga delivers us safely into the hands of the Villagers—My Men exaggerate the Deeds of Valour they had performed—Arrival at Yengué—Project of descending the Ogoulou in a Canoe—Lose our Way—Distant View of the Apono Prairie—Igoumbié—Reach Mokaba—The Ngouyai—March to Nchiengain's—Cross the River—Nchiengain's Village—Reception at Máyolo—Operation of the African Law of Inheritance—March to Ashira-land—Alarm of the Ashira People—Avoid Olenda—Sojourn at Angouka's—Cross the Ofoubou—Quengueza's Encampment—Sorrows of the old King—Devastations of the Plague at Goumbi—Quengueza wants to go to the White Man's Country—Descend the River—Arrival at "Plateau"—Gratitude of the Commi People—Departure for England .. .. Page 371

CHAPTER XX.

PHYSICAL GEOGRAPHY AND CLIMATE.

Great Forest of Equatorial Africa—Scanty Population—Scarcity or absence of large African Animals—Hilly Ranges—River Systems—The Ogobai—French exploring expeditions—Amount of rain—Seasons—Rainy climate of Central Equatorial Africa—Temperature—Heat of the sun's rays—Coolness of the forest shades 400

CHAPTER XXI.

ETHNOLOGY.

Isolation of the tribes in the interior of Western Equatorial Africa—Scantiness of the Population—Divisions of tribes and clans—Patriarchal form of Government—Comparison of Customs between Western Equatorial tribes and Eastern—Laws of Inheritance—Cannibalism—Migrations always towards the West—Decrease of Population—Its Causes—The African race doomed to extinction 424

APPENDIX I.

APPENDIX II.

APPENDIX III.

LIST OF ILLUSTRATIONS.

JOURNEY IN ASHANGO-LAND.

CHAPTER I.

THE VOYAGE.

Objects of the Journey—Preparatory studies—Difficulties in obtaining a passage—Departure from England—Arrival off the Coast—Miss the mouth of the Fernand Vaz—Return up the Coast—Excitement of the Natives—Old acquaintances—Changes in the bar of the River—Choice of a settlement near Djombouai's Village—Bonfires and rejoicings on the river banks—Commencement of disembarkation—Dangerous state of the shore—The boat upset in the breakers—Saved by the Negroes—Loss of instruments and stores.

Early in 1863, after three years' recreation in the civilized countries of Europe and North America, I began to entertain the idea of undertaking a new journey into Western Equatorial Africa. My main object in this journey was to attempt to penetrate still further into the interior than I had done hitherto, taking the route of the Fernand Vaz River, the starting point of my principal expedition in the former journey. I had also a strong desire to fix with scientific accuracy the geographical positions of the places I had already discovered, and to vindicate by fresh observations, and the acquisition of further specimens, the truth of the remarks I had published on the ethnology and natural history of the country. Beyond this, there was the vague hope of being able to reach, in the far interior, some unknown western tributary of the Nile, and to descend by it to the great river, and thence to the Mediterranean.

To qualify myself for such a task, I went through a course of instruction* in the use of instruments, to enable me to project my route by dead-reckoning and astronomical observations, and supplied myself with a complete outfit for this purpose, as well as for taking the altitudes of places above the sea-level. I also learnt practical photography,† and laid in a store of materials necessary to make 2,000 pictures, having felt the importance of obtaining faithful representations of the scenery, natives, and animals of these remote countries. In natural history I did not expect to find many novelties near the coast, at least in the larger animals, but I took pains to learn what was most likely to be interesting to zoologists, and hoped to be able to make many discoveries in the far interior. Besides materials for preserving large animals, I provided myself with a stock of boxes, glass tubes, &c., in order to collect insects, worms, and the like classes of animals, which I had neglected in my former journey. I also took fifty pounds of arsenic for the preservation of stuffed specimens. My hope of traversing the whole of Equatorial Africa to the head of the Nile, although acting as a strong incitement to me, was kept secret, except from a few

* Under Staff-Commander C. George, Map Curator, Royal Geographical Society; to whom I am, besides, much indebted for the trouble he took in selecting instruments for me, and for his care in testing them.

† Under M. Claudet, and his son M. Henri Claudet.

intimate friends. I was resolved, however, that if the achievement of this splendid feat should be denied me, I would spare no effort in advancing as far towards the east as was practicable, and in obtaining accurate information regarding those portions of the country which I might be able to explore.

There is no direct trade between England—or, indeed, between any part of Europe or America—and the Fernand Vaz, and this gave rise to the chief difficulty I had to encounter at the outset. How was I to get there? My outfit was too large to think of transhipping it from one port to another. I must here remind my readers that the mouth of the Fernand Vaz lies about 110 miles to the south of the Gaboon, which is the principal centre of trade in Western Equatorial Africa. What little trade there is is carried on by native boats, which pass from the Gaboon to the negro villages on the banks of the Fernand Vaz, by way of the narrow channels of the delta of the Ogobai River, thus avoiding the detour round Cape Lopez. The negro tribes of the Fernand Vaz have never had much communication with the white man; there is no permanent trading settlement there, although sometimes the captain of a ship may come with his vessel and put up a factory for a short time; indeed, I must add that I was the first to ascend the river and make known its geography, its inhabitants, and its productions. I chose this river as the starting-point of my new exploration because I was already well known to the inhabitants of its banks, through my long previous residence amongst them; they loved me, and my life was safe in their hands, and having acquired some influence over them, I could depend upon obtaining an escort to enable me to advance into the interior. I do not know any other point of the West African coast, between the Congo and the Niger, where I, or indeed any white man, could have any chance of penetrating more than a short distance into the interior. After making some inquiries, I found my best course would be to freight a vessel specially to take me to the Fernand Vaz. I therefore engaged with the owners of the schooner *Mentor*, Captain Vardon, a little vessel of less than 100 tons measurement, and all preparations being complete, embarked on board of her at Gravesend on the 6th of August, 1863.

Although I looked forward with great pleasure to my new journey of exploration, I left old England with a heavy heart. The land where I had received so much kindness and sympathy, so much genuine hospitality, and where I had made so many true friends, had become to me a second home. I could not repress the feeling of sadness which came over me, and the pang I felt at parting was the greater from the thought that I might never return from an undertaking beset with such various perils.

We were detained with a crowd of other vessels off Deal, for several days, by a strong wind from the south-west. I was much struck, part of the time, by the strong contrast between the weather we had at sea and that which prevailed on shore. With us the wind was blowing strong and the sea rough, whilst on land the sun was shining beautifully on the golden corn-fields, and the reapers were at work gathering in the bountiful harvest. My ardent longing to be on shore with them and have a last look at the happy land of England was one day gratified, for Mr. Dombrain, the ship-missionary of Deal, kindly took the captain and myself to the town, and we had a charming drive through the country lanes. I never enjoyed the country so much. Every face we met seemed so pleasant, and Nature seemed so tranquil; I felt that England was more than ever dear to me.

I will not weary my readers by a description of our voyage to the West Coast. As far as the weather and the captain were concerned, it was a pleasant one. We arrived at Accra, a British settlement, east of Sierra Leone, in the Gulf of Guinea, on the 20th of September. According to my agreement with the owners of the vessel, the *Mentor* ought to have sailed direct from this place to the Fernand Vaz, but I now made the discovery that she was ordered to call at Lagos. At this unhealthy spot I declined the invitation to go ashore. We left it on the 2nd of October, and after a few days pleasant sailing came in sight of the Commi Coast on the 8th of the same month.

The part of the African coast in the neighbourhood of the mouth of the Fernand Vaz has a monotonous aspect as viewed from the sea. A long line of country, elevated only a few feet above the sea-level, stretches away towards the south, diversified here and there by groups of trees, and enlivened only at intervals of a few miles by a cluster of palm-clad huts of the natives, amongst which is always conspicuous the big house which the villagers construct for the "factory" that they are always expecting to be established at their village. The mouth of the river itself is very difficult to discover. In my former journey it was recognisable only by the white surf which foamed over its bar, and by the flocks of fish-eating birds hovering in the air above it. The bar, however, seemed now to have shifted, for we passed by it without perceiving it.

We sailed along the coast the same evening, and, after anchoring for the night, still continued the same course, under light sail, the next morning, looking out for some native canoe to come to us, and tell us our whereabouts. At length a canoe put off from the shore and came alongside, and we then discovered that we were several miles to the south of the Fernand Vaz. The head man of the boat recognised me, and thinking at first that I had come to establish a trading post at his village, could not contain his delight. He knew a few words of English, and shouted out: "Put down the anchor; plenty ivory; load the ship in a fortnight!" It was a wretched take-down for the poor fellow to learn that I intended to establish my head-quarters in a rival village on the banks of the river. He wanted to make me believe that Ranpano, the chief of my former place, was dead, and that his village was scattered—this was the old African trick, which I knew too well to be deceived by. The fellow, in his spite and disappointment, on leaving us went out of his way to prevent other canoes from coming to us, and so we were unable to get a pilot.

As we returned up the coast, we saw the natives running about from house to house along the beach in great excitement. In every village the big flag kept by the chiefs for this purpose was hoisted on the top of a long pole to attract the white man ashore to trade, and at night a line of bonfires shone along the coast.

At length, on the morning of the 10th, I recognised the country near the mouth of the river. We shortened sail, and two canoes soon put off and made for the vessel. In the first, as it approached, I recognised my old friend Adjouatonga, a chief of one of the villages belonging to the clan Adjiena, which occupies the mouth of the river. He climbed up the vessel's side, and after shaking hands with the captain, advanced towards me to do the same. On my turning round to him, he stepped back in astonishment, and exclaimed—"Are you Chaillie, or are you his spirit? Have you come from the dead? Tell me quick, for I don't know whether I am to believe my own eyes; perhaps I am getting a kendé (fool)." The good fellow hugged me in a transport of joy, but so tightly and so long that I wished his friendship had been a little less enthusiastic, especially as his skin was dripping with a strong mixture of oil and perspiration. In the second canoe came another old friend, Sholomba, nephew of the chief, Ranpano, of my own village of former days. In short, I was surrounded by a crowd of old acquaintances, and had to listen to a confused account of the chief events that had happened since my departure, related by half-a-dozen eager informants.

The next subject to be considered was how we were to get ashore. Sholomba assured me that the mouth of the Fernand Vaz had changed much for the worse since I had left, and that it would be less dangerous to run a canoe through the surf to the beach than to attempt an entry into the mouth of the river. It was now the beginning of the rainy season, when the winds are less rough than in the dry season, but the surf, under the influence of the steady south-west winds, was still frightful. However, the first landing, in Adjouatonga's boat, which was much steadier than the rest, was made with safety. The frail canoe was skilfully directed towards a promising roller at the right moment, and we were carried on its back with lightening speed to the beach, where we were snatched up by the natives assembled to meet us. After this hazardous landing, I was hurried along amidst a crowd of several hundred savages, all dancing and shouting with frantic joy, across the sandy tongue of land to the banks of the Fernand Vaz, where canoes were ready to take us up the river to the village of Ranpano.

Although I had been absent only four years—years so full of events to me!—time had wrought great changes in the scene of my former adventures. The mouth of the river had altered so much that I scarcely knew it again. The long, sandy, reed-covered spit, which formerly projected three miles from the southern point of the river's mouth, had disappeared, and the sea had washed up the sand so much on the northern side that the village of Elindé, whose chief, Sangala, had given me so much trouble in former times, had become untenantable, and the people had removed. Many little islands had also been submerged or washed away, and I no longer saw those flocks of sea birds which formerly frequented the locality. Paddling up the stream we came to my old settlement, which I had called Washington; it was deserted and in ruins, a few loose bamboos and rotting poles alone remained to show me where it stood. The house of my honest old friend, Rinkimongani, was there, looking like a wreck, for this excellent fellow had gone to his rest and his family was scattered.

After a brief survey of the altered state of the country, I resolved to fix my new quarters at a little village near the residence of Djombouai, two miles above my last place: the situation was a good one, and, besides, it would conciliate the prejudices of the Commi, who opposed my settlement at the old spot on account of the suspicion of witchcraft which attached to it, and which had increased since the death of Rinkimongani. Meantime, the news spread that I had arrived in the country, and for several days people came trooping in by land and water to see their old friend, and the stores of good things he had brought with him. Ranpano was away from home, on the Ogobai River, but messengers were sent to him to hasten his return. I soon felt that I had returned to wild life. At night bonfires were lit, and the crowd of half-dressed and rude, but good-humoured, savages danced around them, and dinned my ears with their monotonous drumming and songs.

It was now necessary to return on board the schooner, and arrange the mode of disembarkation of my extensive outfit and stock of goods. As the mouth of the river had become so unsafe, from the breaking up of the sandy spit, and as no one knew the direction of the deep channels—for the whole breadth of the mouth of the river was one uninterrupted line of breakers—we resolved to land everything on the beach through the surf. But on some days the breakers were so bad, continuing all day long without a single lull, that it was impossible to do anything.

On the 15th of October we made a commencement. Three native canoes were brought alongside, and I began by loading them with my most valuable articles. In one of them I placed all my scientific instruments, sextants, chronometers, prismatic compasses, barometers, &c., besides five large Geneva musical boxes (intended as presents to the native chiefs), and five barrels of salt meat, a case containing 1,500 rifle bullets, a box of medicines, and many other things. Captain Vardon and myself embarked in this boat on account of the value of its cargo, and away we went amidst the cheers of the dusky paddlers.

The two other canoes took the surf first. The rollers were terrific, and the boats seemed buried in the seething spray without a chance of coming out of it safely, but they reached the shore without upsetting. The captain himself had misgivings as to the result of our venture. I advised him to put on his life-belt, but in the excitement of the moment he neglected the precaution. We now came near the ranges of breakers, and our only chance of safety was to ride on the back of one of those smoother rollers which from time to time swelled up and arched gently over, but with headlong speed, towards the shore. We had not, however, the good fortune to be borne by it in safety; our boatmen, in their great anxiety to avoid a mishap, were not venturesome enough, they waited a few moments too long. Instead of carrying us onward, the huge wave broke over our canoe, upsetting it and hurling us to a distance away from it. Heavy, short breakers now succeeded each other with awful rapidity; the sea all around became one mass of foaming billows; and in a few moments we were almost exhausted with the buffetings we received. The negroes who had formed the crew of the canoe, most of whom were my own "boys," companions of my former expedition, swam towards me, and with great exertions kept me from sinking. They assisted me to divest myself of my shoes and my coat, the pockets of which were filled with small weighty articles, and as I became weaker, through the effects of drinking so much salt water, they swam under me and buoyed me up with their own bodies. I caught a glimpse of poor Captain Vardon at a distance from me, struggling with the waves; the men had devoted all their attentions to me, so I shouted to some of them to go and help him. Meantime, several unsuccessful attempts were made by the negroes ashore to launch canoes to the rescue, but they were all swamped one after the other. Nothing could be done until the tumult of the waves subsided; for after the breakers have spent their fury there is usually a lull, and it is during these lulls, which are, however, very uncertain and limited in their duration, that the only chances occur of reaching this difficult shore. When the sea is rough, in the height of the dry season, these lulls do not occur for days together. A favourable moment at length arrived; a canoe reached us, and we were delivered from our perilous situation.

This was the fifth time during my experience of this coast that I had been upset in the breakers, and saved by the exertions of these faithful negroes. After landing, the magnitude of the loss which I had sustained presented itself with full force to my mind. All my astronomical instruments were spoilt by the salt water, and with them the power of carrying out the principal object of my journey. There was no help for it but to submit to a weary delay, whilst a second set was sent for from England.

As soon as I reached the shore, I found myself surrounded by the blacks; the women being conspicuous by their sympathies. A general shout arose —"Who are the people who are jealous of us, desiring the death of our white man?"

In this country all misfortunes are attributed to some evil influence, bewitching the sufferer; and they referred to the jealousy of some neighbouring village, the catastrophe from which I had so narrowly escaped.

CHAPTER II.

THE FERNAND VAZ.

Outlines of the Coast region—The Ogobai—Prairies of the Fernand Vaz—The Commi nation—Distribution of the Clans—Chief Ranpano and his Spells—News of arrival sent to Quengueza, King of the Rembo—Arrival of Quengueza—His alarm at the great wealth I had brought him—A pet Chimpanzee, and his departure for England—Visit to Elindé and the mouth of the river—My illness—Tenderness of Ranpano—King Olenga-Yombi—Grand palaver of Commi chiefs—Permission granted me to ascend the river into the interior—Visit to my old place and to Ilinkimongani's grave—Superstition of the natives—The *Bola Ivoga*—Rabolo's fetich—Departure of the *Mentor* for England.

In my former work on Equatorial Africa, I gave my readers a short account of the neighbourhood of the Fernand Vaz and of the natives who inhabit this part of the West African coast. The country on both sides the river, which flows for some forty miles nearly parallel to the sea-shore, is for the most part level and of little elevation. Between the river and the sea the plain is sandy, and covered with a grassy and shrubby vegetation, with here and there a cluster of trees, and often a fringe of palm-trees by the river side. Travelling southward from the mouth of the river the "islands" of trees become larger, and unite to form a considerable forest, which contains many timber-trees of great size and beauty. This is towards Cape St. Catherine, where, between the river and the sea, lies the inhospitable jungle which forms the principal home of the gorilla, of which I shall have more to say presently.

Towards the north stretches the delta of the great Ogobai River, a much larger stream than the Fernand Vaz, with its network of channels densely fringed with mangrove-trees. The country on the right bank of the Fernand Vaz is thickly wooded, and consists principally of mangrove swamps. Thus, on one side of the broad sluggish stream, lies a tract of dense woodland, and, on the other, an expanse of open prairie. The Ogobai is the only West African river at present known, between the Niger and the Congo, which rises far in the interior and breaks through the great coast range of mountains. One of the channels from the Ogobai combines with the Fernand Vaz a few miles from its mouth. About forty miles up stream the bed of the Fernand Vaz becomes contracted; higher up, wooded hills hem it in on both sides—the portals of the mountainous and picturesque African interior, and the river changes its name to Rembo, meaning *the* River *par excellence.*

The prairies of the Fernand Vaz are not unhealthy. During the dry season, from June to September, a steady, strong, and cool sea-breeze blows over the land, without, however, raising dunes or sandy hillocks of the beautiful white sand which forms the soil of the prairie. All the pools and marshes dry up; and, before the continued dryness has parched up the herbage, the aspect is that of an extensive English park, especially when in the cool hours of early morning a herd of wild cattle (Bos brachyceros) or a troop of antelopes, grazing by a wood-side in the distance, remind one, for the moment, of the cattle and deer of more cultivated scenes. But as the dry season continues, the grass dries up or becomes burnt, and the country then wears a more desolate aspect: the sky is generally overcast. Innumerable flocks of marabouts come to lay their eggs on the prairies; the prodigious number of these birds and their sudden appearance are quite astounding. In the wet season the numerous pools and marshy places afford another attraction, for they teem with life; and I used to notice, especially, the quantity of eel-like fishes which appeared in a mysterious manner almost as soon as the pools began to form, they having no doubt buried themselves in the mud and passed the dry season in a dormant state. Flocks of sand-pipers trot along the sandy margins of the rivers and pools, and numbers of gulls, terns, shear-waters, and pelicans enliven the scene with their movements and their cries. The plain along the banks of the river is dotted with villages of the great Commi tribe of negroes, whose plantations, however, are on the opposite wooded side of the Fernand Vaz, and also along the banks of the Npoulounay channel, as the sandy soil of the plain is unfitted for bananas, sugar-cane, and other cultivated plants and trees. Each village is under the patriarchal government of its hereditary chief, and all are nominally subject to the king of the tribe residing at Aniambié, formerly a large village on the sea-shore near Cape St. Catherine, but now reduced to a few dilapidated huts. The king lives on his plantation.

The clan of the Commi to which I was attached (Abogo) had several villages occupying the banks of the river for a few miles near its mouth. Its present chief—at least the chief of the river-side villagers—was my old friend Ranpano, a slow, phlegmatic negro, with a pleasant expression of countenance and good honest intentions. The quality in Ranpano for which he was most lauded by the negroes was his habit of going to sleep when he was drunk, instead of quarrelling. His authority in the clan was less, however, than that of Olenga-Yombi, the superior chief or king of the Commi tribe, which inhabits the Eliva, or Fernand Vaz district.

The distribution of the population comprised in a clan of these African tribes presents some curious features; for instance, the people under the immediate authority of Olenga-Yombi live near the sea-coast, about thirty miles to the south of the villages of Ranpano; thus they are separated, by numerous villages belonging to other clans, from the rest of their clan-relations. The head chiefship had belonged to the family of Olenga-Yombi for many generations, and it shows the respect these primitive negroes entertain for hereditary rank that they continue to acknowledge the sovereignty of the present representative of the title, although the villages under his immediate authority have declined greatly in population and influence.

If I could succeed in preserving the friendship of these two men and that of Quengueza, the powerful chief of Goumbi, eighty miles further up the river, my objects in coming to the country would most likely be attained, and I should not only meet with no political obstacle, but have all the assistance the coast tribes could give me to enable me to penetrate into the interior. I had brought goods for the trade-loving Commi, to exchange with them for the produce of their country, in order to secure their good will. The people of the West Coast have no consideration for any one but a trader, and even amongst themselves a man is more respected for his trading goods than for the territory or land that he possesses. My first object, therefore, was to settle myself for a few weeks amongst them, and cultivate the friendship of the people and their chiefs. I sent Sholomba up the river to apprise Quengueza of my arrival, and meantime went to pay my court to Ranpano, who had just arrived from the Ogolai.

I knew that Ranpano had arrived during my absence on board the schooner, and I felt vexed that he was not amongst the number of those who waited for me on the beach when the accident occurred. I now learnt that he was in a hut at no great distance. Thither I went, and found the fat, grey-headed old fellow sitting motionless, with grave countenance, over a bundle of fetiches or mondahs, muttering his spells. I drew myself up, trying to look haughty, and reproached him for his indifference to the fate of his old friend, knowing, as he did, the dangers of passing the surf at this season. To all this he remained immoveable as a stone, and replied, pointing to his fetiches, "My white man die in the water? never, whilst I am alive! How could it be?" and, looking round at his people, he repeated, "How could it be?"

I let the old man welcome me in his own way. Even his gloomy superstition could not in the end destroy the natural benevolence of his disposition.

One night shortly after my arrival, after I had retired to bed in the hut lent to me by the negroes, I heard the sound of the native bugle on the river, and the songs of a multitude of paddlers. It was King Quengueza, who had arrived for the purpose of welcoming me back to his country. I got up at once, and found at the door the venerable chief; who received me with open arms, declaring that he could not go to sleep until he had embraced me, and had assured me of his enduring affection. When I despatched Sholomba with a canoe to fetch him, to prevent any doubt on his part, and having nothing else to send him at the time, I sent him a bottle of brandy, the sight of which convinced him at once that it was I and no other. I was truly glad to see this noble old chief, the King of the Rembo, or Upper River. He was a man of great and wide influence, not only on account of his hereditary rank, but also from the energy and dignity of his character. He was fond of Europeans, but I could never induce him to wear in public the fine European clothes I gave him; he had a firm idea that he should die if he put on any dress, as he was still in mourning for his brother, who had died several years before I made the old chief's acquaintance. I felt and still feel the warmest friendship towards this stern, hard-featured old man; and, in recalling his many good qualities, cannot bring myself to think of him as an untutored savage.

Next day Quengueza brought me as a present a very fine goat, the largest I had ever seen in Africa. Goats are regal presents in this part of the continent, and Quengueza had reared the one he brought with the express intention of giving it to me, if I should fulfil my promise of returning from the white man's country. Our formal meeting next day was an important one; and I chose the opportunity to renew our pact of friendship.

After the first cordial greetings were over, I told him, in a set speech, how I had been received in America and Europe, and how his name, and the great service he had rendered me in enabling me to penetrate into the far interior, had become widely known among the nations of white men. I also told him, in a low whisper, that I had brought from one of his well-wishers in England a present of a chest-full of fine things.* The old man rose in his turn, and made an eloquent reply. With the figurative politeness of a negro chief, he assured me that his town, his forests, his slaves, and his wives were mine (he was quite sincere with regard to the last), that henceforth he should have no will of his own, but that I might do whatever I chose, that "my belly should be full every day," meaning that I should never be hungry, and, what was of more importance, he would assist me with all his influence, and even accompany me, in my proposed journey towards the interior, quietly adding, in a tone not to be heard

* My friend, Mr. John Murray, of Albemarle Street, gave me £50 for the purpose of purchasing suitable presents for Quengueza and other chiefs.

by the bystanders, "If you love me, do not say a word to any one that you have brought me any presents."

During the interview I showed Quengueza, amongst other things, a copy of my book 'Adventures in Equatorial Africa,' and pointed out to him the plate which represents him and myself seated in the palaver house of Goumbi. It delighted him amazingly: he shouted, "Am I then known so well in the white man's country that they make my picture?" Then turning with an air of ineffable contempt to the crowd around us, and pointing to the engraving, he said, "Pigs, look here! what do *you* know about the white man? Quengueza is the white man's friend; what would you be without me?" He asked me who made the book. I told him it was the same good friend who had sent him such beautiful presents. He did not forget this; and the next day he put into my hands a handsome leopard's skin, with the request that I would send it to the ntangani (white man) who had put him in a book and sent him so many things to do him good.

Conforming to his wish for strict secresy regarding the presents, I appointed a day on which to receive him alone. He chose an hour in the afternoon when most of his people were asleep, enjoying the usual siesta. He came accompanied by a select party of relatives and wives, for kings in these parts must always be accompanied by some retinue or escort. But his Majesty was determined not to let his people see what I was going to give him. Touching me gently with his elbow, he told me, in a whisper, to send them all away, and not to let any of them come in. Entering my hut alone, he closed the door, and, sitting down, told me that he was ready to see the presents I had brought him.

The first thing that I displayed before his admiring eyes was the coat of a London beadle, made expressly to fit his tall figure, and, to please his taste, it was of the most glaring colours, blue, with yellow fringe, lined with red. There was also a splendid plush waistcoat. As his Majesty does not wear trowsers those articles did not form part of the suit, any more than did a shirt.

"Let us try them on," said the king, in a whisper; but, before doing so, he went to the door to make sure that no one was peeping in. Having put on the robes, and taking in his hand the beadle's staff, which I had not omitted to bring also, he asked for a looking-glass, in which he admired himself vastly; whilst I completed the costume by placing on his head my opera-hat, which, to his utter astonishment, I had caused to spring up from its flattened state. After surveying himself for some time in the glass, with evident satisfaction, he drew himself up to his full height, and strutted up and down the room, "as happy as a king." Having indulged his vanity for a few minutes, he replaced in the chest the various articles of this imperial costume, and proceeded to inspect the other presents.

I had myself brought a large amount of presents and goods for the old chief, and besides these I had many valuable articles of European workmanship, some of which were purchased with money given me by another friend* in England to lay out in presents for African chiefs, which I thought I could not better bestow than on the King of the Rembo. Amongst them were a quantity of silks and fine cotton goods, silver knives, forks, and spoons, gunpowder, trade guns, kettles, and beads for his numerous wives. All were packed in chests secured with lock and key; the chests being an important part of the donation, for the property of an African chief, in this part, is estimated in slaves, wives, and *chests*. The sight of all this wealth almost dumbfoundered the old man. When I commenced showing the contents of the chests to him he stopped me, and said—"Do you love me, Chaillie? Then do not tell the people what you have given me, or they will bewitch me." There was an internal struggle between avarice and fear expressed in his countenance. His fear of witchcraft was a great defect in his character as a chief, for it had led to the depopulation of Goumbi, his capital on the Rembo. Going to the door, he looked out to see that no one was listening; then he knelt down, and clasped my feet with his hands, and, with the stern lineaments of his face distorted by fear, begged me again to keep secret the account of the wealth I had given him. No sooner had he left me than I heard him declaring to his people that the white man had brought him nothing. As I approached, instead of being disconcerted by my appearance on the scene, he repeated the same statement, in a louder voice, but looked towards me at the same time with an expression of countenance that was clearly meant to

* Henry Johnson, Esq., of 39, Crutched Friars.

implore me not to say a word to the contrary. The people were smiling all the while, for they knew better, and were well acquainted with the ways of their beloved old chief. He would not remove the chests to his canoe in the day-time, but came at night, on the eve of his departure, when every one was asleep, and stealthily took them himself, with the aid of two slaves, down to the water-side.

In a few days the vessel was unloaded, and my goods stored in several huts which were secured only by a door tied with a rope of lianas to the bamboo wall. My property, however, was respected, and the honest Commi people did not rob me of a single article. Quengueza returned to Goumbi, and I gradually inured myself again to the climate and ways of the country. I made short excursions in various directions, visited numerous petty chiefs, besides receiving visits from others, and stimulated them and their people to the collection of produce, that Captain Vardon might reload his vessel and return to England. As I have described the coast country at length in my former book, a few incidents only of my stay need be recorded here, together with some stray notes on the natural history, before I commence the narrative of my expedition into the interior.

On the 1st of November a negro from a neighbouring village brought me a young male chimpanzee about three years old, which had been caught in the woods on the banks of the Npoulounay about three months previously. Thomas, for so I christened my little *protégé*, was a tricky little rascal, and afforded me no end of amusement; he was, however, very tame, like all young chimpanzees. Unfortunately Thomas was lame in one hand, several of the fingers having been broken and healed up in a distorted position. This was caused by his having been maltreated by the village dogs, who were sent in chase of him one day when he escaped from his captors and ran into the neighbouring woods. I had Tom tied by a cord to a pole in the verandah of my hut, and fed him with cooked plantains and other food from my own table. He soon got to prefer cooked to raw food, and rejected raw plantains whenever they were offered to him. The difference in tameability between the young chimpanzee and the young gorilla is a fact which I have confirmed by numerous observations, and I must repeat it here as it was one of those points which were disputed in my former work. A young chimpanzee becomes tame and apparently reconciled to captivity in two or three days after he is brought from the woods. The young gorilla I have never yet seen tame in confinement, although I have had four of them in custody, while still of very early age.

One day I witnessed an act of Master Thomas which seemed to me to illustrate the habits of his species in the wild state. A few days after he came into my possession I bought a domestic cat for my house; as soon as the young chimpanzee saw it he flew in alarm to his pole and clambered up it, the hair of his body becoming erect and his eyes bright with excitement. In a moment recovering himself he came down, and rushing on the cat, with one of his feet seized the nape of the animal, and with the other pressed on its back, as if trying to break its neck. Not wishing to lose my cat, I interfered and saved its life. The negroes say that the chimpanzee attacks the leopard in this way, and I have no doubt, from what I saw, that their statement is correct.

My pet preserved his good health and increased in intelligence and gentleness until the departure of Captain Vardon for England. I then sent him home, and on his arrival he was deposited by my friend in the Crystal Palace at Sydenham, where, I dare say, very many of my readers have seen him, and have laughed at his amusing tricks. I am credibly informed that his education at the Palace has become so far advanced that he understands what is going on when his own "cartes de visite" are sold. A feint is sometimes made of carrying off one without paying for it, but Thomas rushes forward, screaming, to the length of his tether, to prevent the irregular transaction, and does not cease his noisy expressions of dissatisfaction until the money is paid down.

Whilst waiting for the erection of a new house and store-rooms, I made several little trips down the river, visiting the Commi settlements and examining the altered state of the river banks. The alterations in the mouth of the Fernand Vaz I found had arisen from the currents of the river and the sea having broken through the long sandy spit, making the embouchure broader but more dangerous, because portions of the spit had been converted into sandbanks with but a small depth of water over them; and, the sand having shifted, no one knew the situation of the deep channel. Old Sangala, the chief of Elindé at the mouth of the river, was dead; and his heir, the present chief, who had taken the name of his predecessor, was a drunkard, and was held in very little estimation. I missed, near the river's mouth, the beautiful little island on which I used to shoot so many water birds, and where, as also on the sandy spit, the grotesque and large crane *Mycteria senegalensis* used to be found, together with thousands of sea-birds of many species. The widows of old Sangala had all married again; but they gave me a warm welcome, especially the old kondé (head wife or Queen) who cooked my food for me whilst I stayed, and became eloquent in recalling the events of the good old times when Sangala was alive. Her husband showed no jealousy at this discourse, for here widows are allowed freely to praise their former husbands.

Death had been busy in other places besides Elindé. At the village of Makombé I found that the chief was dead, and that Ilougou, his heir, who had helped me to build my former settlement of Washington, had been accused of having caused his death by witchcraft, and forced to drink the poison ordeal, which ended in his own life being sacrificed. Similar scenes had been enacted in other villages. It is dangerous in this unhappy country to be the heir of any man who sickens and dies.

The day after my return from visiting the mouth of the river, I was seized with a severe fit of fever, which laid me prostrate for four days. I was obliged to send on board the *Mentor* for a supply of calomel and jalap, as my medicine chest had been lost in the upsetting of the canoe, a box of quinine only having been saved. I was touched during my illness by the great sympathy shown to me by the natives. The most perfect silence was observed round the hut where I lay, day and night; tam-tamming, singing and dancing were forbidden, lest they should disturb me; and the old chief, Ranpano, came and sat every day for hours together by my bed-side. He very seldom spoke, but his countenance manifested the anxiety which the good old fellow felt. He would sometimes say "Chaillie! Chaillie! you must not be ill while you stay in my village. None among my people are glad to see you ill. I love you, for you came to me, and I have no better friend in the world." When he went out he used to mutter words which I did not understand, but which were probably invocations to some spirit to watch over me. Old Ranpano had some strange notions about spirits good and bad, which I think were peculiar to him. One day he took it into his head that he should die if he entered my hut, for he had been told that some one having an aniemba (a witch) had made a *mondah*, and had put it under the threshold of my door, so that, should he enter my hut, the witch would go into him and he would die.

No persuasion of mine could induce the old chief to come into my hut, and after a time I got angry with him, and told him that he ought not to refuse to come and see me. The good old chief immediately sent for some doctors, who, of course, at once declared that it was true that some one wanted to bewitch him, and had put a mondah at my door to kill him. But they said that it could be removed now that the people knew that there was one.

Immediately the ceremonies for banishing the witch began. For three consecutive days they danced almost incessantly, and invoked the good spirits; and one fine morning, whilst I was occupied in writing inside the hut, unaware that any one was approaching, Ranpano came to my door, fired a gun, and entered the hut in a great hurry, muttering invocations and curses; he then became easier in his manners, having as he thought, thus cleared the moral atmosphere.

An event of great importance in relation to my expedition occurred on the 22nd of November and following days. During my absence in Europe the assembled chiefs of the Commi clans under the presidency of King Olenga-Yombi (who had now taken the name of Rigoundo) had passed a law to the effect that no Mpongwé (the trading tribe of the Gaboon) or white man should be allowed to ascend the river Fernand Vaz or the Ogobai. It is the universal rule among the coast tribes of West Africa to prevent, if possible, all strangers from penetrating into the interior, even if it be only to the next tribe, through fear that they should lose the exclusive privilege of trading with these tribes. Indeed every tribe tries to prevent all strangers from communicating with the tribe next in advance of them. The spirit of commercial and political monopoly, so natural to the heart of uncivilized as well as semi-civilized man, is the cause of this; and the rule had only been broken through in my own case, on my former journey, owing to my popularity among the chiefs and the powerful friendship of Quengueza. It was now my aim to get this new law repealed, at least as far as I was concerned; and on the 22nd of November King Olenga-Yombi came in person to my village on the Fernand Vaz, to hold a palaver thereupon.

King Olenga-Yombi still retained his old habits of drunkenness, which I have described in 'Equatorial Africa;' and although it was early in the morning when he came to see me, he was already fuddled with palm wine. I made him a present of a very long blue coat, the tails of which dangled about his ankles when he walked, and a light yellow waistcoat with gilt buttons; with these he strutted about with the true pride of an African king, and they seemed to please him quite as much as the muskets and many other more useful articles which I added to the gift. A single word from Olenga-Yombi might have hindered me from passing up the river; for, although in council the head chiefs of these tribes have no more influence than the other speakers, they have the power of veto in many things. There is a certain spirit of loyalty amongst these Africans which leads them not to disobey a positive prohibition by the superior chief, although he may not have the physical power to enforce obedience. It was important therefore for me to conciliate this drunken negro chief.

The palaver was held in the council-house of the village, a large open shed, chairs being placed for the principal speakers. There was a Mpongwé man present who had recently come from the Gaboon, entrusted by one of the traders there with about eight hundred pounds worth of goods. When the palaver began, I took care that my own case and that of the Mpongwé should be treated of separately. The result was most satisfactory. I was allowed the right of the river, whilst the Mpongwé was refused. Long speeches were made, and the king finally issued his decree that whatever village allowed the Mpongwé trader to pass up the river should be burnt and the plantations destroyed. The speakers argued that I did not go into the interior to trade, but to shoot animals and bring away the skins and bones. "Truly," they said, "we do not know what our Chaillie has in his stomach to want such things, but we must let him go." Orders were given to the *Makaga* to see that the law was executed; and the king concluded by assuring me that not only would no resistance be offered to my progress, but that, when I was ready to depart, he would send some of his own slaves to accompany me. He told me, when we were alone afterwards, that I was his "big white man." "What you say," he continued, "we do, for we know it is for our good." He wished me to go and establish a factory at his village near Cape St. Catherine, saying that he had made a law that whoever robbed a white man should have his ears cut off, and that his people, who were formerly great thieves, did not now steal any longer. On the 25th he departed, after having made me promise to visit him at his village.

On the 27th of November I paid a visit to the ruins of my old establishment, "Washington," and to the burial-place of my faithful guardian Rinkimongani, which were a mile distant from my new settlement. I felt the loss of the honest old fellow more than ever, for the man who now filled the same office, Malonga, the brother of Ranpano, was a tricky knave, whom I disliked thoroughly. The natives told me that Rinkimongani was continually talking of me during my absence, counting the seasons as they rolled past, and carefully guarding the house and gardens, in the firm hope that I should soon return. It was universally believed, of course, that he had been bewitched through jealousy of my friendship for him, and that foul play had been used to cause his death.

I was accompanied by one of my boys to the burial-ground. The road to it from my place led across the prairie and through a few groves of trees to the margins of one of those pretty islands of wood, which diversify the sandy grass-land of the Fernand Vaz. The cemetery was recognisable from a distance by the numerous poles fixed in the ground. Rinkimongani's body had been placed in a box or coffin, for the Commi people are now so far advanced in civilisation that they have adopted the white man's customs in this respect; it is only, however, the head men who are laid in boxes, and they are not interred in the earth, but laid according to the old native habit on the surface, or inserted a small depth into the ground. The wood of my poor old friend's coffin was decayed, and I could see his mouldering bones inside, together with the remains of his valuables that were buried with him, consisting of jugs and pots, a quantity of brass buttons, the remains of a coat, and an old umbrella-stick, which was all that was left of this article, a present from me, and which he always carried about with him. All around were skeletons and bones crumbling to powder, the fragments of mats and cloth which had served the corpses as their winding-sheets, and broken relics which had been reverently buried with the dead. It was a place that one might moralise in—the humble, fragile grave-yard of a tribe of poor negroes, which represented in their eyes quite as much as our proud monuments of stone that will also in their turn disappear.

Returning to the old settlement I saw the house in which Rinkimongani died. It was still standing close to my own place, which had been partly destroyed by fire in the burning of the prairie. All the out-buildings and huts of my men were complete ruins, but the old man's house was in tolerable preservation. The faith of Rinkimongani in my return had overcome his superstitious scruples; for every negro believed the settlement had been bewitched, and wondered at the old man's folly and obstinacy in remaining there after so many had died. It will be remembered that the place was once abandoned on account of its evil reputation during my former residence. As I wandered about the ruins I thought of the many happy hours I had spent here in the days of my Natural History enthusiasm, when I was amassing my collections, and the addition of a new species was the coveted reward of a long day's hunt. The birds which used to build their nests by hundreds in the surrounding trees had forsaken the place; and in the rank grass near the river I saw a huge python coiled up, like an evil spirit on the watch. When I told my companion that I regretted not having returned to the old spot, he looked at me with horror expressed in his countenance. The place was thought to be bewitched and accursed.

All the fixtures and household property of Rinkimongani remained intact, for the *bolá ivoga*, or breaking up of the mourning-time and division of his effects,* had not yet been celebrated. Contrary to African custom, the wives of the deceased had deserted the place before the bola ivoga, on account of its bad reputation. They ought to have remained here in chaste widowhood until the proper time had arrived for the ceremony (generally a year or two after the death of the husband), when the wives, slaves, and other property of the deceased, are divided amongst his rightful heirs, and the house burnt to the ground.

Soon after this the building of my new palm-wood house approached completion, in the little village which I had chosen for my residence, and which I had bought of Rabolo, a petty chief. Nothing remained to be put up except the verandah, but an obstacle existed to its erection which my men dared not remove. This was a formidable *mondah* or fetich, which my friend Rabolo had made in his village before I purchased it, and which I now found was

* See, for a description of this custom, 'Adventures in Equatorial Africa,' p. 289.

close to the site of my house, at what was formerly the entrance to the single street of the village. Almost all the villages in this country have something of this kind at their entrance, constructed to prevent the entry of witchcraft and death, or to bring good luck to the inhabitants. Rabolo's talisman was considered to be a very effective one, for since the village was established, twelve dry seasons ago, no one had died there. This was no great wonder, since there were only fifteen inhabitants in the place.

My builders came to me to say they dared not remove Rabolo's fetich, and prayed me not to touch it until Rabolo came, otherwise there would be a big palaver. It seemed likely I should have some difficulty, for Rabolo had already spent the purchase-money of his village, distributing the goods amongst his wives and numerous fathers-in-law. However, I was firm, and when Rabolo came I was peremptory in demanding that the rubbish should be cleared away. He submitted at last, and commenced to cut down the bushes which covered the talisman, and dig up the mysterious relics. The first thing that I saw turned up was the skull of a chimpanzee buried in the sand; then came the skull of a man, probably an ancestor of Rabolo, and a mass of broken plates, glasses, and crockery of all sorts, which had been placed there to keep company with the *mondah*. He then removed the two upright poles with cross-bar and talismanic creeper growing at their foot, which constituted the protecting portal of the village, the negroes all the while standing around with looks of blank amazement. It is the belief of the negroes that, as long as the creeping-plant keeps alive, so long will the fetich retain its efficacy. A similar plant covered both the heaps of skulls and rubbish. At the foot of this portal and underneath the creeper were more chimpanzee skulls and fragments of pottery. In the ground near the two poles were also two wooden idols. We removed the whole, and I need not tell my readers that no evil consequences ensued. As to Rabolo and his subjects, they flattered themselves that it was this powerful fetich which brought me to settle on this spot. They have, in common with all the negroes of this part of Africa, a notion that there is some mysterious connection or affinity between the chimpanzee and the white man. It is owing, I believe, to the pale face of the chimpanzee, which has suggested the notion that we are descended from it, as the negro has descended from the black-faced gorilla. I heard of other head men of villages making *mondahs* with skulls of chimpanzees associated with skulls of their ancestors, believing that these would draw my heart to them and induce me to give them presents or trust them with goods. I removed all my goods and establishment to the village when my large roomy house and store were at length ready for me, thanks to my good friend Captain Vardon, who had himself worked hard to get them finished. The house was pleasantly situated between the villages of Djombouai and Ranpano.

On the 18th of January, 1864, the *Mentor*, having completed her cargo, sailed for England. It was the first vessel that the Commi people had loaded by themselves with the produce of their country, and they were not a little proud of their achievement. Besides Thomas, I sent by the vessel a live female chimpanzee which I had obtained, and which I christened "Mrs. Thomas." I also sent a collection of skulls of natives, about ninety in number, for the British Museum. I was obliged to pack these skulls very carefully, to prevent the negroes from knowing what it was they were carrying on board the ship.

I had forbidden my lad Macondai to say a word about it. As they placed the box in the canoe, the negroes inquired what was in it. Macondai answered, "Of course, mats for his friends." As soon as the box was on board the ship the mate and the sailors peeped into it, and discovering the contents, begged Captain Vardon to send the box ashore again, as the skulls were sure to bring misfortune and shipwreck. Luckily for me Captain Vardon had too much good sense to pay any heed to their superstitious fears.

Mrs. Tom unfortunately died on the passage, but Tom, as I have already stated, arrived safely in London, and is still living.* I went on board when all was ready, and bade Captain Vardon a hearty good-bye. My boys in the canoe gave three cheers for the crew, as the white sails expanded and the little vessel glided away; and I returned to my solitude in the wilderness with a heavy heart.

* The fire at the Crystal Palace, to which my unfortunate pet fell a sacrifice, occurred whilst these sheets were passing through the press.

CHAPTER III.

EXCURSIONS IN SEARCH OF THE GORILLA AND THE IPI.

Visit to King Olenga-Yombi—Storm on the Fernand Vaz—Land journey to Aniambié—First traces of Gorilla—Form of its tracks—Drunken orgies of the King—Magic Island of Nengué Ncoma—Village of Nkongon Mboumba—Search of the Ipi, or great Pangolin—Its habits—Village of Mburu Shara—Nkengo Nschiego variety of Chimpanzee—Bowers of the Chimpanzee—Group of Gorillas in a plantain grove—Their mode of walking—Horrid form of monomania—Akondogo brings a live Gorilla—Return to the Fernand Vaz—Three more live Gorillas—Account of their capture—Modification of opinions concerning the Gorilla.

During my stay in the country of the Fernand Vaz, before departing for the interior, I made several very interesting excursions. The most important of these were to the residence of King Olenga-Yombi near Cape St. Catherine, on the coast, south of the Fernand Vaz, and to the wooded country in the interior south-east of that place. This part of the country, I have now reason for concluding, is the head-quarters of the gorilla, or the district in which he exists in the greatest number, but where he is wildest and most difficult to get near. I stayed there many weeks, almost wholly occupied in hunting, and had good opportunities of seeing this formidable ape in his native wilds. Some account of these excursions will, therefore, be necessary in this place.

I visited Aniambié, the residence of Olenga-Yombi,

twice during the year 1864, once in February and again in June. During the first excursion, besides hunting the gorilla, I spent some time in search of a large species of pangolin, or scaly ant-eater, called Ipi, which I had not succeeded in obtaining during my earlier travels in this country. We left my village, "Plateau," as I had named it, on the 13th of the month, in two canoes, one manned by eleven men in which I myself embarked, and the other manned by six men.

As my readers will see by the map, the Fernand Vaz runs in the lower part of its course, for about forty miles, nearly parallel to the sea, the space between the river and the sea-shore being a tract of level sandy country covered with grass and isolated groups of trees, and nowhere more than a few miles wide. The nearest road to Aniambié, a sea-shore town, the capital of Olenga-Yombi, is therefore up the stream to a point nearly opposite the town, and then across the tongue of land. A little south of this point, and towards the interior, the level land ceases, and a hilly and more thickly-wooded country commences, where are the plantations of the king.

As we put off from "Plateau" on our first journey, Malonga, an old negro, whom I left in charge of my house and property,* assured me that he had made a fetich to ensure us fine weather, and that we should have no rain. In this country the doctors are not makers, but unmakers, of rain. He was miserably

* Ranpono had named this man to be guardian of my premises whenever I was absent; and the guardian having been named by the chief, he and his people became responsible for the safety of my property.

wrong in his forecast. The evening, indeed, was fine, and the moon shone in a cloudless sky; but soon after the moon had set, about ten o'clock, a thick black cloud arose in the north-east, and before we could run the canoes into a safe harbour, a terrific tornado burst upon us. The sky seemed all ablaze with lightning, and the thunder pealed incessantly. Our canoes were driven ashore, but luckily in a place where the banks were clothed with low trees and bushes. The rain came down in torrents, and we could find no shelter until we reached a small village, where we went ashore, and passed the remainder of the night shivering over our wretched little fire, for the people had neglected to provide a supply of fire-wood.

We stayed here till noon the next day, and then resumed our voyage in the rain till six o'clock, when we arrived at the landing-place, where the path commences that leads to Aniambié. King Olenga-Yombi had here ordered a large shed (ebando) to be built for me, and we found a store of fire-wood and provisions, including a goat, ready for us. The ebando stood on the banks of a little creek, the mouth of which lay opposite the lower end of the Island Nengué Shika.

Inland from this place the scenery is varied and beautiful; stretches of grassy prairie and patches of luxuriant forest. Some parts of the district, however, are swampy, and in these the forest is very rank. Such places are called by the natives "ivolo," which means a wooded bog, and they are the haunts of the gorilla. My first day's chase was not very successful. We hunted with two dogs, and after we had struggled through the thorny and swampy thickets for a long time, one of the dogs broke away from us, and spoilt what might have been very good sport. We heard distinctly the rustling and crashing noise in the bush, which denoted gorillas in the act of feeding, for, in searching for berries, they are continually pulling down the branches of the lower trees, and letting them go again. Before we could get within sight of them we heard a sharp cry, and they then made off. My men agreed with myself that they were two females; but they also added that the male was not far away, and would soon come towards us to see what drove his females off, and fight us. We traversed the jungle for two or three miles, but had not the good luck to see a male gorilla. Foot-tracks were very abundant in the moist soil wherever we came upon bare places. We followed the tracks of the two females until we lost them in the midst of a great number of foot-marks of other gorillas. All around were numerous young trees broken down, and, in an old plantation, we saw some sugar-cane which had been broken, and the stems presented signs of their having been bitten by the gorillas.

I may state in this place that I took particular note, on this day's hunt, of the marks which the feet and hands of the gorilla made in the soft soil. The tracks were very plain, but those of the feet never showed the marks of the toes, only the heels, and the tracks of the hands showed simply the impressions of the knuckles.

During the following days I traversed other patches of jungle lying nearer the sea-shore, and, although unsuccessful with regard to bagging a gorilla, added a number of specimens in other departments of Natural History to my collection. On the 25th of February I proceeded to Aniambié to see the king, who had returned from a big palaver he had had with the Ngobi tribe south of Cape Catherine.

The Ngobi are the next tribe to the Commi, going southward along the coast. They have not yet arrived at that stage of African civilization which forbids selling their own people into slavery. The Mpongwé of the Gaboon and the Commi of the Fernand Vaz, since they have become a little civilized by contact with the white man, have quite abandoned the practice of selling people of their own tribes; such an act would be now looked upon as shameful.

I have already described Aniambié in my former work; all that it is now necessary to say is, that I found it much reduced in its population, and looking very wretched. The king, as usual, was drunk when I arrived. Indeed, he was too tipsy to stand on his legs; nevertheless, he was bullying and boasting in a loud tone of voice. I had not been in his place long before he ordered another calabash full of palm wine, and drank off about half a gallon of it. This finished him up for the day; he fell back into the arms of his loving wives, ejaculating many times, "I am a big king! I am a big king!" The voice soon became inaudible, and he fell asleep.

In the neighbourhood of Aniambié there is one island covered with trees, which is held in great awe. It is called Nengué Ncoma. "Whosoever enters this island," said to me one of my guides, "is sure to die suddenly, or to become crazy and wander about till he dies." This is another of the wild superstitions with which this land is teeming, so fertile are the busy brains of the imaginative Commi people. My guide added that it was the home of a great crocodile whose scales were of brass, and who never left the island. To show the people how vain were their fears, I immediately walked towards the place, and traversed the patch of jungle in various directions. When I came out again the poor negroes seemed stupified with wonder. They were not cured, however, of their belief, for they only concluded that I was a spirit, and that what would be death to them did no harm to me.

Early in the morning of the 26th of February, before the drunken king was awake, I started for Nkongon Mboumba, one of his slave villages, there to hunt the ipi or large pangolin, which was said to inhabit the neighbouring forest. During my former journey I sought in vain for the ipi, it being very rarely met with. The place is situated about ten miles south-east of Aniambié, in an undulating well-wooded country. It is built on the summit of a hill, at the foot of which flowed a charming rivulet, which meandered through the valley for some distance, and then became hidden from the view by the dense forest. This district was wholly new ground to me, as I had not visited it in my former travels. Among the slaves residing here to work the king's plantations were specimens of no less than eleven different tribes. Some old slaves from the far interior seemed very little removed from the Anthropoid apes in their shape and features—lean legs, heavy bodies with pro-

IPI, OR SCALY ANT-EATER.

(Pholidotus Africanus.)

minent abdomen, retreating foreheads and projecting muzzles—they were more like animals than men and women. A Portuguese slave-schooner had just left the coast for the Island of St. Thomas with seventy-eight slaves on board. The king, as well as the chiefs and people, never sell the slaves they have inherited, and I saw some in this village who had lived there fifty years. The children of slaves, also, are not sold. The sale of inherited slaves is contrary to the customs of the country, and, to use their own expression, would bring shame upon them.

The next morning I went with a number of men in search of the ipi. From the description given me by the natives I was sure that I had never before met with this species, and had some hope of its being new to science. The pangolin genus (*Manis* of zoologists) to which it belongs is a very singular group of animals. They are ant-eaters, like the *Myrmecophaga* of South America, being like them quite destitute of teeth, and having a long extensile tongue, the extremity of which is covered with a glutinous secretion, by means of which they catch their prey. But, whilst the South American ant-eaters are clothed with hair, like ordinary mammalian animals, the pangolins have an armour of large scales, implanted in the skin of the upper surface of the body from the head to the tip of the tail, and imbricated or overlapping, like the slates on the roof of a house. The animals look, at first sight, like curious heavy-bodied lizards, but they have warm blood, and nourish their young like the rest of the mammalia.

The ipi lives in burrows in the earth, or sometimes

in the large hollows of colossal trunks of trees which have fallen to the ground. The burrows that I saw were in light soil on the slope of a hill. There are two holes to each gallery, one for entrance and the other for exit. This is necessary, on account of the animal being quite incapable of curving its body sideways, so that it cannot turn itself in its burrow. The bodies of pangolins are very flexible *vertically*, that is, they can roll themselves up into a ball, and coil and uncoil themselves very readily, but they cannot turn round within the confined limits of their burrows. In hunting them we had first to ascertain, by the footmarks, or more readily by the marks left by the trail of the tail, which was the entrance and which the exit of the burrow, and then, making a trap at the one end, drive them out by the smoke of a fire at the other; afterwards securing them with ropes. The freshness of the tracks told us that the animal had entered its burrow the previous evening; for I must add that the ipi is nocturnal in its habits, sleeping in its burrow throughout the day. When it wanders at night the natives say that they can hear the rattling of its large scales.

A long and wearisome day's hunt produced no fruit. We wandered over hill and dale through the forest and streams, leaving the beaten paths, and struggling for hours through the tangled maze, with no other result than to tear our clothes to rags, and cover ourselves with scratches from the thorns and cutting edges of sword-like grasses which grew in many places. I nevertheless persevered, searching the whole country for many miles round, and had, at any rate, the melancholy satisfaction of feeling that I was hardening myself for any amount of endurance that might be required in my future explorations. At length, on the 5th of March, I was rewarded by finding two specimens, an adult female and a young one; the skins and skeletons of both I preserved and afterwards sent to the British Museum. The adult measured about four feet and a half from the head to the tip of the tail. The flesh of the ipi is good eating. Those that I captured were very lean, but I was informed by the natives that they are sometimes very fat. I found, on dissection, nothing but the remains of ants in their stomachs. The tail is very thick, and makes a large track on the ground in walking.

On my return to England I found, as I had expected, that my ipi was a new species; but it appears that, some time after the arrival of my two specimens, another was bought from a dealer, who said that it had come from Dr. Baikie, having been found by him in the neighbourhood of the River Niger. It has been described by Dr. Gray in the 'Proceedings of the Zoological Society,' April, 1865, under the name of *Pholidotus Africanus*, so that it belongs to a different genus from the rest of the African species of these curious animals, which are ranged under *Manis*. It is interesting to find that the animal is more nearly allied to an Indian form than to the other African pangolins. My adult skeleton fortunately turned out a fine and perfect specimen, the largest yet known, and it may now be seen mounted in the collection of the British Museum.*

My first journey to the gorilla district having been unsuccessful in its main object, namely, the capture of a gorilla (although I obtained several skins and skeletons), I resolved to pay it a second visit. The 16th of June saw me again on my way thither.

On the 17th I diverged from my route to visit my friend Mburu Shara, a negro chief, whose village was situated on the right or eastern bank of the Fernand Vaz, just opposite to the landing-place of Aniambié. Mburu Shara was a younger man than African chiefs usually are, but he was one of the finest fellows in the country, and well-disposed towards the white man. I spent three most delightful days at his place, which I had never before visited. Soon after I landed, the villagers came forth, laid mats at my feet, and piled up their presents of plantains; a fat goat was given to me, and my

* The specimen of *Phalidotus Africanus* on which the describer of the species founds his measurements, and the skull of which he figured, I have ascertained, by my own examination in the British Museum, is not the one said to be received from the Niger, but the specimen which I sent. The Niger specimen is very much smaller. I mention this, because Dr. Gray, doubtless through inadvertency, has omitted to mention my name at all in connection with the species. This omission is important only from the circumstance that the locality of the animal, "Fernand Vaz," is also left out; the localities and ranges of species being always considered, and very rightly, important facts in zoological science. I presume there is a possibility of a mistake in the locality of the Niger specimen; however, I may as well mention that I know that a third specimen of the ipi was taken by the natives whilst I was at the Fernand Vaz, exactly the size of the one described as coming from the Niger: but the natives asking too high a price for it, I would not purchase it, and it came into the possession of Captain Holder, the master of the *Cambria*, a vessel trading to Bristol; where the specimen is at present I do not know, but it may possibly be the one Dr. Gray purchased for the British Museum.

reception altogether was most hearty. I hunted in the neighbourhood during my stay. The country was varied in its surface, prairie land and scattered woods. The woods were inhabited by a good many chimpanzees, but the gorilla was not known in the district. We succeeded in killing an adult female chimpanzee of a variety new to me, and called by the natives Nkengo Nschiego. It is distinguished from the common form of the chimpanzee by its face being yellow. All the specimens of the old bald-headed chimpanzee (Nschiego Mbouvé) that I have found had black faces, except when quite young, when the face is white and not yellow, as I have described in 'Equatorial Africa;' and the common chimpanzee, although yellow-faced when young, becomes gradually black as it grows old. There are, therefore, three varieties of the chimpanzee distinguished by the negroes of Equatorial Africa. I do not here include the Kooloo Kamba.* I was extremely sorry at not being able to obtain further specimens of this last-mentioned ape on my present journey; it appears to be very rare. I was told that the Nschiego Mbouvé was also found in these woods.

I found here also several of the bowers made by the Nkengo Nschiego of branches of trees, and they were somewhat different in form from those I found in my former journey. I had two of them cut down, and sent them to the British Museum. They are formed at a height of twenty or thirty feet in the trees by the animals bending over and intertwining a number of the weaker boughs, so as to

* Figured in 'Adventures in Equatorial Africa,' pp. 270 and 360.

form bower, under which they can sit, protected from the rains by the masses of foliage thus entangled together, some of the boughs being so bent that they form convenient seats; on them were found remains of nuts and berries.

I found Olenga-Yombi at his slave-plantation, drunk as usual. His head wife, thinking to appease my wrath at the vile habits of her husband, told me the following curious story of the origin of the vice. When he was quite a child his father used to put him in a big bag which he had made for the purpose, and carry him to the top of a high tree, where he plied him with the intoxicating palm wine. Every day he repeated the dose until the child came to like palm wine better than its mother's milk, whereat the father was greatly delighted, because he wished him to be renowned, when he was grown up, for the quantity of palm wine he could drink. "So you see, Chaillie," she said, "you must not be angry with him, for it is not his own fault." The wife, however, promised he should keep sober whilst I was with him, and the slaves, amusingly enough, in the presence of the king, declared they would throw away every calabash of wine that should be brought to his Majesty.

I had not been at the village long before news came that gorillas had been recently seen in the neighbourhood of a plantation only half a mile distant. Early in the morning of the 25th of June I wended my way thither, accompanied by one of my boys, named Odanga. The plantation was a large one, and situated on very broken ground, surrounded by the virgin forest. It was a lovely morning; the sky was almost cloudless, and all around was still as death, except the slight rustling of the tree-tops moved by the gentle land breeze. When I reached the place, I had first to pick my way through the maze of tree-stumps and half-burnt logs by the side of a field of cassada. I was going quietly along the borders of this, when I heard, in the grove of plantain-trees towards which I was walking, a great crashing noise, like the breaking of trees. I immediately hid myself behind a bush, and was soon gratified with the sight of a female gorilla; but before I had time to notice its movements, a second and third emerged from the masses of colossal foliage; at length no less than four came into view.

They were all busily engaged in tearing down the larger trees. One of the females had a young one following her. I had an excellent opportunity of watching the movements of the impish-looking band. The shaggy hides, the protuberant abdomens, the hideous features of these strange creatures, whose forms so nearly resemble man, made up a picture like a vision in some morbid dream. In destroying a tree, they first grasped the base of the stem with one of their feet and then with their powerful arms pulled it down, a matter of not much difficulty with so loosely-formed a stem as that of the plantain. They then set upon the juicy heart of the tree at the bases of the leaves, and devoured it with great voracity. While eating they made a kind of clucking noise, expressive of contentment. Many trees they destroyed apparently out of pure mischief. Now and then they stood still and looked around. Once or twice they seemed on the point of starting off in alarm, but recovered themselves and continued their work. Gradually they got nearer to the edge of the dark forest, and finally disappeared. I was so intent on watching them, that I let go the last chance of shooting one almost before I became aware of it.

The next day I went again with Odanga to the same spot. I had no expectation of seeing gorillas in the same plantation, and was carrying a light shot gun, having given my heavy double-barrelled rifle to the boy to carry. The plantation extended over two hills, with a deep hollow between, planted with sugar cane. Before I had crossed the hollow I saw on the opposite slope a monstrous gorilla, standing erect and looking directly towards me. Without turning my face I beckoned to the boy to bring me my rifle, but no rifle came,—the little coward had bolted, and I lost my chance. The huge beast stared at me for about two minutes, and then, without uttering any cry, moved off to the shade of the forest, running nimbly on his hands and feet.

As my readers may easily imagine, I had excellent opportunity of observing, during these two days, the manner in which the gorillas walked when in open ground. They move along with great rapidity and on all fours, that is, with the knuckles of their hands touching the ground. Artists, in representing the gorilla walking, generally make the arms too much bowed outwards, and the elbows too much bent; this gives the figures an appearance of heaviness and awkwardness. When the gorillas that I watched left the plantain-trees, they moved off at a great pace over the ground, with their arms extended straight forwards towards the ground, and moving rapidly. I may mention also that having now opened the stomachs of several freshly-killed gorillas I have never found anything but vegetable matter in them.

When I returned to Nkongon Mbounba I found there my old friend Akondogo, chief of one of the Commi villages, who had just returned from the Ngobi country, a little further south. To my great surprise and pleasure, he had brought for me a living gorilla, a young one, but the largest I had ever seen captured alive. Like Joe, the young male whose habits in confinement I described in 'Equatorial Africa,' this one showed the most violent and ungovernable disposition. He tried to bite every one who came near him, and was obliged to be secured by a forked stick closely applied to the back of his neck. This mode of imprisoning these animals is a very improper one if the object be to keep them alive and to tame them, but, unfortunately, in this barbarous country, we had not the materials requisite to build a strong cage. The injury caused to this one by the forked stick eventually caused his death. As I had some more hunting to do, I left the animal in charge of Akondogo until he should have an opportunity of sending it to me on the Fernand Vaz.

I cannot avoid relating in this place a very curious instance of a strange and horrid form of monomania which is sometimes displayed by these primitive negroes. It was related to me so circumstantially by Akondogo, and so well confirmed by others, that I cannot help fully believing in all the principal facts of the case.

Poor Akondogo said that he had had plenty of trouble in his day; that a leopard had killed two of his men, and that he had a great many palavers to settle on account of these deaths.

Not knowing exactly what he meant, I said to him, "Why did you not make a trap to catch the leopard?" To my astonishment, he replied, "The leopard was not of the kind you mean. It was a man who had changed himself into a leopard, and then became a man again." I said, "Akondogo, I will never believe your story. How can a man be turned into a leopard?" He again asserted that it was true, and gave me the following history:—

Whilst he was in the woods with his people, gathering india-rubber, one of his men disappeared, and, notwithstanding all their endeavours, nothing could be found of him but a quantity of blood. The next day another man disappeared, and in searching for him more blood was found. All the people got alarmed, and Akondogo sent for a great Doctor to drink the mboundou, and solve the mystery of these two deaths. To the horror and astonishment of the old chief, the doctor declared it was Akondogo's own child (his nephew and heir), Akosho, who had killed the two men. Akosho was sent for, and, when asked by the chief, answered that it was truly he who had committed the murders; that he could not help it, for he had turned into a leopard, and his heart longed for blood; and that after each deed he had turned into a man again. Akondogo loved his boy so much that he would not believe his own confession, until the boy took him to a place in the forest where lay the two bodies, one with the head cut off, and the other with the belly torn open. Upon this, Akondogo gave orders to seize the lad. He was bound with ropes, taken to the village, and there tied in a horizontal position to a post, and burnt slowly to death, all the people standing by until he expired.

I must say, the end of the story seemed to me too horrid to listen to. I shuddered, and was ready to curse the race that was capable of committing such acts. But on careful inquiry, I found it was a case of monomania in the boy Akosho, and that he really was the murderer of the two men. It is probable that the superstitious belief of these morbidly imaginative Africans in the transformation of men into leopards, being early instilled into the minds of their children, is the direct cause of murders being committed under the influence of it. The boy himself, as well as Akondogo and all the people, believed he had really turned into a leopard, and the cruel punishment was partly in vengeance for witchcraft, and partly to prevent the committal of more crimes by the boy in a similar way, for, said they, the man has a spirit of witchcraft.

The natives of all the neighbouring country were now so well aware that I wanted live gorillas, and was willing to give a high price for them, that many were stimulated to search with great perseverance; the good effects of this were soon made evident.

One day as I was quietly dining with Captain

Holder, of the *Cambria* (a vessel just arrived from England), one of my men came in with the startling news that three live gorillas had been brought, one of them full grown. I had not long to wait; in they came. First, a very large adult female, bound hand and foot; then her female child, screaming terribly; and lastly, a vigorous young male, also tightly bound. The female had been ingeniously secured by the negroes to a strong stick, the wrists bound to the upper part and the ankles to the lower, so that she could not reach to tear the cords with her teeth. It was dark, and the scene was one so wild and strange that I shall never forget it. The fiendish countenances of the Calibanish trio, one of them distorted by pain, for the mother gorilla was severely wounded, were lit up by the ruddy glare of native torches. The thought struck me, what would I not give to have the group in London for a few days!

The young male I secured by a chain which I had in readiness, and gave him henceforth the name of Tom. We untied his hands and feet; to show his gratitude for this act of kindness he immediately made a rush at me, screaming with all his might; happily the chain was made fast, and I took care afterwards to keep out of his way. The old mother gorilla was in an unfortunate plight. She had an arm broken and a wound in the chest, besides being dreadfully beaten on the head. She groaned and roared many times during the night, probably from pain.

I noticed next day, and on many occasions, that the

vigorous young male whenever he made a rush at any one and missed his aim, immediately ran back. This corresponds with what is known of the habits of the large males in their native woods; when attacked they make a furious rush at their enemy, break an arm or tear his bowels open, and then beat a retreat, leaving their victim to shift for himself.

The wounded female died in the course of the next day; her moanings were more frequent in the morning, and they gradually became weaker as her life ebbed out. Her death was like that of a human being, and afflicted me more than I could have thought possible. Her child clung to her to the last, and tried to obtain milk from her breast after she was dead. I photographed them both when the young one was resting in its dead mother's lap. I kept the young one alive for three days after its mother's death. It moaned at night most piteously. I fed it on goat's milk, for it was too young to eat berries. It died the fourth day, having taken an unconquerable dislike to the milk. It had, I think, begun to know me a little. As to the male, I made at least a dozen attempts to photograph the irascible little demon, but all in vain. The pointing of the camera towards him threw him into a perfect rage, and I was almost provoked to give him a sound thrashing. The day after, however, I succeeded with him, taking two views, not very perfect, but sufficient for my object.

I must now relate how these three animals were caught, premising that the capture of the female was the first instance that had come to my knowledge of an adult gorilla being taken alive. The place where they were found was on the left bank of the Fernand Vaz, about thirty miles above my village. At this part a narrow promontory projects into the river. It was the place where I had intended to take the distinguished traveller, Captain Burton, to show him a live gorilla, if he had paid me a visit, as I had expected, for I had written to invite him whilst he was on a tour from his consulate at Fernando Po to several points on the West African coast. A woman, belonging to a neighbouring village, had told her people that she had seen two squads of female gorillas, some of them accompanied by their young ones, in her plantain field. The men resolved to go in chase of them, so they armed themselves with guns, axes, and spears, and sallied forth. The situation was very favourable for the hunters; they formed a line across the narrow strip of land and pressed forward, driving the animals to the edge of the water. When they came in sight of them, they made all the noise in their power, and thus bewildered the gorillas, who were shot or beaten down in their endeavours to escape. There were eight adult females altogether, but not a single male. The negroes thought the males were in concealment in the adjoining woods, having probably been frightened away by the noise.

This incident led me to modify somewhat the opinions I had expressed, in 'Adventures in Equatorial Africa,' regarding some of the habits of the gorilla. I there said that I believed it impossible to capture an adult female alive, but I ought to have added, unless wounded. I have also satisfied myself that the gorilla is more gregarious than I formerly considered it to be; at least it is now clear that, at certain times of the year, it goes in bands more numerous than those I saw in my former journey. Then I never saw more than five together. I have myself seen, on my present expedition, two of these bands of gorillas, numbering eight or ten, and have had authentic accounts from the natives of other similar bands. It is true that, when gorillas become aged, they seem to be more solitary, and to live in pairs, or, as in the case of old males, quite alone. I have been assured by the negroes that solitary and aged gorillas are sometimes seen almost white; the hair becomes grizzled with age, and I have no doubt that the statement of their becoming occasionally white with extreme old age is quite correct.

After reconsidering the whole subject, I am compelled also to state that I think it highly probable that gorillas, and not chimpanzees, as I was formerly inclined to think, were the animals seen and captured by the Carthaginians under Hanno, as related in the 'Periplus.' Many circumstances combine in favour of this conclusion. One of the results of my late journey has been to prove that gorillas are nowhere more common than on the tract of land between the bend of the Fernand Vaz and the sea-shore; and, as this land is chiefly of alluvial formation, and the bed of the river constantly shifting, it is extremely probable that there were islands here in the time of Hanno. The southerly part of the land is rather hilly, and, even if it were not then an island, the Carthaginians in rambling a short distance from the beach would see a broad water (the Fernand Vaz) beyond them, and would conclude that the land was an island.

Gorillas are attracted to this district by the quantity of a little yellow berry, called *mbimo*, growing there on a tree resembling the African teak, and by the abundance of two other kinds of fruits, of which they are very fond, and which grow on the sandy soil of this part of the coast-land; one of these fruits is called *nionien*, about the size of a nectarine, and of the colour of the peach, but not having the rich bloom of this fruit; it is produced by a shrub that creeps over the sandy soil; the other resembles in size and colour the wild plum, and is a fruit of which I am myself very fond.

The passage in the 'Periplus' which I mentioned in 'Equatorial Africa' is to the following effect:—"On the third day, having sailed from thence, passing the streams of fire, we came to a bay called the Horn of the South. In the recess was an island like the first, having a lake, and in this there was another island full of wild men. But much the greater part of them were women with hairy bodies, whom the interpreters called gorillas. . . . But, pursuing them, we were not able to take the men; they all escaped from us by their great agility, being *cremnobates* (that is to say, climbing precipitous rocks and trees), and defending themselves by throwing stones at us. We took three women, who bit and tore those who caught them, and were unwilling to follow. We were obliged, therefore, to kill them, and took their skins off, which skins were brought to Carthage, for we did not navigate farther, provisions becoming scarce."

These statements appear to me, with the fresh knowledge I have gained on the present expedition, to agree very well with the supposition that the bold Carthaginians reached the country near the mouth of the Fernand Vaz in their celebrated voyage, and that the hairy men and women met with were males and females of the *Troglodytes gorilla*. Even the name "gorilla," given to the animal in the 'Periplus,' is not very greatly different from its native name at the present day, "ngina" or "ngilla," especially in the indistinct way in which it is sometimes pronounced. I now think it far more likely that the gorilla was the animal seen and not the chimpanzee, which is generally less gregarious, and is not often found near the sea-coast. As to the theory that Hanno's hairy men and women were some species of baboon, I think that very unlikely; for why would the Carthaginians hang the skins in the temple of Juno on their return to Carthage, and preserve them for so many generations, as related by Pliny, if they were simply the skins of baboons, animals so common in Africa that they could scarcely have been considered as anything extraordinary by a nation of traders and travellers like the Carthaginians.

The gorilla is of migratory habits at some seasons of the year. He is then not found in the districts usually resorted to by him when the berries, fruits, and nuts are in season.

CHAPTER IV.

START FOR THE INTERIOR.

Arrival of a fresh supply of Scientific Instruments—The first Steamer on the Fernand Vaz—Preliminary trip to Goumbi—Astonishment of the Natives at the fire-vessel—Despatch Collections to England—Live Gorilla embarked for London—His habits in confinement—Narrow escape of drowning when embarked—Preparations completed—Last look at the sea—Outfit—Body guard of Commi men—Affecting parting scenes—I am deceived by Olenga-Yombi—The renowned doctor, Oune-jiou-e-niaré—Arrival at Goumbi—Observations to fix latitude and altitude of Goumbi—Quengueza's Invocation of his Forefathers—Disobedient Wives—Excessive Drought—Obindji—Opposition of Bakalai—Arrival of Ashira Porters—Passage of the hills to Olenda.

On the 30th of June, I bade adieu to my friend Olenga-Yombi, and started for Plateau. I hardly left the ebando, when I espied the sail of a canoe that was coming towards us from the direction of the mouth of the river. On our meeting, the men in the canoe shouted out, "Your vessel has arrived." How glad I was—no news could have been more welcome! My men pulled with renewed vigour, and we reached Plateau that night. There I found awaiting me a letter from Messrs. Baring of London, who had kindly sent a vessel with goods and stores for which I had written, and also with a fresh supply of scientific instruments, to replace those spoilt in the surf. My sets were not, however, completed until a month afterwards, when other instruments reached me by way of the Gaboon; my best chronometer was brought me by Captain Vardon on his return voyage from London in September. I had then three sets and was prepared for accidents which might occur in crossing rivers and so forth. I had sent the damaged chronometers and sextants to England through the Rev. W. Walker of the Gaboon; this being the only way I could send them at that time. They went to the Gaboon in a native boat, and were sent by Mr. Walker to the English consul at Fernando Po, who kindly shipped them in the mail steamer for Liverpool. I must here record my thanks to Mr. Graves, now M.P. for Liverpool, who took the trouble to receive the instruments and transmit them to London, where my friends had them repaired or replaced by new ones. Not the least welcome was a box of medicines sent to me by my good friend, Robert Cooke. My kind friends, the American missionaries at the Gaboon, also sent me a supply of medicines and other things. But their letters were not of a kind to bring me much consolation: they were not so hopeful as I was of success in my undertaking, and although they did not so express themselves, I could see they thought I should never return.

An interesting event occurred in July, which is worth recording here. It was the arrival of a French steamer, the first steam vessel ever seen in the waters of the Fernand Vaz. Some of my negroes came into my hut one morning in great consternation, and breathless with running, to say that a great, smoking ship of war had come down the Npoulounay river. I asked how many guns it had. "Ten," they replied without hesitation. The vessel turned out to be a small flat-bottomed river boat forty feet in length, belonging to an old friend of mine, Dr. Touchard (Chirurgien de Marine, 1re classe), which he had bought with the intention of exploring in it the rivers of Equatorial Africa, and which he had lent to the French authorities at the Gaboon; it was now commanded by Lieutenant Labigot of the French Navy. I need hardly say that the ten guns were only products of the imagination of my excited negroes, the vessel had no guns at all. It was ironically named the *Leviathan*, and had been built, originally, as a pleasure boat, for the navigation of the Seine near Paris. It entered the Fernand Vaz by way of the Npoulounay river, having first explored, in company with a larger vessel, the river Ogobai. The present trip was planned simply from a desire to pay me a visit.

The service on which Lieut. Labigot and Dr. Touchard were employed was the completion of the survey of the Ogobai river, which had been commenced three years previously by Messrs. Serval and Griffon du Bellay, the French Government having shown recently great enterprise in the exploration of this region. On neither expedition were the larger vessels able to ascend the Ogobai, on account of the shallowness of the water, the season chosen not being favourable. Lieut. Labigot and Dr. Touchard had, however, the perseverance to ascend in boats, or in the little steamer, as far as the junction of the Okanda and Ngouyni rivers; they were the first Europeans who had reached this point, and it is to be hoped, in the interests of science, that the result of their voyage will soon be made public.

The *Leviathan* afterwards foundered in a squall at the Gaboon, and I was extremely sorry to hear that the loss was not made good to my friend Dr. Touchard by the French Government, but I hope that it has been by this time.

On July 12th we started in the steamer for an excursion to Goumbi, about seventy miles up the river, setting at defiance the law of the Commi that no white man (except myself) should ascend the stream. For the first twenty miles we had a stiff breeze; we had then reached a small village on the left bank where a Portuguese trader, agent for an English house of business, was settled; there we passed the night. On the 13th we started early and reached Goumbi at half-past five p.m.

The apparition of a steam vessel in these solitary waters put the whole country into a state of excitement. The natives came forth in troops from the villages and crowded the banks. Some were stupified; others, recognising me on the deck as we passed, put out in their canoes and paddled might and main in their attempts to catch us. At the point where the river, in descending from the interior, bends from its westerly course, the banks are high and wooded; here the steamer puffed its way right up to the villages before it was seen, and the frightened natives peeped from the top of the banks and ran away again.

Old Quengueza was proud of this visit of the white men in their fire-vessel, and turned towards his attendant Bakalai and Ashira with looks of supreme contempt. We remained in Goumbi all day on the 14th, and, on the 15th, ascended the river to three or four miles beyond the junction of the Niembai. The vain old African chieftain accompanied us unattended, and he seemed thoroughly to enjoy his trip. I made him put on a European coat and cap for the occasion, although nothing would induce him to wear a shirt, and had a chair placed on deck for him to sit upon. Here he remained the whole time, with a self-complacent smile on his grim features which was almost laughable to look at. He took care to let the people of the villages we passed see him, and calculated no doubt on increasing his influence on the river by this important event. At this point we were obliged to stop in our upward progress, on account of the numerous fallen trees obstructing the navigation, and on the 16th we returned to Plateau.

A few days after this excursion with Lieut. Labigot and Dr. Touchard, I was honoured by an intended visit from the British Commodore Commanding the West African squadron, Commodore A. P. Eardley-Wilmot. He called on his way along the coast, in his flag ship, off the mouth of the river, and learning from the master of the trading vessel anchored there that the bar was unsafe for the ship's boats, he left a message for me expressing his regret that he was unable to come up the river and see me. He inquired regarding the preparations for my expedition into the interior. I much regretted being unable to see Commodore Wilmot, who I knew took a warm interest in all scientific enterprises in the countries of Western Africa, and would, I am sure, have done anything in his power to have helped me in my undertaking.

On the 18th of August I despatched by Captain Berridge to England, all the collections in Natural History that I had made up to that date. They included a second collection of skulls of various tribes of negroes, fifty-four in number, in illustration of the Anthropology of this part of Africa; six skins and seven skeletons of the gorilla; one skin and two skeletons of the chimpanzee, two skins and skeletons of the large scaly ant-eater (the Ipi), three skeletons of the manatee, one skeleton of *Genetta Fieldiana*, besides other mammals, and 4500 insects as specimens of the entomology of the Fernand Vaz region. The collection I am glad to say arrived in London safely, and a great part of it was afterwards deposited in the British Museum. I also sent a living specimen of the singular wild hog of this region (*Potamochærus albifrons*), and two live fishing eagles. The hog I presented to the Zoological Society of London, and I believe it is still living in their gardens in Regent's Park.

The whole of the mammals, including the skins and skeletons of the gorilla, I sent to the British Museum, with a request to my honoured friend, Professor Owen, the Superintendent of the Zoological Department, to select any specimens from the collection that the Museum required, and present them in my name to the national collection. I was much pleased to learn afterwards that several of the specimens were accepted. I felt that I had done something to repay the debt of gratitude which I owed to the large-hearted British nation who had so generously welcomed me when I arrived in England, an unknown traveller, from my former arduous journey. One of the male gorillas proved to be a much larger and finer specimen than the former one, which many must have seen at the end of the Zoological Gallery in the museum; it has therefore been mounted and set up in its place, where I would recommend all who wish to see a really fine specimen of this most wonderful animal to go and see it.

The large collection of skulls made in so short a time will surprise many people, especially travellers in other wild countries who find skulls of natives generally very difficult to obtain. But with the money and trade-loving negro many strange things are possible. It was necessary first to overcome the scruples of the Commi people, and this I did by explaining to them why I wanted the skulls; so I told them that there was a strong party among the doctors or magic-men in my country who believed that negroes were apes almost the same as the gorilla, and that I wished to send them a number of skulls to show how much they were mistaken. When I backed up this statement by the offer of three dollars' worth of goods for each skull they might bring, I soon obtained a plentiful supply; in fact, I was obliged afterwards to reduce the price. The skulls brought me were almost always those of slaves from the far interior, who had died in the coast country; and, as corpses are laid simply on the ground in the native cemeteries, the transaction was much simplified. Nevertheless, the sale of a skull was always treated as a secret matter. The negroes would bring them only at night and by stealth, carefully wrapped up in a parcel, and disguising the shape of the contents, or covering the top with a few sweet potatoes, to mislead any one whom they might meet.

Sometimes two negroes engaged in this sort of contraband traffic would meet, by accident, in my house, each with a suspicious-looking bundle under his arm. They would look at each other in a shy, half-ashamed manner, and then burst out laughing, but finally swearing to keep one another's secret. Skull-selling, however, never became an open, public business. One day old Rabolo came to me, his countenance beaming with satisfaction, and said, in a half whisper :—

"Chaillie, I shall have something for you to-night which will make your heart glad."

"What is that?" I inquired.

"Rogala, my little Ishogo slave, is sick, and will die to-night: I know it. You have often asked for an Ishogo head, and now you shall have one."

I was horrified at the old chief's coolness in thus dispensing skulls before their owners were dead, and insisted upon his showing me the sick boy. He led me to the dark shed where the poor slave lay ill. The child was dreadfully emaciated with dysentery, the disease of which a great many slaves die when brought from the interior. He thought himself he was going to die; but I undertook to prescribe for him. I ordered one of Rabolo's wives to give him warm food. I sent them chickens to make broth with, and myself administered quinine and a little wine. In a few days he was much better, and finally recovered. Thus Rabolo was disappointed in his little skull-dealing transaction, but in compensation saved his slave.

Besides these collections I embarked a live gorilla, our little friend Tom, and had full hopes that he would arrive safely and gratify the world of London with a sight of this rare and wonderful ape in the living state; unfortunately, he died on the passage. He did very well for a few weeks, I am told, as long as the supply of bananas lasted which I placed on board for his sustenance. The repugnance of the gorilla to cooked food, or any sort of food except the fruits and juicy plants he obtains in his own wilds, will always be a difficulty in the way of bringing him to Europe alive. I had sent him consigned to Messrs. Baring, who, I am sure, never had any such consignment before. I promised the Captain that he should receive one hundred pounds if he succeeded in taking the animal alive to London.

During the few days Tom was in my possession he remained, like all the others of his species that I had seen, utterly untractable. The food that was offered to him he would come and snatch from the hand, and then bolt with it to the length of his tether. If I looked at him he would make a feint of darting at me, and in giving him water I had to push the bowl towards him with a stick, for fear of his biting me. When he was angry I saw him often beat the ground and his legs with his fists, thus showing a similar habit to that of the adult gorillas which I described as beating their breasts with their fists when confronting an enemy. Before laying down to rest he used to pack his straw very carefully as a bed to lie on. Tom used to wake me in the night by screaming suddenly, and in the morning I more than once detected him in the attempt to strangle himself with his chain, no doubt through rage at being kept prisoner. He used to twist the chain round and round the post to which it was attached until it became quite short and then pressed with his feet the lower part of the post until he had nearly done the business.

As I have before related, I took photographs of Tom, and succeeded very well. These photographs I was unwilling to send home, and kept them until I should have completed my whole series of photographs of African subjects. They are now, unfortunately, lost for ever; for they were left behind in the bush during my hurried retreat from Ashango-land, as will be related in the sequel.

When the last boat which took on board the Captain and the live animals left the shore for the vessel, I trembled for the safety of the cargo, for the surf was very rough. The negroes, however, could have managed to get her safely through if they had not been too careful. They were nervous at having a white man on board, and did not seize the proper moment to pass the breakers; their hesitation was very near proving fatal, for a huge billow broke over them and filled the boat. It did not, happily, upset, but they had to return. Captain Berridge thus escaped with a wetting, and the Potamochœrus and eagles were half drowned. As to poor Tom, the bath, instead of cooling his courage, made him more violent than ever. He shouted furiously, and as soon as I opened the door of his cage he pounced on the bystanders, clinging to them and screaming. A present of a banana, which he ate voraciously, quieted him down, and the passage was again tried in the afternoon with a better result.

At length my preparations were completed. Towards the end of September my canoes were loaded, and I had selected the men who were to accompany me on my journey.

On the 28th I crossed the tongue of land which separated my village from the sea-shore, to test my boiling-point thermometers and aneroids at the level of the sea, preparatory to my departure inland. Having finished, and wishing to be alone, I sent back my negro lad with the instruments and took a last solitary walk along the sands. I watched the long waves breaking on the beach, and my mind gradually turned to the other shores in the far north washed by the same sea: I thought of the dear friends I had left there, and a spirit of sadness filled my mind. I thought of the dangers of the undertaking to which I was pledged, and felt that perhaps I might never more return. I believe there was not a friend, or a person from whom I had received a kindness, that I did not call to mind; and I also thought of those other persons who had tried to do me all the injury in their power, and forgave them from the bottom of my heart. I took a last look at the friendly sea, and prayed God that I might live to see it again.

My expedition was an affair of great importance for the whole of the Commi tribe. Quengueza, who was more disinterested than the other chiefs—for he was actuated only by a sense of the importance the friendship of the white man conferred upon him—came down the river to bear me company; Olenga-Yombi came from Cape St. Catherine to assist in the ceremony of my departure, with an eye to getting as much out of me as he could, and Ranpano, with his nephew and heir, Djombouai, attended to accompany me part of the way.

My stores and outfit filled two large canoes. I had no less than forty-seven large chests of goods, besides ten boxes containing my photographic apparatus and chemicals, and fifty voluminous bundles of miscellaneous articles. I had also in ammunition 500 lbs. of coarse and fine powder, 350 lbs. of shot, and 3,000 ball cartridges. For the transport of these things by land I should require, including my body-guard of the Commi tribe, more than 100 men. I chose for my body-guard ten faithful negroes, some of whom had accompanied me on my former journey. It was on these men that my own safety, among the savage and unfriendly tribes we might expect to meet with in the far interior, depended. I knew I could thoroughly rely upon them, and that, come what might, they would never hurt a hair of my head. It would have suited my plans better if I could have obtained twenty-five Commi men, but this was not possible. Many were willing to go, but their parents objected.

The best of them were my boy Macondai, now grown a stalwart young man and completely devoted to me, and my hunter Igala, a good and faithful friend. Macondai will be recollected by some of the readers of my former book, as having accompanied me on almost all my wanderings in this region. I had brought him, as a present, a double-barrelled gun from England, and he soon became a good shot. He was more attached to me than any of the others, and I could more safely trust him, as he was free from the superstitions and vain fears of his countrymen and cared nothing for fetiches. He was brave and honest, and helped me to guard my property in our long marches in the interior. Igala I considered my right-hand man. He was a negro of tall figure and noble bearing, cool and clear-headed in an emergency, brave as a lion, but with me docile and submissive. In our most troublesome marches he used to lead the van, whilst I brought up the rear to see that the porters did not run away with their loads. I could always rely upon him; and, with twenty such as he, there would be little difficulty in crossing Africa. He was also my taxidermist, for I had taught him to skin and preserve animals. His reputation was great amongst the Commi as a hunter, and he used to make quite a trade by selling fetiches to the credulous people who wished to possess his skill and good luck in this respect. Igala, however, had a weakness; he was too amorous, and his intrigues with the wives of chiefs gave me no end of trouble. Another good man was Rebouka, a big strapping negro, whose chief faults were bragging and a voracious appetite. Then there were Igalo, next to Macondai the youngest of the party, a light-coloured negro, excitable and tender-hearted; and Mouitchi, Retonda, Rogueri, Igala (the second), Rapelina and Ngoma—six slaves given to me by the various chiefs whose friendship I had acquired on the banks of the Fernand Vaz. I dressed my men all alike in thick canvas trowsers, blue woollen shirts and worsted caps. Shirts being the more important article of dress, they had three each. Trowsers I had found it quite necessary for negroes to wear on a march, as they protected the legs from the stings of insects, from thorns, and many other injuries to which they are liable. Moreover each man had a blanket to keep him warm at night. All the six slaves had volunteered to accompany me; they were not forced to go, against their will, at the command of their masters. It would have been much better if all my Commi attendants had been free-men, for some of the slaves afterwards gave me much trouble by ill-conduct, the result of that absence of self-respect and sense of responsibility which the free men alone possessed. Most of these men now handled fire-arms for the first time, and the possession of a gun to the six men who had been slaves all their lives was one of the inducements which made them willing to accompany me.

Nearly all the people of the neighbouring villages came down to see us off. It was an affecting sight to see my negroes take leave of their families and friends. At the last moment, the young daughter of Igala clung to her father, and with a flood of tears begged him not to go with the white man on the *okili mpolo* (the long road). Igala consoled her by saying, "Do not cry, my child, I am coming back; we shall reach the other side, and bring plenty of beads for you from the white man's country." It was the universal belief of the Commi people that we were going across the land to England, and I was obliged to encourage them in this idea, which was the only way of rendering the journey comprehensible to them. My old friend, Captain Vardon, who had lately returned to the Fernand Vaz with the intention of establishing a factory, lent the villagers guns to fire off salvos on our departure, and was not behind hand in wishing me God speed.

On the second of October we left "Plateau:" on the 3rd we reached an *elanlo*, or palaver shed, on the banks of the river where King Olenga-Yombi, together with the other chiefs and people, had to settle some outstanding disputes of the neighbourhood, and to *mpanga nehé*, or "make the land straight," in general. To my great mortification, this council of wise-heads hindered us a whole week. I could not leave at once, as I had to receive from Olenga-Yombi the slaves that he had promised to give me to carry my goods, the payment for whose services he had already received in the shape of presents having that end in view. The palavers were numerous and difficult to settle. They related either to run-away wives (a fertile source of ill-will and bloodshed) or to homicides. When a man is killed here, if only by accident, satisfaction must be given. Deaths by accident are not more excusable than wilful murder. "An eye for an eye and a tooth for a tooth" is the maxim of the tribe, and the settlement of the compensation generally requires a formal palaver like the present one.

As regards runaway wives the laws are very severe. Any wife refusing to remain with her husband, or running away, is condemned to have her ears and nose cut off. Any man debauching his neighbour's wife has to give a slave to the injured husband; and, if he cannot pay this fine, he must have his ears and nose cut off.

They have no laws to punish robbery.

At length, on the 10th of October, I left the place alone and proceeded to the olako where the road to Aniambié commences. Here Olenga-Yombi followed three days afterwards and had the impudence to tell me his slaves had all run away and that I could not have any, as they were all afraid to come with me. I left in disgust, and in company with Quengueza proceeded on my voyage.

We stopped for the night at a small Commi village, where lived a renowned Doctor named Ounejiou-e-niaré (head of a bullock). This was a most singular old man, possessed of much natural acuteness and at the same time a good deal of kindly humour. He was about seventy years of age, short of stature, very thin, and with a remarkably prominent chin, and piercing, deep-sunken eyes. He had the reputation of being a great prophet, and all the Commi people had great faith in what he said. My men asked him whether our journey would be prosperous. He replied that we should go very far, and that a chief would ask Chaillie to marry his daughter, and then if Chaillie gave her all she asked and made her heart glad, she would lead us from tribe to tribe until we reached the far-off sea where we wished to go. This speech inspired my men with new confidence. I must say that I felt very grateful to the old man. We all sorely needed encouragement in the great enterprise we had undertaken, and nothing was better calculated to buoy up the spirits of my half-hearted followers than these oracular sayings.

We resumed our voyage, with quite a little fleet of canoes in company, on the 14th; the heat was intense, and almost insupportable in the confinement of the boat; we paddled till twelve o'clock at night, and towards the afternoon of the next day arrived at Goumbi.

Here friend Quengueza behaved most royally. We revelled in plenty, and, if my object had been merely to stay here, all would have been pleasant. He soon made up his mind to accompany me to the capital of the Ashira country, and resolved to do it in a triumphal sort of way. But he continued to detain me, day after day, long after all our preparations were completed. The presence of a white man with stores of goods gave him consequence in the eyes of the neighbouring Bakalai, and he wished to prolong the novel enjoyment as long as he could. In his great generosity he franked all his wives to my men, but I overheard them one day complaining that the royal ladies were a grasping lot and drove very hard bargains.

During my stay at Goumbi, I undertook several short excursions in the neighbourhood and made observations to ascertain the altitude of the place and its geographical position; which was very necessary, as it was placed on my map by mere calculation of distances travelled. Unfortunately I was unable to obtain lunar distances here, and therefore cannot fix its longitude; but the mean of several observations of the meridian altitude of the planet Mars and of two fixed stars gave the latitude as 1° 35′ 34″ south—*i.e.* no less than 23 miles further south than it had been placed on my former map, where it had been placed simply on calculation of distances travelled. The altitude of the town I found by means of my aneroid barometers to be 143 feet, and that of the hill-top behind the town 238 feet, above the sea-level. From the hill-top a wide view is obtained of the country round. It is hilly, but there are considerable tracts of level low land between the hills, and few of the hills appeared higher than that of Goumbi.

I was obliged to resort to an artifice which I knew would be effective to get Quengueza to move. I pretended to be deeply offended with him for delaying me so long; and, giving Macondai orders to remove my bed away from the village, I left one evening and made preparations for sleeping under a shed at some distance from the place. Night had hardly set in when the old king, discovering my absence, made a great fuss, and, coming to where I lay, expressed his sorrow and repentance. He lay down by my side, and said that he would sleep where I slept.

Thus, by dint of coaxing and threatening, I got

him, at length, to give the order for our departure, after we had spent thirteen days at Goumbi. It was scarcely day-light, on the 28th October, when I was awoke by the beating of the Kendo (royal bell) and the voice of the old chief invoking, in loud tones, the spirits of his ancestors to protect us on our journey. The roll of his ancestors was a formidable one, Igoumbai, Wombi, Rebouka, Ngouva, Ricati, Olenga Yombi; but they were rather the deceased relations whose heads he had preserved in his mondah or alumbi* house. Quengueza was prouder than any chief I knew of the prowess of his deceased relatives, and there were, I believe, men of great bravery and ability amongst them. Quengueza himself was a bold and courageous warrior in his younger days. It is the rule in Western Africa, when chiefs have been warlike and enterprising in the days of their princehood, to become quiet and settled when they succeed to the chief authority, and then the people rob them; for, as they say, if they do not steal from their father, from whom should they steal?

There were great difficulties as usual on the day of departure. Firstly, Quengueza's chaste and faithful wives refused point blank to accompany him. This did not seem to concern him much, for, in every village of the Bakalai, a wife would be offered to him as the lord of the land; but he was greatly excited when his slaves were not ready for the journey. Some of them had hid themselves, and others had run off to distant plantations. A large number of men were absolutely necessary to carry our loads

* For description of the Alumbi house, see p. 180.

when we commenced our land journey. The old chief threatened to shoot them down right and left if they forced him to use strong measures, and in this way about thirty were mustered.

We started at 10 A.M. on the 28th of October, halting at night at the junction of the Niembai and the Ovenga. It being the dry season, and fish plentiful at this place, we resolved to pass the night here. Our camp was a lively one in the evening, for we caught a great quantity of fish; the smoke of many fires ascended amongst the trees on the river's bank, and all had their fill. Jokes and laughter and tale-telling were carried on far into the night.

I was much amused by the story one of the men related about the dry and wet seasons. The remarkable dryness of the present season had been talked over a good deal, and it was this conversation that led to the story. As usual with the African, the two seasons were personified, *Nchanga* being the name of the wet, and *Enomo* that of the dry season. One day, the story went, Nchanga and Enomo had a great dispute as to which was the older, and they came at last to lay a wager on the question, which was to be decided in an assembly of the people of the air or sky. Nchanga said, "When I come to a place rain comes." Enomo retorted, "When I make my appearance the rain goes." The people of the air all listened, and, when the two disputants had ceased, they exclaimed, "Verily, verily, we cannot tell which is the eldest, you must both be of the same age."

The dry season this year was an unusual one for the long absence of rain and lowness of the rivers. The negroes have a special name for a season of this sort, calling it *enomo onguéro*; it lasts five months, and they assure me that it always comes after a long series of dry seasons of the usual length. We have had a few showers, but they have produced no impression. The effect of the tide is perceived as far as the junction of the Niembai, at least at this time of the year (the dry season); above this point the current of the Ovenga is too strong to allow it to pass further. I took here only one meridian altitude of Fomalhaut, and have fixed the latitude by computation of my dead reckoning.

Next day we proceeded up stream. The Ovenga was very low, about twenty feet below the high-water mark of the rainy season; the current was generally three miles an hour, but, in some places, four miles; it was encumbered with fallen trees, and our journey was difficult and slow.

A little before reaching the village of Obindji we found an obstacle in the way of our further progress. The Bakalai had made a fence across the river to bar the passage, leaving only a gap near the shore for small canoes to pass. This had been done on account of some petty trade-quarrel which the people of this tribe had had with their neighbours. Nothing could have happened more offensive to the pride of Quengueza than the erection of this bar without his having been consulted—he, the king of the Rembo (river), travelling in company with his *ntangani!* It made him appear as though he had no authority. As soon as he saw the obstacle his face changed colour, and, getting up in a violent rage, he called for axes and cutlasses. The fence was demolished in a few seconds, a number of Bakalai looking on from the bank armed with guns and spears.

From the 30th October to the 5th November we were detained at Obindji, waiting for porters from the Ashira country to carry my baggage overland. Our camp was pitched on a wooded point of land opposite to the village, and below the junction of the Ofoubou with the Ovenga.

The town of Obindji has been erroneously placed in maps, published since my first exploration of this country, on the eastern bank of the Ofoubou; it is in reality situated on the western side. It is built at the foot of a fine wooded hill; indeed, the whole country around is clothed with forest of great luxuriance and beauty. From the northern bank of the Ovenga, on which our camp was placed, stretches a long point of beautiful white sand; this sand, in the dry season, connects the point with the mainland of the right bank of the Ovenga. The sand is then most delightful to walk on, especially in the early morning, when the natives ramble about to dig up the eggs of a species of fresh-water turtle laid during the night. The turtle was the species that I discovered in my former journey, *Aspidonectes Aspilus.*

I was glad to find my old acquaintance Obindji, one of the chiefs of the Bakalai of the Ovenga, looking as well as ever. He was a faithful ally and friend of Quengueza, who was his superior chief, in the sense of his being king of the river, and having the right of road and trade both up and down. This section of the Bakalai tribe had been led to abandon the migratory and warlike habits which distinguish their brethren, chiefly through the civilizing influences of trade. Their settlement in one of the richest districts of the river, where ebony abounded in the forests, almost necessitated their becoming traders, and they now collect large quantities of this valuable wood, which is getting scarce here. They have adhered loyally to the treaties made many years ago with Quengueza, who allows them to trade on the river on condition that they abstain from war. Their women have, besides, become wives of the Commi in many cases. One of the privileges of Quengueza, attached to his acknowledged sovereignty, is the choice of the wives of the Bakalai chiefs whenever he sleeps at a village. He has the same right over the Ashira; the chief is obliged to give up even his kondé, or head wife, if Quengueza takes a fancy to her, and his host considers it a great honour so to provide for the entertainment of his liege lord.

When the porters arrived, and, on the eve of our departure into new countries, old Quengueza made a speech to my men. "You are going into the bush," said he; "you will find there no one of your tribe; look up to Chaillie as your chief, and obey him. Now, listen to what I say. You will visit many strange tribes. If you see on the road, or in the street of a village, a fine bunch of plantains with ground-nuts lying by its side, do not touch them, leave the village at once; this is a tricky village, for the people are on the watch to see what you do with them. If the people of any village tell you to go and catch fowls or goats, or cut plantains for yourselves, say to them, 'Strangers do not help themselves; it is the duty of a host to catch the goat or fowl, and cut the plantains, and bring the present to the house which has been given to the guest.' When a house is given to you in any village, keep to that house, and go into no other; and, if you see a seat, do not sit upon it, for there are seats which none but the owners can sit upon. But, above all, beware of the women! I tell you these things that you may journey in safety." The speech of the old sage was listened to with great attention. Like most other good advice, it was not followed; if it had been, many of my subsequent troubles would have been avoided.

Twelve more days were occupied in getting ready to start for Olenda. Messengers were sent to Olenda for more porters. Supplies of food had to be fetched from a distance, as there was great scarcity in the neighbourhood of Obindji; *otaitais*, or baskets of a peculiar shape, had to be made for each porter to carry his load on his back; and there were, besides, all the usual delays which are encountered when one has to deal with a body of negroes. Olenda only sent fifty men in all, whilst my baggage required at least a hundred porters. We were obliged, therefore, to send half of it on, and wait for the return of the men to carry the other half. I was quite frightened at the amount of my outfit, although I left behind everything that seemed not absolutely necessary. It was impossible to preserve any sort of discipline amongst these vivacious savages; they struggled and quarrelled over their loads—the strongest anxious to carry the lightest burdens, and loading the youngest with the heaviest; and, when the provisions for the journey had to be divided, there was a perfect scramble for the lots, the biggest and strongest getting the lion's share. The presence of two of King Olenda's nephews, Arangui and Mpoto, who were sent to command the unruly body, was of no avail.

The *otaitai*, or porter's basket, as manufactured by these Africans, is an ingenious contrivance for the carriage of loads in safety on the back. It is long and narrow, being formed of a piece of strong cane-work (serving as the bottom) two and a half feet in length and nine inches in width, with sides of more open cane-work, capable of being expanded or drawn in, so as to admit of a larger or smaller load. Cords of bast are attached to the sides for the purpose of making fast the contents, and the bottom of the basket is closed in by a continuation of the sides, leaving the top-end (the part nearest the head when carried on the back) open, so as to allow of the augmentation of the load at the top. Straps made of strong plaited rushes secure the basket to the head and arms of the carrier. The wicker-work is made of strips of a very tough climbing plant, or *rotang*, and is always a neat specimen of workmanship.

The first party started on the 8th, going up the Ofoubou river, a southern affluent of the Ovenga, in canoes, to the landing-place on the Olenda road. We had about this time several heavy showers, and the Ovenga rose so much that I was obliged twice

OTAITAI, OR PORTER'S BASKET

to shift my hut to a higher position, and the point of land on which I was encamped, with its beach of white sand, became an island. By a series of observations I found the river-level at Obindji to be fifty-four feet above the sea-level. I made many additions to my collections during my stay here. Insects were not numerous, but some of the lepidoptera, attracted to the moist sand at the edge of the water, and floating about the flowering bushes on the skirts of the forest, were very beautiful. Some of the butterflies (*Romaleosoma*) were magnificent, with their green and black wings ornamented beneath with patches of crimson and yellow. These flew very swiftly, and were difficult to capture. Birds were scarce. I hunted in vain for the *Muscipeta Duchaillui*, of which I had only shot one specimen in my former journey.

The porters at length returned, and the remaining loads having been cleared off, Quengueza and I departed from Obindji on the 17th November. Paddling up the Ofoubou, we saw a very young crocodile sunning itself on a log. One of our boys immediately swam off to seize it, but, just as he was about to grasp it by the neck, the reptile slid off and disappeared. It took us three hours and a half to reach the landing-place, Djali Coudié. Here we slept, and commenced our march the next morning (18th) at day-break. At a quarter-past eight we reached a steep hill, Nomba Rigoubou (369 feet), at the summit of which we stopped for breakfast. Then, resuming our march, we arrived at four p.m. at the base of a hill, called Ecourou, where we stopped for the night. There was here nothing to shelter us but an old shed, loosely covered with pieces of bark. I wanted to roof it with fresh leaves, but we were guaranteed against rain by an Ashira doctor who was with us, and who blew his magic horn to drive it away. In the middle of the night a shower fell and almost drenched us. This did not, however, discompose the doctor and his believers, for he said if he had not blown his horn the rain would have been much heavier.

Quengueza was an amusing companion on a march, for the oddities of his character seemed to be endless. He never travelled without his fetich, which was an ugly little pot-bellied image of wood, with a row of four cowries embedded in its abdomen. As he generally wore an old coat when he travelled with me, he used to keep this dirty little thing in one of the pockets. Waking or sleeping the fetich was never suffered to be away from him. Whenever he ate or drank he used to take the image and gravely pass its belly with the row of projecting cowries over his lips, and when I gave him liquor of any sort he would always take it out and pour a libation over its feet before drinking himself. Libations are great features in the religious rites of these Western Africans, as they were amongst the Ancient Greeks. It used to puzzle me where the four sacred cowries came from; they are unknown on the Fernand Vaz, and I believe came across the continent from Eastern Africa.

Next morning (November 19th) we marched over a wild, hilly, and wooded country until eleven o'clock, when we emerged on the pleasant undulating grass-land of Ashira. An extensive prospect here lay before us; to the south extended the Igoumbi Andelo and Ofoubou Orere ranges of hills, and to the north the lofty ridges of the Nkoumou Nabouali, near which lie the Falls of Samba Nagoshi. At two p.m. we entered, in the midst of the firing of guns and great hubbub, the village of Olenda.

CHAPTER V.

VISIT TO THE SAMBA NAGOSHI FALLS.

King Olenda, his great age—Preparations for the journey to the Falls—We cross the Ovigui—Opangano Prairie—Ndgewho Mountains—Bakalai Village—A flock of Gorillas in the Forest—The Louvendji River—Dihaou and the Ashira-Kambas—Navigate the Ngouyai River—The Avia Tribe—Village of Mandji—River Scenery—Nkoumou Nabouali Mountains—Nami Gemba—Village of Luba—The Spirit of the Falls—Village Deity—Arrival at Fougamou, the principal Fall—Legend of Fougamou—Night Encampment—Return to Dihaou—We sup on a poisonous serpent—Forced March through flooded forest to Olenda.

My old friend, King Olenda, gave me a warm welcome. He had changed but little since I saw him last. His age must have been very great; his cheeks were sunken, his legs and arms excessively thin and bony, and covered with wrinkled skin. He seemed to have hardly strength enough to support his own weight. The negroes say he has a powerful fetich to guard him against death. I believe he was the oldest man I ever saw, and to me he was quite a curiosity. Olenda came constantly to see me during the few days I remained in his village. He was never tired of telling me that he loved me like a sweetheart; but, when I called him to give him his present, he became rather too exacting. I said to him, "I thought you only loved me as a sweetheart, but I am afraid you love me for my goods." "Oh, no!" said the old man, smiling, "I love you like a sweetheart for yourself, but I love your goods also."

I have already, in the narrative of my former journey,* given a description of Ashira-land, and the customs of its people; it will be unnecessary, therefore, to recur to the subject in this place. It was not my intention to make any lengthened stay here on my present expedition; but unforeseen obstacles, and an appalling calamity, as will presently be related, kept me here for several months. I had intended to stop in the country only a short time, sufficient to enable me to visit the Falls of Samba Nagoshi, to the north of Olenda. The preparations for this excursion, out of the line of my eastward march, commenced soon after I had paid our porters, and gone through the ceremony of making a suitable present to the king and the principal chiefs.

It will be recollected by some of my readers that I made an abortive attempt to reach these Falls from the Apingi country on my former expedition. I now learnt that my guides in that journey never intended to take me there; orders having been received from the Commi country to that effect, my good friends there being afraid that some disaster might happen to me. No obstacle being now placed in my way, and having the powerful support of my friend Quengueza, Olenda showed tolerable readiness in furnishing me with porters and guides, and we set off on the 1st December.

We started in light marching order; the only heavy baggage being my photographic camera,

* 'Adventures in Equatorial Africa,' chap. xxiv.

which I was determined to take in order to bring away accurate views of the splendid scenery which I expected to behold. Besides three Ashira guides, Arangui, Oyagui, and Ayagui, and two boys to carry the cooking-pots and ammunition, I took with me two *Ashira Kambas*, natives of an outlying district of Ashira-land lying along the banks of the Ovigui river near its junction with the Ngouyai. These, with four of my faithful Commi boys, formed my party. I left my guns behind, taking only my revolvers. My boys carried their guns, but left behind their woollen-shirts and blankets, and everything that was not indispensible.

We left Olenda at nine a.m., and pursued a N.-E. direction until we struck the Ovigui river. We had to cross this on a bridge formed of a single tree-trunk lying about fifteen feet above the water. We passed it with some difficulty, nearly losing my camera, owing to the timidity of the carrier when half-way across. From the eastern bank of the river the path led to the foot of a high range of hills, which bounds the Ashira plain on this side. At four p.m. we encamped for the night on the banks of a small stream. In the evening we had a frightful thunder-storm, and had to lie down for the night in wet clothes.

December 2nd. Resumed our march at six a.m. The path lay along the western foot of the hilly range, through a dense forest, the rich and varied foliage of which was dripping with moisture. Not a sound was heard, as we trudged steadily along in Indian file. At nine o'clock we came upon a beau-

GROUP OF BAKALAI.

tiful prairie encircled by a wall of forest. This prairie was called Opangano. From it I had a clear view of the Ndgewho mountains. At ten o'clock we arrived at a Bakalai village. Like many of the primitive villages of this warlike tribe, it was artfully constructed for purposes of defence. The single street was narrow, barred at each end by a gate, and the houses had no doors in their outer walls. This would effectually guard the place against nocturnal surprise by other Bakalai with whom the villagers might be at war. This mode of construction had also another object, namely, to allow the people to kill and plunder any party of traders whom they might entice into the village and prevent from escaping by closing the two gates. The neighbouring tribes, especially the Ashiras, dread the power and treachery of the Bakalai. The chief of the village was absent. I bought, for a few beads, a quantity of smoke-dried wild hog of one of the inhabitants.

Leaving this place at one p.m., we pursued a north-easterly direction, and passing several other Bakalai villages, two of which were abandoned on account of some one having died there, reached at five o'clock the Lambengue prairie. It rained nearly the whole afternoon, and we had a disagreeable walk through the mire and over the slippery stones of the forest paths. We built sheds, and passed the night in the prairie.

3rd. At six a.m. again on the march. My men were tired with the exertions of yesterday, for we had been wet all day, so, to keep them up to the speed, I led the column myself. We were soon buried again in the shades of the forest. It was a wild, desolate district, and I marched along in anything but a cheerful mood, thinking of the hard task I had imposed upon myself in attempting to cross Africa. I was going along, a little ahead of my party, when my reverie was suddenly disturbed by a loud crashing and rustling in the trees just before me. Thinking it might be a flock of monkeys feeding on some wild fruit-tree, I looked up, peered through the thick foliage, and was thoroughly roused by seeing on a large tree a whole group of gorillas. I had nothing but a walking-stick in my hand, but was so struck at the sight that I was rivetted to the spot. Meantime the animals had seen me, and began to hurry down the tree, making the thinner boughs bend with their weight. An old male, apparently the guardian of the flock, alone made a bold stand, and stared at me through an opening in the foliage. I could see his hideous black face, ferocious eyes, and projecting eye-brows, as he glared defiance at me. In my unarmed condition I began to think of retracing my steps, but the rest of my party coming up at the moment, with clatter of voices, altered the state of things. The shaggy monster raised a cry of alarm, scrambled to the ground through the entangled lianas that were around the tree-trunk, and soon disappeared into the jungle in the same direction as his mates.

How I regretted to have left my double rifle behind me at Olenda! I had this morning even divested myself of my revolvers, having given them to my man Rebouka to carry, as I wished to be in light trim for leading the day's march. We were all

GORILLAS SURPRISED IN THE FOREST.

tired, and more or less unwell from the constant wetting we had had, and from sleeping in damp clothes. The gorillas were ten in number, and of different ages and sizes, but apparently all females except the one male. My men rushed after the beasts with their guns, but the chase was useless; the forest had resumed its usual stillness, and we continued our march.

At noon we arrived on the banks of the Louvendji river, a stream similar to the Ovigui, and flowing from the south towards the great Ngouyai river, in which were the Falls of Samba Nagoshi. We breakfasted on the brink of this pleasant stream flowing through the silent forest; our breakfast, as usual, consisting of boiled plantains, poor fare for the weary traveller whose bones were aching with the effects of overwork and exposure. The altitude of the river-level above the sea, according to my aneroids, was 490 feet.

Resuming our journey about one p.m. we soon got into a district of swamps, and had to wade at times up to the waist. In places where the water was only ankle-deep the mud had a fetid smell. I found that my Ashira companions were taking me by a very roundabout way, and our journey was long and fatiguing, although we accomplished but a very moderate distance in a straight line. Their object was to avoid some of the Bakalai villages, with the inhabitants of which they had trade-palavers remaining unsettled. At half-past five p.m. we came again upon the Ovigui, where we had resolved to pass the night. As we emerged from the jungle, we were not a little surprised to see an encampment of natives. My Ashira companions soon fraternised with them, for they were Ashira Kambas who, with Dihaou their chief, were spending a few days fishing in the river. The chief received me with wild demonstrations of joy, and thanked Olenda for sending the white man to him.

4th. Passed a wretched night. My bed was simply a row of sticks, each about four inches in diameter, laid to protect me from the damp ground, and a foraging party of the horrible Bashikouay ants came in the middle of the night and disturbed us for about an hour, inflicting upon us severe bites.

Early in the morning we embarked on the Ovigui in a long, narrow, leaky, and cranky canoe, provided by the chief to enable us to make the rest of our way by water. The Ovigui was now a wide and deep stream, with a rapid current. We were nearly upset several times in the course of the first hour of our voyage. At the end of the hour we came to the mouth of the Louvendji, which here joins the Ovigui. In my former journey I was under the impression that the Louvendji falls into the Rembo, but it does not. It joins the Ovigui before that river falls into the Rembo. Below this we passed several Bakalai and Kamba villages, which are built a short distance away from the river bank. About four miles from the mouth of the Louvendji we arrived at the village of Dihaou, the chief town of the Ashira Kambas, where we had to stay in order to obtain proper introduction to the Aviia tribe, in whose territory were situated the Falls.

Dihaou is a cluster of three or four little villages, each containing about fifteen houses. Soon after I arrived presents came from the chief: twelve fowls, five bunches of plantains, and a goat. Our welcome was most friendly, and I felt almost sure of attaining the object for which I had come.

5th. We were all glad of rest after the fatigues of our long march. My men all complained of sore feet. In the evening the chief, Dihaou Okamba, made me a formal visit to receive his return present. I gave him a few articles, and the gift, although I felt it to be an inadequate one, for I had not brought goods with me, seemed to please the old fellow very much. I promised him, however, a big coat, a necklace of large beads, and some salt, on my return to Olenda, on condition that he would send one of his sons with me to the Falls. I had forewarned him by message, that I could not make a sufficient return for the goat I heard he intended to give me; but the old man had all the pride and generosity which these African chiefs usually show in dealing with the white man—at least, whilst the friendship is new. He sent back the reply: "I should not like it to be said that Chaillie, the friend of Olenda, Chaillie my ntangani, came to my town, and that I had not a goat to give him to eat; never."

These Ashira Kambas consider themselves a distinct people from the Ashira of the prairie, over which Olenda and other chiefs ruled, and which are called Ashira Ngozai. I could not, however, detect any difference between them worthy of note, either in their *physique* or customs, and the language of the two peoples is the same. By immemorial law of the country, the Ashira Ngozai are allowed to trade direct with the Kambas, but they are not permitted to go beyond them in their trading expeditions. If an Ashira of the prairie wishes to trade with any tribe north of the Kamba country, he is obliged to employ Kambas as his agents, and must remain in Dihaou until the business is arranged. Otherwise he is compelled to leave his goods in the hands of some Kamba man, and trust to him in bartering them for produce with other tribes. I believe there was not a single Ashira Ngozai who had ever seen the Samba Nagoshi Falls, so effectual are the political barriers which are opposed to the travels of natives beyond the limits of their own and adjoining tribes.

We had the usual difficulty in getting away from Dihaou. The African is never in a hurry to resume a march, and it gratifies the pride of the chief and gives him consequence amongst his neighbours to have the ntangani in his possession. Arangui, nephew of Olenda, who was my chief guide, gave me some trouble with his fears that the villagers wished to bewitch him through jealousy of the white man's friendship. I found it necessary, on the 6th of December, to address a speech to the chief and his subjects, telling them that I must go forward without further delay to the Samba Nagoshi, that I had to *sherra mpaga*, "a wager to win," that our feet had rested long enough, and, finally, that I must be off the next day. Dihaou and his people, as usual, retired a short distance to deliberate, and returned, the chief saying that it should be as I wished; that no harm should come to me from the Aviia people, for they were all his friends, several of his sisters were married amongst them, &c., &c.

7th. The canoe given me for the voyage was a leaky, rotten affair, and on trial I found that it would not contain all our party, with my instruments and the provisions for the journey. I was obliged to leave three men behind with half the plantains. Even then the wretched vessel was only an inch and a half above the water. It seemed to me to be running too great a risk to trust my chronometers on such a journey. If the canoe upset we might swim or scramble ashore, saving what we could, but the loss of the watches would put an end to lunar observations, which I felt to be one of the principal objects of my expedition. So I determined to confide them to Dihaou till my return. The three men we left out of the canoe were to go a tedious march by land and meet us at the Falls.

We left the town at a quarter to nine a.m. and entered the great Rembo (the river Ngouyai) at ten minutes past ten a.m., the distance being about ten miles. It was with some pride that I greeted again this fine river, which I had the honour of discovering on my former journey, at the upper part of its course in the Apingi country;* up to the present time I was the only white man who had ever embarked on its waters.

The Ovigui, at its junction with the Ngouyai, is

* 'Adventures in Equatorial Africa,' p. 439. In the Apingi country it is called the Rembo (river) Apingi, under which name I described it *loc. cit.*

about thirty-five yards broad, and is, at this time of the year (the rainy season), a deep stream. The banks are clothed with uninterrupted forest, leaving only little entrances here and there at the ports of the villages, which lie backwards from the river. Silence and monotony reign over the landscape, unenlivened by the flight and song of birds or the movement of animals.

After a few miles' pull down the Ngouyai, we arrived at a village of the Aviia tribe, called Mandji. As soon as we stepped ashore, the timid villagers—men, women, and children—set off to run for the forest, and all the shouting of my Ashira Kamba companions was for some time of no avail. We took possession of the empty huts, and the people, after the assurance that we had not come to do them harm, dropped in one by one. Confidence had not quite been restored when a gun fired by my man, Rebouka, on the beach, again put to flight the timid savages. This time one of our Ashiras had to follow them into the thicket and coax them to come back.

It was the dirtiest village I had yet seen in Africa, and the inhabitants appeared to me of a degraded class of negroes. The shape and arrangement of the village were quite different from anything I had seen before. The place was in the form of a quadrangle, with an open space in the middle not more than ten yards square, and the huts, arranged in a continuous row on two sides, were not more than eight feet high from the ground to the roof. The doors were only four feet high, and of about the same width, with sticks placed across on the inside, one above the other, to bar the entrance. The place for the fire was in the middle of the principal room, on each side of which was a little dark chamber, and on the floor was an *orala*, or stage to smoke meat upon. In the middle of the yard was a hole dug in the ground for the reception of offal, from which a disgusting smell arose, the wretched inhabitants being too lazy or obtuse to guard against this by covering it with earth.

The houses were built of a framework of poles, covered with the bark of trees, and roofed with leaves. In the middle of the village stood the public shed, or palaver-house, a kind of town-hall found in almost all West African villages. A large fire was burning in it, on the ground, and at one end of the shed stood a huge wooden idol, painted red and white, and rudely fashioned in the shape of a woman. The shed was the largest building in the village, for it was ten feet high, and measured fifteen feet by ten. It is the habit of the lazy negroes of these interior villages—at least, the men—to spend almost the whole day lying down under the palaver-shed, feeding their morbid imaginations with tales of witchcraft, and smoking their condoquais.

We stayed in this wretched abode of savages only to take our mid-day meal. A little before two p.m. we were again *en route*. The river scenery was most beautiful; glorious vegetation clothed the banks, and through breaks in the forest we caught frequent glimpses of blue hills beyond. But the number of deserted villages we passed imparted a saddening effect to the landscape. The country seemed depopulated. No groups of people were seen, happy at their work; no songs of boatmen were heard, paddling their canoes over the pleasant stream. The craven superstitions of these wretched people, and the horror of remaining in any place after a death has occurred, are the causes which lead to the abandonment of their dwellings. Where the people of this neighbourhood had gone to I could not ascertain. No wonder that these interior tribes make no advance in industry, wealth, and culture, whilst such customs exist.

About three miles below the Aviia village, we came in sight of the Nkoumou Nabouali peaks, which appeared to extend from N.N.W. to S.S.E. There were four distinct ranges of hills in view from this spot, Nkoumou Nabouali, the highest, being the second in point of distance from us. A little after three o'clock we began to hear the roar of the Falls, and soon after we put ashore at Luba, another village of the Aviia tribe, which was the nearest to the Falls.

A little below this village there are two large rocks in the middle of the river, or a little nearer to the left bank, called *Nami Gemba*. In the dry season these form dangerous rapids; and the current, rushing at headlong speed between the obstructions to its course, creates a loud noise which is heard at a considerable distance. I made the discovery on my present visit to this part that it was these rapids of Nami Gemba which my guides represented as the Falls of Samba Nagoshi, on my former journey, when in search of the Falls from the Apingi country. I then arrived within hearing distance, but did not actually see them; indeed, I believe my guides themselves did not know where the true Samba Nagoshi were situated.

Apaka, the head man of the village, was taken unawares by our arrival, and had not time to run away from us like the rest of the people. When I approached him, his heart was visibly beating with fear under his shining skin. Movema Baka, my Ashira Kamba guide, however, soon pacified him. The village is called Luba, and was a far cleaner place than the one we had visited higher up. The houses were hidden in the shade of plantain-trees, but the people were short of food, and we not only missed our usual introductory presents, but found great difficulty in purchasing anything to eat.

The chief informed me, in the course of my conversations with him, that the Ishogo tribe did not dwell on the banks of the river to the east, but a little more than a day's journey in the interior, in a N.E. direction, and that another tribe, the Aco, probably a branch of the Shekiani, which I described in 'Equatorial Africa,' lay between them and the river.

As will be seen in the sequel, I visited the Ishogos afterwards in the southern part of their territory. If the information given me by Apaka was correct, this tribe must occupy a narrow extent of territory stretching in a curved form, nearly parallel to the bend of the Ngouyai from the north-west to the south-east.

I asked Apaka to show me the village mbuiti, or

idol, which, it appears, was of the female sex, but he told me that she still remained in the place the people inhabited before they came to this village. To my question why she was not brought with them when they removed, he replied that it was a serious matter to disturb and carry the mbuiti, for it displeased her, and very often those who carried her and the people of the village died one after the other. Thus it is always with these poor Africans, death is always attributed to some supernatural cause or to witchcraft. I had often noticed, in passing abandoned villages, the mbuiti house standing, apparently kept in a good state of preservation, but did not before know the reason. When they resolve to remove the idol, the people accompany it singing songs, and dancing and singing are kept up for days afterwards. Apaka told me that his mbuiti was a very good one; for when she told them it was a good time to go and fish or hunt, they were sure to succeed in getting plenty of food.

At the further end of the village I noticed a detached and ruinous hut, which appeared, from the smoke issuing from the roof, to be inhabited, so I had the curiosity to peep in, thinking it was the house where they kept some of their idols. A most hideous object met my view; a miserable old woman, a mere skeleton, covered with wrinkled skin, lay feebly moaning on a mat. She moved a little when I looked in, and this showed me she was alive. The poor creature, old and therefore useless, had evidently been placed here and abandoned. Such was the famine that reigned in the village, that it was unlikely any food could be given to her. It is in sickness and old age that the life of the savage is most hideous to contemplate. No one in the village seemed to care for the forlorn creature.

8th. The Nkoumou Nabouali mountains lie to the westward of this place; the Ashaukolo range lies many miles further, on the S.E. of Lake Jonanga of the Ogobai, visited lately by the French exploring party under Lieut. Serval. Several chiefs of surrounding villages came in to-day soliciting presents, on account of my having come to see the great mbuiri (spirit) of their river, Samba Nagoshi, but I stoutly refused to fee any chief but Apaka, who would give me a guide to the Falls. Salt from Cape Lopez and European cloth have reached this remote spot. The women wore heavy brass wire round their necks, and lighter wire round their ankles. The young girls go naked, with the exception of a small apron of leaves in front; most of them were better-looking than the Ashira belles.

At Luba the river is very broad, and the rapid takes the name of Nagoshi. Nagoshi is but a rapid. There is an island just above, and sometimes the natives go there in their canoes to fish.

10th. Started for the Falls. We took, for some distance, a path which followed the course of the river, and then descended a steep bank to the margin of the river itself. Here we beheld the first rapids. The bed of the stream was encumbered with boulders of rock of various sizes, through which rushed the water with great force. We followed the river margin for about two hours, scrambling over rocks and crossing several streams which here enter the Ngouyai, some of them so deep that my companions had to swim across and cut down a tree that I might scramble over, for it was very important that the instruments I carried with me should not get wetted. At last we could get along no further by the river margin, and had to ascend the bank into the forest, through which we continued our way to the Fougamou, or principal Falls.

We walked through the jungle for about three quarters of an hour, with the roar of the cataract constantly within hearing, so that I conjectured there was more than one fall. At length we emerged on the brink of the stream, and saw before us a broad seething torrent, madly rushing down between steep and rocky banks with deafening roar. It was not a cataract, but a torrent of fearful velocity and grand proportions, leaping in huge billows, as though the whole of the water of the river dropped into a chasm and bounded out again, over ridges of rock; the scene was rendered more magnificent by the luxuriant tropical foliage of the banks, and the steep hills rising on each side, and clothed to their summits with glorious forest. The width of the stream was not so great as at Lulu, and the torrent roared along one mass of foam as far as the eye could reach.

My Aviia guide now informed me that he had mistaken the path through the forest, and that this was not the Fougamou. It was, in fact, the torrent below the Falls. We had to retrace our steps, ascending the steep declivity, and after a scramble along the rugged hill-side of a mile or so, we came in view of the object I had come so far to see. The stream here was broader (about 150 yards in width), but a rocky island in the middle, covered with trees, breaks the fall of water into two unequal parts, only one of which could be seen from either side. The right-hand Fall was about seventy yards wide, the water rushing in immense volume down a steep incline. Besides the island several detached islets and masses of rock divided this body of water, so that the cataract did not present one imposing sheet of water, as I had expected, and the total fall was only about fifteen feet. The rocks were of red granite, both in the middle of the Falls and on the mainland. It seemed to me that the greatest body of water poured over the right-hand Fall. The left-hand Fall was partly concealed from our view by the rocky wooded islet, and the water appeared not to rush down there with the same force.

The sight was wild, grand, and beautiful; but it did not quite impress me with the awe that the rapids below inspired. We see here the river Ngouyai, after flowing through the Apingi valley in the interior, and receiving the waters of the Ovigui and many other streams, bursting through the barrier of the hilly range which separates the interior of Africa from the coast-land. The high ridges which have been broken through by the river rise on each side, covered with varied forest, and the shattered fragments encumber the bed of the stream for miles. The falls and rapids must vary greatly according to the season, and the amount of water in the river. At the foot of Fougamou my aneroids gave an altitude of 347 feet above the sea-level.

We had brought my photographic camera down to the foot of the Falls, and I ordered a tree to be felled in front in order to get a clear view, finding a large snake twisted round one of its branches, as though it had come there to listen to the music of the waters. The day, however, was cloudy, and after several unsuccessful attempts, I was obliged to give up the intention of taking views of the scenery. I wanted to encamp for the night near the place, and make another trial the next day. But at this suggestion my Aviia guide took great fright, and intimidated my other followers by saying that Fougamou would come in the night and roar with such anger into our ears that we should not survive it; besides which, no one had ever slept there.

Like all other remarkable natural objects, the Falls of the Ngouyai have given rise, in the fertile imaginations of the negroes, to mythological stories. The legend runs that the main Falls are the work of the spirit Fougamou, who resides there, and was in old times a mighty forger of iron; but the rapids above are presided over by Nagoshi, the wife of Samba, who has spoiled this part of the river in order to prevent people from ascending and descending. The Falls to which the name Samba is given lie a good day's journey below the Fougamou, but, from the description of the natives, I concluded they were only rapids, like Nagoshi above. The Fougamou is the only great fall of water. It takes its name from the spirit (mbuiri), who is said to have made it, and who watches it constantly, wandering night and day round the Falls. Nagoshi, the rapid above, takes its name from a spirit said to be the wife of Samba, as I have already stated.

A legend on this subject was related to us with great animation by our Aviia guide, to the following effect: In former times people used to go to the Falls, deposit iron and charcoal on the river side, and say, "Oh! mighty Fougamou, I want this iron to be worked into a knife or hatchet" (or whatever implement it might be), and in the morning when they went to the place they found the weapon finished. One day, however, a man and his son went with their iron and charcoal, and had the impertinent curiosity to wait and see how it was done. They hid themselves, the father in the hollow of a tree, and the son amongst the boughs of another tree. Fougamou came with his son and began to work, when suddenly the son said, "Father, I smell the smell of people!" The father replied, "Of course you smell people; for does not the iron and charcoal come from the hands of people?" So they worked on. But the son again interrupted his father, repeating the same words, and then Fougamou looked round and saw the two men. He roared with rage, and to punish the father and his son, he turned the tree in which the father was hidden into an ant-hill, and the hiding-place of the son into a nest of black ants. Since then, Fougamou has not worked iron for the people any more.

The sky being cloudy all day, I could not take observations to fix the latitude of the rapid, Nagoshi, but as I took a series of bearings, and a meridian altitude of a star at Mandji, and was careful in registering my dead reckoning in the journey from the junction of the Ovigui to the Falls, the position can be fixed with tolerable accuracy. This will enable geographers to clear up much that was doubtful in the cartography of this part of Africa.

It was nearly dark when we had packed up the camera, and we had a difficult walk to accomplish before reaching the place where we intended to pass the night, namely, a fishing encampment of Aviia people on the banks of the river. We were still struggling through the entangled forest when night came on, and through breaks in the foliage we could see the misty moon peering through the light clouds. The loud roar of cataracts and rapids accompanied us every step of the way, and the uncertain track lay over broken and stony ground near the river. Scrambling through thorny bushes, climbing and wading, we at length reached the olando (encampment) at half-past eight p.m. On the road Igalo, who was just before me, killed a venomous snake which was lying in the path. It had a hideous triangular flat head, and fangs of enormous length.

To my dismay the olando was full of people, and there was scarcely room to move under its shelter. I was quite exhausted with fatigue and hunger; my hands and legs were bloody with the laceration of thorns, and my clothes wet through. At length I lay down by the side of one of the fires and thus passed the night. My Commi men were greatly discontented, and Macondai cursed the *okenda i nialai* (the good-for-nothing journey), which did not take us a step nearer to London.

The next morning, the 11th, I succeeded in ascending, in a frail canoe, part of the river which was difficult to navigate, being full of rocks and small islands. In many places the river seemed broader than at Luba. One of the many islands was called Olenda.

Leaving the chando, I returned to Luba. The scarcity of food here had reached starvation point, so we lost no time in continuing our journey to the Ovigui; we had just sufficient plantains left to last us; the river was rising fast, and the current was very strong. I found the Ngouyai had risen about four and a half feet in three days.

In ascending we kept close to the right bank, in order to get a good view of the Nkoumou Nabouali. When the highest part of the mountain bore W., then the summit, which had appeared only as a single peak, showed distinctly two sharp peaks. Trees covered the peaks to the summit. I named this conspicuous mountain Mount Murchison, after my honoured friend Sir Roderick Murchison, the illustrious President of the Royal Geographical Society of London. In my former travels I had estimated the distance of Nkoumou Nabouali from Olenda at sixty miles, being misled by my recollections of the appearance of the peak of Fernando Po. I now found the distance was only thirty-five miles. A few miles below the junction of the Ovigui the Ngouyai seems to run parallel to the hilly ridges, which are five or six miles distant. At the little Aviia village Mandji, where we passed the night, I succeeded in taking the meridian altitude of α Eridani, the resulting latitude being 1° 16′ 26″ S.

12th. In early morning a dense fog enveloped the forests and the broad river; we could not see the opposite bank. We reached the Ovigui at ten minutes past eight a.m. On its banks we stopped at a small village, the chief of which gave us a bunch of plantains and a fowl, and the people sold me a quantity of smoke-dried fish for my men. How we enjoyed the meal after the famine of the previous three days! At half-past two p.m. we arrived at Dihaou; the chief was absent fishing.

13th. The good old chief Dihaou returned this morning, and expressed unaffected delight at seeing me. As usual I heard a harrowing tale of witchcraft in the course of the day. Few weeks pass away in these unhappy villages without something of this kind happening. A poor fellow was singing a mournful song, seated on the ground in the village street; and on inquiring the cause of his grief, I was told that the chief of a village near his having died, and the magic Doctor having declared that five persons had bewitched him, the mother, sister and brother of the poor mourner had just been ruthlessly massacred by the excited people, and his own house and plantation burnt and laid waste.

14th—16th. Delayed at Dihaou by Arangui's trading affairs. Took three observations for latitude, which gave the position of the village as 1° 21′ 3″ S.

17*th*. It was useless to think of ascending the Ovigui in a canoe, as the current had become so strong with the heavy rains, and the canoe was too small to carry all our party; so we were ferried across to the opposite side, where a path commenced leading to Olenda. Our march for several miles led through forest. About four p.m. a storm burst upon us, and we arrived at an old olando, where we were to pass the night, drenched to the skin.

As we were entering the shed, eager to find a shelter from the soaking rain, my men gave a sudden shout of alarm, and all started backwards, tumbling over a fallen log, and floundering in the mire. The cause of their fright was a huge poisonous snake which lay coiled up on the ground within the shelter. The snake was of a species considered by the negroes to be the most poisonous of all the kinds known in Western Africa, the *Clotho nasicornis*. In colour it can scarcely be distinguished from the ground and dead leaves on which it crawls. It is of great thickness round the middle, tapering very suddenly at the tail, and its head is very large and hideous, being triangular in shape, and having an erect process or horn rising from the tip of its nose.

One of our Ashira men killed it. They were delighted with their good fortune, for, being large and fat, it furnished them, when roasted, with a good supper; some of the meat was boiled for broth, and the rest was carefully packed away for another meal. After our arrival at Olenda, I saw the Ashira man roast and eat the head of this poisonous snake: when I examined it I did not see the poison fangs, probably they had been extracted.

18th. Travelled all day, reaching the Opangano prairie at five p.m.

19th. On the march again by daylight, through a fearful storm with deluges of rain. The rain fell in such sheets, that we had difficulty in seeing the path before us, and it lasted till eleven o'clock. One or two rain-falls of this kind happen every wet season. I was afraid my watches would have been spoiled, but the leather case proved a good protector. This case had been given to me by my good and honoured friend, Sir George Back; and was of the same pattern as the one used by him in his celebrated Arctic voyage. The kind letters I received from him just before my departure for the interior were full of good and valuable advice, and will always be gratefully remembered by me. We waded for hours through water up to the ankles. The rivulets we crossed had become too deep to ford, and as I could not swim, trees had to be felled, to fall across and serve as a bridge. I felt that another night passed in the forest would be almost insupportable, besides the great risk of fever to which we should be exposed. We pushed forward at our best speed, crossed the Ovigui, and at length, at half-past five p.m., arrived at Olenda utterly exhausted.

Quengueza came out to meet me. As soon as I reached my hut I had a bath of warm water, took a cup of tea and a dose of quinine, and went to bed.

The forced marches, exposure and privations of this arduous journey, laid me up for several days. I suffered much from a pain in the left side in the neighbourhood of the heart, which was accompanied with fever, and distressed me much. I had also rheumatic pains in my shoulder. My faithful Macondai also had a slight attack of fever, which, however, gave way to a few doses of quinine.

I made also another excursion about this time, to my friend the chief Adingo, whose village is situated at the foot of the Igoumbi Andele mountains, south of Olenda. As a description of this neighbourhood is given in 'Equatorial Africa,' it is unnecessary here to repeat further details of this excursion. I need only say that I have now named the fine wooded peaks of Igoumbi Andele after my much respected friend Professor Owen.

CHAPTER VI.

ASHIRA-LAND.

Grand Palaver to discuss the route into the interior—I am forbidden to pass through the Apingi country—Messengers sent to the Chief of Otando—Changes in Ashira Customs—Decrease of Population—The *Potamogale Velox*—Its habits—My former description of this Animal—Visit to Angouka—Immense Plantation of Plantain-trees—Quarrel with Mpoto, nephew of Olenda—Difficulties and anxieties—First rumours of the Small-pox.

Dec. 23rd, 1864. To day there was an assembly of the head-men of Ashira-land, presided over by King Olenda, to discuss the important subject of my journey towards the east. My intention was to have followed the same route from Olenda as I took on my former expedition, namely, through the Apingi country. But obstacles to this arrangement were raised by Olenda and the Ashira people, who argued that my best course would be to proceed to the Otando country, lying a little to the south of Apingi.

I learnt, in the course of the palaver, the cause of Olenda's opposition. It appeared that after I had left the Apingi, the people could not comprehend what had become of me, and Remandji their chief had much trouble with them. They declared he had hid me in the forest, with the intention of keeping me for himself. So they came in a body to ask him what had become of me. They also demanded that he should give them some of the presents I had given him. A few days afterwards Remandji died, and his son shortly followed him. The cry of witchcraft of course was raised, one party saying that some of the neighbouring people had killed their chief, through envy of his possession of the ntangani, whilst others (and these prevailed) said that I had killed him, wishing, on account of the friendship I had for him, to carry him with me to my own country. The present chief, I afterwards learnt, had secretly sent messengers to Olenda to warn him against forwarding me through his country. He said that he did not want to follow the "spirit," as Remandji and his son had done, but would prefer to stop at home and eat plantains. The present world was good enough for him.

Such is a fair sample of the wild fancies and whimsical superstitions of these strange people, which interpose the most irritating obstacles to the progress of the African traveller. It was clear I must renounce my project of travelling through Apingiland, with such a charge hanging over my head.

After a long discussion and many irrelevant speeches, it was decided that I should go through the Otando country, and that Olenda should send forthwith a messenger to the chief, apprising him of the intended visit, and requesting him to send a party of men to help in carrying my baggage. This is the best, and, indeed, the only plan of getting from place to place in this part of Africa.

I now anticipated but a short delay in Olenda, as on the arrival of men from Otando I should pack up and be off at once. Meantime I occupied myself in practising in photography, taking astronomical observations, and adding greatly to my collections in Natural History. By a numerous series of observations which I took here, the latitude of Olenda has been found to be 1° 44′ 22″ S., the longitude 10° 30′ 34″, and the altitude above the sea-level 526 feet.

A few rambles about the Ashira prairie showed me that the population had much diminished, since my visit six years previously. Many of the villages which then studded its grassy slopes and hollows had disappeared. It is true that some of the head men had removed their people to new villages in the woods, which surround the prairie; nevertheless, I believe the total number of the people had been much reduced. The tribe was once superior to all their neighbours in industry and cleanliness, and in the quality of their clothing and ornaments. A deterioration was now plainly visible. The well-woven dengui which the people used to wear had almost disappeared, and in its stead I saw only garments of thin, dirty, cotton cloth. A few of the older women alone were decorated with copper rings round the neck. The young people had also abandoned the practice of filing their front teeth, and I noticed a total change of fashion in the dressing of their hair, increasing commerce with the Rembo having had the result of their adopting Commi fashions. The tribe have now constant intercourse with the Commi, and of late years the warlike Bakalai have married many of their women and of course taken them away.

The 28th of December was a happy day to me; for I succeeded in what I had been long wishing for, the acquisition of specimens of the curious otter-like animal *Potamogale velox*. It was one of my most interesting discoveries on my former journey, and I had given a description of it which was published in the 'Proceedings of the Boston Society of Natural History for 1860' (vol. vii. p. 353). I had been unable to bring home more than a skin of this animal; and when it was made the subject of one of the ungenerous attacks made at that time upon me, I was unable to produce evidence, in a skeleton or specimen of the perfect animal, of the truth of the account I had given of it. I had examined the living animal, and had described it from remembrance as allied to the otters. But my critic, from an examination of the skin, only ridiculed my statement, and declared that it did not even belong to the order under which otters are classed, but was a rodent animal. He proposed even to do away with the name I had given it, and to call it *Mythomys*, in commemoration of my supposed fabulous statement. It may be imagined, then, how glad I felt in obtaining two specimens of the Potamogale. I preserved the skeletons as well as the skins of both, and wished that I could at once have sent them to London to vindicate my statements.* Some weeks afterwards, when at Máyolo, I obtained four more specimens.

* Independently of my specimens, an example of the Potamogale velox came into the hands of Professor Allman, of Edinburgh, who was the first to announce that I had accurately described and classified the animal. See Professor Allman's Memoir in the 'Transactions of the Zoological Society,' vol. vi., pt. I., p. 1.

The Potamogale lives in many of the shady and rocky streams near Olenda, gliding under water with great velocity after its prey. On opening the stomachs of all my specimens, I found only fresh-water crabs in those I found at Olenda. At this season of the year, the waters are all turbid with the floods, and I imagine that the Potamogale, unable to find fish, which are his ordinary food, has to content himself with crustacea, which he finds about their holes, under the rocks and stones on the banks of the rivulets. Three of those found at Máyolo had fish in their stomach, and one had crustacea. The animal is not found in the Ngouyai or other large rivers of the country, but is confined to the smaller streams. In the dry season it is seldom to be found anywhere.

One of my excursions in the neighbourhood of Olenda was to the village of my former friend the chief Angouka, situated ten miles N.W. of the capital. I may here say that, although I speak of Olenda as the capital of Ashira-land, it was by no means the largest village in the country. It is a peculiarity of this part of Africa, that the residence of the head chief, or king of a tribe, is often a smaller place than the villages of the subordinate chiefs. The size of a royal village depends on various circumstances, chiefly on the personal character of the king. If he is of a conciliatory and unsuspicious, and, at the same time, of an energetic disposition, he may attract a large number of people around him; but if he is quarrelsome, or more than usually suspicious of witchery, &c., the minor chiefs and the people will keep out of his way. It will be seen hereafter that the slave-village of King Olenda, in the neighbouring woods, was a much larger and better-ordered settlement than his own town.

Angouka, like many other chiefs, had moved his village since I last visited the country. We passed through the remnants of it on our way. Strange to say, these people seem to leave their villages just as the fruit-trees, which they have planted with considerable labour, have begun to bear. My faithful friend Quengueza accompanied me, and Angouka gave us a hearty welcome. In remembrance of his former kindness to me, I presented the chief with a big coat, a white shirt, a piece of fine cloth, and a necklace of large beads. We feasted heartily on an antelope which had been killed just before our arrival.

The most remarkable feature about Angouka's place was the great extent of his plantain-groves. It was the largest plantation of this tree I had ever seen in Africa; there being, according to my calculation, about 30,000 trees, most of them planted about five feet apart. Each tree would bear, on an average, half a dozen shoots, which would in time grow to trees, but the natives generally cut all these away except two or three. The bunches of plantain produced by each tree weighed from 20 to 40 lbs., but I found many weighed as much as from 80 to 120 lbs. No cereal could give in the same space of ground so large a supply of food. There were many varieties; some bear about six months after the sprouts are planted, others eight or ten months, and others again not before eighteen months; these last generally bear the largest-sized bunches. The sight of this great plantation, with the magnificent foliage covering the gentle hollows and slopes, was most pleasing; nothing had so much delighted me for many months. It was within the borders of the forest which skirts the prairie, the trees of which had not been all felled, but killed by barking their trunks, and making fires at their bases. In early morning a light mist hung over the landscape, and veiled with thin clouds the forest slopes of the neighbouring hills.

The first days of the New Year were spent by me in much anxiety of mind. There were, in the first place, many unpleasant disputes with the Ashira people, on account of the intrigues of my Commi men with the native women, and these led to a quarrel between me and Mpoto, Olenda's nephew, who was very violent. Mpoto was a hot-headed negro, never well-disposed towards strangers. He came, with the intention of making a disturbance, one morning from his village, which was within a short distance from Olenda, and singling out my head man, Igala, pointed a loaded gun at his head. I was obliged to interfere, otherwise blood would have been shed, and only prevented him from firing by levelling a revolver at him. All my men had seized their arms, and a general *mêlée* was imminent. Igala behaved like a brave fellow as he was, facing the enraged Mpoto when the muzzle of the gun was within a few feet of his head, and you could not see a muscle move in his fearless countenance. Olenda interposed afterwards as peace-maker, and Mpoto was so terrified at the old man's threatening to curse him, that he bent down, and, taking hold of the patriarch's feet, implored his forgiveness. I threatened and chastised my men, but all my endeavours to put a lasting end to the evil were fruitless.

There was next the long delay in the arrival of the porters expected from Otando, and I was afraid some hitch had occurred. At last a party of men arrived from the chief of Otando, bringing an invitation for me, accompanied by the present of a goat; but, whilst we were engaged in collecting a sufficient number of Ashira porters to aid in transporting my baggage, a third and most serious cause of anxiety arose, which ultimately had well nigh put an end to my expedition.

Elanga, one of Olenda's nephews, was taken ill with a disease which the natives had never before seen. It was described to me, and I thought I recognised in the description the symptoms of small-pox. The next day the news came from a neighbouring village that Elanga had died. There was a great deal of mourning and wailing among the people; and all the inhabitants of Olenda, with the exception of the old king, went to join in the wild manifestations of grief. Now, Elanga was one of the Ashira men who had been to Obindji to fetch my baggage, and a suspicion of foul play or witchcraft, as usual, arose in the minds of the Ashira people, which, in addition to the other causes of unfriendliness, threatened to embarrass my movements. After the lapse of a few days, two other cases of the disease occurred, also in men who had carried my goods from the Bakalai country. I began to be alarmed, for I knew what havoc such a pestilence would cause amongst these people if it gained head. But I had no fear for myself, for I had been, fortunately, re-vaccinated in London a fortnight before I left England, little thinking what I should have afterwards to pass through.

The first step I took was to keep my Commi men away from the places where the disease had shown itself. This was remarked by the people, and their suspicions were strengthened. They began boldly to accuse me of having introduced the *evira* (thing that spreads, *i.e.*, the plague), or, as they sometimes called it, the *opunga* (a bad wind), amongst them; they declared that I had brought death with me instead of bringing good to the people; that I was an evil spirit; that I had killed Remandji, king of the Apingi, and so forth. Hence arose angry disputes. Quengueza, never a very good-tempered man, grew furious. He asked them whether they thought that he, the king who held the passage of the Rembo, had come with his white man into the bush amongst these pigs of Ashira to be cursed? Old Olenda held Quengueza in great respect, and invariably sided with him in our troublesome disputes with the Ashira people. Some days passed in this way. I strove my utmost to get away from the place before the disease had made further progress. Olenda had sent orders round to the neighbouring villages for porters to assemble in the village; and thus in a few days I hoped to be on the march, and to find health and pleasure in the hilly and wooded country, which intervenes between Ashira and Otando.

CHAPTER VII.

THE PLAGUE IN ASHIRA-LAND.

Breaking out of the Small-pox Epidemic—Noble Conduct of Quengueza—Departure of Quengueza's People—Illness of the Porters—My Commi Body-guard refuse to leave me—Departure of part of the baggage to Otando-land—Quengueza returns to Goumbi—Letters from Europe—Death of Mpoto—Death of King Olenda—His burial—Cemetery of the Ademba Chiefs—Wailing for the dead—Death of Retonda—Arrival of Messengers from Máyolo—Distrust of the Natives—Trickery of Arangui—I am robbed by the Ashira People—Diminution of the Pestilence—Quengueza's message to the people of Olenda.

At length the calamity which I had so much dreaded came upon us; the plague broke out with great violence in Olenda village, causing obstacles to the progress of my expedition which had well nigh proved fatal to it. The first victim was the head wife of Olenda himself. The awful scourge spread with a rapidity that frightened me. Several of the mourners who had been to Elanga's funeral had fallen ill of the disease. This was not to be wondered at, considering their style of mourning, the relatives and neighbours all surrounding the corpse, touching and even embracing it, whilst crying out, "Do speak to us—do not leave us! Oh, why do you die?" I had urged Olenda not to allow these mourning ceremonies to take place, telling him of the results that would follow. None of the people of the surrounding villages would come near us. In a few days more than half the people of Olenda caught the infection. I became alarmed for the safety of the noble old Quengueza and his men; and my first desire was to see him free from the danger, and returning to his own country. But he refused to leave me. "Chaillie," said he, "I cannot go back. I came here to see you through this country, and I should feel shame to leave you in your troubles. What would the Commi people say? They would laugh at me, and say, 'Quengueza had no power to help Chaillie on his way.' No, I shall not leave you!"

A favourite little slave of Quengueza's, named Rigoli, soon after this was attacked by the disease. It was now in our camp, and there was great danger of my own men falling ill. I was obliged to make the most stringent regulations, forbidding them to hold intercourse with the natives, to use any of their utensils, or to smoke their condoquais. It was in vain, however, that I tried to get Quengueza to send away his little boy. When I went to see him, I found, to my horror, that he had got the boy in his hut, laid on a mat near his own, and was nursing him with the tenderest care. If the noble old fellow had caught the disease himself, it would have completely put an end to my expedition; besides, many of his own people were going in and out of the hut, and all my quarantine regulations were totally upset. To my expostulations the old man only replied, "If I get the plague, it will be God's (Aniembié's) palaver, but I can better take care of Rigoli here." Notwithstanding my annoyance, the scene raised Quengueza more than ever in my estimation, and showed me, under the coarse skin of the savage, the noble heart of a man who had but the promptings of generous instinct to guide him.

A few days afterwards Quengueza, at my earnest persuasion, sent away all his people, and used his influence with Olenda to get me again a number of porters to continue my journey. The Ashira tried to persuade Quengueza to leave me, promising him they would take care of me. The old chief had a very stormy palaver with Olenda, and taunted him with his inability to send me forward on my journey. He threatened to return to Goumbi and tell the people how powerless Olenda was, or else to take me to the Bakalai, who would do better than the Ashira had done. Olenda was stung by these reproaches, and undertook at once to send for his nephew, Arangui (the same who had taken me to the Samba Nagoshi Falls), to guide me to the Otando country.

Three times I had mustered porters for my onward journey, and had each time been disappointed through the poor fellows falling ill of the epidemic before even the packing of the loads was completed. I had now given away a large quantity of my goods, and had much reduced my baggage; but still it would require more men to carry it than were now in a condition to work in Olenda's village. Thirty men were all that could be mustered at the command of Olenda, and they are so proud that they would not go to another clan to get porters from among their friends. The bargaining for pay was the most difficult I had ever experienced. The rascals knew the difficulty I was in, and increased their demands accordingly. The cunning of these people is not to be matched by that of the wiliest diplomatist of our race. When settling the price of their services, all the older men took my part in the haggling match, beating down the demands of the younger ones; of course, looking forward to the natural reward of their partizanship in higher pay for themselves. This was a deep-laid manœuvre to get higher wages for the whole, and was planned secretly by the entire party beforehand; for, when all were paid, the young men returned and refused point blank to go with me unless I paid them at the same rate as the older ones, who, said they, have no loads to carry.

My plan now was to get all my own men away from the small-pox by sending them on first with part of the goods to the Otando country, under the guidance of Arangui, myself intending to follow with the rest of the baggage on Arangui's return. To this arrangement my faithful lads would not agree at all. They conferred together, and then told me they would not leave me here alone. "Who," said they, "in the midst of this fearful sickness, is to cook for you, and wash your clothes? These Ashira may poison you, by putting the gall of a leopard into your food. Some of us must remain with you, come what may!" I was obliged to accede to their wishes, and chose five of them to remain with me, Macondai, Ngoma, Igala (Quengueza's slave), Igalo, and Rétonda. The rest, Igala, Rebouka, Mouitchi, Rapolina, Rogueri, together with the porters, who comprised all the disposable men of Olenda's clan, departed on the following morning. This division of my party was a great mistake on my part; it tempted the Ashira people to form a plot to plunder me, as will presently be related.

Quengueza now left me to return to Goumbi. Before his departure I took a photographic likeness of him, and was glad to have this memento of so excellent a fellow. He believed I was now well on my way to the white man's country, and told me not to forget to bring him back a big bell, a silver sword, a brass chest, and plenty of fine things. On parting he took my two hands in his own, blew on them, and invoked the Spirits of his ancestors to take care of me. I looked after him as he disappeared in the tall grass of the prairie, and returned sorrowful to my hut, for I felt that I had parted from the best friend I had in Africa.

The men from Goumbi, who came to accompany Quengueza back to his home, brought me a large parcel of letters and newspapers from my friends in England, France, and the United States. They had come by the mail-steamer to Fernando Po; had been transmitted thence in a sailing vessel to the Gaboon, and forwarded to the Fernand Vaz in a native canoe. From my village they had been sent up to Goumbi by a negro messenger. Notwithstanding the many changes of conveyance, no injury was sustained, and, as far as I could learn, nothing was missing.

How I revelled in the kind letters of my many friends, so full of encouragement and good wishes! They were as manna in the wilderness to me, and gave me new strength of resolution to carry out my undertaking at a time when I was thoroughly disheartened. The letters of Sir Roderick Murchison and Professor Owen, especially, gave me new life. Amongst the papers which I received, there was a copy of 'The Times' containing an article on the death of Captain Speke. It was the only sorrowful news that came, and I felt sad in reflecting how precarious and uncertain was life. A brave and strong man, who had gone through all the dangers of a march through the interior of Africa, had thus fallen by accident, after his safe return to his home and his family!

The parcel contained, besides other papers, numbers of the 'Illustrated London News' and 'Punch.' These were, afterwards, extremely useful to me, as they never failed to give amusement to the negroes of the villages I stayed at, and they were always thought much of by the head men as presents. The unsophisticated African has a great liking for printed paper and books, especially when they have plenty of engravings.

After Quengueza's departure the small-pox increased its ravages. Not a day passed without its victims, each fresh death being announced by the firing of guns, a sound which each time pierced through me with a pang of sorrow. From morning to night, in my solitude, I could hear the cries of wailing, and the mournful songs which were raised by the relatives round the corpses of the dead. The curses of the natives fell thick on me as the author of their misfortunes. To these miseries another one was soon added in the shape of famine. There was no one left to gather food; and my men in searching for it in the neighbouring villages were driven back and threatened with death by the terror-stricken inhabitants, who believed that we were the carriers of the plague and of the famine.

All Olenda's wives were down with the disease; but, happily, the king himself remained my friend, and as long as he had food he shared it with us. But sorer trials than famine were in store for us. One wretched night a sudden wailing burst forth, and soon became general throughout the village. It was the announcement of the death of Mpoto, the favourite nephew and heir-apparent of Olenda. The tremulous and feeble voice of poor old Olenda was heard in the early morning singing the plaintive songs of grief. The death of Mpoto was imputed by the people to me, on account of the quarrel I had had with him; and a general complaint was made that, whilst all the Ashira were falling ill, the white man's people were untouched. We were in great danger of being attacked by the enraged people of Mpoto, and had to keep watch for some time with loaded revolvers ready at hand. Soon after this came the final blow—Olenda himself sickened and died! He was the last of his clan to be struck down with the disease, if, indeed, it was the small-pox of which he died. In fact, he, Macondai, and I, were the only people remaining well at that time, for my three other faithful lads had, to my infinite grief, fallen ill with the worst type of the infection; Ngoma, especially, was a great sufferer, for the skin sloughed off his body in large patches; his face was swollen up, and the putrid smell that came from his body was dreadful. He lay beside my bed; for there was no hut but my own in which I could put him. Igala, Quengueza's slave, was in almost as bad a state.

No one can imagine the anxiety I felt when, one morning, Olenda complained to me of burning heat and thirst. The fever increased in the course of the next two days, and with it weakness and drowsiness, but without any external appearance of small-pox. When I sat by his bedside, the old man, seeing my sorrowful countenance, would say, "Do not grieve, Chaillie; it is not your fault; you have not caused my illness, I know it." On the third night a sudden cry of anguish from house to house in the village, the meaning of which I knew too well, told me that my only remaining friend was no more. He died, I was told, without suffering; going off, as it seemed, in a quiet sleep. Shortly before his death he had enjoined upon his people that they should take care that no harm came to me.

I was afraid that Olenda's subjects would not be so tolerant as he himself was, and would accuse me of having caused his death. I had taken a photographic likeness of him a few days before his illness, to the great wonderment and fear of the few people who were well enough to watch the process. I wished now that I had not done it, for I thought it would be sure to create suspicions of my having practised magical arts to cause his death. Happily, matters took another turn. His relatives had been so touched by my evident sorrow at the old man's illness and death that they came to me afterwards, and, instead of accusing me of causing his death, consoled me, saying that although Olenda was dead, his clan had not died with him; he had left people behind him, and they would carry out his wishes, and see that I had porters to take my baggage to Otando. This day Macondai fell ill. A high fever, the precursor of the small-pox, seized him, and for a week I knew not whether I should lose my beloved boy, as the eruption did not come out. And now I was indeed alone, with no one to help me. I had to fetch water, to search for firewood, and to cook for myself, as well as for all my poor stricken followers.

The villagers exerted themselves to procure food for me. Those who were now well enough crept towards the plantation to get plantains for me; and even the invalids, men and women, sent me offerings of food, saying, "We do not want our stranger to be hungry."

Poor Olenda was buried in the cemetery of the chiefs of the Ademba clan, the clan of Ashira over which he had been the head. I say buried, although this term hardly applies to the custom followed by these people of exposing the corpse above-ground. The cemetery was in a little grove of trees just outside the village. I gave the people powder to fire a salute at the funeral, and they came and begged from me an umbrella to bury with him, this being an article which it was thought very necessary and desirable to bury with their chief. There was great grief on the burial-day; the women shaved their heads, dressed themselves in rags, and besmeared their bodies with ashes; and as the body was carried out of the village, cries of anguish and lamentation were heard; all the people shouting out, "He will not take care of us any more—he will not speak to us any more. Oh, Olenda, why have you left us! Oh, Olenda, why have you left us!" Two days afterwards I went myself to the cemetery. The corpse of the old chief was placed on the ground, in a sitting posture, enveloped in a large European coat which I had given him, and by his side was the umbrella; the head looked already like a skull, covered with dry, wrinkled, parchment-like skin. By his side lay a chest containing the various presents I had given him, and also plates, jugs, cooking utensils, his favourite pipe, and some tobacco, and a fire was burning, which the people keep alight day and night by the corpse of a chief, sometimes for many weeks. There was also a plate of victuals, brought, according to the custom of these people, for the corpse to eat, and renewed daily for some time. The aspect of the place was not cheering, as may well be imagined; all around lay the bones of the ancestors of the Ademba chief, in various stages of decay. For several mornings after his burial, the people came to me and declared that they had seen Olenda the previous evening, walking in the village, and that he had told them that he had not left them entirely, but would come from time to time to see how they were going on. I have no doubt they believed what they said, as their imaginations were greatly excited during this dreadful period.

The once cheerful prairie of Ashira had now

become a gloomy valley of the dead; each village was a charnel-house. Wherever I walked, the most heart-rending sights met my view. The poor victims of the loathsome disease in all its worst stages lay about in sheds and huts; there were hideous sores filled with maggots, and swarms of carrion flies buzzed about the living but putrid carcases. The stench in the neighbourhood of the huts was insupportable. Some of the sick were raving, and others emaciated, with sunken eyes, victims of hunger as well as of disease. Many wretched creatures from other villages were abandoned to die in the bush. How I bewailed my hard fate, and wished myself back amid the health and comforts of Europe, even though it were only as a street-sweeper in one of its cities!

To add to my sorrows and losses in this unhappy time, one of my Commi boys, Retonda, sickened and died. His disease was not, however, the prevailing epidemic, but a kind of cholic attended with violent vomiting. He was the only one of my Commi body-guard that I lost on the journey; he was a plucky fellow, and I felt much his loss. We buried him, wrapped up in a mat, with the usual honours, firing a salute over his grave.

A few days before the death of Olenda, a number of men, sent by the king, arrived from Máyolo's town in Otando. The news they brought was not very favourable to the prospect of my onward march. There had been a meeting of the head men to consider the matter of my visit; and the conclusion arrived at was that I ought not to be allowed to come, seeing that I carried the *evira*, or plague, wherever I went. Máyolo himself, however, was favourable, and took upon himself the responsibility of inviting me to his village; but I was not to be allowed to visit the other chiefs. The Apono people, beyond the Otando country, had also sent word that they should oppose my progress.

The Otando messengers had some visits to make in the neighbourhood, and left me with the promise that they would return in two days; in the meantime I and my men were busily employed packing up, with the hope of soon being on the march. Three days elapsed, and then, to my great vexation, I heard that the Otandos had hastened back in fright to Máyolo. This was most unfortunate. They had seen the sickness and desolation of the Ashira villages, and were now returning in their fright to spread the horrid news throughout Otando-land, and to confirm the impression that I was the cause of it all.

Several weeks passed away in solitude, anxiety, and suspense. I waited day after day in expectation of seeing Arangui return from Máyolo, that I might proceed with the rest of the goods. The small-pox was gradually diminishing, from sheer lack of victims for further ravages; but the Ashira people had grown more distrustful, and something was evidently going wrong. At length three of my men suddenly made their appearance from Máyolo. They had left all well, but, to my surprise, told me that Arangui had left two days after their arrival in Máyolo, and must therefore have long ago arrived in Ashira. Some underhand movement was evidently going on, protably with a view to plunder me, and I suspected Ondonga to be at the bottom of it, as it was he who had repeatedly told me that Arangui still remained in Otando. I soon learnt, on further inquiry, that several of the loads had never reached Máyolo at all, that the porters had gone back to their plantations with them, no doubt by orders of Arangui, who would have a large share of the spoil afterwards; the porters had scattered themselves along the forest road, some sleeping in one place and some in another, and almost every load had been rifled of part of its contents. My men had been tired of waiting for me, and they told me that the Otando messengers, who had returned in such hot haste, were driven from Ashira-land by the threats of Arangui, who had seized one of them, and made him prisoner. Thinking that something was wrong, my men had resolved to despatch three of their number, well armed, to know the cause of my detention.

I was now in a very unpleasant position. It was no satisfaction to hear that Arangui had shown violent anger on the discovery of the robbery, for I well knew the hypocrisy of the African character. I had been shamefully robbed, with the connivance of the head men of Olenda, and in addition one of Máyolo's messengers was detained a prisoner, without whose release I should never be allowed to enter the Otando territory. I told my men to say nothing about the robbery, my object being not to excite any fears of punishment until I had obtained porters to enable me to get away from the place.

It was a difficult matter to conceal my indignation,

PRISONER IN SCHOOL.

especially when I saw that all the people of the village knew how I had been plundered. I detected them often whispering secretly and casting furtive glances towards my hut; but orders had been given to every Ashira man, woman, and child to keep the matter secret from me, and not a single one betrayed it. It is wonderful how even the young children here are taught to be "discreet." I was obliged to act the hypocrite and pretend that I believed Ondonga was ignorant of the arrival of Arangui. The day following the arrival of my men, Ondonga, Mintcho, and several others came to me and told me they would endeavour to persuade Arangui to give up the man. Arangui was obstinate, and neither the arguments of his friends nor my threats could prevail upon him. It appeared that two years previously the Otandos had seized a relative of his, and still kept him in nchogo (the native stocks). Here was a sample of the complicated difficulties a poor African traveller has to contend with. At length Arangui fell ill; and, in his superstitious fears that I had caused his illness, he released the man, but with limbs so cruelly lacerated by the wooden blocks in which he had been confined, that he was unable to move for several days afterwards.

Meantime the news of Olenda's death and my detention had reached Goumbi, and Quengueza had sent word that he must come and fetch me back, that Olenda had left no people to carry the white man's goods to the next country, and so forth. The men who brought the message told us (what I afterwards learnt to be true) that all the negroes who had accompanied Quengueza from Olenda had died, either on the way or after their arrival at Goumbi. The reproach of Quengueza stung the Ashira people to the quick, and they now bestirred themselves in reality. It was, however, very difficult to get porters together, although Ondonga aided me with all sincerity, for they did not want to have to go to another clan for people. I was obliged at last to grant them all they wanted, which was to abandon to them all the apparatus and goods which I could not carry any further into the interior, for want of porters.

I finally succeeded in obtaining about twenty men, including five Apingi belonging to Mintcho, whom I was obliged to propitiate with the present of a gun, to induce him to join us with this strong reinforcement. I had to give up besides to the porters the greater part of my ammunition, all my sugar, tea, and every spare article of clothing. One of the principal men, Ayagui, son of Olenda, who accompanied me on my former journey, when he had received the whole of his pay, said in the coolest manner that he should keep that as recompense for having taken care of two of my men, and that neither he nor his slaves would go with me without further wages. Although boiling with indignation at this act of rascality, I was obliged to yield. I was entirely in the power of these rapacious scoundrels. With these tribes it is not only that they are seeking to gratify their own cupidity in thus fleecing a traveller, but mingled with it is a jealousy of the next tribe's having a chance in their turn of participating in the plunder of the white man.

CHAPTER VIII.

FROM OLENDA TO MÁYOLO.

Departure from Ashira-land—Passage of the Ovigui—Slave Village of King Olenda—A Slave Chief—Difficulties with the Porters—More Robberies—Illness of Macondai—Leave him behind—The Otando Range of Hills—Picturesque Cascade in the Forest—Cross the Louvendji—More difficulties with the Porters—Hunger in the Forest—Men sent to Máyolo for Relief—A Night in the Forest—Myth of Atungulo Shimba—Koola Nut-trees—Search for Food—Meet with a Gorilla—A Hungry Night—Unselfish act of the Ashira—Help arrives from Máyolo—Mpegui Nuts—Arrival in Otando-land.

March 16th. At length, after many months of weary delay, the hour arrived for our departure from the Ashira settlement. I had suffered in this unfortunate place more than words can describe; racked with anxiety on account of the fearful epidemic which had dogged my footsteps, and which the credulous natives accused me of introducing amongst them, tortured with the threatened failure of all my schemes, robbed and cheated by the head men and their subjects. My party of ten men had become reduced to seven. Retonda was dead; Igala (Quengueza's slave) was left behind, although much better; and Rogueri, the slave given to me by Makaga Nchango, had run away. But as he was an inveterate thief, I did not regret his loss. Yet I should have been happy, if I could have felt that the dreaded plague was left behind us, for we were now again *en route* towards countries never before visited by a European, and I was buoyed up by the hope of making new discoveries. I and my men left Olenda at four o'clock in the afternoon; our porters were to start with Ondonga at daylight the next morning.

As my readers may perceive on examining the map, my route, on leaving Olenda, was a different one from that followed on my former journey. I was then bound for the Apingi country to the north-east of Olenda; my present destination was Otando, lying south-east by east of the Ashira villages.

About a mile or so east of Olenda commences the great forest which bounds the eastern side of the Ashira prairie; and just within its borders flows the impetuous Ovigui. This river descends from the slopes of the Igoumbi Andele Mountains, south of Ashira-land, and skirts the western foot of the hilly range which separates the Ashira from the Otando country. It drains, with its numerous tributaries, the whole of the valley enclosed between the wooded ranges east and west of the Ashira prairie. I crossed it at a different place from that described in my former journey, but by a similar bridge—a slippery log lying across the torrent, with a rope of lianas stretched from tree to tree to hold on by. There had been a very heavy rain the previous night, and the Ovigui had overflowed its banks, forming three channels separated by islands. Many a tall tree stood in the water, and fallen trunks and branches were washed down, or lay stranded and quivering in the current. In crossing I had a mishap, for, before I could grasp the balustrade, my foot slipped, and I fell headlong into a deep hole, from which I was extricated with difficulty. My arms and watches were fortunately not at all damaged by the bath, and I was glad to find that it did not damp the charges in my revolver, for, on reaching the opposite bank, I fired them all off, not a little to the surprise of the negroes, whose respect for the weapon was thereby very much increased.

A march of about a mile beyond the river brought us to a large plantation, the chief slave settlement of the late King Olenda. It comprised a large extent of land cleared from the forest, and contained a village inhabited by the slaves, three or four hundred in number. I was greatly astonished to find the houses better built than in the town of Olenda, and the whole village more neat and orderly. The plantation extended over a picturesque and undulating tract of ground, with brooks of crystal water in the hollows. In places where these cool streams flowed under the shade of trees, their banks were most delightful, being overgrown with rich vegetation, and the trunks and branches of the trees overhead covered with vines and parasitic plants. The great quantity of plantain-trees in the open ground, with their gigantic, glossy leaves, the patches of ground-nuts, and the light green blades of the sugar cane, gave a pleasant aspect to the place, and hid the charred trunks and stumps of trees which are otherwise so unsightly in these clearings.

The slave village had its chief, himself a slave, and all called themselves the children of Olenda.

He was an Ashango man, a chief in his own country, and probably sold into slavery on account of witchcraft. He was a savage of noble bearing, and apparently of good disposition. He had several wives and a large family of children. The other slaves called him father, and he exercised quite a patriarchal authority over them. These plantations supply the household of the chief of the clan with food, and his wives have also small patches of clearing in the same place, which they cultivate themselves with the help of others. The majority of the slaves were inherited by old Olenda, and a great number had known no other master. This village was not the only slave-farm owned by the late chief, but it was the largest of them.

I found here very stringent sanitary regulations against the prevailing epidemic. Every one showing the first symptoms of the small-pox was instantly carried away to a neighbouring village, or collection of huts, set apart for the purpose. This was full of patients, and was called by the negroes the small-pox village.

We spent the night here, and early the next morning Ondonga arrived with the porters. The first disagreeable news I heard was that several of them had run away before starting, taking, of course, their pay with them. I next discovered that three of my boxes were missing. Notwithstanding the protestations of Ondonga, I was convinced that he was at the bottom of another plot to rob me in the midst of my troubles. He appeared, however, rather alarmed at what had been done, and in the course of the day the boxes were brought in, but they had been opened and rifled of half their contents. At this, Ondonga pretended to be in a violent rage with the unknown thieves, and declared in a loud voice that there should be war against those who had dared to rob his white man. For a moment I thought he was sincere, and that, being young, his authority as successor to Olenda was not sufficiently established over his unruly clan to prevent me from being robbed by his subjects. The old slave-chief joined in the well-acted cry of indignation, and actually put spears into the hands of his sons, and bid them go forth with the rest to demand the restitution of my property. They then all hurried out of the place, shouting, cursing, and vowing death to the thieves.

Next day a portion of the missing things was brought in, but the contents of the principal box, which contained my photographic apparatus, were never made good; two of the focussing glasses had been taken or destroyed, and also the two black curtains.

A greater calamity to me than the loss of my property, and the desertion of several frightened porters which followed, was the illness of my faithful companion, Macondai, who had been at last struck down with the small-pox. We could not delay our journey, and I had great reluctance to leave him behind, on many accounts. When we resumed our march he tried to walk with us, but he became so ill that we were forced to come to a stand. I held, as was my custom in cases of difficulty concerning the safety of our party, a palaver with my faithful body-guard, but to my proposition that I should remain behind and take care of Macondai they opposed a decided negative, on account of the risk of further robberies if I sent the goods on without accompanying them myself. The poor lad himself prayed us to leave him. "All your porters will desert you," said he, "if you do not go on, and you will never reach Máyolo." We finally decided to leave Igalo with him at a plantation in the neighbourhood, and Oudonga promised, with every appearance of good will, to send people to take care of him.

We now continued our march. The country became more and more picturesque at every step. We were seven days on the road between the slave village and Máyolo; but this included considerable stoppages, for the distance, in a straight line, is only a little over thirty-five miles. The road is a narrow track through a most varied and picturesque but dense forest, clothing the hills and valleys of the mountain range, which extends in a north and south direction, between the Ashira and the Otando territories. I call this the Otando range; it is not a continuous ridge, but is broken up into a great number of hills, of greater or less elevation, with steep slopes and narrow valleys; the highest elevation at which I crossed the range was about 1,200 feet. The hills are of primitive rock; and numerous blocks of quartz lay strewed along the path nearly all the way. Quartz crystals also covered the beds of the sparkling brooks that flowed at the bottom of every valley, all running in a northerly direction. The forest did not contain many timber trees of gigantic size, but the treesgrew everywhere close to one another and were matted together by a net-work of woody lianas, amongst which I noticed a great quantity of the climbing ficus, which produces gum elastic. It was impossible to see far on either side of the path; in many places there was a dense growth of underwood, including dwarf species of palm-tree, and the ground was strewn all over with wrecks of the forest in the shape of broken and rotting branches, up-turned trees, and masses of decaying leaves.

It was most toilsome marching up the steep hills, encumbered with the weight of our loads. A few miles south-east of the plantation, we came unexpectedly upon a most enchanting sight. One of the numerous tributaries of the Ovigui here descends from the upper valleys, down the broken hill-side, in a most lovely cascade, filling the neighbouring forest with spray and favouring the growth of countless ferns and glossy-leaved plants. The forest nook looked like a place of enchantment, decked out with the choicest productions of the vegetable world. There was, however, throughout the whole march a great scarcity of animal life. Scarcely once did we hear the voices of birds, and at night, as we lay round the fires of the bivouac, all was still as death in the black shades of the forest.

On the morning of the second day of our march we came to the river Louvendji, which I crossed, at a point lower down, on my former journey to the Apingi country. It is rather smaller than the Ovigui and different in character, having a rocky bed and water of crystal clearness; both flow to the north, the Louvendji discharging itself into the Ovigui a little above the junction of the latter with the Ngouyai. The banks of the Louvendji nourished many tall palm-trees and gigantic ferns, which are absent from the hilly and drier grounds.

I should have much enjoyed this part of my journey if I had been free from anxiety on account of the porters in whose hands my goods were entrusted. But guides and porters alike were bent on plundering me still further. I found it impossible to keep them all together. All sorts of excuses were invented for lagging behind, and I soon made the discovery that they were hiding their provisions in the bush—a sign that they intended to rob me and run away by the same road.

On the first and second nights I ordered all the loads to be piled up near to the shed under which I slept, but on the third night, when we were assembled together to sleep, Mintcho and several of the porters were not forthcoming. They had stayed behind and did not overtake us till the next morning. On their arrival, Mintcho took the bull by the horns and told me to look into some of my boxes, for he thought they had been opened and plundered. He accused others of being the thieves, and mutual recriminations ensued, which ended in several of the porters laying down their loads and running away, and the rest (including some of the thieves) declared that it was of no use going any further, as the white man had been robbed and would not give them their pay. On opening some of the boxes I found a great number of valuable articles had been stolen, including two bottles of old brandy, a reserve in case of illness, and the loss of which was very vexing, as it was portion of a present made me by a valued friend in London.* I was imprudent enough, at first, to accuse Mintcho of knowledge of the thefts, a step which nearly led to my being left alone in the wilderness. I was obliged to retract, and allay his fears by saying that I did not hold him responsible. My readers must bear in mind that Mintcho was all along the principal thief, together with the men he had with him, who obeyed his orders in everything. It was only by a temporizing policy, and by appealing alternately to their vanity and to their fears, now coaxing and now threatening, that I could hope to avoid the hard fate of being left alone in this inhospitable forest. Towards the evening of the fourth day we came to a standstill; so many porters had run away, that there were no longer men enough to carry our goods.

The weather was stormy, and it was almost impossible to shelter ourselves from the rains which fell every night. We could find no large leaves to make a good thatch for our sheds, and what with the discomfort caused by the frequent thunder showers, and the necessity of keeping watch over my goods, I got very little rest. As time went on, hunger came to add to our miseries. Negroes never take more than two or three days' provisions on a march, plantains being so heavy; and as a large portion of what they carried on the present journey had been hidden in

* Charles White, Esq., of Lime Street, London.

the bush, we were now reduced to very slender rations indeed, although still about fifteen miles distant from the nearest village of the Otando.

I gathered our party together, and consulted with them as to what was best to be done. To my suggestion that some of the Ashira men should go forward to Máyolo and ask for porters, Mintcho and his friends opposed a decided negative. Neither would they allow two of their men and two of my Commi boys to go to Máyolo. They were afraid, in short, of being detained and punished by Máyolo for having robbed me. I finally resolved to send Mouitchi, with the Otando man who had been Arangui's prisoner. He departed with the promise of returning in two days with men to carry our goods, and a supply of food.

I was now left with the Ashira rascals, eight in number, and with only two of my faithful Commi men to aid me in keeping watch over them. We were encamped in a small open space in the loneliest and gloomiest part of the forest, on the top of a long sloping path which led into a deep valley on the Otando side. We were absolutely without food, and went supperless to bed, myself and my two men Rebouka and Ngoma having agreed to watch in our turns the Ashira, who pretended to be asleep in their olakos on the opposite side of the road. My baggage, alas! still too large and the cause of all my troubles, lay piled up beside our camp fire in front of us.

We whiled away the early hours of night in talking of Quengueza and the country by the sea-shore, or in relating and listening to legends and fables. This latter amusement was always to me a pleasant way of passing the time. The memory of the Equatorial African is well stored with parables, fables, and extravagant stories of one kind or another. Having improved my acquaintance, on the present journey, with several of the native languages, I was able to note down almost every story I heard, and thus accumulated a large collection of them. The following legend, connected probably with some natural phenomenon in one of the neighbouring rivers, is a sample of these African stories:—

Atungulu Shimba was a king who attained the chief authority in his village by right of succession, and built eight new houses. But Atungulu had sworn, that whosoever should quarrel with him he would eat him. And so it really happened until, finally, after eating his enemies one after the other, he was left alone in his dominions, and he then married the beautiful Arondo-ienu, daughter of a neighbouring king.

It was Atungulu's habit, after his marriage, to go daily into the forest to trap wild animals, with the Ashinga net, leaving his wife alone in the village. One day Njali, the eldest brother of Arondo-ienu—for Coniambié (King of the Air), their father, had three sons—came to take back his sister out of the clutches of Atungulu Shimba; but the king arrived unexpectedly and ate him up. Next came the second brother, and he was also eaten. At last came Reninga, the third brother, and there was a great fight between him and Atungulu, which lasted from sunrise till midday, when Reninga was overpowered and eaten like his two brothers before him.

Reninga, however, had a powerful fetich on him, and came out of Atungulu alive. The King, on seeing him, exclaimed, "How have you contrived this, to come back?" He then smeared him and Arondo-ienu with *alumbi* chalk, and putting his hands together, blew a loud whistle, saying afterwards, "Reninga, take back your sister." He then went and threw himself into the water, to drown himself, through grief for the loss of his wife.

Before dying, Atungulu Shimba declared that if Arondo-ienu ever married again, she would die; and the prophecy came true, for she married another man and died soon after. Her brother Reninga, thereupon, through sorrow for the loss of his sister, threw himself into the water in the place where Atungulu died, and was drowned.

At the spot where Atungulu Shimba died, a stranger sees, when he looks into the deep water, the bodies of the king and Arondo-ienu side by side, and the nails of his beautiful wife all glittering like looking-glasses. From that time, water has obtained the property of reflecting objects, and has ever since been called by the name of Arondo-ienu, and people have been able to see their own images reflected on its surface, on account of the transparency given to it by the bright nails of Arondo-ienu.*

As the day dawned hunger came, but there was

* Ienu means "looking-glass" in the languages of tribes near the sea.

no food to be had. There was no help for it, but to divide our party and go in search of something to eat in the forest; some, therefore, went to look for *Koola* nuts, and others took their guns and wandered in search of monkeys, or any other game they might find. The whole day passed, however, without anything being found, and we again went supperless to sleep.

It was unfortunate for us that Koola nut-trees were so scarce in the part of the forest where we now lay, for this valuable nut is generally an unfailing resource at this season of the year. The natives never think of taking with them much food on a journey in the season when Koola nuts are ripe, but trust in finding their daily bread, as it were, under the trees. The tree is one of the tallest and finest in these forests. It grows singly, or in small groups, and yields so abundantly that, when the nut is ripe, the whole crown appears one mass of fruit. The nut is quite round, and has a very hard shell, so hard that it has to be broken with a stone. The kernel is about as large as a cherry, and is almost as compact in substance as the almond. It is very nourishing and wholesome; about thirty nuts are enough for a single meal. The wild boar feeds on them in the nut season, and becomes extremely fat with the nutritious diet.

The next day I went also myself into the bush, accompanied by an Ashira boy, and leaving Rebouka armed to the teeth to watch my baggage. I was so much weakened with hunger and anxiety that I could scarcely walk. For a long time I could find no traces of game of any kind, and was about to retrace my steps, when I heard the unmistakeable roar of the gorilla. For the moment I forgot my fatigue, and the old spirit was once more aroused within me. I plunged forward into the thick of the forest, breaking, as I went along, small boughs to enable me to find my way back, and tearing my clothes with the thorny underwood. The roar became nearer, and seemed to shake the ground under me. I heard the rustling of the branches, and fancied there must be more than one. The excitement of the moment was great, and was increased by the prospect of obtaining food for all our party. Suddenly the roaring ceased. I stopped, thinking that it was a male which was perhaps preparing to advance on me. But I listened in vain; the beast had fled. When I reached the spot, I saw nothing but broken branches of trees. I measured some of these with my thumb, and found boughs of five inches diameter broken in two by the powerful grip of this monster of the forest. Although disappointed in my chase, I was glad to find a corroboration of the explanation I had given, in my former volume, of the wearing down of the animal's front teeth, for some of the branches bore plainly the tooth marks.

I returned weary and hungry to the camp, and tried to sleep under my shed. But I could not sleep, and, in my prostrate condition, visions passed through my mind of the many good dinners I had eaten at the hospitable boards of my friends in Europe and America. Strange to say, dinners which I had entirely forgotten now recurred to my memory with an almost morbid vividness. I could tell every dish, and recalled the pleasant savour of many good things which I felt there was no hope of my ever enjoying again.

Towards evening things began to mend. The Ashira returned from their chase successful, having killed two monkeys. How strange are the contradictions in the African character! These men who had so remorselessly plundered me, and with whom my relations had been for a long time none of the pleasantest, came forward with great disinterestedness and gave the whole of the meat up to me. I refused however to take it, and told them that as it was of their own procuring they were to divide it amongst themselves. They insisted, however, upon giving me the lion's share, which I did not a second time refuse. I divided it into equal portions between my Commi men and myself, and a most hearty and refreshing meal we made off our monkey.

On the following day, hour after hour passed and no arrival from Otando. The Ashira men began to feel uneasy. They thought something was in preparation against them; that Máyolo was mustering a force to come and punish them for their treachery to the white man, and for their imprisonment of an Otando subject. I had great difficulty, as the day wore on, to prevent them from leaving me; they tried at first to get their pay from me, but, on my refusal, threatened to run off without it. It was only by holding up before them the certainty of Quengueza making war on the Ashira if they forsook me entirely, that I finally prevailed on them to remain.

At length voices were heard in the valley on the Otando side, then the report of a gun, and up bounded the long line of Otando men, headed by Rapelina, to the rescue, laden with provisions, and merry as crickets. Máyolo had sent for my own use a stock of *Mpegui* nuts, two fowls, and plenty of plantains. The arrival was most welcome, for we were again helpless with hunger. We had been again without food all day, and it was now evening.

Mpegui nuts are the product of a large tree which grows abundantly in some parts of the forest, but is nowhere planted by the natives. The nut is quite different in form from the Koola nut already described. It is round, but the kernel is three-lobed and full of oil. The oily nature of the nuts enables the natives to manufacture them into excellent cakes, by pounding them in a wooden mortar, and enclosing the pulp in folded leaves, and then subjecting it to the action of smoke on a stage over a wood fire. They eat it generally with meat as we do bread, but when animal food is scarce it forms a good reserve, and is very palatable, seasoned with a little salt and pepper.

After a good night's rest—the first that I had had for a long time—we arose refreshed in the morning, and the horns of the Otando men at sunrise blew the signal for our departure. There had been again heavy rain in the night, and the rain-drops on the leaves of the forest trees glittered in the early sunlight. A thin mist hung over the deep valley before us, and in the coolness of the early hour we marched off at great speed, determined not to spend another night in the solitude of the forest.

Nothing occurred worthy of mention during the remainder of our march except the crossing of a deep river, another of the tributaries of the Ngouyai, about ten miles west of Máyolo. This stream is called the Oganga, and for me it was a new discovery, as I did not see it on my journey to the Apingi country in 1858. It is a deep river at all seasons of the year. We traversed it by a bridge, formed of the trunk of a colossal tree which lay across it. We were delayed a short time on the banks of the stream by the men stopping to gather and eat Koola nuts, vast quantities of which lay beneath a group of trees of this species that grew here. We were approaching the end of our journey, and the blue sky began to appear through the breaks in the crowns of the trees ahead.

CHAPTER IX.

MÁYOLO.

Arrival at Máyolo—Reception by the Chief—Discovery of more Losses—I accuse the Ashira—Their Flight—Seizure of a Hostage—Gathering of the Head men of Otando—Máyolo falls ill—I am attacked by Fever—Great Heat and Thunderstorm—Arrival of Macondai and Igalo—Their Ill-treatment by the Ashira—Loss of Photographic Camera and Chemicals—Surgical Practice of the Otando—A Female Doctor—Matrimonial Squabbles—Máyolo's health improves—Witchcraft Ordeal—My Speech to the People—Speech of Máyolo—Curiosity of the Otando—A Female Duel—The Bashikouay Ants—A Precocious Thief—Máyolo again falls ill—Good news from the Apono country—Astonishment of the Natives at the Musical-box and Magnets—Climate of Máyolo—Deposit of Dew—The *Ololicnus*—Recovery of Macondai—The Alumbi Fetich—Departure from Máyolo.

At length, on the evening of the 24th March, we emerged from the gloom of the forest into an open tract of grass-land, the Otando prairie, where everything seemed light and cheerful after the dark shades to which we had been so long accustomed. A wide stretch of undulating country lay open before us; the foreground of which was formed by prairie, the rest appearing as a continuous expanse of forest with long wooded ridges in the distance, one behind the other, the last and highest fading into blue mist in the far distance. From the margins of the forest the land gradually sloped, and signs of population were apparent in sheds and patches of plantation. A beautifully clear stream flowed near the prairie and past the plantations towards the Ngouyai. A denser tract of forest, with lofty trees and numerous palms stretching across the distant landscape, marked the course of the great river Ngouyai which watered these fertile plains. As we approached the village of Máyolo, we fired off the customary signal-shots, and these brought a response of the same kind. The chief of the village possessed only one old Tower-musket, *minus* the stock, which had long been worn out; it was still, however, a good gun. Powder was a scarce article in this inland country, and nothing but the hope of getting more from me could have induced Máyolo to waste his small stock.

A number of men soon made their appearance, and led us, with loud cheers, to the palaver-house of the village. The beating of the kendo was then heard, and Máyolo himself was seen in the street advancing towards us; his body streaked with alumbi chalk, and muttering mysterious words as he slowly marched along. On being seated, and after stopping the beating of the kendo, he looked towards my Ashira guides, and exclaimed, "So here he is at last, the great Spirit with his untold wealth!" Then, turning to me, he told me of the great trouble he had had with the Otando people, who had tried all they could to dissuade him from receiving me, saying that I brought the plague and death wherever I came. He said he had vainly argued with them that I could not be the cause of the plague, seeing that the disease was already amongst them long before they had heard of the white man being even in the Ashira country. My heart warmed towards the sagacious old man for these sensible words, and we exchanged vows of friendship in face of the gaping crowd assembled around us.

Máyolo was the principal chief of the Otando country, and it was my interest to conciliate him as much as possible. He was a man of striking appearance; tall, broad-shouldered, and very light-coloured for a negro. His eyes were small and piercing, and there was in them far more intelligence than is usually seen in negroes. His right hand had lost several of its fingers through the bursting of a gun, for he had been, in his younger days, a great elephant-hunter, and his bravery was well known all over the neighbouring country. He had a pleasant expression of features, notwithstanding that his face was daubed with ochre-coloured chalk of various shades; one cheek being red and the other nearly white, including the circuit of the eyes. His people seemed to regard him with great reverence; and, in their looks, one might read the thought, "What a great man you are, O Chief! your fame it is that has brought the great Spirit amongst us!"

After Máyolo retired, a present of a large goat and two enormous bunches of plantains was brought in. We were almost famished, and had a great feast that evening. It was astonishing to see the quantity my Commi men could consume. Negroes can stand hunger well for a few days, but they make amends for it when food is put before them in abundance. Whilst dinner was preparing I went to see my man Igala, who was ill of the small-pox, in the hut where the goods were stored which I had sent with him. I found he had the confluent and worst form of the disease; the poor fellow seemed much pleased when I shook hands with him, and showed him I was not afraid of him. The Máyolo people had wanted to remove him from the hut, but he had refused to leave the goods which I had put under his care.

The next morning, on opening my japanned boxes to take out medicine for Igala, I made fresh discoveries of the extent to which I had been robbed by these rascally Ashira. All the bottles containing medicines —castor-oil, calomel, laudanum, rhubarb, julap—were gone; besides a thermometer, two sun thermometers, several tins of preserved meats, camera, photographic chemicals, beads, and many other things. They were the boxes that had formed part of the cargoes of Mintcho, Ayágui, and the Apingi men. I could scarcely contain my vexation, and thoughts of being forced, for sheer lack of goods and instruments, to relinquish my object of penetrating further into the interior, flashed across my mind.

I now accused Mintcho boldly of the robbery, taking care to seize his gun and his two slave-bundles* beforehand. But the hypocritical rascal pretended to be in a rage with others for having robbed me. He worked himself into the appearance of violent passion, foaming at the mouth, and exclaiming, "Let me go back, Chaillie; I will find out the robbers, and shoot them if they do not give up everything you have lost." Ayágui came in at this juncture, with a gun which Rebouka had lent him to go out shooting that

* The slave-bundle is a parcel of goods amounting to the value of a slave, which the head men carried on the march, to buy slaves with on their own account.

morning. It was necessary to disarm this man, but he refused when I requested him to deliver up the gun. The situation was now a critical one; for, if I allowed the Otando people to see how I could be plundered, and afterwards set at defiance, the example would be fatal to the success of my expedition. I appealed to Máyolo, telling him that the goods of which I had been robbed were intended as presents for him, and that the gun which Ayágui refused to give up was also his property. This was a manœuvre of mine, and was quite successful; the Otando and their chief forthwith ranged themselves on my side, but Ayágui was not disarmed without great difficulty, for he threatened to fire on the first man who approached him. At this I called my four men together, ordered them to level their muskets at him, myself pointing my revolver, and this brought him to reason. The gun was handed over to Máyolo.

Mintcho and the rest now made for the forest on their way home; but, wishing to secure one of them as a hostage for the restitution of my property, we pursued them, and Rebouka seized one of them. To my vexation, instead of one of the men, he seized a boy, the son of my good Ashira friend, Adingo. The guilty fugitives at this were terribly frightened, but I took pains to let them know, before they were out of hearing, that we should do no harm to the boy, but would restore him as soon as my goods were brought back. Igala, though very ill, said if he had known what I wanted to do, he could have seized Mintcho himself.

Our prompt action in this matter had the effect

which I desired. It inspired the Otando people with fear and respect for us, and showed that, though few, we were not to be trifled with.

I now turned to our little prisoner. Poor fellow! he was a mere boy, about twelve years of age, and my heart felt for him as I heard his moans when passing by the hut, for Rebouka had secured him so tightly with cords that he could not move a limb. He said to me, with tears in his eyes, "Oh, Chaillie! you are my father's great friend; I am but a child, and cannot run away. They will come back with all your stolen things; Mintcho told me so. Oh, Chaillie! I suffer so much. I am your boy. Did I not refuse to leave you, but followed you to the Otando country? Do loosen the cords which hurt me so much." I ordered Rebouka to slacken the cords, which he did, but remonstrated terribly at my imprudence, telling me that I wasted my pity on the boy; that I did not know negroes; that negroes were not children at that age. "Do you think," said he, "that a child could have come from the Ngouyai to the Otando country with the load this boy has carried?" We then secured him under the verandah of my hut, and set a watch over him during the night. Máyolo also urged me to keep a good look-out on the boy; for then all my property would be sure to come back to me.

Rebouka was right. The cunning little fellow escaped before the morning. He contrived to wriggle free of the cords which bound him, and fled whilst the guard was absent for a few moments. His escape was a great loss to me, for, had I succeeded in keeping him, all the goods I had been robbed of would have been certainly restored—the boy being the son of a chief who had great influence over the Ashira.

In the afternoon there was a gathering of the head men of the neighbouring villages, belonging to Máyolo's clan, and much speechifying and excitement. Máyolo swelled with pride on introducing the white man to them, and as I spread out the goods I intended for each of them as payment for the men they had sent to my assistance, he exclaimed, pointing at the goods: "Look! this is the sort of plague the white man brings among us. Would you ever have had any of these fine things if I had not invited him to come?" The appeal was not to be resisted. They all went away at the end of the palaver in good humour, and the next morning brought into the village presents of fowls, goats, ground-nuts, and plantains. Máyolo and the other chiefs said they would disprove the slander of the Ashiras, who wanted to keep all my goods for themselves and said there was nothing to eat in Otando-land. After this there were more speeches, and then the important ceremony, for me, of making return presents to all the donors. I had previously shown Máyolo what I intended to give, and he had remonstrated with me for giving them too much, saying they did not know the value of the things. I adhered, however, to my purpose, and was rather astounded to hear Máyolo, on coming out of the hut, tell the chiefs that he had been persuading me to give each of them a good present! On their sides they tried to look dissatisfied, and demanded more. This I resisted, and made a show of taking back the whole. They all laughed and said, "No, we were only trying it on;" and looking at one another, they added, "He *is* a man!" which means he is not to be humbugged, and is a high compliment.

We had been only four days in Otando-land, when, to my great sorrow and vexation, Máyolo fell seriously ill. Thus it was my fate to see another chief cast down after my arrival in his country. Should Máyolo die, I felt that my expedition must come to an end, for it would be impossible to drive the idea out of the heads of the superstitious negroes that my presence was the cause of the death of their chiefs. Night after night I was kept awake with anxiety, listening to the moans of the sick man. The heat of the weather, too, in the early days of April, was most stifling. A conflagration of the prairie round the village also came to add to our troubles, for I had great difficulty in removing the ammunition and goods from my hut in time to avoid a disaster. On the 1st and 3rd of April I over-exerted myself in taking several solar observations. The heat in the shade was about 92° Fahr., and in the sun it reached 130° or 135° Fahr. I took, at night, several lunar observations, ascertaining the distances between the moon and Venus and between the moon and Spica, and obtained also several meridian altitudes of stars. The sky was so clear that I was anxious not to let the opportunity pass of obtaining these observations. My exertions, however, combined with my heavy anxieties and the loss of my goods, brought on an attack of fever. It was fortunate that the scoundrel had not robbed me of all my stock of quinine and calomel.

The great heat of the weather culminated on the evening of the 5th of April, and we then had a most terrific storm, with claps of thunder exploding over our heads that made the whole place shake with the concussion. At the second explosion I felt a shock in my right leg, and a sudden jerk, which for the moment frightened me. Deluges of rain accompanied the electric explosion, and the weather became much cooler. Heavy rain fell again on the evening of the 6th, but the weather afterwards cleared up, and the moon shone beautifully.

Though far from well, I took a meridian altitude of Dubhe, so that now I was sure of my latitude, having taken several good observations.

April 8th. Amidst all my cares a gleam of sunshine lights me up now and then. To-day one source of anxiety was taken off my mind in the arrival of Igalo with my poor boy Macondai. The Otando people seemed as much pleased as I was that all my party were now reunited. The state of Macondai was, however, a great drawback to my rejoicing. I went to the hut, to which Igalo had led him, to see my faithful companion, but was horrified on beholding him. His head was swollen and covered with pustules, the nose seemed literally eaten up, and his body was in the same state. But the worst sight was one of his legs; it was so swollen that it looked more like the foot of an elephant than that of a human being, and there was an appearance of gangrene commencing. I had known Macondai from a child, and loved him.

A cold chill ran through me at the thought that he would not recover; I felt that I was to blame in bringing these faithful fellows all the way from the coast, to suffer and die amongst what were to them a foreign people.

Igalo and Macondai now related the events which had happened in Ashira-land after my departure. They told me that Ondonga, the heir of Olenda, who had promised to take care of Macondai, removed them, on my departure, to another hut, which he told them belonged to his father-in-law, who would attend to the sick boy. He gave out that he himself was going to Olenda village, but would return in two days, and borrowed the cutlass I had left to take with him. Ondonga never returned, and the owner of the hut, on his appearance, demanded payment of them for lodging. A few days afterwards, Mintcho, Ayágui, and the others made their appearance. They said I had refused to pay them until Macondai and Igalo had rejoined me, and told Macondai to make haste to be well; but the owner of the hut, returning some time after their departure, told them the truth, namely, that I had retained their bundles, and refused to pay them, until my stolen property was restored. He told them also that the robbery had been planned beforehand between Ondonga and Mintcho. After this they had a visit from four Ashira people, who resorted to artifice to get Igalo out of the way for a few moments, telling him that he ought to go and fetch water to wash the sick boy's sores, and then, whilst Igalo was gone to the brook with the water-jar, decamped with both the guns and all their other property, laughing at poor Macondai in his helpless state. After this he resolved to leave the wretched place, Macondai crawling slowly, supported by Igalo, who carried sufficient plantains for the journey.

How I thanked my stars that I had not listened to the advice of those scoundrels to leave all my property in the woods. Out of all my thermometers I had now only one left, the centigrade, and but two aneroids to measure the height of mountains. I felt much the loss of my two thermometers, with which I measured the power of the sun, for I was exceedingly interested in these observations. The mountain aneroids and all my watches I always carried myself in a little japanned box. I felt the loss of my camera most keenly, for it was one of the things I had looked forward to with the greatest pleasure, to bring home a splendid and unique series of photographs of this inland country. This hope was now at an end; and the many months I had spent in learning the art, and the tedious practising in the coast country, to the great injury of my health, were all in vain. The thieves had also stolen a number of photographic views I had taken of villages and natives, and of the live gorillas. I had been at very considerable expense in purchasing a complete apparatus and a supply of the best chemicals, and it was very annoying to think it should all be wasted in this way. I thought how much my friend, M. Claudet, would grieve, who took so much pains to instruct me in the art—and all his labours given freely, for the love of science. They had also carried off my cooking implements, working tools, &c.

I heard a few days afterwards that two of the Ashira thieves had died soon after their return. I wonder whether they had swallowed some of my chemicals! It was the belief of the people that I had caused their death in some mysterious way for their robbery of my property, and I was considered a most potent wizard.

On the 9th of April we had a tornado and rain at half-past eight in the evening. For hours, flash after flash of lightning was seen all round the horizon, except between the west and south. The heavens seemed ploughed up by the flashes. I have remarked that the wind generally blows from the south-east, but sometimes in the morning it blew from the mountains between Máyolo and the Ngouyai country. On the 12th we had a tremendous tornado, the heaviest, I think, that we have had this year. It came from the north-east.

April 20th. The weather still continued oppressively hot. At ten a.m. to-day the thermometer in the village marked 92° 30′ Fahr.* I took my instrument into the neighbouring forest and found that the temperature there fell to 84° 20′, and remained so until near four o'clock. When I returned to the village at a quarter-past four p.m. the thermometer stood at 92°. The great humidity of these dense shades causes an agreeable coolness, and I have noticed that when rain has fallen during the night there often remains some moisture on the surface of the leaves at two p.m., showing how slow, com-

* For the convenience of the reader I have converted centigrade into Fahrenheit.

paratively speaking, is the evaporation in these shady places. Whether it was owing to the heat of the weather, or to the low situation of Máyolo (for the prairie lies in a valley only 496 feet above the sea-level), I cannot tell, but I was unwell during the whole of our stay here, and was never free from feverishness and an oppressive sensation in the head, which were extremely dispiriting. Nevertheless, I was determined not to give way to feelings of lassitude, and took my daily bath in the sparkling rivulet which meandered through the prairie towards the forest.

Some days after, an eruption of very small red pimples almost covered my body. I then thought that the small-pox had been checked by my having been vaccinated.

Since my arrival in Máyolo, I have been computing my lunar observations, a very fatiguing task in this hot climate.

Every day since I have been here we have had thunder and lightning. As I look towards the mountains in the east, heavy black clouds hang continually over the country, and it seems to rain there unceasingly. The people, pointing to that country, say it is the "Mother of Rain." Here, at Máyolo, since the 12th, we have had alternately rain and sunshine—one day a tornado, the next day a clear blue sky. Since the sun has been east of the moon, I have only been able on one day to take the distance between the sun and moon.

On the 22nd of April I saw a curious example of the surgical practice of the Otando people. In the stillness of the afternoon, when the heat of the vertical sun compels every one to repose, I was startled by loud screams, as though some unfortunate being was being led to death for witchcraft. On going to the place, I found a helpless woman, who was afflicted with leprosy, and suffering besides under an attack of lumbago, undergoing an operation for the latter disease at the hands of the Otando doctor and his assistants. They had made a number of small incisions in the back of the poor creature with a sharp-pointed knife of the country, and were rubbing into the gashes a great quantity of lime-juice mixed with pounded cayenne-pepper. The doctor was rubbing the irritating mixture into the wounds with all his might, so that it was no wonder that the poor creature was screaming with pain, and rolling herself on the ground. It is wonderful to observe the faith all these negroes have in lime-juice mixed with cayenne pepper. They use it not only as an embrocation, but also internally for dysentery, and I have often seen them drink as much as half a tumblerful of it in such cases. The pepper itself I believe to be a very useful medicine in this climate, for I have often found benefit from it when unwell and feverish, by taking an unusual quantity in my food.

Whilst I am on the subject of native doctoring, I must relate what I saw afterwards in the course of Máyolo's illness. I knew the old chief had been regularly attended by a female doctor, and often wondered what she did to him. At length one morning I happened to go into his house when she was administering her cures, and remained, an interested spectator, to watch her operations. Máyolo was seated on a mat, submitting to all that was done with the utmost gravity and patience. Before him was extended the skin of a wild animal (*Genetta*). The woman was engaged in rubbing his body all over with her hands, muttering all the while, in a low voice, words which I could not understand. Having continued this wholesome friction for some time, she took a piece of *alumbi* chalk and made with it a broad stripe along the middle of his chest and down each arm. This done, she chewed a quantity of some kind of roots and seeds, and, having well charged her mouth with saliva, spat upon him in different places, but aiming her heaviest shots at the parts most affected. Finally, she took a bunch of a particular kind of grass, which had been gathered when in bloom and was now dry, and, lighting it, touched with the flame the body of her patient in various places, beginning at the foot and gradually ascending to the head. I could perceive that Máyolo smarted with the pain of the burns, when the torch remained too long. When the flame was extinguished the woman applied the burnt end of the torch to her patient's body, and so the operations ended.

It seemed to me that there was some superstition of deep significance connected with the application of fire in these Otando cures. They appeared to have great faith in the virtues of fire, and this is perhaps not far removed from fire-worship. I asked the old woman why she used this kind of remedy, and what power she attributed to fire, but her only answer was that it prevented the illness with which Máyolo had been afflicted from coming again. The female doctor, I need scarcely add, had come from a distance; for it is always so in primitive Africa—the further off a doctor or witchfinder lives, the greater his reputation.

The wives of West African chiefs are almost as independent as their lords and masters. They have their own plantations, and have their own little property. When quarrels arise between them and their husbands, I don't think the latter always get the best of it, for wife-flogging is but very seldom resorted to by the men here. The following is a sample of the matrimonial disputes which I witnessed during my stay at Máyolo:—

Máyolo was greatly enraged one day because his head wife—a young woman about twenty years of age, and remarkable for her light-coloured skin and hazel eyes—had mislaid or wasted his tobacco, a very precious drug here. He threatened to take away the pipe or condoquai, which is common property to man and wife, and so prevent her smoking any more. Instead of being frightened, the young wife retorted that the plantain-stem of the pipe was her own property, and that she would take it away, and what was he to do then?—for he had not plantain-trees of his own, they were all hers. The dispute soon waxed fierce, and she then threatened to set fire to his house. At this the old man laughed heartily, and dared her to do it. It was the most serious squabble I had witnessed; if Máyolo had been well in health at the time, and more seriously angry, the worst that would have happened would have been a flogging for the beloved wife. She might have then run away; but any great act of cruelty does not enter the heads of these mild-tempered people, except as the punishment of witchcraft.

Towards the end of April I was glad to find a decided change for the better in Máyolo's health. Macondai was also much improved, and I now saw some prospect of moving forwards towards the east. Unfortunately my hopes were soon after again cast down, by Máyolo's favourite wife and one of his nephews falling ill of small-pox. Máyolo, who was as anxious as I was to be off before the dry season set in, on account of the plantations he had to make, was now in great trouble. He rose the next day before daylight, and proclaimed aloud in the street of his village, before the people had gone out of their houses, that some one had bewitched the place, and that the *mboundou* (poison ordeal) must be tried. Notwithstanding the love he seemed to have for his young wife, fear of the disease had the upper hand; he sent her away to the village of her own people, where the plague was now raging, there to remain till she either died or became well; the nephew was ordered into the woods, and people sent to build him an olako, or shed; his own wife, who was to attend on him, was to be prohibited from entering the village. These were strong sanitary measures. I was racked with anxiety and vexation. This abominable plague seemed to follow me everywhere. I had learnt from Macondai that the chiefs of Ashira Kamba, and especially Mbana and his wife, who had cooked for us when in the Kamba country, had died of the disease after I had left. I had succeeded in preventing the news from spreading in Máyolo, for my men had the good sense never to say a word about anything that might retard my progress; but it filled me with grief to think that I should be thought to bring nothing but death to so many poor, kind-hearted people.

The "finding out" or trial in the witchcraft case came off on the 27th of April;* Máyolo being convinced that neither himself, his wife, nor his nephew, would have been ill if some one were not bewitching them, and seeking to cause their death. A celebrated doctor had been sent for from a distance, and appeared in the morning decked out in the most fantastic manner. Half his body was painted red and the other half white, his face was daubed with streaks of black, white, and red, and of course he wore around his neck a great quantity of fetiches. The villagers were assembled and the doctor had commenced his divinations when I arrived at the place, a witness once again of this gloomy ceremony, which was different from that of the Commi people seen formerly by me, as related in 'Adventures in Equatorial Africa.' The doctor counterfeited his voice when speaking, in order to impress on the people a due sense of his supernatural powers of divination; all the painting, dressing and mummery have the same object in view, namely to strike awe into the minds of the people. A black earthenware vessel filled with water, and surrounded by charmed ochre and

* This ordeal—the *pona oganga* of the Commi—is here called *ogambi*, or *ogambé*.

fetiches, served the purpose of the looking-glass used by the coast tribes. The doctor, seated on his stool, looked intently and mysteriously into the water, shook his head, then looked into a lighted torch which he waved over it, made contortions with his body, trying to look as ugly as he could, then smoked the condoquai (pipe), repeated the mummeries over again, and concluded by pronouncing that the persons who were bewitching the village were people belonging to the place. This oracular saying put the people into great consternation; they all began to appear afraid of each other; the nearest relatives were made miserable by mutual suspicions. Máyolo then rose and exclaimed in an excited manner that the mboundou must be drunk, appointing the following morning for the ceremony, as the people had eaten to-day, and the poison must be drunk on an empty stomach.

At sunrise the next morning the village was empty. All had gone to a little meadow encircled by woods, a short distance away, to take part in the ceremony. Who were the suspected persons was kept secret, partly because they were afraid I would interfere. I thought it, however, better policy not to do so, but attended to witness the proceedings and to ascertain whether they differed from those followed on similar occasions near the coast. On entering the assembly I gave them the usual salutation, and shook hands with Máyolo. It soon appeared that the suspicions of the people fell upon three of Máyolo's nephews, his consecutive heirs, it being thought natural that they should wish to get rid of him. I noticed that the whole body of the people took an active part in the affair; the doctor not openly naming anybody as the guilty parties. It was the people themselves who originated the suspicions, and they showed by their clamour how they thirsted for victims. Máyolo and the doctor remained silent.

The nephews in vain protested that they were innocent, and declared that the accusation was a lie; but they added that there were others who wanted to bewitch their uncle. They became enraged at the pertinacity of their accusers, and swore that the people should pay dearly for making them drink the mboundou. They said they were not afraid to drink it, for they were not wizards and would not die.

Some of the relatives of the nephews and some of the people of the village now retired to a short distance to prepare the poison. Roots of the mboundou were then scraped, and a vessel filled with the fragments, on which water was poured; a kind of effervescence then took place, and the water became of a red colour, like the root itself. Sufficient was made to serve as a good draught to each of the accused. When the water becomes red, it is considered good mboundou, and ready to kill any wizards. The drinkers of the mboundou are not allowed to witness the preparation, but their representatives may, to see that fair play is used. When at length the poor fellows were brought into the middle of the circle of excited spectators, it was horrid to see the ferocity expressed in the countenances of the people; it seemed as though their nature had entirely changed. Knives, axes, and spears were held ready to be used on the bodies of the victims if they should succumb under the ordeal; if the accused should become unsteady under the influence of the poison and stumble, the now quiet crowd would become suddenly frenzied and unmanageable. All seemed eager for the sacrifice of victims to their superstitious fears. It is chiefly through the immunity with which they can drink the poison that the doctors obtain such power over the people; and no wonder, when so many people die under it. The mboundou is a most violent poison. This was proved by the analysis of its roots which I caused to be made after my former journey.

A breathless silence prevailed whilst the young men took the much-dreaded cups of liquid and boldly swallowed the contents; the whispering of the wind could be heard through the leaves of the surrounding trees. But it was only of short duration. As soon as the poison was drunk, the crowd began to beat their sticks on the ground, and shout, "If they are wizards, let the mboundou kill them; if innocent, let it go out!" repeating the words as long as the suspense lasted. The struggle was a severe one; the eyes of the young men became bloodshot, their limbs trembled convulsively, and every muscle in their bodies was visibly working under the potent irritation. The more acute their sufferings became, the louder vociferated the excited assembly. I was horror-stricken, and, although I would gladly have fled from the place, felt transfixed to the spot. I knew that if they fell I should have no power to save them, but should be forced to see them torn limb from limb. At length, however, the crisis came—a sudden shiver of the body and involuntary discharge—and the first intended victim had escaped. The same soon after happened to the second and to the third. They gradually came back to their former state, but appeared very much exhausted. Some people never get over the effects of drinking the mboundou, although they pass the ordeal without giving way. They linger for a long time in a sickly condition, and then die. The trial was over, and the doctor closed the ceremony by himself drinking an enormous quantity of the poison, with a similar result to that which we had witnessed in the young men, only that he appeared quite tipsy; in his wild and incoherent sayings, whilst under the influence of the drink, he stated that the bewitchers of Máyolo and the bringers of the plague did not belong to the village, a decision which was received with great acclamation. Máyolo was rejoiced that the wizards or witches did not belong to his own people, and the whole people were wild with joy: guns were fired, and the evening passed with beating of drums, singing, and dancing.

To protect the village from the wizards who might enter it from the neighbouring villages, and who had been accused as the cause of Máyolo's troubles, the doctor, accompanied by the whole of the people, went to the paths leading to Máyolo from other villages, and planted sticks at intervals across them, connecting the sticks by strong woody creepers, and hanging on the ropes leaves from the core of the crowns of palm-trees. It is a recognised law among these people that no stranger can come within these lines. When

I asked Máyolo what he would do if any one was to force the lines, he said that there would then be a grand palaver, but that there was no fear of such an event, for it never happened. Another reason for planting the lines was of a sanitary nature: small-pox was prevalent in several neighbouring villages, and Máyolo wished to prevent the relatives of the wives of his villagers (for people generally marry girls of distant places) from coming on a visit to them. I learnt to-day that the Otando man, who had accompanied me from Olenda, had since died of the plague, and the people of other villages had naturally come to the conclusion that his being in contact with me was the cause. He was one of Máyolo's fathers-in-law. It is marvellous how firm Máyolo adheres to the faith that I have nothing at all to do with the introduction of the plague. His influence is so great amongst his people that many have now come round to his opinion, and others dare not openly declare the contrary.

Two days after the pona oganga I called my people, and Máyolo and his people, together, and made a formal and resolute demand to be furnished with guides and porters to the Apono country. The speech which I made on this occasion was, as nearly as I can translate it, in the following words; I spoke in similitudes, African fashion, and used African expressions:—

"Máyolo, I have called you and your people together, in order that you may hear my mouth. When one of your people goes to the Ashira country to make trade, his heart is not glad until his friends there have given him trade, although he may have been well treated in the meantime, had plenty given him to eat, and a fine woman lent him as a wife. When you go to the Apono country in order to get a slave on trust from your friend the chief, or some large tusk of ivory from an elephant he has killed, you are not satisfied until he has sent you back to your village with the slave or the ivory; and your friend never fails to send you back with your desire granted. It is the same if you go to a man whose daughter you are very fond of, and who has promised to give her to you as a wife. For if, when you go to his house to get his daughter, instead of her he gives you plenty of food, your heart is not glad, though you have plenty to eat. The food will taste bitter, for it is not what you came for!

"So it is with me: I am not happy. I have not come to you, Máyolo, to make trade, to get slaves and ivory, or to marry your daughters. If I had come for these things, I am sure they would have been given to me long ago. (The assembly here all shouted 'Yes! they would have been given to you long ago!')

"But you all know that I have not come for these things. I told you when I came, and you knew it before, that I wanted to go further away. I love you and your people. (Interruptions of 'We know you love us.') You have been kind to me and to my men. Though some of them have slept with your women, you have done nothing to them. You have given us plenty to eat; you have stolen nothing from my men or from me; I have been here as if in my own village. (Here they cried out, 'It is your own village; you are our king,' Máyolo leading the chorus.) If I wanted to get angry with you, I could not find a single cause for it. (At this Máyolo stiffened himself up and looked around, quite proud.) A few days after my arrival you, Máyolo, fell ill. You have a good head; you know that I did not make you ill. I was very sorry to see you ill, for I have a heart like yourself. How could I like to see Máyolo, my only friend, ill? (Here Máyolo smiled, and looked prouder than ever.) I love you, and I love your people for your sake. (Shouts of 'We are all your friends.') I am not an evil Spirit; I do not delight in making people ill; I do not bring the plague, for it was in your country before I came. (Loud shouts of 'Rovano!'—it is so.) My own people have also been ill; how could I make them ill? Macondai, my beloved boy, who has been with me from a little child, has been more ill than any other of my men; how could I wish to make him ill? I sit by spreading death and disease before me that I can go into the interior? If you wanted to go amongst other tribes, would you spread illness before you? So it is with me; to go into the interior I must make friends. The plague goes where it likes and asks nobody. The people are afraid of me; they do not see that I bring them fine things: beads, looking-glasses, cloth, and red caps for their heads. These are things that I wish to leave with the people wherever I go.

"Now, Máyolo, you are getting better. You have a saying among yourselves that a man does not stand alone in the world; he has friends, and there are no people who are without friends. You Otando have friends among the Apono and Ishogo people, where I want to go. If you ask trade of these friends, they give it to you. I come to you to ask you the road. Come and show me the road through the Apono country; it is the one I like the best, for it is the shortest. I will make your heart glad, if you make my heart glad. I have things to give you all, and I want the news to spread that Máyolo and I are two great friends, so that after I am gone people may say, 'Máyolo was the friend of the Oguizi.'"

The last part of the speech was received with tremendous shouts of applause, and cries of "Rovano! Rovano!" Máyolo joining in with the rest. When I had finished I sat down on my footstool.

Máyolo deferred his answer to the next day, as all his people were not present, and we then had another palaver, which I hoped would be a final one. The men were seated round in a semi-circle, the women forming a cluster by themselves, and in front was stationed a boy holding a goat, by the side of which were two bunches of plantains; my own people were also present. Máyolo began his speech, and, as is customary, addressed a third person, Igala, saying:—

"When a hunter goes into the forest in search of game, he is not glad until he returns home with meat. So Chaillie's heart will not be glad, until he finishes what he wishes to do. I have heard what Chaillie has told me. I am *a man*. Chaillie, the Oguizi (Spirit) has come to Máyolo; I am Máyolo; there is no other Máyolo but me. I am ashamed at this long delay; I have a heart, and Chaillie shall go on. I know that some people, jealous of me, have told you that I have palaver in the upper country; that I have taken their slaves on trust, and am in debt to them; but it is a lie. The people are afraid of Chaillie; we all know that he is a Spirit; from the time our fathers were born, his like has never been seen. The news has spread that he brings disease and death wherever he goes; and so the people are afraid of him. I have been ill, but it is not he that has caused it, but other people who want to bewitch me, because of the good things that he has given me. I will go myself, in three or four days, to visit an Apono chief, a friend of mine, and will tell him that Chaillie eats like ourselves, drinks like ourselves, that he plays with our children, talks to our women and men, and does us good. I am Máyolo, and Chaillie shall go on his way, and then his heart will be glad."

Then turning to me, he said: "During the days you have to wait, take this goat and these two bunches of plantains, and eat them. We shall soon be on the *long road*, but I must feel the way first; we must do things little by little. You cannot catch a monkey, unless you are very careful in going to it."

I answered one of their sayings. "If you had said 'Wait, wait,' and I saw that you were not telling me the truth, the goat you have just given me could not be good, and I would have returned it to you, for it would taste bitter; but I believe you."

Thus I had to content myself, whilst Máyolo was

exerting himself to open the way for me into Apono-land. In the afternoon I made Igala cut, with a lancet, into the abscess on Máyolo's shoulder, which gave him great relief after the discharge of the matter. The good fellow thanked me very much, and we became better friends than ever. Next day he was so much elated with the improvement in his health, that he got tipsy on a fermented beverage which he had prepared two days before he had fallen ill, and which was made by mixing honey and water, and adding to it pieces of bark of a certain tree. The long standing had improved the liquor in his eyes, for the older the beverage, the more intoxicating it becomes. All the people of the village had a jollification in the evening to celebrate the recovery of their chief; Máyolo being the most uproarious of all, dancing, slapping his chest, and shouting "Here I am alive; they said I should die because the Spirit had come, but here I am."

During all the time he was ill he had been continually looking forward to this "jolly treat." He had several of the jars of the country full of the fermented beverage. Fortunately, he was very inoffensive when under the influence of drink. Scarcely able to stand steady, he came up to me, crying out, "Here I am, Chaillie, well at last. I tell you I am well, Oguizi!" and, in order to prove it to me, he began to leap about and to strike the ground with his feet, saying, "Don't you see that I am well? The Otando people said, the Apono said—as soon as they heard that you had arrived in my village—'Máyolo is a dead man!' As soon as I fell ill, they said, 'Máyolo will never get up again!' But here I am, alive and well! Give me some powder, that I may fire off the guns, to let the surrounding people know that I am well!"

I quietly said, "Not to-day, Máyolo, for your head is still weak."

He laughed, and went away shouting, "I knew the Oguizi did not like to see me ill. I am Máyolo! I will take him further on!"

Throughout the month of April I frequently regaled myself with what I used to consider a very good dinner: that is, a haunch of monkey cooked on the grillo. Formerly I had always had a great aversion to eating monkeys (not, however, from any ideas about their relationship to man), but hunger and the scarcity of other animal food had compelled me lately to make many a meal on these animals. This is the height of the monkey season in Otando-land, the season lasting through March, April and May, during which months they are so fat that their flesh is really exquisite eating. I know of no game better or more relishing; the joints must be either roasted or grilled, to bring out the flavour of the meat to perfection. At all other times of the year except these three months monkeys are lean, tough, and tasteless. It is the same with the wild hog of these regions; from February to the beginning of May, when the fattening Koola nut is ripe and falls in abundance from the trees, the wild hog gets something like an overfed pig at home, and the meat is delicious eating. I felt to-night that I had dined well, and did not envy Sardanapalus his dainties, for I doubted whether this luxurious monarch ever had fat monkey for dinner. I recommend all future travellers to cast aside their prejudices and try grilled monkey, at least during the months I have mentioned. They will thank me for the advice. Many wild fruit trees are now in full bearing and the monkeys have splendid feed. I finished my dinner with pine-apple as dessert; the season, however, is now past for pine-apples, it began when I entered the Ashira country and lasted during the whole of the time of my stay there.

Máyolo after his recovery became more friendly than ever. He was naturally of an inquisitive turn of mind, and in his frequent conversations with me occupied all my time in answering his questions. One day he came with all his people and all the women of the village, to ask me a number of questions. He first asked how the women worked our plantations? I told him women did no field-work with us. They were astonished to hear this, and still more to hear that plantains and cassava were almost unknown in my country. They all shouted, "Then what do you eat?" I explained to them that we had always plenty to eat. I told them that we had bullocks like their wild cattle, which remained tame in our villages like their goats, and that we taught them to carry things. They would hardly believe me, when I added that in their own country there were tribes of black men who owned tame oxen. Continuing the subject, I said that there were countries in which even elephants were tamed, and taught to carry people on their backs. At this a wild shout of astonishment arose from the assembly, and remembering that I had a copy of the "Illustrated London News" containing an Indian scene with elephants, I went and fetched it to prove that I told them the truth. There was a rush forward to look at the picture over Máyolo's shoulders. They all recognised the animals as elephants, and expressed their astonishment at the men on their backs; above all, they wondered to see the animals represented as tied by the feet and kept quiet. 'Punch,' the travellers' friend, excited their wonder greatly. They all exclaimed, "What a fine cap he wears!" and asked me if I had any like it. They were quite disappointed when I told them I had not.

Then came numerous questions about white men. How they stared when I told them that our houses were made of stone, the same material as was found on their mountains. The last question was a delicate one; it was, "Do white men die?" I wished them to remain in their present belief that we did not die, for their superstitious feeling towards me was my best safeguard; so I feigned not to hear the question, and turned their attention to another subject.

The people generally, and especially the women, became emboldened after this long chat; and I could see some of the buxom matrons laughingly conferring with one another, as if on some important business. At last one of them, bolder than the rest, said: "We have seen your head and your hands since you have been among us, but we have never seen what the rest of your body is like; it would make our hearts glad, if you would take off your clothes and let us see."

This polite request I of course flatly refused to comply with, and they did not press it. Another request they made I was able to grant: this was to talk the Oguizi language. I gave them a few samples of French and English, but I very much doubt if they could perceive the difference. They believe that all white men belong to one people, and of course, beyond the fact that they land on their shores from the great sea, know nothing of the different nations of the world or where they are situated. When I asked them where they thought the Ngouyai river ended, they answered, "Somewhere in the sand."

After our long conversation I felt tired and went for a walk over the prairie. This pleasant day was ruffled in the evening by a violent quarrel between two Ashira married women, one of them being a stranger who had come to Máyolo on a visit to her friends. It appeared that one of the men of the village called this woman towards him; and his wife, on hearing of it, asked her husband what business he had to call the woman, and, getting jealous, told him she must be his sweetheart. The husband's reply being, I suppose, not altogether satisfactory, the enraged wife rushed out to seek her supposed rival, and a battle ensued. Women's fights in this country always begin by their throwing off their *dengui*, that is, stripping themselves entirely naked. The challenger having thus denuded herself, her enemy showed pluck and answered the challenge by promptly doing the same; so that the two elegant figures immediately went at it, literally tooth and nail, for they fought like cats, and between the rounds reviled each other in language the most filthy that could possibly be uttered. Máyolo being asleep in his house, and no one seeming ready to interfere, I went myself and separated the two furies.

In the meantime Oshoumouna and the men sent by Máyolo to open the way for me into Apono-land, returned last night, frightened away by the reception they had met with from the people of the Apono village to which they had gone, and which is situated on the right bank of the Rembo Ngouyai. As soon as they said who they were, and that they had beads with which to buy some salt—for the Apono trade a good deal in salt, paying for it in slaves—the villagers shouted out, "Go away! go away! We don't want to have anything to do with the Oguizi, or with the people who have come in contact with him! We do not want your beads! We want nothing that came with the Oguizi!"

This news filled me with sorrow. Máyolo tried to comfort me; but my prospects were indeed dark and gloomy.

May 6th. After taking several lunar distances to-night between the moon and Jupiter, and feeling tired, as I generally do after night observations, I went into a little shed behind my house and took a cold shower-bath—at least, an imitation of one—by splashing water over me; I find this very refreshing and cooling before retiring to rest. I then went into my chamber; but I came out of it again faster than I entered, for I had stepped into a band of Bashikouay ants, and was quickly covered with the nimble and savage little creatures, who bit me dreadfully. I was driven almost mad with pain. I did not dare to light paper or apply fire to the invading horde of ants, inside the place, on account of the quantity of gunpowder stored in my chamber; thus I had to abandon my house to the irresistible ants, who had become perfect masters of it. I at once called my men, and we succeeded in finding the line of the invading host outside of the house; to this we applied fire, and burnt many thousands of them; but it was not until half-past two in the morning that the house was cleared.

When I rose, feverish and unrefreshed, the next morning, I found the Bashikouays again in the house. This time they emerged from a number of holes which had newly made their appearance in the ground near my house, and which were the mouths of the tunnels or galleries leading from their subterranean abodes. I was thankful that it was daytime, for if it had been night they would not have been long before paying me another visit. An invasion of a sleeping-chamber by these ants at night is a very serious matter, for an army of Bashikouays swarming over the body during sleep would wake a person up rather disagreeably. There can be no doubt that if a man were firmly tied to a bed so that he could not escape, he would be entirely eaten up by these ants in a short space of time. I have heard that men have been put to death for witchcraft in this way. Happily their bite is not venomous. We poured boiling water down the newly-made galleries and over the columns of ants that were issuing from them, so that they were again driven away, and we were saved from another invasion.

May 10th. I witnessed to-day a striking instance of the inborn cunning and deceit of the native African. My people had spread out on mats in front of my hut a quantity of ground-nuts, which we had bought, when I observed from the inside of the hut a little urchin about four years old slily regaling himself with them, keeping his eyes on me, and believing himself unnoticed. I suddenly came out, but the little rascal, as quick as thought, seated himself on a piece of wood, and dexterously concealed the nuts he had in his hand under the joints of his legs and in the folds of his abdominal skin; then looked up to me with an air of perfect innocence. This, thought I, is a bright example of the unsophisticated children of nature, whom some writers love to describe, to the disadvantage of the corrupted children of civilization! Thieving, in these savage countries, is not considered an offence against the community; for no one complains but he who has been robbed. My precocious little pilferer would therefore have no teaching to prevent him from becoming an accomplished thief as he grew older.

In the evening, as I was computing the lunar distances I had taken, I was startled by the sudden screech of a woman. I went out immediately, and found that it was the mbuiri woman, who had been suddenly seized with the spirit of divination—the mbuiri having entered into her. She raved on for some time, the theme of her discourse being the *eciva* or plague.

May 14th. My misfortunes will never terminate! Máyolo has another abscess forming. I begin to think I shall never get beyond this Otando country. Máyolo, however, assures me that he will send his nephew onward to Apono to prepare the way for us. He told me our great difficulty would be to get ferried across the river, which could only be done by the aid of the chief of Mouendi, a village near the banks of the Ngouyai. I went to my hut and selected a present for the Apono chief, a bright red cap, a string of beads, and some powder; and in giving them to Máyolo to send by his messenger, I told him to say I should bring him many other fine things when I came myself. It was necessary to overcome the scruples of the Apono, who dreaded a visit from me lest I should bring evil on their village.

May 15th. Máyolo's messenger returned to-day with the joyful news that the Apono chief would receive us. The chief had sent a kendo as a return present to Máyolo, with the words "Máyolo has given me birth, how can I refuse him what he asks? Tell him to come with his *ibamba*. Máyolo has not died through receiving the Spirit; why should I die?"

Many people of Máyolo's clan came to-day to see, before I left their country, the many wonderful things I had brought with me; and Máyolo himself, though not very well, could not resist the temptation to leave his hut and join the sightseers. I first brought out a large Geneva musical box, and having wound it up inside my house, set it down on a stool in the street. On hearing the mysterious sounds they all got up, looked at each other, then at me and the box, to see whether I had any communication with it, and worked themselves into such a state of fright that when a little drum inside beat, they all took to their heels and ran away as fast as they could to the other end of the village, Máyolo leading the van. I went after them, and tried to allay their fears, but their belief was not to be shaken that a devil was inside the box. They came back, but would not sit down, holding themselves ready to run again, if anything startling occurred. They were completely mystified when they heard the music still going on although I was walking about at a distance from the box, holding no communication with it. I remained away from it a long time walking about in the prairie, and the music was still going on when I returned, to the great perplexity of the simple villagers. I offered to open the box to show them that there was no devil inside; but as soon as I touched the lid with that intention, they all started for another run; so I did not open it.

I showed them an accordion; and, being no player myself, made simply a noise with it, which pleased them amazingly. They were more pleased with it than with the musical box, for there was no mystery about the cause of the noise to alarm them. Then I got out a galvanic battery, and experimented on such of them as I could persuade to touch the handles. When they felt the shock they cried out "Eninda!" this being the name of a species of electric fish found in the neighbouring streams. They all cried, "Why did you not show us these things before?" Finally, after showing them pictures and other objects—the portraits of the Movers of the Address in the 'Illustrated London News' attracting their notice more than anything else—I exhibited my large magnet, which I knew would astonish them. I asked one man to come near with his Apono sword, and staggered him by taking it out of his hand with the magnet. I asked for other swords, and knives. All were handed to me at arm's length, for they were afraid of approaching the magical instrument, to which the red paint gave additional terrors. When they saw their knives and swords sticking to the magnet without dropping, sometimes by the edges and sometimes sideways, they all shouted out: "He is surely an Oguizi (Spirit) to do these things." I invited them to take the instrument in their hands, but they dared not; Máyolo's curiosity eventually overcame his fears, and he handled the magnet with the air of a man who is doing something very courageous. At the conclusion of the exhibition the old chief exclaimed that I was immensely rich, and that if I was not a king I must be next in rank to the king in my country. He was astonished when I told him that the kings of the white men had probably never heard of me. He thought I was telling him a very wicked story, and did not believe me.

The day previous to this I had a good laugh at the alarm of one of these simple Otando people, when using my boiling-point apparatus to ascertain the height of the place. I was engaged in taking the observation, when a native, attracted by curiosity, came to see what I was doing. He looked earnestly at the aneroids, then at the bull's-eye lantern on the top of which was the little kettle where water was to be boiled, and then at the thermometer screwed into the kettle: when he had finished his inspection he withdrew to a distance, in a state of bewilderment and fear that was comical to behold; but I pretended to be taking no notice of him. These people fancy that I travel with all sorts of fetiches and am possessed of supernatural power—a belief which I did not try to upset, as it stood me in good stead. I now lighted the lamp and proceeded to boil the water; as soon as the negro saw the steam ascending, and heard the bubbling of the water, his courage finally gave way, and he fled with the utmost precipitation.

My photographic apparatus, or at least what remained of it, was much admired by friend Máyolo. He was the most inquisitive man of his tribe, none of whom were wanting in curiosity, and he was never weary of asking me questions and inspecting my wonderful stores. When I first took out the photographic tent from its box, he was amazed, after seeing it fixed, to discover what a bulky affair could come out of so small a box. After fixing the tent I withdrew the slide and exposed the orange-coloured glass, and invited the mystified chief to look through it at the prairie. At first he was afraid and declined to come into the tent; but on my telling him that he knew I should never do anything to harm him, he consented. He could not comprehend it. He looked at me, at my hands, then at the glass, and believed there was witchcraft at the bottom of it. After Máyolo had come out of the tent unharmed, the rest of the negroes took courage, and my tent was made a peep-show for the remainder of the day.

The climate of Máyolo seems very variable and uncertain; and night after night I was disappointed when preparing to take lunar distances or meridian altitudes of stars, by the sudden clouding of the heavens. The sky would often be very clear and settled, inducing me to get my sextant in order, prepare a quicksilver artificial horizon, and note the index error; but a thick mist would suddenly arise and put an end to all operations. But now and then I had magnificent nights, so that I succeeded in taking a pretty long series of observations for latitude and longitude before I left Máyolo; so complete are they, that the position of the town may be considered as well fixed; but I should fail were I to attempt to describe the difficulties and disappointments I had to contend with in completing them. There was something rather remarkable also about the deposit of dew. I remarked that at Máyolo and Ashira the grass was often very damp before sunset, when the sun had disappeared behind the mountains. It was so damp that it wetted my shoes in walking through; and, at ten minutes after sunset, dew drops were plentiful along the edges of the plantain leaves, even on those trees which the sun had shone upon just before disappearing below the horizon. The dew drops glittering on the margins of these beautiful leaves looked like crystal drops or gems, appearing the brighter from the contrast with the velvety green hue of the magnificent foliage. One evening I watched closely the first appearance of these dew drops. At a quarter past five, before the sun had quite disappeared behind the hill-tops, I counted thirty-six drops of dew on the leaves of one tree; but three quarters of an hour later the edges of the leaves were quite surrounded with water. The sky at the same time was very clear, only a few clouds near the horizon could be seen. At six o'clock the grass was not sufficiently damp to leave water-marks on my boots; so that it is to be concluded that the leaves of the plantain are the first to condense the invisible vapour of the atmosphere. Up to the present time (May 18th) I have only twice seen the sky entirely free from cloud since my arrival at Fernand Vaz from England.

On the 16th of May, whilst I was in the prairie at a short distance from Máyolo, studying the habits of the white ants, I was aroused from my meditations by sudden screams from the town. I was afraid something tragical was taking place, and made haste for the village. I found the place in an uproar; all caused by an influx of poor relations. It appeared that the news of the vast wealth Máyolo had obtained from the Oguizi had spread far and wide over the neighbouring country, and, getting to the ears of the old chief's numerous fathers-in-law and brothers-in-law, some of them had journeyed to his village with a view to getting a share of the spoils, their greediness overcoming their fear of me. The people of the village had been plagued to death with these avaricious guests, for they were all thought to have become rich since I am living amongst them. As time is of no importance to the African, and during their stay they were living at the expense of the villagers, it was no easy matter to get rid of them. The fathers-in-law praised the beauty and all the good qualities of their daughters married to the chief, hinted that he had got a cheap bargain in this one and had not paid enough for the other; and some of them actually threatened to take away their daughters unless something more was given. Poor Máyolo, sick of the worry, had asked me for various things to give them in order to get rid of them, but they were insatiable.

The row this morning was between Oshoumouna, Máyolo's nephew, and his father-in-law, arising out of these unsatisfied demands for more pay. The old man was very discontented, saying, that though he had given him his daughter, he had not had a single thing given him by the Oguizi. It was in vain that Oshoumouna assured him that I never gave presents for nothing. Whilst I was absent, the father-in-law had ventured to use force to take away his daughter. It is a very common thing in Africa for a father-in-law to take away his daughter, if he is not satisfied with the husband's conduct. Oshoumouna took no notice of the abduction, and the row was caused by the father-in-law, enraged at this coolness, proceeding to demolish his son-in-law's house. A general *mêlée* ensued; old Máyolo rushed out and belaboured the aggressor with a club; the women screamed, and a fearful uproar took place. As usual, the object was to see who could make the most noise, and in this contest the father-in-law was no match for the villagers.

The discomfited father-in-law left the village, and

took his daughter with him, saying that her husband should never see her again; but the damsel gave her father the slip before night and returned to her husband. There was general rejoicing in the village, and Oshoumouna bragged greatly of the love and fidelity of his wife, although she accounted for her return by saying that she loved the place where the Oguizi was, for there she could get beads.

During the latter part of my stay at Máyolo, I had in my possession a beautiful little nocturnal animal, of the Lemur family, an *Otolicnus*, called by the negroes *Ibola*. It is nocturnal in its habits, and has immensely large eyes, and a fur so soft that it reminded me of the Chinchilla. I had it about a fortnight. The species lives in the forests, retiring in the day time to the hollows of trees, where it sleeps till the hour of its activity returns; but it sometimes also conceals itself in the midst of masses of dead boughs of trees, where daylight cannot penetrate. In broad daylight you could see by the twinkling of its eyes and its efforts to conceal itself, that light was painful to it. At first I had no means of protecting it during the day, and the delicate little creature used to cover its eyes with its tail to keep out the light. Nothing but ripe plantains would it accept for food. I was much grieved one morning to find the poor Ibola dead, for it had become quite tame, and liked to be caressed.

My boy Macondai was now entirely recovered, with the exception of sore eyes, from which many negroes suffer after the small-pox has disappeared; some lose their sight from the effects of the disease;

one only of my men was afflicted in this way, Mouitchi, who became blind of one eye. One of Máyolo's fathers-in-law was quite blind from this disease. All my Commi companions having thus got over the danger, with the exception of Rapelina, who had not had the disease, I was anxious only for Máyolo, whose abscess was still slowly progressing and confined him to his house. As the time approached for our departure, a marked increase of attention and kindness was noticeable on his part. Every day a present of eatables came to my hut cooked by his head wife; one day a plateful of yams, another day a dish of cassava, and so forth. But I suspected a trick was being played upon me, having recently become acquainted with an African custom, of which I had not previously heard, and which consisted in serving, in dishes given to a guest, powder from the skull of a deceased ancestor, with a view to soften his heart in the matter of parting presents. This custom is called the *alumbi*.

I had long known of the practice of preserving in a separate hut the skulls of ancestors, but did not know of this particular use of the relics. In fact, a person might travel in Africa for years without becoming aware of this singular custom, as no negro will divulge to you the whole details of such a matter, even should he be one of your best friends.

Most travellers in this part of the continent are puzzled to know the meaning of certain miniature huts which are seen standing behind or between the dwelling-houses, and which are held sacred. No one but the owner himself is allowed to enter these little huts; but Quengueza's great friendship for me overcame his African scruples in my case; and I was permitted, on my return from the interior, to examine his *alumbi*-house. These erections are spoken of by travellers as fetich-houses; and if, perchance, a stranger is allowed to 'peep into one, he sees a few boxes containing chalk or ochre, and upon a kind of little table a cake of the same, with which the owner rubs his body every time he goes on a fishing, hunting, or trading expedition. The chalk is considered sacred, and to be smeared with it serves as a protection from danger. If you are a great friend, the chalk of the alumbi will be marked upon you on your departure from the residence of your host. But the boxes generally contain also the skulls of the ancestors of the owner, at least those relatives who were alive during his own life-time; for, on the death of such a relative, his or her head is cut off and placed in a box full of white clay, looking like chalk, where it is left to rot and saturate the chalk; both skull and saturated chalk being then held sacred. The skulls of twin children are almost always used for the alumbi.

When a guest is entertained of whom presents are expected, the host, in a quiet way, goes from time to time into the fetich-house and scrapes a little bone-powder from a favourite skull, and puts it into the food which is being cooked as a present to the guest. The idea is, that, by consuming the scrapings of the skull, the blood of their ancestors enters into your body, and thus, becoming of one blood, you are naturally led to love them, and grant them what they wish. It is not a pleasant subject of reflection, but I have no doubt been operated upon on previous journeys; being now, however, aware of the custom, I refused the food, and told Máyolo I cared very little to eat of the scraped skull of his grandfather. Of course, Máyolo indignantly denied it; he said he had offered me food out of pure love for me.

The last days of May were employed in re-packing my large stores of baggage. It was a most laborious task; everything had to be sorted, and all that was not absolutely necessary secured in packages to be left behind. How I wished it were possible to travel through Africa with a lighter load! Amongst the things to be left behind were the remains of my photographical outfit; I packed them up with a heavy heart, so much did I regret being unable to continue taking photographs. Notwithstanding the lightening of my loads, I still required forty-five porters to carry them.

A few days before my departure we held a grand palaver, and I made my request for the requisite number of porters. All wished to go, and, to the credit of Máyolo, I must say that I never had less trouble in arranging the terms of payment. To Máyolo himself I gave all the goods that I had set apart to leave behind, owing to the necessity of lightening my baggage, including all that remained of my photographic apparatus. I had given to him more presents than to any other chief, with the exception of my staunch friend, King Quengueza. He was overjoyed at the splendour of the presents, but said, "Truly, goods and money are like hunger; you are filled to-day, but to-morrow you are hungry again!"

CHAPTER X.

THE OTANDO AND APONO REGION.

Geographical Position of Máyolo—Splendour of the Constellations as seen from the Equatorial Regions—The Zodiacal Light—Twinkling of the Stars—Meteoric Showers—The Otando and Apono Plains, or Prairies—The Otando People a branch of the Ashira Nation—Their Customs—Filing the Teeth—Tattooing—Native Dogs.

FROM Olenda eastwards, as attentive readers of my former and present narratives will be aware, the countries I traversed were new ground, not only to myself, but to any European; it is, therefore, necessary that I should give such details as I am able, in the course of my journey, about the various portions of the country, their inhabitants and productions.

Unfortunately, the volume of my journal, which contained the diary of my march from Olenda to Máyolo, and of more than two months of the latter part of my stay in this place, was lost, with nearly the whole of the rest of my property, in my hurried flight from Ashango-land. It was the only volume out of five that was missing. It contained the observations which I took for altitudes of the range of highlands separating the Ashira from the Otando districts; and I am, therefore, unable to give a full account of this range, which is an important feature in this part of Africa, as separating, together with the lower hilly range west of Olenda, the coast-lands from the great interior of the continent. I remember, however, that some part of the country was more than 1,200 feet above the level of the sea, as shown by the aneroids.

The town of Máyolo I determined, by a long series of observations, to lie in 1° 51′ 14″ S. lat., and 11° 0′ 37″ E. long., and 496 feet above the sea-level.

At Máyolo, the contemplation of the heavens afforded me a degree of enjoyment difficult to describe. When every one else had gone to sleep, I often stood alone on the prairie, with a gun by my side, watching the stars. I looked at some with fond love, for they had been my guides, and consequently my friends, in the lonely country I travelled; and it was always with a feeling of sadness that I looked at them for the last time, before they disappeared below the horizon for a few months, and always welcomed them back with a feeling of pleasure which, no doubt, those who have been in a situation similar to mine can understand. I studied also how high they twinkled, and tried to see how many bright meteors travelled through the sky, until the morning twilight came and reminded me that my work was done, by the then visible world becoming invisible.

I shall always remember the matchless beauty of these Equatorial nights, for they have left an indelible impression upon my memory.

The period of the year I spent at Máyolo (April and May) were the months when the atmosphere is the purest, for after the storms the azure of the sky was so intensely deep, that it made the stars doubly bright in the vault of heaven.

At that time the finest constellations of the Southern Hemisphere were within view at the same time. The constellation of the Ship, of the Cross, of the Centaur, of the Scorpion, and the Belt of Orion, which include the three brightest stars in the heavens, Sirius, Canopus, and α Centauri.

The planets Venus, Mars, Saturn, and Jupiter were in sight.

The Magellanic clouds—white-looking patches, especially the larger one—brightly illuminated as they revolved round the starless South Pole, contrasting with the well-known "coal-sack" adjoining the Southern Cross.

The part of the Milky Way, between the 50° and 80° parallel, so beautiful and rich in crowded nebulæ and stars, seemed to be in a perfect blaze between Sirius and the Centaur; the heavens there appeared brilliantly illuminated.

Then looking northward, I could see the beautiful constellation of the Great Bear, which was about the same altitude above the horizon as the constellations of the Cross and of the Centaur; some of the stars in the two constellations passing the meridian within a short time of each other; γ Ursæ Majoris half an hour before α Crucis, and Benetnasch eleven minutes before β Centauri.

Where and when could any one have a grander view of the heavens at one glance? From α Ursæ Majoris to α Crucis, there was an arc of 125°. Then, as if to give a still grander view to the almost enchanting scene, the zodiacal light rose after the sun had set, increasing in brilliancy, of a bright yellow colour, and rising in a pyramidal shape high into the sky, often so bright that it overshadowed the brightness of the milky way and the rays of the moon, the beautiful yellow light gradually diminishing towards the apex. It cast a gentle radiance on the clouds round it, and sometimes formed almost a ring, but never perfect, having a break near the meridian; at times being reflected in the east with nearly as much brilliancy, if not as much, as in the west, and making me almost imagine a second sunrise.

I had noticed this yellow glow before at Olenda in March, where it was sometimes very bright; but it was only at Máyolo I began to write down observations upon it. April and May were the months when the light showed itself in its greatest brilliancy. It often became visible half an hour after the sun had disappeared, and was very brilliant, like a second sunset. It still increased in brilliancy, and attained often a very bright orange colour at the base. It rose in a very distinct pyramidal shape, which sometimes, if I remember well, must have extended about 40°, the bright yellow gradually becoming fainter and fainter at the top. The brilliancy and duration varied considerably on different days, and also the breadth and height. It could be seen most every day when the sky was clear; and as it faded away, it left behind it a white light, which also showed itself in the east. It was generally the brightest from a quarter to seven to half-past seven, but there were exceptions; sometimes it would be later, and at times the glow would fade and then reappear with fresh strength; but generally the increase and decrease of brilliancy was uniform. It was seldom discernible after ten o'clock.

Unfortunately the book containing these observations on the light has been lost, but a few notes on it are scattered here and there in my journal.

April 13th. The weather has been cloudy, with a few showers. . . . . To-night the sky presents a magnificent appearance after sunset. The glow coming from the west was so bright that it overshadowed the brightness of the Milky Way. I could only distinguish it above the Sword of Orion; the glow was the brightest below the planet Mars, and the base of the pyramid reached, on the south, the part of the Milky Way at the foot of the Cross. At the north point of the horizon its extent was about the same.

April 15th. The weather has been cloudy until past noon, and to-night the sky is clear though a little hazy. The glow of light coming from the west is beautiful, and is quite white; at seven o'clock it was still of great intensity, though it had diminished. I do not remember to have seen it so bright before.

May 6th. Yesterday the bright yellow light which appears after sunset was magnificent, and could be seen above the trapezium in Orion notwithstanding the strong moonlight, the moon being then nearly at the full. Indeed, I have never seen the zodiacal light shine so brightly; one might fancy, if it was not towards the west, the dawn of morning coming.

May 14th. After sunset I observed a phenomenon

that much surprised me; the zodiacal light had its counterpart in the east.

Now I will make a few observations on the twinkling of stars. Some persons have believed that, in our northern latitudes, the stars twinkle more than within the tropics. I spent this last summer at Twickenham at Mr. Bishop's observatory, and have watched the scintillation of the stars, and I doubt much if this conclusion is right; unfortunately, I have also lost the notes I had made on this subject. I remember distinctly that one of the stars of the Belt of Orion twinkled until it reached the zenith; others twinkled to a considerable altitude. There were nights when they seemed to twinkle more than at other times.

While watching the stars, in the southern heavens, it appeared to me that α Centauri was changing to a ruddy colour. It was certainly not so white as β Centauri, and often, through a light mist so common there, I could recognise it through its reddishness. I should say, that it was only with the naked eye that these observations were made.

The most southern star of the constellation of the Ship (ε Argûs), distant from Canopus about 17° 43′, was quite red to the eyes.

In regard to the April shower of meteors, I only saw them few in number; there was nothing to compare with the number of those I observed this year at Twickenham, in company with the distinguished astronomer, Mr. Hind; but many were far brighter. Almost every night, while observing at Máyolo, I could see brilliant meteors, many of which seemed to emanate from the direction of Leo, though its altitude was very high.

All the inquiries I made concerning the fall of aerolites have been fruitless; the negroes never saw any, though I suppose that, as in every other country, some may have fallen, but they are buried in these impenetrable forests.

Máyolo lies on the western edge of an undulating plain about twenty miles broad, stretching between the Ashira ranges of hills and the higher ridges of Ashango in the interior; this plain averaging about 400 feet above the sea-level, and the hilly ranges running nearly north-west and south-east. The plain is covered in many places with a clayey soil, but in other parts with masses of fragments of ferruginous sandstone. It is watered by the Ngouyai and its affluents, which river flows in a north-westerly direction, and, cutting through the hilly range north of Ashira-land, forms a junction some thirty miles further down with the Okanda (apparently a still more important stream); both together then form the great River Ogobai, which pursues a south-westerly direction through the coast-plains to the Atlantic.

The plains east of Máyolo are inhabited, as will presently be seen, by the Otando and the Apono tribes. These plains consist chiefly of undulating grass-land, diversified by groups of trees, or small circumscribed tracts of forest, in which are many magnificent timber-trees; the banks of the river are almost everywhere lined with trees for a hundred yards or more from the water's edge. Now and then the prairie reaches to the water-side. The grass-lands extend in a north-west and south-east direction, and the numerous negro-villages are generally built in the prairie. Some of the wooded islands or isolated patches of forest are many miles in length; the prairies are covered with tall grasses and shrubs, without any mixture of bushes or trees. The soil of the forest tracts is generally more fertile than that of the prairies, and it is within their shades that the plantations of the people are situated. The Otando villages round Máyolo are surrounded by groves of plaintain-trees; and the broad magnificent leaves of these trees form a striking contrast with the grass that surrounds them.

I have little to remark respecting the Otando people. They are a branch of the Ashira nation, speaking the Ashira language, and having a similar physical conformation to the people of that tribe, together with the same superstitions, customs, arts, warlike implements, and dress; but they do not seem to be so industrious in the manufacture of the grass cloth.

I found many of the people not very dark-skinned. They had various fashions as regards their teeth. Many file the two upper incisors in the shape of a sharp cone, and the four lower ones are also filed to a sharp point. Others file the four upper incisors to a point. A few among them have the two upper incisors pulled out. They tattoo themselves on the chest and stomach, but keep the face smooth. Among the young people very few have their teeth filed: the custom is dying out.

One day, in my rambles near Máyolo, two of my native dogs had a severe fight with a very large white-nosed monkey (*cercopithecus*), and came back to me in a dreadful state, especially my dog Andeko, who, being always the first in a fray, generally came off worse than his comrade. In this encounter with the white-nosed monkey, he had the flesh of his fore-leg bitten through to the bone, and his upper lip was cut in two by a terrible gash. Andeko was famous for his courage. He had at different times taken alive young gorillas, young chimpanzees, and young boars.

These native dogs are keen, active animals; they are seen in the interior of purer blood than in the Commi country, where they have become much changed by crossing with European dogs of various breeds, brought by trading vessels. The pure bred native dog is small, has long straight ears, long muzzle, and long, curly tail—very curly when the breed is pure. The hair is short and the colour yellowish, the pure breed being known by the clearness of this colour. They are always lean, and are kept very short of food by their owners; in fact, they get no food except what they can steal. Although they have a quick ear, I do not think highly of their scent. My head man, Igala, keeps a large number of dogs for hunting at his plantations in the Fernand Vaz. They are good watch-dogs, but are often destroyed by leopards in the night. As I have stated in 'Equatorial Africa,' hydrophobia is unknown in this part of the continent. I have only now to confirm that statement; it appears, therefore, conclusive that heat is not the cause of this terrible disease.

CHAPTER XI.

ANTS.

The White Ants of the Prairies—The Mushroom-hived Termes—Interior of their Hives—Three classes in each Community: Soldiers, Workers, and Chiefs—Their mode of building—The Tree Ants—Curious structure of their Hives—Their process of constructing them—The Bark Ants—Curious tunnels formed by them—The Forest Ants—Large size of their Shelters or Hives—The stinging Black Ant.

DURING my stay at Máyolo, I occupied a great part of my leisure hours in studying the habits of the many different species of white ants (Termites), the nests of which are very conspicuous objects in the prairie. The study of these curious creatures was most fascinating, and it was a source of great enjoyment to me in the midst of so many cares and anxieties. The ants are of wonderful diversity, both in form of body, head, and so forth, and in architectural tastes. I began to form a collection of them, putting specimens of the different kinds, in their various stages, in little glass tubes filled with spirits, having brought an assortment of these tubes for the purpose of preserving minute insects. The loss of this collection in my retreat from Mouaou Kombo I felt most keenly, as I had hoped the specimens would have explained much that still remains obscure in the history of these curious insects. It prevents me also from giving the proper scientific names to the different varieties, each of which builds a different kind of nest; the natives have only a general name for all the species.

Mushroom-hived Termes.—Let us begin with the species which builds the mushroom-shaped edifice. These singular hives, shaped like gigantic mushrooms, are scattered by tens of thousands over the Otando prairie. The top is from twelve to eighteen inches in diameter, and the column about five inches; the total height is from ten inches to fifteen inches. After the grass has been burnt they present a most extraordinary appearance; near Máyolo they are met with almost at every step. They are not all uniformly built, as they appear at a distance, but differ in the roundness or sharpness of their summits. I opened a great number of these, and followed up my researches day after day into the habits of their inhabitants. These and all similar edifices are built to protect the white ants against the inclemencies of the weather, and against their enemies, which are very numerous, and include many predaceous kinds of fellow ants.

The mushroom-shaped hive is not so firmly built in the ground but that it can be knocked down by a well-planted kick. It is built of a kind of mortar after being digested in the stomachs of the ants, When felled, the base of the pillar is found to have rested on the ground, leaving a circular hollow, in the middle of which is a ball of earth full of cells, which enters the centre of the base of the pillar, and the cells are eagerly defended by a multitude of the

NESTS OF MUSHROOM ANTS AND TREE ANTS.

([illegible].)

soldier class of the ants, which I took to be males, all striving to bite the intruder with their pincer-like jaws. On breaking open the ball—which, when handled, divided itself into three parts—I always found it full of young white ants in different stages of growth, and also of eggs. The young were of a milky-white colour, while the adults were yellowish, with a tinge of grey when the abdomen is full of earth. Besides these young ants, there were a great many full-grown individuals, whom I took to be females, and who appeared to be the workers or labourers described by entomologists. These have not elongated nippers like the soldiers, but have very bulky abdomens, and they are inoffensive. We shall see presently what their distended abdomens are used for. Besides these soldiers and workers, I always saw, whenever I broke a hive, a very much larger specimen than the other two, which came in from the inner galleries, looked round, and went away again. These large ants were very few in number. There were, therefore, three distinct sets of individuals. To these large ones I shall give the name of head men or chiefs.

In order to examine the rest of the structure I often took an axe and broke the nest into several pieces; but the material was so hard that it required several blows before I succeeded. I tried then to make out the structure of the chambers and galleries of which the interior was composed. But before I could do this, I was somewhat perplexed at discovering that there was another distinct species of white ant mixed up with the proper architects of the edifice. The soldiers of this other species were much smaller and more slender, and, as I broke the pieces, these two kinds fell to fighting one another. On close inspection I found that these slender fellows came out of cells composed of a yellow earth, whilst the others inhabited cells of black earth. The yellow colour was due to a coating of some foreign substance on the walls of the cell. The chambers inhabited by the slender species did not communicate with those peopled by the lords of the manor; they seemed rather to be inserted into the vacant spaces or partition walls between the other cells. No doubt they had intruded themselves, after the building had been finished, from under the ground. In the fight the larger kind showed no mercy to the smaller. It was quite marvellous to witness the fury with which the soldiers of the one kind seized the bodies of the others with their powerful pincer-jaws, and carried them away into their own chambers. The soldiers of the slender kind also possessed long pincer-like jaws, and I noticed in one instance, when a worker of the larger kind had seized a small worker, who was in her last struggle for life, that one of these slender soldiers flew to the rescue, and snapping into the soft abdomen of the assailant, twice its size, let out its contents; the slender one then fell from the pincers that had gripped her, but life was extinct. The rescuer came, examined the body, and seeing that she was dead, went away and disappeared; if she had been only wounded she would probably have been carried away, as they do the young. I may here remark that, with the exception of the head, the body of the termites is exceedingly soft. On examining the structure of the soldiers, it is evident that their powerful pincer-jaws are made for wounding and piercing, while the structure of the workers shows that their pincers are made for the purposes of labour. Nothing astonished me more than this impetuous attack; my attention was intense on this deadly combat; the weaker species knew the vulnerable point of his formidable enemy, who was too busy to protect himself. A further examination showed me that the mushroom-like cap of the whole edifice was composed of both black and yellow cells. This curious mixture of two species, each building its own cells and yet contributing to form an entire and symmetrical edifice, filled me with astonishment. The wonder did not cease here, for in some of the mushroom-like heads there was still a third kind quite distinct from the other two, and not a white ant.

The mushroom nests are built very rapidly, but when finished they last, in all probability, many years. The ants work at them only at night, and shut out all the apertures from the external air when daylight comes, for the white ant abhors daylight; and when they migrate from an old building to commence the erection of a new one, they come from under the ground. Sometimes they add to their structures by building one mushroom-head above another; I have seen as many as four, one on the top of the other. The new structures are built when the colony increases; new cells must be found for the new comers. The shelter is quite rain-proof.

I passed hours in watching the tiny builders at

their daily labours in the cells, which I was enabled to do by laying open some of their cells, and then observing what went on after all was quiet. So soon as the cells are broken, a few head men or chiefs are seen; each one moves his head all round the aperture, and then disappears into the dark galleries, apparently without leaving anything. Then the soldiers come; these do no work, but there must be some intention in these movements; they no doubt were on guard to protect the workers. I was never able, even with my magnifying glass, to see them do anything. The workers then come forward, and each of them turns round and ejects from behind a quantity of liquid mud into the aperture, and finally walls it up. They come one after the other, and all of them leave their contributions; this is done first in a row from one end of the aperture to another, then each ejection is put on the top of the other with a precision that would do honour to a bricklayer or stonemason. The question to me was to know if the same ants went away to eat more earth and came again. How much would I have given to be able to see into the dark recesses of the chambers! but I do not see how this will ever be done. The apertures of the cells were only closed during the day, and during the following night the part of the structure which I had demolished was rebuilt to its original shape. Some of them brought very small grains of sand or minute pebbles, and deposited them in the mud; when demolishing their shelter, I saw several cells filled with these little pebbles, which I had also collected and preserved.

Soon after others came and closed up the cell. The earth which they eat can be seen shining through the thin skins of their bodies, but I was unable to see where it was stored in the interior of the edifice. The mud is mixed with gluey matter, through the digestion, when it is ejected, and with this material the little creatures are enabled to build up the thin tough walls which form their cells, and, in course of time, the firm and solid structure of the entire nest. Sun and rain are equally fatal to the white ants; thus it is necessary that they should build a hive impervious to light, heat, and rain. I have put white ants in the sun, and they were shortly afterwards killed by its heat. I thought each cell was, perhaps, inhabited only by one ant, but the great number I saw in each mushroom-like edifice made it quite improbable that it should be so.

I believe these white ants of the prairie are quite a different species from those which live in subterranean dwellings, and which make their appearance suddenly through the floor of one's hut and devour all substances made of cotton or paper; these are very fond of eating wood, and are often found in dead trees. In these species, the sense of smell, or some other sense equivalent to it, must be very acute. One may retire to bed in fancied security, with no sign of white ants about, and in the morning wake to find little covered ways overspreading the floor and chests of clothing and stores, and the contents of the chest entirely destroyed, with thousands of the busy ants engaged in cutting the things with their sharp jaw-blades. Everything made of wool or silk is, however, invariably spared. At Máyolo this kind of ant was very abundant, and was a cause of much anxiety to me.

Tree Ant.—Now that I have tried to the best of my abilities to give an account of what I call the mushroom-building white ant, I will speak of another species which lives in the forest, and which is often a near neighbour of the other. In the forest there is a species which makes its hives or nests between the ribs of the trunks of trees. The nests are from four to seven feet long, and six to eight inches broad, and are formed externally of several slanting roofs, one above the other. The ants that make these structures have long black bodies and white heads, and are unlike the mushroom-building ants.

The structure begins from the ground in a somewhat irregular cylindrical piece of walling or building about a foot high, but varying to as much as eighteen inches, and full of cells and galleries; then occurs the first slanting roof. The larger the structure, the more of these slanting roof-like projections it possesses, and they become smaller towards the top, the middle roof being the broadest; sometimes a few inches will separate one roof from the other; the roofs communicate with each other through the cells by the same cylindrical piece of masonry; the material of which the whole is built is very thick, hard, and impermeable to rain. The structure of this ant is not common in the forest; but having found a nest in the prairie near Máyolo, I had not to go far to study them.

I frequently broke open portions of this singular structure, and tried to observe the movements of the inhabitants in the interior of their dark chambers. As in the mushroom hives of the prairie, I found numbers of little pale young ants in the cells; there were also a few head men or chiefs, soldiers, and workers, the soldiers doing no work, whilst the workers were full of activity; the immature individuals moved but slowly, and seemed very delicate; the very young ones did not move at all. Whenever I broke into the cells, the first care of the adults was always to place the young progeny out of danger; this they did by taking them up in their mouths and carrying them into the inner chambers. Those, however, who could walk unaided were driven in. As soon as the young ones had been taken into the cells, the soldiers came to the apertures of all the cells that had been broken, to defend the breach from any enemies that might come: and then the workers began to work with great rapidity. In breaking the structure I killed a few of the young ones—the adults came to them, and seeing them dead, left them on the field.

I observed the soldiers engaged in an occupation which was at first incomprehensible to me, but I afterwards came to the conclusion that it was the act of tracing with their mouths the outline of the work of closing up the cells, which was to be completed by their fellow ants the workers. The soldiers came and stood at the opening of every broken cell in a row, quiet for a little while, then they disappeared. By the movement of their heads I thought they might be taking some earth away, but I was not able to see this with my magnifying glass. I thought also that they might be throwing some moisture in order to dampen the soil where the walls were to be built, there again my magnifying glass failed me. The worker ants would then come in and apply their mouths intently to the bottom of the cells in the places where the mud had been ejected by the others, and this was done so frequently that it appeared a regular occurrence. It was interesting to watch the regularity with which the ants worked, in compact rows, side by side, until the chambers were covered in. Before building, they carried away the little pieces of clay which had been broken off, and which were in their way. The material they used for building seemed to me almost the same as that of the mushroom-building ants. After having disposed of their loads, the ants disappeared, and others took their places; what I wanted to find out was whether the same ants came again, but, as in the case of the mushroom-building ants, I was not able to settle this point. The head men were far less numerous in proportion to the total population of the community than in the mushroom hives. The ants of this species only once rebuilt their hive in its original shape, after I had broken it. When I again destroyed part of it they only closed the open cells.

In this kind of building the slanting roof prevented the rain from getting in; but in the mushroom hives, if the damage had not been entirely repaired, the rain would have penetrated the structure.

Bark Ant.—Another much smaller species of white ant is found under pieces of loose dry bark on the forest trees, on which they feed. The colonies were composed of a very scanty number of individuals, and the ants were so small and obscure that it was not easy to detect them. They always choose trees that are old and have these scales of loose bark on their trunks from place to place. It is under these small patches or scales that the ants live. They feed on the wood, and build covered ways, or rather tunnels, which start from the ground and communicate to the different places where the colony has scattered itself. Now and then, scraping under the bark, I found that the settlement had moved somewhere else as soon as they had come to the green of the tree. The material which this ant uses to build its tunnels is not earth, but wood-dust. This proves clearly that these white ants, with, perhaps, the exception of one species, build their nests of the same material as they eat, but not till after it has passed through their stomachs, and received an admixture of glutinous fluid. The quantity thrown by this little species was so minute that I could hardly have seen it with the naked eye. They worked exactly like the others I have just described. I was unable to recognise the three distinct classes of individuals. There seemed to be only two sets—soldiers and workers. They worked very slowly when joining the broken portions of the tunnels I had demolished. This was accounted for by the extreme smallness of the particles of material ejected by them, and also by the fact that, in consequence of the tunnel being very narrow, only one or two ants could work at the same time.

Forest Termes.—Now I come to another species of white ants much larger than those I have described before, and building far larger structures.

The shelters of this ant are found in the forest, and are rather uncommon; they are always found single, their light yellow colour makes them quite conspicuous in the midst of the dark foliage by which they are surrounded; this yellow colour comes from the soil which the ants use in building, and which they get from below the black loam.

The height of the structure I examined was four feet and a half, and the diameter at the broadest part two feet and a half; after breaking one sinuosity I found the cells to be about one inch and a half in length and about half an inch in height, each cell corresponding with the others by corridors or round tunnels varying from half an inch to one inch in length, and about a quarter of an inch in diameter.

In demolishing the sides, I found that the thickness of the wall was only one inch before the cells were found; but I found the earth at the top much harder than on the sides, as though the builders had put a much larger quantity of glutinous matter in this part of the structure.

After demolishing three inches of this yellow top of the nest I came suddenly to another layer, half an inch thick, full of little holes or cells, so small that they had no doubt been built on purpose for the ants

NEST OF FOREST ANTS

to remain there alone, but for what reason they required to remain alone I was unable to discover; at that time there were no ants there.

Then with the axe I gave a powerful blow, and demolished another part of the structure, which disturbed the ants from their dark chambers. I saw there the three different classes of ants: the head men, very large, with whitish body and black head (these were but few in number); the workers, with short and thick body and broad head, but not so large as the chiefs; and, thirdly, the soldiers, not so large as the workers, more slender, and possessing longer nippers. These three distinct classes were the inhabitants of this curious structure.

As I was looking at these ants, my attention was suddenly called to watch their movements. The soldiers came and, ranging themselves round the broken cells, took their stand and remained immovable. Then the workers came; each carried between its pinchers a small particle of yellow clay, which some of them collected from the broken pieces, and which stood in my sight, while others came with their loads from the cells; there were sometimes two or three busy together at the same time and in the same cells. Each ant came and put down its particle of wet clay with the utmost precision, and then with its head moved it right and left, and by so doing succeeded in making the bits stick together, and so finished the wall. Each bit was put by the side of the one left by the previous worker, who had gone to fetch more, for here I saw the same ant go and fetch fresh pieces of the same clay, which came from the structure I had broken. I observed that they never went outside the cells to get their materials. No masons could have worked more systematically.

But how could the clay which I saw them take dry become suddenly wet? I took a small reed and advanced it quietly towards some; they made a spring at it (for these ants' bites are far worse than the others) and seized it with their nippers, and then threw upon it a little whitish thickish matter, the same stuff that made the clay wet and ready for building purposes. During the working time not one of the largest class was in sight. The soldiers kept watch, and it was only just before the wall was closed that they retired.

As in the other species, only a single class out of the three worked. This ant is not the Termes bellicosus of Smeathman; which erects far larger buildings, and is rather well known on the coast of Africa. It has been described by several travellers; but I have never met with a single specimen. M. Serval, in his 'Exploration of the Ogobai,' mentions having seen an ant-hive four metres high. This would correspond with the height of the sheltered hives built by the Termes bellicosus. In them Smeathman found only labourers and soldiers—fighting ants, as he calls them. Smeathman gives a most graphic and interesting account of this species. From his account it would appear that the Termes bellicosus builds the sheltered hives in the same way as the forest ants do. Professor Owen kindly lent me Smeathman's paper, which was published in 1781.

I have never been able to find a single winged specimen of any white ants whatever, but I found unwinged queens in the mushroom hives.

The Môgôkora Ant.—Often, while I was walking in the Olando prairie, another ant attracted my attention; it was called by the natives Môgôkora; it is a ground ant. Many hours I have spent in studying its habits. These ants are of a black colour; many of them are an inch in length, and they are the largest species of ants I met with. They possess long and powerful nippers, and, when once they have seized an insect, they never relinquish their hold; and they have often to struggle very hard before overpowering their victim. Considering the large size of the insects which I have seen them master, I judge that their strength must be enormous. They wander solitarily over the prairie, and it was only after the grass had been burnt, that I could study them thoroughly. They seem to scour it in search of prey; insects and caterpillars being their food. They inhabit holes or subterranean chambers, and seem never to move very far from their abodes; as soon as they have captured an insect they make for their galleries, and enter them with their victim, which they devour at leisure. I never saw them eat their prey out of their dens. These holes or subterranean chambers are scattered over the prairie, and each ant seems to know the one that belongs to it. When they find an individual of their own species dead, they carry it off to their den.

These dens are found almost always on the declivity of hills, so that the water may not enter them so easily when it rains; in despite of this, many are found drowned after a heavy storm, so that the species is not very abundant; besides, the burning of the prairie must also destroy many. Their bite is very painful, and is felt for a long time afterwards. When trodden upon they emit a strong smell. I have never been able to find out the nest of these ants, and have never seen a winged one.

The Ozhoni Ant.—This is a much smaller species than the Môgôkora; it is found in the prairie and on the borders of the forest. Like the former it is essentially a ground ant. It seems more voracious than its powerful neighbour, for they capture their own species alive and devour them. I have often assisted at these fights. The attacking party is sure always to be larger than the attacked, which, though much weaker, offers great resistance, knowing what will be its fate if it cannot escape. The ants wrestled together, and sometimes the attacked succeeded in escaping, but generally they are recaptured.

If one of the ants is not strong enough to overpower its victim or drag it along, then two or three will unite to help it.

The sting of this species reminded me almost of the sting of a bee, and I have myself suffered intensely from it—once for more than two hours, in despite of the ammonia which I applied to the sting.

The Stinging Black Ant.—I have only noticed this species in the Otando country; it is very scarce and only found in the forest, climbing along trunks of trees. These ants are almost as large as the Môgôkora, and they are also of a dark black colour, and shaped more like a bee than any other ant I have seen. Their sting is quite of the size of that of a bee, they are very quick in their motions, and are very difficult to capture if they have once been missed. Their sting is the most painful I ever felt, but happily the pain does not last long.

CHAPTER XII.

MÁYOLO TO APONO-LAND.

Leave Máyolo—Cross the Nomba Obana Hill—River Dooya—Arrival at Mouendi—Timidity of the Inhabitants—The Chief Nchiengain—Arrival of Apingi Men—Loss and Recovery of a Thermometer—Nocturnal Reflections—African Story of the Sun and Moon—Smelling the White Man's Presents—Passage of the Ngouyai—Hippopotami and Crocodiles; seasons of their scarcity and abundance—Arrival at Dilolo—Opposition of the Inhabitants to our entering the Village—Pluck of my Commi Boys—Arrival at Mokaba—My system of a Medicine Parade for my Men.

Our preparations being finished, we left Máyolo on the 30th of May, at half-past eight in the morning. The good chief accompanied us, and our party consisted of about thirty men, including twenty porters, all heavily laden with my baggage. My own load was, besides a double-barrelled gun and two revolvers, fifty ball cartridges, thirty bullets, six pounds of shot, and a quantity of powder and caps; altogether about forty pounds weight.

The whole of the villagers came to bid me good-bye—the women were especially demonstrative in their adieux. I gave them a parting present of beads. As we left the village, they all shouted, "The Oguizi is going! the Oguizi is going! we shall never see him more!" It was with a heavy heart that I bade adieu to these good-natured people.

For three hours we followed a course nearly due

east over the open grass-land of Otando. About seven miles from Máyolo we ascended a high hill, part of an elevated ridge, called Nomba Obana; from its summit a beautiful view is obtained towards the west, as far as the dividing range between Otando and Ashira; on the eastern side an equally extensive prospect opens out towards the higher ranges, amongst which dwell the Ishogo, the Ashango, and other tribes; but directly east there was a gap in the range, for north and south the mountains were higher. The continuous forest which clothed the hills, green on the nearer ranges and shading off to misty blue on the distant ones, gave an air of solitude to the scene. The eastern slope of Nomba Obana was precipitous, and red sandstone rocks lay about in wild confusion.

In the valley were the ruins of a village that had been abandoned by Máyolo. This was the second village he had abandoned within less than two years. If any one dies, Máyolo immediately moves off, saying that the place is bewitched.

About three miles east of Nomba Obana we crossed a small river called Dooya. It was fordable at this season, but during the rains it must be a considerable stream. Marching onwards, always in an easterly direction, we arrived, at half-past four, at the village of the Apono chief Nchiengain, which is called Mouendi. The territory of the Apono tribe lies chiefly to the south-east of this place.

We halted before entering the village, at the request of Máyolo, to arrange the order of going in, for it was necessary to avoid anything that might give alarm to the timid savages, who had never before received a similar visitor. The passage of inhabited places would henceforward be the most difficult part of our journey; as long as we had nothing but forests, rivers, and mountains to traverse, provided we could get plenty of food, all would go well; but to contend with the superstitious fears, restless curiosity, and greedy avarice of the chiefs and villagers was a serious matter. It was settled that Máyolo, who was the friend and *nkaga* (born the same day) of Nchiengain, should go first, and that the rest should follow at intervals one by one. We marched towards the entrance of the village in dead silence.

As we approached, the people who first caught sight of us, began to flee. The women cried out as they ran with their babes in their arms, "The Oguizi! (Spirit) the Oguizi! He has come and we shall die!" They wept and shrieked; I heard their cries with dismay, but did not know till afterwards that the small-pox had already swept through this village.

When we reached the middle of the village, there was not a soul remaining except Nchiengain himself and two men, who stood with fear depicted in their countenances near the ouandja (a kind of house open in front) of the chief. Nchiengain, however, had given his consent to our coming, and seemed to have inwardly resolved to brave it out. He had fortified himself against evil by besmearing his body with great streaks of the alumbi chalk, and hanging all his fetiches around him.

The persuasive tongue of Máyolo soon calmed his fears. He gathered courage to look me steadily in the face. I then addressed him in the Ashira language, and recounted the treasures in beads, caps for the head, coats, and cotton prints that I had brought for him; finally he began to smile and took my proffered hand. Beads were promised to the women, and gradually the people came back to their houses. Máyolo finished up with a lengthy speech in the African manner, proving to him that I did not bring the plague. Towards evening I went round the village, looked into the huts, laughed with the people, and distributed beads. Good humour was restored, and the remark became general that the Oguizi was a good Spirit after all.

I took meridian altitudes of Arcturus and α Crucis before retiring to bed, although exceedingly fatigued after our long march and the great load I had carried. I found, by these observations, that my course had been due east.

31st May. Nchiengain is a tall, slender old negro, with a mild and timid expression of features. He is the leading chief of the Apono tribe in these parts; but his clan is now, I hear, almost extinguished. His village is one of the finest and cleanest I have yet seen, the houses being neat, built chiefly of bamboo, or strips of the leaf-stalks of palm-trees, and arranged in symmetrical lines. I have measured the street, and find it to be 447 yards long and 18 broad. The houses are small and quite separate from one another; the height of the roof is about seven feet; and each house has its little verandah in front, under which the inhabitants take their meals and sit to smoke and chat. The soil on which the village stands is clayey. I notice that many of the men have their two middle upper incisor teeth pulled out, and the two next to them filed to a point. Some of the women beautify themselves in a similar way; they also endeavour to improve their looks by tattooing themselves in long scars on their foreheads, between their eyebrows, and on their cheeks in a line with the middle of the ear.

The people of Nchiengain's village are all Bambais or Bambas—that is, the children of slaves, born in the country. The women are the prettiest I have seen in Africa; and many of them had very small feet and hands, which I have remarked is the case with many of the negroes of Equatorial Africa.

Although the chief seems to be of a good disposition, I found him no better inclined to forward my journey than any of the others I had had dealings with. Like the Olenda people, he wanted the chief who had brought me to his place to leave me in his hands; this being the first step necessary to enable the rapacious negroes to get all they could out of me at their leisure. Máyolo was firm in his demand to have me forwarded across the Rembo in two days, and I supported his arguments by feigning anger at the chief's proposal, and refusing to eat the presents of food he had made me. Our palavers lasted all this day and the next. I gave him a quantity of goods, but, as was to be expected, he expressed his dissatisfaction, with a view to get more out of me. I left Máyolo with him, and by some means or other he persuaded him to be contented.

What could I do with a man who believed that I made all these things myself, by some conjuring process? for it is thus that Nchiengain argued with Máyolo: "The cloth and beads and guns cost him no trouble to make; why does he not give me more of these things which do me so much good?" "Máyolo," he would continue in course of his many palavers with him, "you eat me with jealousy. Why do you want yourself to take the Oguizi to the Ashango country? why not go back and leave him to me? I want it to go far and wide that the Oguizi and Nchiengain are big friends." At length he offered himself to accompany me across the Rembo, and to give me some porters, for our loads were too heavy for our present numbers. It was the passage of this river (the upper Ngouyai) that offered our next difficulty; it was too wide and deep to ford or swim across, and we needed a good canoe to ferry the party over.

June 1st. A number of Apingi men came up the river to-day from their villages, which are situated a few miles lower down, on the river banks, towards the north or north-west, but belonging to a different clan from Remandji's, which I visited in my former journey. They fraternised with the Apono, and we had great noise, tam-tamming, and confusion. They brought about 100 bunches of plantains for sale, which my men purchased. I find the Apingi are generally lighter and redder in colour than the Apono, and they are not so well-made a people or so handsome (or less ugly) in features. But there are no sharp lines of distinction between these African tribes. They intermarry a good deal with each other, and, besides, the chiefs have children with their slaves who are brought from various tribes, far and near. The Apingi were not so much accustomed to me as the Apono were, and whenever they caught sight of me they fled. The noise made by these fellows was quite unbearable.

I took a walk into the neighbouring woods; and on my return, going to look at the thermometer hung under the verandah of my hut, I found it had been stolen. This was too much to be borne, as it was the only thermometer remaining to me after the plundering of the Ashira. I felt that I must use energetic measures to recover the instrument, so I seized two men who were running away from the heap of plantains in front of my hut, and calling on my Commi boys to cock their guns, I sent for Nchiengain and said that I would shoot a man if the instrument was not returned to me. Nchiengain and the Apono declared that the Apingi were the thieves. Two chiefs who were with the Apingi protested that the theft was committed by none of their men, that they did not come to steal, &c., &c. My strong measures, however, had the desired effect; the thermometer, fortunately unbroken, was found shortly after lying on the ground near a neighbouring hut. Many of the Apingi were armed with spears, but they are not so warlike as the Apono. They are more accustomed to the water, and build large canoes, which they sell to the Apono.

June 1*st*. I paid the new Apono porters to-day. We were obliged to have seven more men than before, as the loads were so heavy that the former number was insufficient, and three of my people had the skin worn off their backs on the march from Máyolo. To-night the air was colder than I ever recollect to have found it in Western Africa. The sky was cloudless but hazy—as, indeed, it often is in the interior, in the clearest weather during the dry season—a reddish halo surrounded the moon. I sat up as usual to take lunar distances and altitudes of stars. Indeed, I seldom retire before one a.m., and enjoy the silent nights, when the hubbub and torment of a crowd of whimsical, restless savages are stilled by sleep. I sometimes stretched myself on the ground after the work was done, and enjoyed the contemplation of the starry heavens, thinking of the far-off northern land, lying under constellations so different from these of the southern hemisphere. My thoughts would wander to my distant friends in Europe and North America, and my eyes would fill with tears when I dwelt on the many acts of kindness I had received from them. Did they now think of the poor lonely traveller working out his mission amidst savages in the heart of Africa!

I was not always so solitary in taking my nightly observations, for sometimes one or other of my men or Máyolo would stand by me. Of course I could never make them comprehend what I was doing. Sometimes I used to be amused by their ideas about the heavenly bodies. Like all other remarkable natural objects, they are the subjects of whimsical myths amongst them. According to them, the sun and moon are of the same age, but the sun brings daylight and gladness and the moon brings darkness, witchcraft and death—for death comes from sleep, and sleep commences in darkness. The sun and moon, they say, once got angry with each other, each one claiming to be the eldest. The moon said: "Who are you, to dare to speak to me? you are alone, you have no people; what, are you to consider yourself equal to me? Look at me," she continued, showing the stars shining around her, "these are my people; I am not alone in the world like you." The sun answered, "Oh, moon, you bring witchcraft, and it is you who have killed all my people, or I should have as many attendants as you." According to the negroes, people are more liable to die when the moon first makes her appearance and when she is last visible. They say that she calls the people her insects, and devours them. The moon with them is the emblem of time and of death.

I was much amused to-day. Some of the inhabitants of a neighbouring Apono village, who had been most hostile to my coming to their country, having since heard that I had brought no evil or sickness with me here, now came to see me. As soon as my friend Nchiengain saw them, he went up to them in great anger, crying out, "Go away, go away! Now that you have smelt niva (my goods or presents), you are no longer afraid, but want to come!" So the men went away without my speaking to them.

June 2nd. Towards evening both Nchiengain and Máyolo got drunk with palm wine, and their ardour to go forward with me was something astonishing. They say they are going with me far beyond the

Ashango; they are *men;* they will even travel by night, as there will be the moon with us.

I wanted to obtain one of the idols of the Apono, so to-day, on asking Nchiengain, he took me out of the village along a path which led to a grove of trees, and thence he sent his head wife to a mbuiri house to fetch an idol. When it came, I found it so large (it was, in fact, a load for one man) and so disgustingly indecent, that I was obliged to refuse it. I felt that if I accepted it I should be like the worthy mayor in the well-known story, who received the present of a white elephant. Like other idols which I had seen, it was a female.

The villagers have the largest *ngoma*, or tam-tam, I have ever seen. It measures very nearly nine feet in length, and the hollowing of the log must have cost the Apono a great deal of labour. Many of the people are drunk to-night, following the example of the two chiefs. I had always heard from the slaves near the coast that the Apono were a merry race, and I now find it so with a vengeance. Since my arrival here there has been nothing but dancing and singing every night. I distributed beads among the women, and this has had a great effect. So we are all good friends together.

June 3rd. We left Mouendi with a great deal of trouble this morning. Nchiengain and Máyolo wanted to renew the libations of the previous evening, and, in fact, were half-drunk soon after daylight; but I went to the hut where the symposium was going on, and, kicking over the calabashes of palm wine, sent the chiefs and their attendants to the right-about. I could not, however, get Nchiengain away, and we started without him. I wondered afterwards at the good-nature of these people, who saw with composure a stranger knocking over so large a quantity of their cherished beverage. They did not resent my act, but only grumbled that so much good liquor was spilt instead of going down their throats.

We reached the banks of the river, distant about three miles from the village, at two p.m. The Ngouyai was here a fine stream, nearly as wide as the Thames at London Bridge, and from ten to fifteen feet deep, flowing from the S.S.W.

It was now the dry season, when the water is about ten feet below the level of the rainy season. The yellow waters formed a curious contrast to the dark green vegetation of its banks. I could not but admire the magnificent trees which towered above the masses of lower trees and bushes growing from the rich soil; some of them grew on the very brink of the stream, and their trunks were supported by erect roots, looking like May-poles, eight or ten feet high, and projecting in places over the water. Openings in the wall of foliage revealed to us the interior of the jungle, where the trees were interlaced with creepers of all kinds, especially the india-rubber vine, which is here very abundant.

I was surprised to find Nchiengain's flat-bottomed canoe, or ferry-boat, large and well-made. It carried my party and baggage across in seven journeys. We finished at half-past four p.m., and encamped for the night on the opposite side. Nchiengain arrived at the river-side, reeling drunk, just as we were shoving off with the last load, and I told the men to pretend not to hear his shouts for the return of the canoe to embark him, so he had to come over alone when we had all landed on the other side.

I was struck with the scarcity of animal life on and near the river. But the rich and open valley through which it flows must teem with Natural History wealth in its varied woods; we could not expect to see much amid the noise of our crossing, and in the short time we remained in the district. There were no aquatic birds in sight, not even pelicans. The water was too deep and there were too few sand and mud banks for hippopotami; for I have always noticed that these animals are found only in rivers which abound in shallows. If the rivers have shallows in the dry season only, then hippopotami are to be seen there only in the dry season. It is the same with crocodiles. In the seasons of flood one may travel for weeks without seeing a single individual of either species in rivers and lakes which nevertheless swarm with them in the dry season. Thus it is with the lake Anengue of the Ogobai, which I described in my former work as full of crocodiles, although when Messrs. Serval and Griffon Du Bellay visited it, after me, in 1862, they were unable to see any of these reptiles. Indeed, I myself found none on my first visit to the lake, as related in 'Adventures in Equatorial Africa;' on my second visit I was surprised to find them so abundant. Even a month or a fortnight makes a great difference, and one wonders where all the crocodiles come from. It is well known to travellers that fishes are very scarce in seasons of flood, and abundant in the dry season, in the same rivers. The scarcity and abundance, of course, are only apparent; the total population of the water must remain pretty nearly the same all the year round, but we are apt to lose sight of the fact that the area of the waters of any river with many arms and lakes must be immensely greater in the flood season than in the dry, and thus the population is more scattered and hidden from view.

4th. We left the banks of the river at a quarter-past six a.m. Shortly afterwards we passed through an Apono village, and at half-past eight a.m. came to three Ishogo villages close together. All three probably belonged to the same clan, and they contained a considerable population. It was no new feature to find a settlement of a tribe living in the middle of a district belonging to another tribe. The Ishogos had been driven by war from their own territory, and have thus intruded on unoccupied lands within the territory of their neighbours.

The Ishogos of these villages knew that I was to pass through the places. They had heard of the untold wealth I brought with me, and were annoyed when they perceived my intention to pass on without stopping. The villages are built in an open grassy space; and as soon as the caravan came in sight the excitement was intense. Women, children, and armed men came around, shouting and entreating; some running along the line of march, with goats in tow, offering them as presents if I would stay with them, even if it was only for a night. It is the custom in all these villages to offer a present of food to a stranger if the inhabitants wish him to stay with them; and the acceptance of the present by the stranger is a token of his intention to remain in the place for a time. They offered also ivory, and slaves, and the more I refused the offers, the more pertinacious they became. Their sole wish, of course, in asking me to stay, was to get as much as they could of the coveted goods I brought with me. It was droll to see, when I stopped in my walk, how they fled in alarm to a distance, and then stood still to gaze at me. Two of the chiefs followed us for miles, with their proffered present of a goat each trotting along by their sides. They finally gave in and went back, saying to Máyolo and Nchiengain that it was their fault that I did not stop. Our Apono companions mourned over the goats that I might have had: they thought only of their share of the meat, as the animals, when killed, would have been cut up and distributed amongst them.

About mid-day we halted in a beautiful wooded hollow, through which ran a picturesque rivulet. There we stopped about an hour and breakfasted. The direct easterly path from here led to a number of Apono villages; these we wished to avoid in order to escape a similar annoyance to that which we had undergone in the morning from the Ishogos, and so struck a little more southerly, or S.S.E. by compass. Our road lay for three hours over undulating prairie land, with occasional woods; one of the open spaces was a prairie called Matimbié irimba (the prairie of stones) stretching S.E. and N.W.

At the S.E. end of the prairie we came to a village called Dilolo. Our reception here was anything but friendly. We found the entrance to the one street of the village barricaded and guarded by all the fighting men, armed with spears, bows and arrows, and sabres. When within earshot, they vented bitter curses against Nchiengain for wanting to bring the Oguizi, who carries with him the *evica* (plague), into their village, and prohibited us from entering if we did not want war. The war drums beat, and the men advanced and retired before us, spear in hand. We marched forward nevertheless, and the determined fellows then set fire to the grass of the open space leading to the village barricade. Wishing to avoid an encounter, and also the fire which was spreading at a great rate over the prairie, we turned by a path leading round the village; but when we had reached the rear of the place, we found a body of the villagers moving in the same direction, to stop our further progress. Most of them appeared half-intoxicated with palm wine, and I now felt that we were going to have a fight. Presently two poisoned arrows were shot at us, but they fell short. Nchiengain then came up and walked between my men and the irritated warriors, begging me not to fire unless some of us were hit. The villagers, seeing that we made no display of force, became bolder, and one of them came right up and with his bow bent threatened to shoot Rapelina. My plucky lad faced the fellow boldly, and, showing him the muzzle of his gun, told him he would be a dead man if he did not instantly put down his bow. All my Commi boys came up, and ranging themselves on the flanks of our caravan with their guns pointed at the enemy, protected the train of porters as they filed past. I was glad to see also our Apono companions taking our part; they got enraged with the villagers, and some of them laid down their loads, and rushed to the front waving their swords. Strange to say, not one of the villagers came near me, or threatened me in any way. I watched the scene calmly, and surveyed the field where war might at any moment break out. Behind us the country was all in a blaze, for the fire had spread with great rapidity. The Apono porters being so resolutely on our side, I had no fear as to how the conflict would end. If we had been travelling alone, without guides and porters, we should have had a serious fight, and it is probable my journey would have come to a termination here in a similar way to that which afterwards happened in Ashango-land; but it is a point of honour with these primitive Africans that they are bound to defend the strangers whom they have undertaken to convey from one tribe to another. Had I not been deserted by my guides in the village where I was finally driven back, as will be hereafter narrated, I should have been enabled to continue my journey. We went on our way, Nchiengain shouting from the rear to the discomfited warriors that there would be a palaver to settle for this, when he came back.

I was prouder then ever of my boys after this, and profited by the occasion to strengthen them in their determination to go forward. There was no going back after this, I told them; they all shouted, "We must go forward; we are going to the white man's country; we are going to London!"

We continued our march till half-past four p.m., when we encamped for the night in the middle of a wood, where there was a cool spring of water, close to a cluster of Apono villages. It appeared that these people also dreaded our approach on account of the *eviva*. In the evening we heard the cries of the people, the weeping of the women, and the beating of the war drums. The burthen of their lamentations was "O Nchiengain, why have you brought this curse upon us? We do not want the Oguizi, who brings the plague with him. The Ishogo are all dead, the Ashango have left; it is of no use your taking the white man to them; go back, go back!" We slept with our loaded guns by our side; the war drums ceased beating about 10 o'clock. My men were tired and foot-sore, on account of the sharp stones and pebbles of the prairie paths.

June 5th. At daylight this morning I got up and looked out over the broad prairie, quite expecting to see a war-party watching us through the long grass; but to my agreeable surprise, I saw no signs of war. Shortly afterwards a deputation of three men came from the village to try to persuade Nchiengain not to pass through, on account of my bringing death wherever I went. But the trusty and sensible old chief, in a long speech, showed them that it was a foolish alarm about my bringing the *eviva*, and that the plague came quite independent of me, for it had passed through his village long before the Oguizi had come near it. The argument seemed to have a good effect; they retired, and shortly afterwards both Nchiengain and Máyolo were sent for to the village; this was followed by a messenger arriving for me.

When I came into the open space chosen for the meeting, at some distance from the village, I was not a little surprised to see about 200 of the villagers assembled, all gravely seated on the grass, in a group of a semi-circular form. As I advanced towards them, I was amused to see the front row getting uneasy and wriggling off into the rear, followed by the next row, and so on. They put me in mind of a flock of sheep or a herd of deer in a park, when confronted by a man walking slowly up to them. Nchiengain, who appeared to have great influence here, and to be acknowledged as a superior chief among the Aponos, succeeded at last in arresting their laughable rear movement. He then addressed me, saying that he had sent for me to tell me that the villagers wished me to leave the wood in which I was encamped, and to move to the top of a grassy hill a little further off. If I did that all the people would come and see me, and bring me food, and on the following day would be willing that I should continue my journey.

I declined this proposal, as the top of the hill was too much exposed to the heat of the sun, and I preferred the cool shade of the wood. They finally let me have my own way, and my encampment for several hours afterwards was thronged with people. They all said that the report of my bringing the *eviva* had been spread abroad amongst the tribes for a long distance in the interior by the Ashira people.

Late in the afternoon, three head men of neighbouring villages came to invite us to their respective villages. One of the elders was from a large place not far distant, called Mokaba, and Máyolo recommended me to go to this village in preference to the others, because its representative had offered us the greatest number of goats, namely, three. When I gave my decision, the other two chiefs were greatly annoyed, and we were very near having a serious row amongst them. Nchiengain was too far gone in intoxication, having had a drinking bout with the chiefs of the village where we now were, to accompany us. As we moved off, the two disappointed elders followed, and continued to pester us. One of them had the boldness to come up to me and try to lead me off to his village; it was droll to witness his fright when I turned sharply on him: he stepped backwards trembling with fear, and waved his leather fan before him, crying, "Oh, don't, Oguizi!" After a short march we entered the more friendly town of Mokaba, amidst the shouts of the whole population. I was alarmed at night in finding Máyolo very feverish and unwell. I had noticed the first symptoms when at Mouendi.

I am happy to say that my own men now enjoy much better health than they did at the commencement of our expedition; for, strange to say, these negroes cannot bear as much fatigue and hardship as I do, and generally after a long march or a hunt they fell ill. But I could never make them come and tell me as soon as they felt the first symptoms of being unwell, so, at fixed periods—once a fortnight, or once a month, according to the season—they were summoned to my "dispensary" to be dosed all round. I had fixed days for the different medicines: one day was castor-oil day, another was blue-pill or calomel day, a third was the "feast of Epsom salts." They all had to come up in single file, and, one after the other, were ordered to swallow their dose. Now and then one or two of them tried to escape the medicine parade; and, when I called them up, each had some ready excuse for his non-attendance, but in vain. This was generally on castor-oil day, for they said that they did not mind the other medicines, but that this was "so bad;" and many were the wry faces that were made before the dose was swallowed by the entire company. However, I found that my plan had very good results, as my men had much better health than they had before I adopted it.

CHAPTER XIII.

THE MARCH THROUGH APONO-LAND.

Mokaba—Curiosity of the People—Renewed illness of Máyolo—His return to Otando—Nchiengain's Speech—The Apono agree to take me to the Ishogo country—Description of the Apono Tribe—Their sprightly character—Arts—Weapons—Population—Description of Mokaba—Palm wine—Drunkenness—Ocuya Performance—Leave Mokaba—River Dougoundo—Arrival at Igoumbié—Invitation from the elders of the village to remain there—Manners of the Ishogos—Description of Igoumbié—The Ishogo huts—Arrival at Yengué, in Ishogo-land.

June 6th. Mokaba and most of the other villages of the Apono tribe are situated in an open tract of undulating country, partly wooded and partly open prairie. The distance of the town from Máyolo is not more than twenty-seven miles in a direct line, and the altitude above the sea-level is scarcely so great as at that place, being only 414 feet, whilst Máyolo is 406 feet; but Mokaba, as I afterwards found, was within a short distance of the Ngouyai, and lay in the valley of the river, whilst Máyolo lies on the lower slope of the mountain range which separates Otando from Ashira-land. Close to the village, on its eastern side, are some fine wooded hills, which give the place a very picturesque appearance when viewed from the western side. The successive mountain ranges towards the east are not visible from the Apono plain, although they formed grand objects from the Otando

MOKABA. APONO VILLAGE.

country, rising in three terrace-like ridges one behind the other. On the other hand, looking towards the west, I could see the fine hilly range beyond Otando, stretching in a semi-circle to the Ashira Kamba territory, and joining, on the north, the range which trends eastward from that point towards the Ashango mountains.

The curiosity of the Mokaba people is most troublesome, so that, although the villagers have been so much more friendly than those we passed yesterday, I have not been much more comfortable. The place swarms with people, and I have been haunted, at my encampment, by numbers of sight-seers. The way they come upon me is sometimes quite startling; they sidle up behind trees, or crawl up amongst the long grass until they are near enough, and then, from behind the tree trunks, or above the herbage, a number of soot-black faces suddenly bob out, staring at me, with eyes and mouth wide open. The least thing I do, elicits shouts of wonder; but if I look directly at them they take to their legs and run as if for their lives.

June 7th. I cannot describe how low-spirited I feel at the condition of poor Máyolo this morning. I fear his days are numbered. He has a burning fever, and was too ill to speak to me, or even to recognise me, when I entered his hut. The Otando men, who are with us, are to carry him back to his place this afternoon. I thought it just possible that he might have been poisoned by some of these hostile villagers. But he is a hard drinker and has been intoxicated almost every day, so that this may have been the cause of his illness. His people begin to recollect that he was first taken ill the day after he had a dispute with his children about beads; and if he dies there will be a frightful witchcraft palaver in Otando. I shall feel his loss greatly, for, besides being a staunch friend, he speaks the Commi language a little, which I understand better than I do any other of these African idioms. He has been therefore a good guide in every way. Fortunately our long stay at Olenda and Máyolo has enabled me to acquire the Ashira language to some extent.

Before the Otando men departed, I went and bid good-bye to Máyolo, but he was too ill to recognise me. After his departure I entreated Nchiengain to hurry me off as quick as he could. He said "You are in as great a hurry as if you had killed somebody." I gave to each of Máyolo's men and to his wife a parting present, and my Commi boys gave them their old garments. The Mokaba people took alarm at night in seeing me look at the stars with my instruments; and the chief, accompanied by his people, came and told me they would build a shed for me at a distance from the houses, as they were afraid of the mysterious work I was doing. I firmly refused, saying that they had made me come to the house where I was staying, and that now I would not remove.

June 8th—9th. Still at Mokaba, waiting for porters. Messengers came on the 9th for Nchiengain to return to his village, as one of his men had died; they brought also the news that Máyolo had been vomiting blood. This was most distressing intelligence for me. If Máyolo dies I am afraid his death will be imputed to me. I made presents to the chiefs and elders of Mokaba, to keep them in good humour, and gave a gun to Nchiengain.

It is settled that nineteen Apono porters are to accompany me to the Ishogo country with their chief Kombila.* Nchiengain returns to his own place. Before he left me we assembled all our new men, and he made a speech to them whilst I distributed the pay. He told them how Olenda had delivered me to Máyolo and Máyolo to him, and that now they must take me safe to the Ishogo people, who would pass me over to the Ashango, and so on. They were to see that I had plenty of goats and plantains, and then if their task was well done they would receive their reward as he and his people had done.

These speeches always have a good effect for the moment, the excitable negroes become enthusiastic about the journey, and promise even more than they are required to do. When Nchiengain was about to leave, he delivered up to me a plate and a kettle which he had borrowed of me when we first became acquainted, that he might show the people how great

* As proper names may be of some utility in the study of the native languages, I subjoin the names of my porters:—

Head man, Kombila. Second in command, Mbouka.

Ipandi,	Kassa,	Bouabouhou,
Foubou,	Mondjego,	Djembé,
Batali,	Mombou,	Boulingué,
Njomba,	Badinga,	Nchago,
Mouzamba,	Miyendo,	Moueti,
Moussoumbi,	Mafoumbi,	Mouaelou.

a man he had become to possess such utensils. When he came to borrow them, he said, "Nchiengain must eat off a plate, and must cook his food with the Oguizi's kettle; so that the people may know that Nchiengain is his friend." I had quite forgotten the loan, and felt pleased at this display of the old man's honesty. He gave us all his blessing as he started, and shouted to me, "I have done all I can for you! I have not slighted you! my good wishes go with you."

As I am about to leave the Apono country, I must say here a few words about this tribe of negroes. They are no doubt a branch of the great Ashira nation, like the Ashira Kamba, the Ashira Ngozai, and the Otando, all of whom, as well as the Aponos, speak the Ashira language. The Ashangos also speak the Ashira language, although they are divided from the Aponos by the Ishogo, who speak an entirely different language. But the Aponos are distinguished from all the other branches of the Ashira nation by their sprightliness of character; and they are clean and well-looking. Their villages are larger, better arranged, and prettier than those of the Otando and Ashira Ngozai. Each house is built separate from its neighbours, and they attend to cleanliness in their domestic arrangements. Their country is an undulating plain, varied with open grassy places covered with a pebbly soil, and rich and extensive patches of woodland well adapted for agriculture, in which they make their plantations. I cannot make an estimate of the total population of the tribe; their villages were numerous along our line of march from Mouendi, but we travelled probably through the most thickly-peopled district.

As I have already said, the Aponos, both men and women, are distinguished by their habit of taking out the two middle upper incisors and filing the rest, as well as the four lower, to a point. The women have for ornament tattooed scars on their forehead; very often these consist of nine rounded prominences similar in size to peas, and arranged in the form of a lozenge between their eye-brows, and they have similar raised marks on their cheeks and a few irregular marks on the chest and abdomen, varying in pattern in different individuals. They also rub themselves with red powder derived from the common bar-wood of trade. They dress their hair in many ways, but never form it into a high mass as the Ashira used formerly to do, as I have described in 'Equatorial Africa.' The Aponos do not practise tattooing so much as the Apingi, who decorate their chests and abdomens with various kinds of raised patterns. I once asked an Apingi man why his people covered themselves with such ugly scars; he replied that they were the same as clothing to them. "Why," retorted he, "do you cover yourself with so many curious garments?" The Apingi seem to be a small tribe, and the territory they occupy is a narrow strip along the banks of the Ngouyai. They and the Ishogos speak the same language.

The Aponos are a warlike people, and are rather looked up to with fear by the Apingi and the Ishogos, whose villages are close to theirs. They are not such skilful workers in iron as the Fans, or as some other tribes further to the east. The iron-ore which they use is found plentifully in some parts of their prairies; it occurs in lumps of various sizes, and is dug from the soil; the deeper they dig the larger and purer are the lumps. They melt it in little thick earthenware pots, holding about a pint each, and use, of course, charcoal in tempering the metal. Their anvils are large and well-made, but the construction of them is apparently beyond their ability, as all the anvils which I saw came from the Abombo and Njavi tribes, who live further towards the east. The Abombos and Njavis manufacture also a superior kind of straight sword four feet long, the handle of which is made of wood and is in the shape of a dice-box, through the middle of which the handle-end of the sword passes.

The bows of the Aponos are very different from those of the Fans, which I described and figured in 'Adventures in Equatorial Africa;' they are not nearly so powerful, but, at the same time, not so clumsy; they are of very tough wood, and bent nearly in a semi-circle, with the chord measuring about two feet, and the string of vegetable fibre. The arrow is rather heavy; the head is of tempered iron, triangular in shape, and prolonged in a tubular form for the insertion of the shaft; the shaft is not secured into the head, so that when the arrow enters into the body of a man or animal, the sharp triangular lance-head, coated with poison, remains in the wound, whilst the shaft drops out. The arrows are kept in cylindrical quivers made of the bark of a tree, and not in bags.

Their spears, also, are different from those of the Fans, and are similar to those described by Burton, Grant, Speke, and other travellers, as used by the tribes of Eastern Equatorial Africa.* They are much heavier and clumsier than the spears of the Fans, and cannot, therefore, like them, be thrown to a distance. The head is lance-shaped, without barbs, and a foot in length. In fight they are used for thrusting, at close quarters. Swords are the most common weapons with these people; they might, however, be more properly termed sabres than swords, being curved, and having wooden handles. The metal of which the blades are made, although pretty well tempered, by means of the charcoal used, is full of flaws. Some of the people use round shields made of wicker-work. Each of my Apono porters carried a sabre, besides his bow and quiver of arrows. The possession of a sword is a mark of manhood with these people, and all the young men think it honourable to obtain a sword before they acquire a wife. In fact, the chief things coveted by the young dandies of the tribe are a sword, a grass-web cap of the country, and a handsome *dengui*, or garment of striped grass-cloth. The red worsted caps which I carried, as part of my stores, immediately drove their native caps out of fashion, and, indeed, created a perfect *furore*. It was a sure way of gaining the good will of an Apono man to present him with one of these caps.

* 'Adventures in Equatorial Africa,' p. 60.

Like the Ashiras, the Aponos are industrious weavers of grass-cloth, which forms the clothing of both sexes. The cloth is woven in small pieces with a fringe, called *bongos*, and is sometimes beautifully fine; when several *bongos* are sewn together, the garment is called a *dengui*; the women wear only two pieces, or *bongos*, one on each side, secured at the top over the hips, and meeting in front at the upper edge.

It might be supposed, from the frequency with which I met with villages on the march, that the Apono country was thickly inhabited, especially as the villages were large, a few of them containing about a thousand inhabitants. But it must be recollected that the high-roads, or pathways, along which we were obliged to march, were the roads leading from one village to another. I travelled, therefore, through the peopled part of the country. Away from these main pathways there were vast tracts of prairie and some wooded land remaining in their original desert condition.

Upon the whole, I liked the Aponos, and got on very well whilst in their country. They showed themselves to be honest, and were faithful in carrying out the engagements they entered into with me, in spite of the numerous palavers we had. I lost none of my property by theft whilst I was amongst them.

The village of Mokaba is large and well-arranged; its site, as I have before remarked, is picturesque, and, in short, it was the prettiest village I have ever seen in Africa. There are upwards of 130 houses or huts, which, as in other West-African villages, are so arranged as to form one main street. But, in Mokaba, several houses are connected so as to form a square, with a common yard or garden in the middle, in which grow magnificent palm-trees. Behind the houses, too, are very frequently groups of plantain and lime-trees. The village being thus composed of a series of small quadrangles and back-gardens containing trees with beautiful foliage, the whole effect is very charming. In the rear of the houses, amidst the plantain-groves, they keep their goats, fowls, and pigs. This was the only village where I saw tame pigs. I was struck with the regularity of the main street; but, besides this, there was another narrower street on each side of the village, lying between the backs of the houses and the plantain-groves, and kept very neat and closely-weeded. Each house has in front a verandah, or little open space without wall, occupying half the length of the house; the other half, in equal portions on each side, forms apartments in which the owners sleep and keep their little property. When a man marries, he immediately builds a house for his new wife; and, as the family increases, other houses are built; the house of each wife being kept separate. The palm-trees in the quadrangles are the property of the chief man of each group of houses; and, being valuable property, pass on his death to his heir, the next brother or the nephew, as in other tribes. Some of these palm-trees tower up to a height of 60 feet, and have a singular appearance in the palm-wine season from being hung, beneath the crown, with hollowed gourds receiving the precious liquor.

The large quantity of palm-trees in and around the village furnish the Aponos of Mokaba with a ready supply of their favourite drink, palm-wine; for, as I have said before, they are a merry people, and make a regular practice of getting drunk every day as long as the wine is obtainable. I often saw them climb the trees in early morning, and take deep draughts from the calabashes suspended there. Like most drunken people, they become quarrelsome; and being a lively and excitable race, many frays occur. Happily the palm-wine season lasts only a few months in the year: it was the height of the drunken season when I was at Mokaba. I saw very few men who had not scars, or the marks of one or more wounds, received in their merry-making scrimmages. Their holidays are very frequent. Unlimited drinking is the chief amusement, together with dancing, tam-tamming, and wild uproar, which last all night. They are very fond of the *ocuya* performances. The ocuya is a man supporting a large framework resembling a giant, and whimsically dressed and ornamented, who walks and dances on stilts. In Mokaba, he appears in a white mask with thick open lips, disclosing the rows of teeth *minus* the middle incisors, according to the Apono fashion. The long garment reaches to the ground, covering the stilts. It struck me as a droll coincidence that his head-dress resembled exactly a lady's bonnet, at least the resemblance held good before chignons came into vogue; it was surmounted by feathers and made of the skin of a monkey. Behind, however, hung the monkey's tail, which I cannot say has its parallel in European fashions, at least at present.

June 10th. We left Mokaba at a quarter-past ten, a.m., having been detained since sunrise by the effects of the palm wine. Every one of my porters was more or less tipsy; and after they had drunk all the wine there was in the village they had not had enough, but went into the woods to fetch down the calabashes that had been left on the palm-trees to catch the liquor. About an hour before starting we had a heavy shower of rain, which lasted a few minutes. It was the first rain we had had since we left Máyolo.

Leaving Mokaba, we pursued a direction a little north of east. The ground soon began to rise, and we entered on a richly-wooded hilly country, in which were numerous plantations and villages of slaves belonging to the head men of Mokaba. At a plantation called Njavi, my aneroids showed me that we were 200 feet above Mokaba. This place is called Njavi probably on account of the plantation being worked by slaves from the Njavi country.

We halted here a short time, for some of the porters were not very strong on their legs.

From Njavi I could see the mountains where the Kamba people live. They seemed, after leaving a gap, to unite with a range on this side. The gap was a continuation of the valley in which flows the Rembo Ngouyai.

At twenty minutes to two we came to the dry bed of a stream with a slaty bottom, which ran from N.E. to S.W. Shortly afterwards, we crossed village, if there was any. Since I have left Mouendi I cannot find out that there are any head men or chiefs in the villages, but there seemed to be a certain number of elders, who hold authority over their respective villages. Here three elders, beating the kendo, came and presented me, each one, with a goat and several bunches of plantains—prefacing their presents with three tremendously long speeches.

At a glance I perceived that I was among quite a different people from those I had hitherto met with. The mode of dressing the hair, both with men and women; the shape of their houses, each with its door; the men smeared with red powder; all these points denoted a perfectly different people.

I was glad to remain for a couple of nights at Igoumbié, for I wanted to take as many observations as I could.

After I had distributed some beads among the women in the evening, a few became more friendly—especially as my Apono porters were never tired of praising me. They seemed also to be much pleased at seeing that, of the three goats which the people of their village had presented to me, I had given two to my porters.

I was very much amused with these Ishogos, especially with the women. When they thought I was not looking at them, they would partially open the door of their hut and peep out at me. As soon as I looked at them, they immediately closed the door, as if greatly alarmed. When they had to go from one house to another, and had to pass the hut in which I was located, and at the door of which I was seated, they hurriedly crossed to the other side of the street, putting their hand up to the side of their face so that they might not see me—apparently with a view to avoid or avert the "evil eye." My Aponos were very indignant at this, and said, with an air of evident superiority, and as though they had been with me all their lives, "When have these men of the woods seen an Oguizi before?"

Though I was very tired, yet I did not go to bed until I had taken several meridian altitudes of stars, in order to ascertain my latitude. The process caused the greatest astonishment to the natives.

June 11th. Igoumbié is the largest village I have met with yet, and forms one long and tolerably broad street. I counted 191 huts; each hut has a wooden door, and is divided into three compartments or chambers. The houses are generally placed close to each other, not wide apart like the houses of the Aponos. There are many of the curious alumbi houses scattered about. A large mbuiti or idol house stands about halfway down the street, with a monstrous wooden image inside, which the villagers hold in great reverence. The village being so large, the inhabitants seem to have thought it required several palaver-houses, for I noticed four or five. The palaver-house is an open shed, which answers the purpose of a public-house, club-room, or town-hall, to these people; they meet there daily to smoke and gossip, hold public trials or palavers, and receive strangers. What was most remarkable, there was here an attempt at decorative work on the doors of many of the houses. The huts, neatly built, with walls formed

[illegible] HOUSES, WITH ORNAMENTED DOORS.

of the bark of trees, had their doors painted red, white, and black, in complicated and sometimes not inelegant patterns. These doors were very ingeniously made; they turned upon pivots above and below, which worked in the frame instead of hinges. Each house is of an oblong shape, about twenty-two feet long by ten or twelve feet broad; the door being in the middle of the front, three and a half feet high and two and a half feet broad. The walls are four and a half feet high and the highest part of the roof is about nine feet.

I could not sleep last night on account of the noise made by these Ishogos. They sang their mbuiti songs until daylight, marching from one end of the village to the other. When at a distance their singing did not sound unpleasant, but when close by it was almost deafening. During the day I made friends with the Ishogos, and gave them sundry small presents. Many of the women came and gave me bunches of plantains, sugar cane, and ground-nuts, and seemed much pleased when I tasted them.

In the evening the atmosphere was very clear, and I was glad to be able to take some more meridian altitudes and a good many lunar distances.

By the time I had written down my journal, and recorded my astronomical observations, it was half-past two in the morning, and, after a hard day's work, I was glad to get to bed, especially as we had to leave Igoumbié early the next morning.

June 12th. We took leave of Igoumbié a little before eight a.m. The people seemed unwilling to let us go, and the elders begged us to stay another day. At nine we passed over a high hill called Ncoondja. A number of Apono people from a village a few miles off, including four of their head men, accompanied us for some distance. Some tampering took place with my Apono porters, and I had great difficulty in preventing them from throwing down their loads and going back. It was an awkward position to be placed in; but, by dint of coaxing and promising extra pay if they would accompany Kombila to the place to which he and they had agreed to take me, they resumed their loads, and we continued our march.

We passed two Apono villages near together; and halted for breakfast by a small stream of water near the second one. We were soon surrounded by villagers bringing fowls and plantains. The noise and confusion were so great that I went away alone for a walk in the thick of the forest, leaving my men to bargain for fowls and eggs. All the villagers wanted to get some of my beads.

We resumed our march at half-past twelve. Kombila annoyed me much by slinking behind, and getting drunk with another of my men, named Mbouka, an elder of Mokaba, who at the last moment said he would accompany us for *a walk*. Under one pretext or another they had remained behind; and as they had told the villagers to follow them "with the drink," when they knew that I was far enough off, they took their libations. They both made their appearance after causing a long delay, and Mbouka had a calabash of palm wine in one of the country bags, which I detected, the bag being of a great size.

I was resolved to put a stop to this, so forced the man to give up his bag, and poured the wine out on the ground, to the great dismay of Kombila, and to the extreme indignation of Mbouka, who grieved that the earth should receive the wine that would have so rejoiced his stomach. He protested that I ought to pay him back the beads he had paid for the wine. This palm-wine drinking had been for some time a great annoyance to me. Our porters squandered their pay (which consisted chiefly of beads) in buying wine at the villages, and were thus spending all their money before we reached the journey's end. I was glad that at Igoumbié there were no palm-trees, so they could get no wine there: besides, the Ishogos of that place are far more sober than the Aponos. What with this, and other interruptions and squabbles, and losing the path for some time, we made but little progress to-day, although we marched till dark.

June 13th. We left our encampment at half-past six a.m. The Apono porters threatened again to leave their loads unless I gave them an increase of pay; but I was determined to resist this imposition, and declared I would shoot down the first man that mutinied. My Commi boys kept close watch over the rascals during our morning's march.

We travelled in an easterly direction. In the course of an hour we crossed the Bouloungou, a dry stream, similar to those we had crossed on the 10th; its bed was slaty, as was the hill down which it flowed. We have met with no quartz blocks or granite since leaving Mokaba. The paths along which we have marched have been covered with fragments of ferruginous sandstone, the corners and edges of which hurt the feet of my men very much. We passed over a hill of considerable elevation, but, my aneroids being packed away, I did not stop to unload and take the altitude. Eastward, it sloped down rapidly until we reached a fine valley, with miles of plantations of ground-nuts. Finally, we came to Yengué, an Ishogo village, almost as large as Igoumbié, situated on the banks of a river called Ogoulou, one of the affluents of the Ngouyai.

Before entering the village, we stopped until all the porters were collected together. Then Kombila and I took the lead, followed by my Commi men, after whom came the Apono porters. We marched through the street of the village—the villagers looking at us, open-mouthed—until we reached the large ouandja, which was almost at the farthest extremity of the village; Kombila all the time exclaiming to the alarmed villagers, "Do not be afraid; we have come to see you as friends!"

Kombila then went and spoke to some of the elders, who came to me, and presented fowls and plantains—the presence of my Apono guides, whom they knew to be on good terms with me, re-assured them: and, after a short delay, they allotted a house to me and my Commi boys; while my Aponos went to lodge with their friends.

CHAPTER XIV.

JOURNEY THROUGH ISHOGO-LAND.

Village of the Obongos or Dwarf Negroes — Their Dwellings — Absence of the Inhabitants — The Elders and People of Yengué — Arrival of the Chief of Yengué — War Dance of the Aponos — Ceremony of the Mpaza — An uproarious Night — Good conduct of the Apono Porters — The River Ogoulou — Geographical Position and Altitude of Yengué — Passage of the Ogoulou — March to the Plateau of Mokenga — Eastern Limits of Ishogo-land — Quembila King of Mokenga — Palavers — Contention between Chiefs for the possession of the "Ihamba"—Panic in Mokenga — Re-adjustment of Baggage — Ishogo Porters.

On our way to Yengué, in traversing one of the tracts of wild forest through which runs the highway of the country, we came suddenly upon a cluster of most extraordinary diminutive huts, which I should have passed by, thinking them to be some kind of fetich-houses, if I had not been told that we might meet in this district with villages of a tribe of dwarf negroes, who are scattered about the Ishogo and Ashango countries and other parts further east.

I had heard of these people during my former journey in the Apingi country, under the name of Ashoungas; they are called here, however, Obongos. From the loose and exaggerated descriptions I had heard on my former journey, I had given no credence to the report of the existence of these dwarf tribes, and had not thought the subject worthy of mention in my former narrative. The sight of these extraordinary dwellings filled me with curiosity, for it was really a village of this curious people. I rushed forward, hoping to find some at least of their tenants inside, but they had fled on our approach into the neighbouring jungle. The huts were of a low oval shape, like a gipsey tent; the highest part—that nearest the entrance—was about four feet from the ground; the greatest breadth was about four feet also. On each side were three or four sticks for the man and woman to sleep upon. The huts were made of flexible branches of trees, arched over and fixed into the ground at each end, the longest branches being in the middle, and the others successively shorter, the whole being covered with large leaves. When I entered the huts, I found in each the remains of a fire in the middle of the floor.

It was a sore disappointment for me to miss this opportunity of seeing and examining these people. We scoured the neighbourhood for some distance, but could find no traces of them. A few days afterwards, at Niembouai, as will presently be seen, I was more fortunate.

As usual, the king was not in the village. But one of the elders took great care of me; so after a while I called him into my house, and made Kombila tell him that I had not come to do them harm, but good. Then I put on his head a bright shining red cap, and round his neck a string of very showy beads. As he came out of my hut, the shouts of the people were deafening. I then distributed a few beads among the women. My Aponos did the same, and to-night the ice is partly broken, and the people are very friendly with me. Kombila having told the women that I was very fond of sugar-cane and ground-nuts, they brought me some, laying them at my feet. In return I gave them beads, and chatted with as many as I could get to talk to me.

June 14th. The man whom I suppose to be the head chief of Yengué arrived in town this afternoon. It appears that he had fled through fear at my approach, and had gained confidence only on hearing that I was not such a dreadful being as he had imagined. The news of the red cap I had given to the elder had reached his ears; for the first thing he asked me was whether I would give him one also. He told me that he had also heard that I had given beads to some of his wives, and to other women in the village. Last night I heard a man walking in the streets of the village and saying, in a tone of voice like that of a town crier: "We have an Oguizi amongst us. Beware! There is no mondah to prevent us from seeing him during the day, but let no one try to see him in his house at night, for whoever does so is sure to die." It was one of the elders walking through the village and making this proclamation in the usual way in which laws are announced in this country.

After the arrival of the chief, things looked quite promising. A formal reception palaver took place in the open street, the Apono people seated in a row on one side, and the Ishogos on the other. Kombila stated at great length, as usual, the objects of my journey, and the king answered in a speech of greater length still. The chief gave to Kombila, as presents for me, two goats, ten fowls, nine bunches of plantains, and a native anvil. The ceremony finished in a kind of war-dance, in which the Aponos took part.

This kind of dance is called by the Aponos M'muirri. It is a war-dance, performed only by the men, and is remarkable for the singular noises the dancers make, yelling and beating their breasts with both hands, like the gorilla, and making a loud vibrating noise with their lips resembling the word "muirri." The men form a line, and, in dancing, advance and retreat. The dance waxes furious as it goes on, and the noise becomes deafening. After it was over, the uproar was continued by the whole village joining in the festivities, singing, beating the tam-tam, and rattling pieces of wood together, until my head reeled again.

The noise was continued throughout the night; and, as it was impossible to sleep, I got up at four o'clock and walked in the fresh morning air. The people were then parading up and down the street, singing loud and long enough to make them hoarse for a month after. At daylight I heard the voice of the chief proclaiming something or other, and immediately afterwards there was dead silence throughout the village.

The singing and dancing during this uproarious night were partly connected with a curious ceremony of this people, namely, the celebration of the *mpazu*, or the release from the long deprivation of liberty which a woman suffers who has had the misfortune to bring forth twins.

The custom altogether is a very strange one, but it is by no means peculiar to the Ishogos, although this is the first time I witnessed the doings. The negroes of this part of Africa have a strange notion or superstition that when twins (mpaza) are born, one of them must die early; so, in order, apparently, to avoid such a calamity, the mother is confined to her hut, or rather restricted in her intercourse with her neighbours, until both the children have grown up, when the danger is supposed to have passed. She is allowed during this time to go to the forest, but is not permitted to speak to any one not belonging to her family. During the long confinement no one but the father and mother are allowed to enter the hut, and the woman must remain chaste. If a stranger goes in by any accident or mistake, he is seized and sold into slavery. The twins themselves are excluded from the society of other children, and the cooking utensils, water vessels, &c., of the family are tabooed to everybody else. Some of the notions have a resemblance to the nonsense believed in by old nurses in more civilized countries; such as, for instance, the belief that when the mother takes one of the twins in her arms something dreadful will happen if the father does not take the other, and so forth.

The house where the twins were born is always marked in some way to distinguish it from the others, in order to prevent mistakes. Here in Yengué it had two long poles on each side of the door, at the top of which was a piece of cloth, and at the foot of the door were a number of pegs stuck in the ground, and painted white. The twins were now six years old, and the poor woman was released from her six years' imprisonment on the day of my arrival. During the day two women were stationed at the door of the house with their faces and legs painted white—one was the doctor, the other the mother. The festivities commenced by their marching down the street, one beating a drum with a slow measured beat, and the other singing. The dancing, singing, and drinking of all the villagers then set in for the night. After the ceremony the twins were allowed to go about like other children. In consequence of all this trouble and restriction of liberty, the bringing forth of twins is considered, and no wonder, by the women as a great calamity. Nothing irritates or annoys an expectant mother in these countries so much as to point to her and tell her that she is sure to have twins.

The tribes here are far milder than those found near Lagos, or in East Africa, where, as Burton mentions, twins are always killed immediately on their being born.

June 15th. I awoke this morning rather unwell from having had so disturbed a night; and when the king came to shake hands with me—a custom I had taught him to adopt—I refused his proffered hand, saying that I was angry, and annoyed at the disturbances of the past night. Whereupon the mild-tempered chief promised that the next night they should sing a long way from my resting-place. We then became better friends than ever.

In the evening I gave him his present. He came

alone, having requested me to give it to him at night, so that the people might not see what he got. I also gave a handsome present to his head wife.

As my Apono porters had now brought me to Ishogo-land, and had shown themselves discontented several times during the march, I called them all together this morning, and told them I did not wish them to take me any further, but would pay them and send them back to their country. At this Kombila came forward and begged of me not to mind what the boys had said. To leave me here in a village of strangers would fill him and them with shame. They had hearts, and would not think of going back to their own country, before taking me to the place to which they were bound. He said the chief of this place to which he wished to take me was a true friend of his, and that not until he had delivered me into his hands could he dare to show himself again in Mokaba. All the porters applauded the speech, and declared their readiness to go further on; and said, laughing, that I must not mind what they did, as they were only trying to get something more. This is a sample of the uncertainty of all dealings with these fickle, but not wholly evil-minded, savages. The chief of the Ishogo village to whom we are bound is, I am now told, to take me forward into Ashango-land.

The river Ogoulou, on the banks of which Yengué is situated, is a fine stream forty or fifty yards broad, and of great depth in the rainy season. It is now about ten feet deep, and I perceived that it was fifteen feet lower than the highest water-mark. The banks of the river show signs of a very considerable population; for about a mile on each side the valley is full of plantations both new and old; the most extensive plantations of ground-nuts I ever saw in Africa are found here—they extend along the slopes of the banks of the river for miles. I once thought a small steamer might reach this place from above the Samba Nagoshi Falls, but I was told on my return journey that there was an obstruction in the shape of rapids a few miles below Yengué. By taking the meridian altitude of two stars, I found the latitude of Yengué to be 2° 0′ 49″ S. I could not take lunar distances to determine the longitude, as the sky was constantly covered with a leaden veil of cloud at night. The altitude above the sea-level is 369 feet; this seems a low elevation, but Yengué lies in a valley much depressed below the general level of the country. The river flows through a most beautiful country, and is the largest feeder of the Rembo Ngouyai above the Falls, that I have seen.

June 16th. This morning, whilst making preparations for the continuation of our journey, a deputation arrived from an Apono village some miles south of Yengué, the chief of which was a brother of Kombila, bringing us an invitation to visit it on our way. The chief promised to take us from his village to the Ashango country. I declined the offer, as the route would have taken me too far south, and I had already diverged more towards the south than I had intended.

The Yengué people were afraid I should take their canoes by force to cross the Ogoulou, and when I was about to start had hidden them in the jungle. It required a long parley to bring them to reason. At length three ferry-boats were brought, one old and rotten. The owner of this last boat was an old man, who knew how to drive a very hard bargain: he required four measures of powder for the loan of the boats, and when I had given him four asked five, when I had given him five he raised his demands to six, and so on. It finished at last in the usual way by my indignantly refusing his demands; he then came round to more moderate terms,—the more readily, because he saw that the other two boat-owners were ready to take us at my price—and we embarked, all Yengué crowding down to the water-side to see us off, the chief himself leading me to the boat.

After crossing the Ogoulou (which I have named the Eckmühl in honour of a dear friend in France) we passed through a tract of forest varied with numerous plantations of the natives, the river flowing through a fertile alluvial valley, between ranges of hills.

Before we had emerged from the river valley we passed through several Ishogo villages; the country then began to rise, and we marched over a hilly district, all covered, as usual, with impenetrable jungle. The forest paths were narrow, and the most varied and strange forms of vegetation rose on either side. We were delayed some time on the way waiting for stragglers. At two p.m. we reached an elevated plateau, and a little before three arrived at the Ishogo village of Mokenga, about six miles to the eastward of Yengué, and 160 feet higher than that town.

The place appeared deserted when we entered, all the doors were closed, and we took possession, undisturbed, of a large unoccupied shed. A few men soon afterwards were seen peeping at us from afar with frightened looks. Kombila shouted to them, "How is it that when strangers come to your village you do not hasten to salute them?" They recognised some of the Aponos, and shouted back, "You are right, you are right!" Then they came to us and gave us the usual salutation of the Ishogos, which is done by clapping the hands together and stretching them out, alternately, several times. We returned the compliment in the same form, and then ensued much tedious speechifying on the part of Kombila, who related all that had happened to us since we commenced our expedition; what fine things I gave to the villagers among whom we stayed; how, when we stopped at Yengué, and the people of Yengué wanted them to leave me with them, they refused, and said they would take me to the Ashango country; and that now they said they would stay with me until they brought me back safe to Mokenga.

Then Kombila cried out, with all the might of his stentorian voice, "If you are not pleased, tell us, and we will take the Spirit to another village, where the people will be glad to welcome us."

Then all the elders of the village withdrew together, and shortly returned, saying, "We have heard what you have said; we are pleased, and gladly welcome the Spirit."

They then told us that the king was not in the village. I noticed that every time I came into a new village, the king ran away. They added that they would send for him; meantime, food was brought to us, as is always the custom on such occasions, and things looked pleasant.

The "M'bolo" salutation common to the Mpongwés of the Gaboon and all the tribes of the Ogobai is unknown in this interior country.

June 17th. Last night, as some of my men were fixing their mosquito nets outside the huts, they were told by the Mokenga people that they had better sleep inside and secure well the doors, as leopards were roaming about the village, and had lately killed many of their dogs and goats. They added that in a neighbouring village a leopard had killed several people. So careful were they of my safety, that a body-guard of three of my men came to protect me whilst I was out taking meridian altitudes of α and β Centauri and Arcturus. One of them fell asleep before my work was half done, and made the rest of us laugh by snoring most boisterously. This sort of thing generally happened when any of the negroes pretended to keep watch whilst I was out in the night taking observations. I was once startled at midnight by hearing a formidable snore close to where I stood. Looking on the ground I saw my man Igalo fast asleep, his gun by his side. Kicking him gently, I asked him why he was not in his hut. He replied: "Do you think I could leave you here alone at night amongst people who use poisoned arrows? No; I keep watch." I laughed at the poor fellow's style of keeping watch, but felt, nevertheless, glad of this proof of his good intentions. I was annoyed to find my second boiling-point apparatus broken to-day; I have now only one left. My aneroids and boiling-point thermometers have corresponded well so far.

June 18*th*. The king made his appearance to-day, thinking that the bad wind or plague I had brought with me had now had time to blow away. He was clad in grass-cloth, and wore a covering on his head in shape somewhat resembling a turban. On his arrival a grand palaver was held; the Ishogo people ranging themselves on one side, and my Apono attendants and Commi body-guard on the other. According to the usual formula, Kombila commenced the speechifying, beginning with a history of my progress through the interior from the beginning. Like the chiefs described by Captain Burton in Abbeokuta, these Africans would begin their long rigmaroles from the time of Adam if they could. At last Kombila came to the enumeration of the presents I had received from the chief of Yengué, and he drew the conclusion that he of Mokenga ought to give at least as much. The allusion to goats, fowls, and plantains drew forth great cheers on the part of my Apono attendants, for thoughts of gourmandizing were always uppermost in their minds, and the faces of my own boys brightened also; for they are quite as fond of good feeding as my Aponos.

In the middle of the palaver an amusing scene occurred. Our pertinacious friend, the brother of Kombila, and chief of a neighbouring Apono village, had been to his place and returned with a present for me of two goats, with the purpose of bribing me to go by way of his place to Ashango-land. The jealousy of the Ishogos was aroused; they seized the men who had brought the goats, and said: "Do you think we have no goats to give the Ibamba and no men to take him to the Ashango country? Take back your goats; he will not go with you; we will ask him his mouth (intention)." Of course my answer was that I should go forward with the Ishogos, for a march by way of the Apono village would take me out of my direct easterly course. The word "ibamba," which was now commonly applied to me, is the Ishogo equivalent of the Commi term "ntangani" or white man.

I had thoroughly secured the friendship of these Mokenga villagers. It is wonderful how the distribution of a few red caps and beads softens the heart of the primitive African. They were determined to stick to me, and Kombila's brother was discomfited. More speeches followed from the elders of Mokenga, the kendo of King Quembila was beaten, the presents were brought out, and the king, with one of my red caps stuck on his head, accepted my proffered hand, and all things were pleasant.

The sky has been cloudy all day, the sun shining only for half an hour towards eleven a.m. A similar state of the atmosphere has existed for several days past, the clouds generally clearing away about seven in the evening, but the sky remaining filled with haze, and at the rising of the moon becoming cloudy again. I have not been able to see the moon at all in the morning, and have been unable to take a lunar distance.

June 19th. A panic seized the Ishogos at night. The news somehow spread through the village (no one could tell who brought it) that in all the villages I had gone through the people were dying fast, especially those to whom I had given things. The fear was so great that many of the women took the beads I had given them and threw them away in the woods. Happily Quembila took my part, and said it was not true, but that the people of other villages originated the report through jealousy. I assembled the villagers together, and addressed him in the usual way by parable. "When you marry a woman," I said, "she loves you, she brings you plenty of food, she presents you with the fish she catches in the forest streams; are you then to flog her? (Cries of "No, no!") But it is this which happens when I come to your village. You give me food, you give me a house to live in, your women are kind to me—how, then, can I bring evil on you?" They all shouted: "You are right, the Ishogos are jealous of us; they spread bad news to prevent us getting some of your good things." Many of the young men came forward and offered themselves as porters to take me to the Ashango country; while the chief and the elders came and presented me with a goat as a peace-offering, saying they were sorry for what the people had done, and for the offence they had given me by being afraid of me.

June 19th. It being thus agreed that the Ishogos should take me to the Ashango country, I dismissed my Apono party this afternoon, after calling them all together and giving to each a parting present in addition to their pay, which they had already received. I also gave them a goat for food on their way back. These parting presents always produced a good effect, both on the people I dismissed and the fresh ones I was about to engage. The Aponos departed in good humour and full of thanks. We were all glad to get rid of these troublesome though well-meaning Aponos, as we then thought them; but we found reason afterwards to regret them, as they were far better workers than the lazy Ishogos.

June 20th. The diminution of my stores necessitated a re-arrangement of the loads. All the *otaitais* (porters' baskets) were opened, and the contents re-sorted. This travelling life is not a lazy one; I am busy from morning till night, and the quiet hours after the people have retired to rest are the only time I have for writing my journal, projecting my route, and writing out three copies of my astronomical and other observations. In the daytime, besides the time wasted in almost incessant palavering, I am beset by crowds of gaping villagers from sunrise to sundown. At night I have got into the habit of waking frequently and going out to watch for chances of taking observations for longitude and latitude; chances not of frequent occurrence in this cloudy climate at this time of the year.

These savages do not seem to sleep at night, for they sing and dance and beat their tam-tams until morning. They seem to be afraid of darkness, believing that night is the time when the spells of witchcraft are the most potent.

June 21st. I engaged eighteen Ishogo porters, paying them, as customary, their wages beforehand, and promising them further pay if they performed their engagements to my satisfaction. I also gave a present to each of the elders who had given me goats, fowls, or plantains. King Quembila is too old and feeble to accompany me, so I am to have as guide one of the leading men, named Mokounga.*

* The following are the names of my Ishogo party:—

Head man, Mokounga.

Mokanbi,	Nchiengani-orere,	Makounga,
Mokambiyengo,	Mondjo,	Mopnia,
Nchiengani,	Doutal,	Maniloka,
Maduta,	Moganguè,	Madjambi,
Makiina,	Matomba,	Nchanda.
Madilako,	Mandja,	

ISHOGO FASHIONS. OBLIQUE CHIGNON

CHAPTER XV.

FROM ISHOGO TO ASHANGO-LAND.

The Ishogos—Their Modes of dressing the Hair—Ishogo Villages—Picturesque Scenery—Granitic Boulders—Grooved Rocks—Leave Mokenga—Cross the Dongou—Continued Ascent—Mount Migoma—The River Oliganga—Boundaries of Ishogo and Ashango-lands—Arrival at Magonga—Plateau of Madombo—Mutiny of Ishogo Porters—An unfriendly Village—Elevated Country—Arrival and friendly Reception at Niembouai—The King's Wives—Prejudices of the Commi Men—Hear of a large River towards the East—The Ashangui Tribe—The Obongos.

The Ishogos are a fine tribe of negroes; they are strongly and well built, with well-developed limbs and broad shoulders. I consider them superior to the Ashiras in physique, and I remarked that they generally had finer heads, broader in the part where phrenologists place the organs of ideality. With some of them their general appearance reminded me of the Fans. The women have good figures; they tattoo themselves in various parts of the body—on the shoulders, arms, breast, back, and abdomen—and some of them have raised pea-like marks similar to those of the Apono women, between the eye-brows and on the cheeks. Both men and women adopt the custom of pulling out the two middle incisors of the upper jaw, but this mode of adding to their personal attraction is not so general as among the Aponos;

many file their upper incisors and two or three of the lower ones to a point.

The men and women ornament themselves with red powder, made by rubbing two pieces of bar-wood together; but their most remarkable fashions relate to the dressing of the hair. On my arrival at Igoumbié, I had noticed how curious the head-dresses of the women were, being so unlike the fashions I had seen among any of the tribes I had visited. Although these modes are sometimes very grotesque, they are not devoid of what English ladies, with their present fashions, might consider good taste: in short, they cultivate a remarkable sort of chignons. I have remarked three different ways of hair-dressing as most prevalent among the Ishogo belles. The first is to train the hair into a tower-shaped mass elevated from eight to ten inches from the crown of the head; the hair from the forehead to the base of the tower, and also that of the back part up to the ears, being closely shaved off. In order to give shape to the tower, they make a framework, generally out of old pieces of grass-cloth, and fix the hair round it. All the chignons are worked up on a frame. Another mode is to wear the tower, with two round balls of hair, one on each side, above the ear.

A third fashion is similar to the first, but the tower, instead of being perpendicular to the crown, is inclined obliquely from the back of the head, and the front of the head is clean shaven almost to the middle. The neck is also shorn closely up to the ears.

BONGO FASHIONS.—HORIZONTAL CHIGNON

The hair on these towers has a parting in the middle and on the sides, which is very neatly done. The whole structure must require years of careful training before it reaches the perfection attained by the leaders of Ishogo fashion. A really good chignon is not attained until the owner is about twenty or twenty-five years of age. It is the chief object of ambition with the young Ishogo women to possess a good well-trained and well-greased tower of hair of the kind that I describe. Some women are far better dressers of hair than others, and are much sought for —the fixing and cleaning of the hair requiring a long day's work.

The woman who desires to have her hair dressed must either pay the hair-dresser or must promise to perform the same kind office to her neighbour in return.

Once fixed, these chignons remain for a couple of months without requiring to be re-arranged, and the mass of insect life that accumulates in them during that period is truly astonishing. However, the women make use of their large iron or ivory hairpins (which I described in 'Equatorial Africa') in the place of combs. The fashion of the "*chignon*" was unknown when I left Europe, so that to the belles of Africa belongs the credit of the invention The women wear no ornaments in the ears, and I saw none who had their ears pierced; they are very different from the Apingi in this respect. Like the women of other tribes, they are not allowed to wear more than two denguis, or pieces of grass-cloth, by way of petticoat. This stinted clothing has a ludicrous effect in the fat dames, as the pieces do not then meet well in the middle.

The men also have fancy ways of trimming their hair. The most fashionable style is to shave the whole of the head except a circular patch on the crown, and to form this into three finely-plaited divisions, each terminating in a point and hanging down. At the end of each of these they fix a large bead or a piece of iron or brass wire, so that the effect is very singular. The Ishogo people shave their eyebrows and pull out their eyelashes.

The native razor, with which both men and women shave themselves, is a kind of curved and pointed knife made of iron, well worked and tempered with charcoal, the cutting edge being the convex side. It is four or five inches long and has a wooden handle. Slabs of slaty stone are used as whetstones.

The Ishogo villages are large. Indeed, what most strikes the traveller in coming from the sea-coast to this inland country, is the large size, neatness, and beauty of the villages. They generally have about 150 or 160 huts, arranged in streets, which are very broad and kept remarkably clean. Each house has a door of wood which is painted in fanciful designs with red, white, and black. One pattern struck me as simple and effective; it was a number of black spots margined with white, painted in regular rows on a red ground. But my readers must not run away with the idea that the doors are like those of the houses of civilized people; they are seldom more than two feet and a half high. The door of my house was just twenty-seven inches high. It is fortunate that I am a short man, otherwise it would have been hard exercise to go in

ISHIKIO FASHIONS.—VERTICAL CHIGNON.

UNYORO FASHIONS. MALE HEAD-DRESS.

and out of my lodgings. The planks of which the doors are made are cut with great labour by native axes out of trunks of trees, one trunk seldom yielding more than one good plank. My hut, an average-sized dwelling, was twenty feet long and eight feet broad. It was divided into three rooms or compartments, the middle one, into which the door opened, being a little larger than the other two.

The wealth of an Ishogo man, contained in his hut, consists of numerous baskets and dishes or large plates made of wicker-work, and a large stock of calabashes to contain water, palm oil, and palm wine, all which are suspended from the roof. The baskets and wicker-work plates are made either of reeds or of the rind of a kind of wild *rotang*, divided into thin strips. The calabashes are hardened by long exposure to smoke, in order to make them more durable A highly-valued article is the cake of tobacco, carefully enveloped in leaves and suspended, like the rest of the property, from the roof. Numerous cotton-bags and cooking-vessels are hung about, or stored away, and on the walls are the bundles of the cuticle of palm-leaves, of which their bongos are woven.

The Ishogos are a peaceful tribe, and more industrious than tribes who live nearer the sea-shore. Very few of them bear scars or signs of hostile encounters. Offensive weapons are not common; at least they are not carried about on ordinary occasions. I saw very few spears and bows and arrows carried in that way, but swords are more general, and they carry these along with them in their friendly visits from one village to another. In these respects they differ much from their neighbours the Aponos, who are very warlike. Their villages are surrounded with palm-trees, and they are not sparing of the favourite intoxicating beverage obtained from them; but they do not become, like the Aponos, boisterous and quarrelsome over their cups. They are altogether milder in character. On the other hand, it must be said to their discredit that they are far more given than the Aponos to sell their kindred into slavery. There can be no doubt about this, judging from the much larger proportion of Ishogos than Aponos met with in slavery amongst the coast-tribes. This, however, may be due to the fact that the Ishogos sold into slavery go down the Rembo Ngouyai, and reach the country between Cape Lopez and Fernand Vaz; while most of the Aponos sold reach the coast by way of Mayomba. In fact, the goods the Aponos get, especially the salt, come from that direction, as far as I could judge from the direction indicated to me by them. The borders of Ishogo-land, near the Apono country, had been visited by the small-pox before my arrival, and indeed were not yet quite free from it. The Ishogos speak the same language as the Apingi, which, as I have already remarked, is quite distinct from the Ashira idiom.

The Ishogo people are noted throughout the neighbouring tribes for the superior quality and fineness of the *bongos*, or pieces of grass-cloth, which they manufacture. They are industrious and skilful weavers. In walking down the main street of Mokenga a number of ouandjas, or houses without walls,

ISHOGO LOOM AND SHUTTLE.

are seen, each containing four or five looms, with the weavers seated before them weaving the cloth. In the middle of the floor of the ouandja a wood-fire is seen burning, and the weavers, as you pass by, are sure to be seen smoking their pipes and chatting to one another whilst going on with their work. The weavers are all men, and it is men also who stitch the *bongos* together to make *denguis* or robes of them; the stitches are not very close together, nor is the thread very fine, but the work is very neat and regular, and the needles are of their own manufacture. The bongos are very often striped, and sometimes made even in check patterns; this is done by their dyeing some of the threads of the warp, or of both warp and woof, with various simple colours; the dyes are all made of decoctions of different kinds of wood, except for black, when a kind of iron ore is used. The bongos are employed as money in this part of Africa. Although called grass-cloth by me, the material is not made of grass, but of the delicate and firm cuticle of palm-leaflets, stripped off in a dexterous manner with the fingers.

Mokenga is a beautiful village, containing about 160 houses; they were the largest dwellings I had yet seen on the journey. The village was surrounded by a dense grove of plantain-trees, many of which had to be supported by poles, on account of the weight of the enormous bunches of plantains they bore. Little groves of lime-trees were scattered everywhere, and the limes, like so much golden fruit, looked beautiful amidst the dark foliage that surrounded them. Tall, towering palm-trees were scattered here and there. Above and behind the village was the dark green forest. The street was the broadest I ever saw in Africa; one part of it was about 100 yards broad, and not a blade of grass could be seen in it. The *Sycobii* were building their nests everywhere, and made a deafening noise, for there were thousands and thousands of these little sociable birds.

Mokenga, being on the skirts of the interior mountain ranges, its neighbourhood is very varied and picturesque. The spring from which the villagers draw their water is situated in a most charming spot. A rill of water, clear and cold, leaps from the lower part of a precipitous hill, with a fall of about nine feet, into a crystal basin, whence a rivulet brawls down towards the lower land through luxuriant woodlands. The hill itself and the neighbourhood of the spring are clothed with forest, as, in fact, is the whole country, and the path leads under shade to the cool fountain. I used to go there in the mornings whilst I was at the village to take a douche-bath. In such places the vegetation of the tropics always shows itself to the best advantage; favoured by the moisture, the glossy and elegant foliage of many strange trees and plants assumes its full development, whilst graceful creepers hang from the branches, and ferns and liliaceous plants grow luxuriantly about the moist margins of the spring.

Not far from Mokenga there was a remarkable and very large boulder of granite perched by itself at the top of a hill. It must have been transported there by some external force, but what this was I cannot undertake to say. I thought it possible that it might have been a true boulder transported by a glacier, like those so abundant in northern latitudes. Although I visited it and examined it closely, I found no traces of grooves upon it. On my way from Mokaba to Yengué, I saw no boulders of quartz or granite.

My visits to this enormous block of granite were so numerous that they attracted the notice of the natives, and I was not a little surprised, one fine morning, to find the village in a state of great excitement about the rumour that the boulder was not in the same place as it had always been, and that the Oguizi had moved it. The people dared not mention their suspicions to me; indeed, they were so much alarmed that they fled from me; but they surrounded my men, and, with every mark of fear and superstitious excitement, asked them why I had moved the stone. It was in vain that my men attempted to laugh them down, and even when some of them went with the villagers to examine the huge block, it was impossible to make them see that the block had not moved; such was the effect their preconceived ideas had upon their vision.

Whilst I am on the subject of boulders and signs of glaciers, I may as well mention that, when crossing the hilly country from Obindji to Ashira-land, my attention was drawn to distinct traces of grooves on the surface of several of the blocks of granite which there lie strewed about on the tops and declivities of the hills. I am aware how preposterous it seems to suppose that the same movements of ice which have modified the surface of the land in northern countries can have taken place here under the equator, but I think it only proper to relate what I saw with my own eyes.

I called three of the elders to my hut, and gave them each a present, including a red cap apiece. The people said they would have a dance in the evening, in order to show me how the Ishogos danced. I am now quite friendly with them all, and they seem to like me and my people.

June 22nd. We left Mokenga at twenty minutes past eleven a.m. Before we started, a number of women brought us little parcels of ground-nuts to eat on the road; they really seemed sorry to see us depart. Soon after leaving the village we began again to ascend rising ground. After we had been an hour on the road, my aneroids gave an altitude of 738 feet. About three or four miles from Mokenga we crossed a little stream called Dongon. At an Ishogo village named Diamba, which we passed about two o'clock, I saw two heads of the gorilla (male and female) stuck on two poles placed under the village tree in the middle of the street. In explanation of this I may mention here that in almost every Ishogo and Ashango village which I visited there was a large tree standing about the middle of the main street, and near the mbuiti or idol-house of the village. The tree is a kind of Ficus, with large, thick, and glossy leaves. It is planted as a sapling when the village is first built, and is considered to bring good luck to the inhabitants as a talisman: if the sapling lives, the villagers consider the omen a good one; but if it dies they all abandon the place and found a new village elsewhere. This tree grows rapidly, and soon forms a conspicuous object, with its broad crown yielding a pleasant shade in the middle of the street. Fetiches, similar to those I have described in the account of Rabolo's village on the Fernand Vaz, are buried at the foot of the tree; and the gorillas' heads on poles at Diamba were no doubt placed there as some sort of fetich. The tree, of course, is held sacred. An additional charm is lent to these village trees by the great number of little social birds (*Sycobius*, three species) which resort to them to build their nests amongst the foliage. These charming little birds love the society of man as well as that of their own species. They associate in these trees sometimes in incredible quantities, and the noise they make with their chirping, chatting, and fuss in building their nests and feeding their young is often greater even than that made by the negroes of the village.

The villagers at Diamba, who had heard how we had treated the Mokenga people, entreated us to stop here for the night, but I would not consent.

The country became more and more mountainous as we travelled onward; but the path led through thick woods, and we could not obtain extensive views except in places where trees had been felled for plantations. Through one of these breaks I saw two high hills, one called Migoma, and another Ndjiangala.

Our road led us over Mount Migoma, and from it I had a magnificent view of the country to the south and south-east. Ranges of hills, all wooded to the summit, stretched away as far as the eye could reach. By compass, I found the ranges to tend N.W. by W. and S.E. by E. We passed, in the course of the evening, two other Ishogo villages; and, at five p.m., fixed our encampment for the night near the foot of a hill called Mouida, on the banks of a beautiful stream, called Mabomina. We had travelled about ten miles since leaving Mokenga.

June 23rd. Our night was not a very tranquil one, as our Ishogos had to keep watch in turns on account of the leopards prowling about. I had myself very little sleep, having no inclination to be made a meal of by the hungry animals.

At eight a.m. we left the leaf-thatched sheds which we had built for our last night's shelter. At ten, we reached the banks of the Odiganga, a picturesque stream, one of the tributaries of the Ngouyai. At the place to which our path led us the stream was fordable at this season, the water reaching only to our hips, but a few yards lower down the stream was very deep. It is only at certain points that the river is fordable. During the rains it becomes so deep and dangerous that the natives have to cross it on a raft secured by ropes to the trees on either bank. The Odiganga forms the eastern boundary of the Ishogo territory, and runs towards the south-west. There are two Ishogo villages near the right bank, and an Ashango village on the left. The two tribes are curiously intermixed in the Ishogo villages; on one side of the street Ishogos dwell, and on the other side Ashangos; they are probably related by marriage, and thus live in company; or it may be that the various clans, which are fast diminishing in numbers, unite together in order to form a large and populous village.

After we had forded the Odiganga—which was by no means an easy task, owing to the strength of the current—we reached the village of Magonga. I may here remark that the villages I have seen in this country never run parallel to, or along the banks of the rivers, but at right angles to them—one end of the village generally being near the water.

At this Ashango village my Ishogo porters found many friends and fathers-in-law; and, although we had marched only five miles to-day, they pleaded fatigue in order to have an idle day with them. Mokounga made all sorts of excuses to put a stop to the march; so, much against my will, I had to order a halt. The villagers, to propitiate me, brought me as a present a goat and some plantains.

June 24th. I find that old Mokounga, my Ishogo leader, is a man of no influence amongst his countrymen. When I gave him orders to pack up and march this morning, the porters took very little notice of his directions, and wanted to stay another day. Happily, I had among them a man of more power than the leader, named Maduta, whose family was partly Ashango, and who aided me in my endeavours to move my party forward. After much ado, we succeeded in leaving the village at nine a.m. The disappointed villagers followed us as we marched out, and endeavoured to entice some of the porters to remain; they all cursed Maduta, and said that they would settle accounts with him if he came back to their village, as he was the cause of the Ibamba's not remaining with them, and of their not getting beads enough. It required some firmness on our part to keep them all in order; so, as our porters were ready, I ordered Igala to lead the van, gun in hand, and one by one we filed through the street, I bringing up the rear.

We had hardly cleared the village when we commenced the ascent of a steep hill called Madombo. It was so steep in some places that we had to help ourselves up by the aid of the bushes. In many parts recently fallen trees lay across the path, and these had to be climbed over. Thorny climbers and briars tore our clothes, and the porters struggled on, venting curses against the many obstacles that lay in their way. The summit formed an extensive table-land, the mean altitude of which, according to my aneroids, was 1226 feet. We marched over this elevated plateau for about three miles, and then descended a little, stopping for breakfast on the banks of a rivulet called Mandjno.

Before we resumed our loads, the porters came to me in a body, and mildly asked me to give them each a few beads to enable them to purchase ground-nuts in the Ashango villages. I told them that I was willing to have given them beads at Magonga, and I opened my bags and distributed a few amongst them; but I was not a little surprised immediately afterwards to find that a mutiny had been resolved upon. They began to complain that I had been more liberal to the Aponos than to them—that I had given them a great many things, for they saw them; and the chief spokesman, the same man who had been the chief cause of our troubles at the last village, had the impudence to say to his comrades, "If he will not give us more beads, let us leave him." The whole body then laid down their loads, and said they would return to their homes. This was a critical moment; I felt that an energetic step was necessary to put an end to such insubordination. I gave the order to my Commi men to arm, and, in a few moments, the resolute fellows stepped forward and levelled their guns at the heads of the offenders. I told them to go now, and they would see how many would reach the other side of the brook alive. The movement had its due effect—they all held out their hands and begged to be forgiven. These little mutinies I found were all arranged beforehand; they are attempts at extortion, and the rascals in planning them agree not to proceed to extremities. In a short time they had again taken up their loads, and we marched off at a quick pace; the porters becoming quite cheerful, laughing and chattering as they trudged along.

In the course of an hour after this, we arrived at a large Ashango village, called Oyégo or Moyégo, through which we passed without stopping; the inhabitants, who seemed to be more astonished at my boots than at anything else, cried out, "Look! he has feet like an elephant!" The road all the way was very hilly; at one part I found the elevation 1486 feet, so that the land here was higher than the plateau of Madombo.

At four p.m. we reached another Ashango village. I was unwilling to accept the hospitality of this place owing to the noise and annoyance caused by the villagers, in fact I felt that my head would not stand it, and so fixed my camp at a short distance from it; erecting as usual slight sheds of poles thatched with leaves.

June 25th. The altitude of my encampment was 1480 feet above the sea-level. The thermometer at six a.m. marked 72° Fahr., and at noon only 73°. In the early morning a thick mist lay over the magnificent woodlands, and half hid the village and surrounding palm-trees from our view. Ahead of us were hills that rose much higher than our present position; we were now at length in the heart of the mountainous country in the interior of Africa.

It is very curious that one side of the street of this village is peopled by the Ashango, and the other side by the Njavi tribe. This was the only opportunity I had of seeing people of the Njavi tribe; it appeared that they had been driven westward to this place by the enmity of a powerful tribe, of whom I shall have to speak further on—the Ashangui—whose country lies near theirs on the east; for the territory occupied by the Njavi lies between Ashango-land and the country of the Ashangui. These Njavi were the shyest and most timid negroes I had ever met with. They would never allow me to enter their houses, and were filled with fear when I merely looked at them.

The streets of all the Ashango villages I have yet seen are less broad than those of the Ishogo villages.

As to the inhabitants, my first impressions were unfavourable. They brought us no food either for sale or presents, and the few men who came to our camp spent all the time in tedious speechifying, of which I was by this time heartily sick. My Ishogo men again began to show signs of discontent, this time not against me but against the villagers; they said, "If there is nothing to eat, let us be off. We do not stop at villages where goats are not given to the Oguizi!" The rascals knew very well that the goats would be given to them to eat. I fed my porters well, for many were induced to come from hearing the stories told by the Aponos of the great number of goats they had eaten while with me. In truth it is enough to weary a man out. It is a tremendous task that I have undertaken. The ordinary difficulties of the way, the toilsome marches, the night watches, the crossing of rivers, the great heat, are as nothing compared with the obstacles and annoyances which these capricious villagers throw in our way. I begin to dread the sight of an inhabited place. Either the panic-stricken people fly from me, or remain to bore me by their insatiable curiosity, fickleness, greediness, and intolerable din. Nevertheless I am obliged to do all I can think of to conciliate them, for I cannot do without them; it being impossible to travel without guides through this wilderness of forests where the paths are so intricate; besides, we could not make our appearance in the villages without some one to take us there and say a good word for us. The villagers are frightened enough of us as it is, although we come with their friends. I am forced to appear good-tempered when, at the same time, I am wishing them all at the bottom of the sea. They surround my hut, hallooing and shouting; as soon as I make my appearance they run away. When I re-enter my hut, they all come back again and recommence shouting for me. During the few days I remain in a village I go about from house to house, distributing beads to the women, coaxing the children, and allaying by smooth speeches the fears and prejudices of the men. I sit by their fire-side. If they are eating, I ask them for some of their food and taste it—this always pleases them vastly.

And after all these exertions to win their favour and friendship, I never knew for certain, when we entered a village, whether we might not be received with a shower of poisoned arrows.

June 26th. There was again a thick mist this morning, lasting from sunrise to nine a.m. We had succeeded in buying two goats at this frightened village. As I had been unable to take meridian altitudes of stars at Magonga, I hoped to have done so here: but the state of the weather unfortunately prevented my doing so. Having no further inducement to stay, and a deputation from the next village, called Niembouai, having arrived to invite us there, I was resolved to resume the march early this morning. When, however, we were getting our loads ready, the head man Mokounga and two of the porters were missing, having sneaked away to feast and drink in company with their friends in the village. I fairly lost temper over these people, and went into the village determined to use force, if necessary, to drag them away. I found one of them in a hut, seated by the side of the fire, with a huge pot of plantains nearly ready for breakfast. On his refusing to come I knocked him over with the butt-end of my rifle. An energetic demonstration of this kind never fails; but one is obliged to be sparing of such displays, as they tend to have the effect of frightening everybody away for good. The man in falling knocked over the pot of boiling plantains; so there was a great hubbub, which roused the whole village, the woman loudly cursing the man for being the cause of her pot being broken. Mokounga came forth from his hiding-place, begging forgiveness in the most abject manner; and as I drove the fellows to the camp, the chief came along the street beating his kendo to allay my wrath, and I began to regret my Apono porters.

At length we were again *en route*. For several miles we continued to ascend; and whenever we could obtain a view through breaks in the forest we saw higher ground towards the east and south-east. Huge rocks of ferruginous sandstone bordered the line of our route. Our entry into Niembouai was a pleasant affair compared with our reception at most of the other villages. This was chiefly owing to one of the elders of Niembouai having been at Mokenga while I was there; and who, having returned before us, had prepared the inhabitants. There was no shyness displayed, nor were there any attempts to run away. The best house in the village had been prepared for me. It belonged to the elder who had met us at Mokenga, and who now claimed me as his guest, and, according to the custom of the country, no one disputed his claim.

Before we entered the village, our Ishogo porters, with the usual greediness of these negroes, resolved to make halt and eat our only remaining goat; their only motive being to avoid being required to share the meal with their relatives in Niembouai. Africans are most confirmed gluttons; and, although used to their displays of voracity, I was annoyed at the conduct of my porters on this occasion, for nothing would do but we must halt by the roadside, kill the goat, and make a fire, although there was no water near the place.

June 27th. The king of Niembouai, like most of the other monarchs of these regions, did not show himself on my arrival—he was absent until about noon to-day. I have been told that the reason why the chiefs keep away from the villages until I have been in them some time is, that they have a notion that I bring with me a whirlwind which may do them some great harm; so they wait until it has had time to blow away from the village before they make their appearance.

Presents and food for sale came in early, and we were well supplied to-day. I was much pleased at the respectful and quiet behaviour of the people. The Niembouaians must have heard of my dislike of impertinent curiosity and noise, and are trying their best to be better behaved than other people. However this might be, I resolved to reward their good conduct by exhibiting to them some of the wonders I had brought with me. I informed the elders of my intention, and the people came in great numbers and formed a circle round me. The musical box was brought out, wound up, and set playing. The people were mute with amazement; at first they did not dare to look at the musical box, afterwards they looked from me to the box and from the box to me, evidently convinced that there was some communication between me and it. Then I went away into the forest, the musical box still continuing to play. When I came back there was still the same mute amazement. The box was still playing, and the people seemed to be spell-bound, not one could utter a word. When I saw that the tunes were played out, I shouted out as loud as I could "Stop!" and the silence that ensued seemed to surprise them as much as the music had done before. Then taking my revolver I fired several times, and my men fired off their guns. Whereupon with one accord the Ashangos cried out, "Truly the Spirit has come among us!"

So soon as this wild excitement had somewhat subsided, the accordion was brought out. With this instrument I made a noise, for I do not know how to play upon it. The same silence followed; and when now and then I played the high notes in a tremulous manner, the people all raised their arms in a state of nervous excitement; indeed I could not understand the strong effect the instrument had upon their nerves. The king, during the performances, was continually beating his kendo, and speaking to the spirits of his ancestors. I had not exhibited these marvels at any village since I left Máyolo. The astonishment, the childish wonder and mystification of these primitive people, who had probably never yet seen any article of civilized manufacture, except beads and articles of brass, may easily be imagined. Beer-bottles are to be seen now and then in the interior, and it is astonishing how far inland they have penetrated. They are held in very high estimation by the chiefs, who covet nothing so much as a black bottle to hang by their side, and contain their palm wine; they consider the bottle far superior to the native calabash for this purpose; no doubt, because it comes from a foreign country. If any of the wives or slaves of a chief have the misfortune to break a bottle, there is a fearful row. The performances had an exceedingly good effect on the minds of the people with respect to the feelings with which they regarded us. In return I asked the king to let me see his alumbi-house, to which he went every day, both in the morning and also a little before dark. In the evening he always lighted a fire, then beat his kendo, and spoke to the spirits of his ancestors. As the little hut was close to my lodging, I could hear what was going on; and could now and then distinguish my own name in his invocations. Though he had promised to take me into his alumbi-house, he always put off doing so with one excuse or other.

The king was blessed with numerous wives, and one of them, the queen (*koulé*, or head wife) was a nice-looking young girl, not more than seventeen or eighteen years of age. She was not shy, as most of the wives of chiefs were in the countries we had lately passed through; she cooked for me and gave plantains to my men. To gratify her, I made her a present of a goat—at least, I was going to do so, but Mokounga laughed heartily at the idea. "Do you not know," says he, "that the Ashango and Ishogo do not allow their women to eat goats?" This, indeed, was the fact, although I had not particularly noticed it in my passage through the villages. Women or girls are not allowed to eat the flesh of goats or fowls. I suppose they are prohibited because the men wish to reserve such scarce articles of food for themselves. It is only amongst the Commi and Mpongwé that this prohibition does not exist or has been abolished. I withheld my intended present, and gave the young lady a string of my best beads instead.

To-day I gave a good lecture to my Commi boys, especially to Macondai. These negroes of the coast have an extraordinary contempt for the negroes of the interior, and I had noticed a growing disposition in them, as we marched eastward, to insult even the elders and chiefs of the villages we passed through. Some days ago I observed Macondai, whilst standing near an Ishogo man, turn aside from him with an expression of disgust and spit on the ground; and to-day, when one of the king's nephews took a seat by his side, he got up and said he must get out of the way of that slave, he stank so. Although this was spoken in the Commi language, the Ashango man understood it and was very angry, and unpleasant consequences might have ensued if I had not interfered; so I called Macondai aside and gave him a sound scolding. The rest of my Commi companions took the same view of the matter as Macondai. They said they were superior to these Ashangos; *they* were not bushmen nor slaves (meaning that the Ashangos are sent to the sea-shore to be sold); *they* did not file their teeth nor rub themselves over with powder; and more to the same effect. I told them they were all of the same race, and that there was a time when their own tribe, the Commi, sold their fellows into slavery. Of course my men obeyed me, and abstained afterwards from openly showing contempt for the chiefs; but my arguments did not convince them that the Ashangos had the same natural rights as they had themselves. I often heard them say, "How is it possible that Chaillie can think us to be of the same blood as these slaves?"

We had a drizzling rain from half-past six p.m., lasting all night.

June 28th. The ground is soaked after so many hours of steady rain, and this is in the middle of the dry season. There is evidently no sharp distinction between the seasons in these high inland regions.

I was told to-day, and it was repeated to me in every place afterwards, that there is a tribe called Ashangui, very numerous, and clever workers in iron, who live a few days' march further on towards the east, on the banks of a large river. This river must either be the Congo or some unknown stream flowing towards the great river. It is remarkable that the people in most of the Ashango villages were very anxious to get gunpowder from me; the porters wanted to be paid partly in powder, and many of the villagers were provided with a little measure made of a hollowed gourd expressly for the purpose of measuring the powder that they received from me in payment of food and so forth. I wondered at first why they were so anxious to obtain gunpowder, as they had no guns and were even afraid of handling one; so I asked them what they wanted to do with the powder they got from me, as they had no guns. They replied that a tribe called Ashangui, living beyond the Njavi and Abombo, bought it and gave them iron for it; that all the iron they had came from there, that there was a good deal of iron "*in the land;*" that all the anvils came from there, and that their swords, spears, and arrow-heads, in fact, all their edged implements, were made of iron bought from that country. The iron from the West Coast sold by the trades does not reach so far inland as this place.

We must conclude, from their buying the powder, that the Ashangui are in possession of guns, which they obtain from traders on the Congo. From Niembouai eastward I found beads were not uncommon, and these must have been obtained by way of the Congo and through the Ashangui; in fact, all the natives told me they came up the large river: they got also copper from Europe. I inquired about the *Sapadi*, or people with cloven feet—a mythical race, believed in by all negroes, and, according to the reports of Ashango slaves on the coast, living in this country—but, as I had expected, their country was now said to be a long way further on. It is very likely that these stories about the Sapadi originate in accounts of the Obongos or hairy dwarfs, who are really inhabitants of Ashango-land, as we shall presently see.

CHAPTER XVI.

ASHANGO-LAND.

Cloudy Skies of Ashango-land—Grand Palaver—Ishogo Porters dismissed—The Village Idol—Religious Rites—Visit to an Obongo Village—Abodes and Habits of the Dwarf Race—Measurements of their Height—River Ouano—Singular Ferry—Mount Mogiama—Its Altitude—Village of Mongon, its Latitude, Longitude, and Height above the Sea-level—Village of Niembouai Olomba—Its picturesque Site—Bashikouay Ants—Ascend Mount Birogou Bouanga—Its Altitude—More Troubles—Robbed by the Ashango Porters—Summary Measures—Resume our March—Arrive at Mobana—Departure of a Bride—Arrival at Mouaou Kombo.

June 29th. The sky in this elevated region is almost constantly clouded or hazy. All day yesterday it was either clouded or overspread with a thick haze; the sun was dimly seen only for a few minutes about four o'clock, and at night the moon did not remain visible long enough to enable me to take lunar observations. To-day it is the same, much to my annoyance, as I wished to take a lunar distance.

A grand palaver was held to-day. The elders of Niembouai were all mustered, seated in a half-circle on the ground, and smoking their long pipes—which are about three feet in length—with imperturbable gravity. The great number of old people seen here was quite remarkable, and the fact speaks well for the healthiness of the climate or the absence of wars and deaths on account of witchcraft. The people here, and also among the Ishogos, seemed to have more respect for old men than in other tribes.

It required a long explanation by Maduta and Mokounga to convince the wise men that I had not come to their country to buy slaves and ivory, but simply to travel from one tribe to another. They had to recount as usual all the stages of my progress and enumerate the different chiefs who had helped me on from tribe to tribe. Maduta is related to some of the villagers by marriage, and this favoured our arrangements; he dwelt particularly on the many offers I had had, on the way, to stay at villages, and how I had refused them in order to have more presents to give away to the good people of Niembouni. This announcement was received with tremendous cheers, and cries of "Rovano!" (that is so). They on their part, he said, must outdo the other places in the magnitude of the presents of food they had to make me. He finished a long rigmarole, which took him about an hour to deliver, by saying that the Ishogos had now fulfilled their duty in bringing me safely to Ashango-land, and that the duty, or, as their language expressed it, the "shame" (or point of honour) remained with the Niembouni people to carry me on a stage further.

The Ashangos unanimously shouted "We have shame, we will pass the Oguizi on." Speeches then set in on their side, and the palaver broke up, to the satisfaction of all parties, after three hours' duration.

After this business was over I finished the payment of the Ishogo porters, by distributing amongst them the parting presents. I then gave them a goat for food on the way, and they set off to march back to their homes, not without bidding me a kind good-bye. Nothing pleases these people so much as these parting presents, as they are unexpected.

This evening I went to see the village idol, or mbuiti (the patron saint as it may be called), and to witness a great ceremony in the mbuiti-house. As with the Aviia and other tribes, the idol was a monstrous and indecent representation of a female figure in wood; I had remarked that the further I travelled towards the interior, the coarser these wooden idols were, and the more roughly they were sculptured. This idol was kept at the end of a long, narrow, and low hut, forty or fifty feet long and ten feet broad, and was painted in red, white, and black colours. When I entered the hut, it was full of Ashango people, ranged in order on each side, with lighted torches stuck in the ground before them. Amongst them were conspicuous two mbuiti men, or, as they might be called, priests, dressed in cloth of vegetable fibre, with their skins painted grotesquely in various colours, one side of the face red, the other white, and in the middle of the breast a broad yellow stripe; the circuit of the eyes was also daubed with paint; these colours are made by boiling various kinds of wood, and mixing the decoction with clay. The rest of the Ashangos were also streaked and daubed with various colours, and by the light of their torches they looked like a troop of devils assembled in the lower regions to celebrate some diabolical rite; around their legs were bound white leaves from the heart of the palm-tree; some wore feathers, others had leaves twisted in the shape of horns behind their ears, and all had a bundle of palm-leaves in their hands.

Soon after I entered, the rites began. All the men squatted down on their haunches, and set up a deafening kind of wild song. There was an orchestra of instrumental performers near the idol, consisting of three drummers with two drumsticks each, one harper, and a performer on the sounding stick, which latter did not touch the ground, but rested on two other sticks, so that the noise was made the more resonant. The two mbuiti men, in the meantime, were dancing in a fantastical manner in the middle of the temple, putting their bodies into all sorts of strange contortions. Every time the mbuiti men opened their mouths to speak, a dead silence ensued. As the ceremony continued, the crowd rose and surrounded the dancing men, redoubling at the same time the volume of their songs, and, after this went on for some time, returning to their former positions. This was repeated several times. It seemed to me to be a kind of village feast. The mbuiti men, I ought to mention, had been sent for from a distance to officiate on the occasion, and the whole affair was similar to a rude sort of theatrical representation. The mbuiti men, like the witchcraft doctors, are important persons among these inland tribes; some have more reputation than others, but in general those who live furthest off are most esteemed. At length, wearied out with the noise, and being unable to see any meaning or any change in the performances, I returned to my hut at half-past ten.

June 30th. The altitude of Niembouai I found to be 1896 ft. above the level of the sea. I succeeded in obtaining observations both for latitude and longitude. The village lies in 1° 58′ 54″ S. lat. and 11° 56′ 38″ E. long.

I had heard that there was a village of the Obongos, or dwarfed wild negroes, somewhere in the neighbourhood of Niembouai, and one of my first inquiries on arriving at the place was naturally whether there was any chance of my seeing this singular people, who, it appears, continually come into their villages, but would not do so while I was there. The Ashangos themselves made no objection, and even offered to accompany me to the Obongo village. They told me, however, that I had better take with me only a very small party, so that we might make as little noise as possible. Two guides were given me, and I took only three of my men. We started this morning, and reached the place after twenty minutes' walk. In a retired nook in the forest were twelve huts of this strange tribe, scattered without order, and covering altogether only a very small space of ground. The shape of the huts was the same as that I have before described in the deserted Obongo village near Yengué. When we approached them no sign of living creature was to be seen, and, in fact, we found them deserted. The huts are of such slight construction, and the Obongos so changeable, that they frequently remove from one place to another. The abodes were very filthy; and whilst my Commi men and myself were endeavouring to examine them, we were covered with swarms of fleas and obliged to beat a retreat. The village had been abandoned by its inhabitants, no doubt on account of their huts being so much infested with these insects.

Leaving the abandoned huts, we continued our way through the forest; and presently, within a distance of a quarter of a mile, we came on another village, composed, like the last, of about a dozen ill-constructed huts, scattered about, without any regular order, in a small open space. The dwellings had been newly made, for the branches of trees of which they were formed had still their leaves on them, quite fresh. We approached with the greatest caution, in order not to alarm the wild inmates, my Ashango guides holding up a bunch of beads in a friendly way; but all our care was fruitless, for the men, at least, were gone when we came up. Their flight was very hurried. We hastened to the huts, and luckily found three old women and one young man, who had not had time to run away, besides several children, the latter hidden in one of the huts.

The little holes which serve as doors to the huts were closed by fresh-gathered branches of trees, with their foliage, stuck in the ground. My Ashango guides tried all they could to calm the fears of the trembling creatures; telling them that I had come to do them no harm, but had brought some beads to give them. I finally succeeded in approaching them, for fear seemed to have paralysed their powers of moving. I gave them some beads, and then made my Ashango guides tell them that we should come back the next day with more beads, to give some to all the women; so they must all be there. One of the old women, in the course of a short time, lost all

APPROACH TO THE CAMP OF THE OBONGO DWARFS.

her shyness and began to ridicule the men for having run away from us. She said they were as timid as the nchendc (squirrel), who cried "Qué, qué," and in squeaking she twisted her little body into odd contortions, with such droll effect that we all laughed.

When I brought out my tape to measure her, her fears returned; thinking perhaps that it was a kind of snake that I was uncoiling out of its case, she trembled all over; I told her I was not going to kill her, but it required another present to quiet her again. I accomplished my task at last. I also measured the young man, who was adult, and probably a fair sample of the male portion of his race.

We then returned to Niembouai. I had waited an hour, in the vain hope that the men might come back to their huts. By the way, the Obongo women seem to know how to tell lies as well as their countrywomen of larger growth; for when I inquired where the rest of the people were, they at once replied that they were gone into the forest to fetch firewood and to trap game.

The next day (*July 1st*) I went again to their village, and saw only one woman and two children. I had not come early enough, the birds had flown. Luckily the woman was one of those I had seen the day before. I gave her and the children a number of beads. Then suspecting that the mother of the children was in the hut close by where they stood, I went to it, took off the branch that had been put at the entrance to signify that the owner was out, and then putting half of my body into the hut, in the best way I could, I finally succeeded in seeing in the dark something which soon after I recognised as a human being. My Ashango man called to her, telling her not to be afraid. I was then told that she had lost her husband a few days before, when they lived in the now deserted village which I had seen on my way hither. She had over her forehead a broad stripe of yellow ochre.

I desired my Ashango guide to ask the women where they buried their dead; but he told me I had better not ask the question, as they might get frightened, and the woman who had just lost her husband might cry.

I gave the poor widow some beads, and then left them again; my old friend Misounda (for she told me her name) inviting me to come back in the afternoon, as the men would then have returned from the woods. I accordingly returned in the course of the afternoon, but no men were to be seen.

On a subsequent visit, I found the village deserted by the women as well as by the men—at least, as we approached it, the women, who had heard us, ran into their huts; among them I caught sight of my old friend Misounda running to hide herself. This was doubly disappointing, as I had flattered myself that I had quite tamed her. When we entered the village not a sound was to be heard, and the branches of the trees had been put up at the doors of all the huts, to make us believe that the people had all gone into the woods. My Ashango guide shouted aloud, "We have come to give you more beads; where are you?" Not a whisper was heard, no one answered our call; but there was no room for any mistake, as we had seen the women enter the huts. I therefore went to the hut of my old friend, Misounda, took off the branch, and called her by name, but there was no answer. It was so dark inside that I could see nothing; so I entered, and tumbled over the old woman. Finding that she was detected, she came out, and pretended that she had been fast asleep. Then she called out the other women, saying that I was not a leopard come to eat them, and that they need not be afraid.

In the course of other visits which I made to the village during my stay at Niembouai, I succeeded in measuring five other women. I could not help laughing, for all of them covered their faces with their hands; and it was only in the case of Woman No. 1 that I could get any measurements of the face. Unfortunately I could not take the same measurements for all. I did the best I could under such circumstances. In order to allay their fears, I tried to measure one of my Ashango guides, but he refused, being as much frightened as the women. The measurements are as follows:—

		Ft.	In.
Woman No. 1, total height		4	4½
,,	between the outer angles of the eyes	0	5¼
,, No. 2, total height		4	7¼
,, No. 3, considered unusually tall		5	0¼
,,	round the broadest part of the head	1	9¾
,,	from the eye to the ear	0	4
,, No. 4, total height		4	8
,,	round the head	1	10
,,	from the eye to the ear	0	3¾
,, No. 5, total height		5	0
,,	round the head	1	9
,,	from the eye to the ear	0	4½
,, No. 6, total height		4	5
,,	round the head	1	10¼
,,	from the eye to the ear	0	4½
Young man, total height		4	6

The colour of these people was a dirty yellow, much lighter than the Ashangos who surround them, and their eyes had an untameable wildness about them that struck me as very remarkable. In their whole appearance, physique, and colour, and in their habitations, they are totally unlike the Ashangos, amongst whom they live. The Ashangos, indeed, are very anxious to disown kinship with them. They do not intermarry with them; but declare that the Obongos intermarry among themselves, sisters with brothers, doing this to keep the families together as much as they can. The smallness of their communities, and the isolation in which the wretched creatures live, must necessitate close interbreeding; and I think it very possible that this circumstance may be the cause of the physical deterioration of their race. Their foreheads are exceedingly low and narrow, and they have prominent cheek bones; but I did not notice any peculiarity in their hands or feet, or in the position of the toes, or in the relative length of their arms to the rest of their bodies; but their legs appeared to be rather short in proportion to their trunks; the palms of their hands seemed quite white. The hair of their heads grows in very short curly tufts; this is the more remarkable, as the Ashangos and neighbouring tribes have rather long bushy hair on their heads, which enables them to dress it in various ways; with the Obongos the dressing of the hair in masses or plaits, as is done by the other tribes, is impossible. The young man had an unusual quantity of hair also on his legs and breast, growing in short curly tufts similar to the hair of the head, and all the accounts of the Ashangos which I heard agreed in this, that the Obongo men were thickly covered with hair on these parts of their body; besides, I saw myself, during the course of my stay at Niembouai on my return, male Obongos in the village, and although they would not allow me to approach them, I could get near enough to notice the small tufts of hair: one of the men was black. The only dress they wear consists of pieces of grass-cloth which they buy of the Ashangos, or which these latter give them out of pure kindness, for I observed that it was quite a custom of the Ashangos to give their old worn *denguis* to these poor Obongos.

The modes of burial of these savages, as related to me by my Ashango companions, are curious. The most common habit is to place the corpse in the interior of a hollow tree in the forest, filling up the hole with branches and leaves mixed with earth; but sometimes they make a hole in the bed of a running stream, diverting the current for the purpose, and then, after the grave is covered in, turning back the rivulet to its former course.

The Ashangos like the presence of this curious people near their villages because the Obongo men are very expert and nimble in trapping wild animals and fish in the streams, the surplus of which, after supplying their own wants, they sell to their neighbours in exchange for plaintains, and also for iron implements, cooking utensils, water-jars, and all manufactured articles of which they stand in need. The woods near their villages are so full of traps and pitfalls that it is dangerous for any but trained woodsmen to wander about in them; I always took care not to walk back from their village to Niembouai after night-fall; for in the path itself there were several traps for leopards, wild boars, and antelopes. From the path, traps for monkeys could be seen everywhere: and I should not at all have relished having my legs caught in one of these traps. I was surprised at the kindness, almost the tenderness, shown by the Ashangos to their diminutive neighbours. On one of my visits to the village I saw about a dozen Niembouai women, who had come with plantains to exchange for game, which they expected to be brought in by the men. As the little hunters had not returned from the forest, they were disappointed in this errand; but seeing that the Obongo women were suffering from hunger, they left nearly all the plantains with them as a gift, or, perhaps, on trust, for outside the hut they were cooking roots of some tree, which did not seem to me very nourishing.

The Obongos, as I have said before, never remain long in one place. They are eminently a migratory people, moving from place to place whenever game becomes scarce. But they do not wander very far; that is, the Obongos who live within the Ashango territory do not go out of that territory—they are called the Obongos of the Ashangos—those who live among the Njavi are called Obongo-Njavi—and the same with other tribes. Obongos are said to exist very far to the east, as far, in fact, as the Ashangos have any knowledge. They are similar to the gypsies of Europe—distinct from the people amongst whom they live, yet living for generations within the confines of the same country. They plant nothing, and depend partly for their vegetable food on roots, berries, and nuts, which they find in the forest; indeed, the men spend most of their days and many of their nights in the woods, and it was partly on this account, and their excessive shyness, that I was unable to examine them closely, with the solitary exception of the young man above described. When they can no longer find wild animals in the locality where they have made their temporary settlements, they are sometimes apt to steal food from their more civilized neighbours, and then decamp. Their appetite for animal food is more like that of a carnivorous beast than that of a man. One day I enticed the old woman, whose heart I had gained by many presents of beads, to Niembouai, simply by promising her a joint of goat-flesh. I had asked her if she was hungry—without answering me, she drew a long breath, drawing in her stomach, to make me understand that it was very empty. When she came, I tried to put her off with a bunch of plantains, but she stuck tenaciously to my hut until I had fulfilled my promise of giving her some meat, repeating the word, *elava*, *elava* (goat, goat). Through her and an Ashango interpreter I took down a few words of the Obongo language, which I add in the Appendix to this volume; it will be seen that it contains words of Ashango; indeed their dialect is a mixture of what was their own original language and the languages of the various tribes among whom they have resided for many years past. I was told that now and then one of them will leave his people, and come and live among the Ashangos. My guides were kind enough to inform me that, if I wanted to buy an Obongo, they would be happy to catch one for me.

July 4th. I find that palavers are common in the Ashango country. A man of Niembouai had been put in *nchogo* by the men of another village, on account of some palaver; and the people of the other village now came to Niembouai to see if the palaver could not be settled, "For," said they, "you men of Niembouai are rich, now that you have the Spirit with you." Several elders spoke on each side, each one trying to speak louder than the one who had preceded him. Finally, the chief of Niembouai gave the complainant a string of the large beads I had presented to him.

Then another Ashango came, bringing a slave to his father-in-law in Niembouai, in payment for the daughter he had given him in marriage: the speeches on the occasion of the presentation of the slave lasted about three hours.

On another occasion, an Ishogo came to get a slave in repayment of a *Neptune* he had trusted to a friend at Niembouai,* and got into a furious rage, on finding that no slave was forthcoming. He protested loudly that he was tired of being put off, and that he was not going to be cheated of his Neptune.

My astronomical observations at this place, unfortunately were not all noted down in my journal. I see by my memoranda, that on the 1st and 4th of

* A *Neptune* is a brass dish worth 3s. 6d. to 4s.

July I took the distances between the Moon and Jupiter; on the 4th, the weather became cloudy, and I failed in taking the observations I had hoped to have obtained. When the moon, the planet Saturn, and the star Spica were sufficiently low in the heavens to be taken with the artificial horizon, the sky was too cloudy to permit of the observation.

July 5th. We were delayed three more days in Niembouai through the illness of Ngoma, one of my Commi boys. I paid the new Ashango porters on the 2nd, and had some difficulty in getting them away after the two days' delay without giving them more.* With them departed Mokounga.

We started at ten a.m., led by Magouga, an influential man of Niembouai, whose guest I had been during my stay here. The path gradually descended into the valley of the Ouano, a river which falls into the Odiganga. I found on reaching its banks, about three miles east of Niembouai, that we had descended more than 600 feet, the altitude being 1285 feet.

* The names of my Ashango porters were as follows:—

Magouga—Head man,

Adoombo,	Mayombon (the 2nd),	Mokela,
Mayombon,	Mouabagou,	Madoungou,
Dishclo,	Ibalo,	Manlaga,
Moquangué,	Dilako,	Mamagué,
Divangui,	Dishcio,	Badinga,
Moabekkai,	Bengouia,	Mayoubon.

Besides these we had eight porters to carry the loads of my Commi men and a varying number followed to carry the provisions and kettles; but I omitted to take their names. We had also generally with us three or four old fellows who followed us from village to village, expecting to feed well on the road, and at the end of a few days to get something for speech-making; for they thought they helped me wonderfully in this way.

The Ouano was about 30 or 40 yards wide, and too deep to be forded.

We crossed this stream by a singular kind of ferry. The boat or raft was formed of two logs of light wood, fifteen feet long, and a flooring of laths, tied by their ends to the logs, so as to form a rude vessel four or five feet broad. The boat was propelled by the ferrymen across the current, and, to prevent its being swept down stream, it was attached, by means of a stout creeper looped at the end, to a rope stretched between trees across the river. Upright sticks were fixed in the side-beams of the raft for the standing passengers to hold on by. Our party were transported across the stream by means of this contrivance in five journeys. In the rainy season, when the current is very strong, this ferry must be very useful. I had never before seen a ferry of this kind in Africa.

About one p.m. we crossed a high hill called Mogiama, the summit of which was 2264 feet above the sea-level. Soon after, we passed a small Ashango plantation, with a few huts on its borders and patches of the wild tobacco-plant and of the hemp. The tenants of the huts had fled at our approach, and we cooked our dinner at the forsaken fires of the settlement. My Ashango porters insisted upon killing their goat here. When I asked them why they had not killed and eaten it at Niembouai, they replied that they were afraid their own people would have asked them for some of the meat. I then asked them why they did not wait until we had reached the village to which we were going. Their reply was the same—the people there also would ask them for some of the meat. They succeeded in eating the whole of the goat at one meal; after which they came to me saying, "You see we have eaten the whole of it. Ashango people have big stomachs—we do not want any one to help us to eat the goats that you will give us. It is a bore that people cannot be allowed to eat their meals in quiet, without others coming to ask them for some of the food." I could not help laughing; for these very fellows had been plaguing my men at Niembouai every time we killed a goat; and they used to make such a terrific noise, praising the meat, and begging for some of it, that I often had to come out of my hut, and drive the whole lot of them away.

The country continued very hilly, and we made *détours* to avoid the steep ascents. At length, a little before the sun set, we reached the village of Mongon. Many of my porters had relatives here, and we were received in a friendly manner. We passed the night in the village, and I was fortunate enough to take several lunar observations, which gave 12° 3′ 37″ E. long., and I found the latitude to be 1° 56′ 45″ S. I was only able to take one meridian altitude; but it was a very successful one, and may be relied upon. The place is the most elevated I have yet found, being 2488 feet above the sea-level. I was glad to find we had made a little northing during the day's march.

July 6th. I had great difficulty in getting my men away this morning. They wanted to spend the day idling and drinking with their friends, who had given them a fat goat to present to me that I might consent to the delay; but I made a firm stand against these manœuvres, and forced the porters to take up their loads by pointing my revolver at their heads, while I took old Magouga by the arm, and led him forward. We left at about eight a.m., and after two hours' march arrived at a small village called Niongo, where we stopped for breakfast.

The importunities of the villagers and their chief delayed us here nearly three hours. I was getting annoyed at these repeated delays, for, at this rate of travel, when should I get to the Nile? It was now nearly a year since I left the coast. At last, I told the chief that if he was so fond of me I would tie him with ropes and carry him with us; we were allowed, after this, to depart without further trouble. Of course I refused the proffered goat; for it is an universal rule with these tribes that, a present being received by a stranger from the villagers, he is bound to make some stay in the place. The refusal of the present of food is a token that you do not wish to remain, and hence the pertinacity of these people in trying to force goats and so forth upon us, when we are passing a village. After an hour's march we were again brought to a stand-still, by the porters laying down their loads and demanding more pay. This was the Ishogo scene over again, and terminated in the same manner, by the vigorous measure of bringing my Commi men up with the muzzles of their guns levelled at the heads of the offenders, followed by their sudden repentance, and their laughing over the affair, as usual, saying, "Let us stop a while and

BIBLIOTECA NAZIONALE
NAPOLI

AN AFRICAN GROUP, NOW AT WIMBLEDON.

have a smoke. Do you think we would leave you in the woods? People may be left in a village but not in the forest."

About four p.m. we reached the village called Niembouai Olomba, or "Further Niembouai," to distinguish it from the other place of the same name which I will call Niembouai West for the sake of distinction. We had made but eight miles in a direct line in four hours' march; but the road lies over a succession of hills and narrow valleys, everywhere thickly wooded; and travelling is most toilsome, heavily-laden as we all were.

We were received with great joy by the chief, who is the "father," head chief, or king of this clan of Ashangos. Houses were allotted to us; presents of goats and plantains were laid at my feet; and I was glad to find that the old chief had not run away. He had one of the mildest expressions of face I ever saw; was tall, and about 60 years old. Of the two goats he gave me, I gave one to my Ashango porters. As they went away with it, I heard one say, "We did not know that he would give us one!" This plan of feeding my porters well has a very good effect on the villagers, and helped me in the difficult task of getting fresh porters.

The people of Niembouai Olomba were shy, but many of them had seen me at Niembouai West. Like all the villages in these mountains, it is surrounded with groves of plantain-trees. Goats are very abundant, and the goat-houses are scattered here and there throughout the village. Swallows were flying over the streets, and numerous birds were singing, perched on the surrounding tall trees, behind the plantain-groves. In the street of the village is seen, now and then, the stump of an old tree, which time has not been able to destroy: for here, wherever the people settle or plant, the trees have to be cut down, and the stump and roots are left to perish by the action of time. Niembouai Olomba is a large village containing about 184 houses. Formerly this and Niembouai West constituted one town (*i.e.*, the population all lived in one place), and it must have been then a very large village for this part of Africa. Nearly all the houses have bee-hives fixed to the walls, and the honey is beautifully white and well-flavoured. Wax is very abundant in Ashango-land, and of a fine quality; as it is not used by the natives, it will probably become a valuable article of export at some future day. I was struck with the simplicity of construction of the bee-hives; they were made simply of the bark of trees, rolled up so as to form a cylinder, thus imitating a hollow tree in which bees make their hives in the wild state. The ends of the cylinder are closed with pieces of bark, in which holes are made for the entrance and the exit of the bees; wooden hoops are fixed at each extremity to keep the cylinder in shape.

Although the Ashangos are certainly quite a distinct tribe from the Ishogos, for they speak a different language, I do not notice any striking difference in their appearance or habits. Their language, as I have said before, is the same as that of the Ashira. In one particular they contrast advantageously with the tribes nearer the coast, namely in the amplitude of their clothing. All are well clothed with the beautiful grass-cloth of the country. I did not even see any naked children. The denguis or robes of chiefs are of unusually large size, and are worn generally very gracefully. They seem to tattoo themselves rather more than the Ishogos do; and the women do not pierce their ears for ear-ornaments; their head-dress is the same as that of the Ishogo women, but they do not seem to take so much care of it. Although the streets of the Ishogo villages were broader, the houses of the Ashangos are larger than those of their neighbours. Both tribes adopt the custom of taking out their two middle upper incisors, and of filing the other incisors to a point; but the Ashangos do not adopt the custom of filing also the upper incisors. Some of the women have the four upper incisors taken out. They submit to this process, in order to be considered the leading belles of the village. All of them, both male and female, shave off their eyebrows and pluck out their eyelashes, and both tribes smear themselves with ntchingo, or red powder.

Beating the women is here of very rare occurrence, I am told; and I have not, myself, seen a single case of woman-beating. In fact, the women have their own way, in many things. Almost every Ashango carries a sword, made by the Shimba and Ashangui tribes. When a sword is sold, the business is always transacted *en famille*. Their other weapons are spears and poisoned arrows. They do not make any iron here, but get it from tribes further east.

They have the reputation of being more quarrelsome than the Ishogos, and of being greater liars. This sin of lying is, unfortunately, thought of little matter in this part of the world. They are not drunkards, like the Aponos, though palm-trees are abundant throughout the district, and they drink the palm wine, but in moderation. They know also how to extract oil from the nuts of the oil palm-tree, which is here very abundant.

July 7th. Niembouai Olomba lies at the foot of a fine wooded hill, on a ridge between two deep narrow valleys or gorges, one running east and west and the other north-east and south-west. The wind from the south blew cool and refreshing, both last night and this morning. At six a.m. the thermometer stood at 68° Fahr., with a clear sky and a bright sun. Along the deep valley towards the east I had a magnificent view of the rising sun. It was the happiest morning I had had for a long time, and I felt invigorated with the cool breeze, after the close heat of the forest-paths and crowded villages during the last few weeks. Towards two p.m. the sky became cloudy again.

July 8th. Last night, as I was quietly lying on my bed, I was aroused by a rustling and scratching noise in the hut, and the flying of numerous cockroaches, some of them alighting on the back of my neck, which, by the way, produces one of the most unpleasant sensations I know of. I knew it must be an invasion of Bashikouay ants, and started up and called my men. The active creatures were already on my bed, and I was lucky in making my escape without being half devoured by them. They were attracted, no doubt, by a quarter of goat's meat hanging in the chamber, for, unfortunately, my sleeping-room is obliged to be also my store-room. The men hastened to fetch hot ashes to spread over the floor, which was black with the shining bodies of these most destructive ants, who come to their work in dense masses. Had their progress not been checked they would have finished our goat-meat in a very short time, for they were already climbing the walls, and we had to sweep them down on the hot cinders, not daring to apply a torch to the wall of such a combustible edifice as an Ashango hut. After killing thousands in this manner the remainder were scared away, and I spent the rest of the night in peace.

I have given an account of this ant in my 'Adventures in Equatorial Africa,' and have little to add regarding it in this place. But one can never cease to wonder at the marvellous habits and instincts of these extraordinary creatures, whose natural history is still but imperfectly known. The individuals which form the armies of the Bashikouays are only the worker or neuter caste of the species. It is well known that the males and females of ants, which alone propagate their kind, are winged, and take no part in the various kinds of industry which render ants such remarkable insects. The armies of the Bashikouays seem for ever on the march, clearing the ground of every fragment of animal substance, dead or alive, which they can obtain or overpower; and, so furious are their onslaughts on the person of any one who steps near their armies, that it is difficult or impossible to trace the columns to their nests, if indeed they have any. The Bashikounys are of several distinct species; and, in each species, the workers or neuters are of many gradations of size and bulk, but all are of shining reddish or black colour, with heads of a square or oblong form. While on the march, they do not attack insects, only when they halt and then spread themselves out in foraging parties.

In the afternoon I ascended one of the hills which form so grand a feature in the landscape close to Niembouai. An almost perpetual mist shrouds the summit of this hill, which is called Birogou Bouanga. By recording observations of the boiling-point and two aneroid-barometers at the summit, and striking the mean, I found the altitude to be 2574 feet above the sea-level. The leaves of the trees and bushes were quite wet at the summit, whilst below, near the village, the herbage was dry, showing the effect of the cap of mist or cloud which covers the hill-top.

When I first spoke of going up the mountain, the villagers expressed themselves willing to go with me, and several promised to accompany me to the summit; but, when I actually got ready to start, they declined to do so—their fellow-villagers telling them not to go with the Oguizi. I began to fear that I should not be able to accomplish the ascent. Finally, two of my porters from Niembouai West offered to go with me; then two of the villagers agreed to show us the path to the top. When we all reached the summit, the two villagers stared to see me bring out my policeman's lantern, and screw my boiling-point thermometer to the kettle; but their astonishment was beyond measure when I produced instantaneous fire with a lucifer-match. They trembled all over, and became speechless. My two porters looked at them with evident contempt, saying, "You see now what kind of spirit we have brought to you." Gradually they got less frightened, and at last came close to me and watched my proceedings with manifest interest.

From the summit of Birogou Bouanga I could see the country for many miles round. The mountains appeared to be, for the most part, of nearly equal height. Here and there, on the declivity of the hill round Niembouai Olomba, were large tracts of the forest that had been felled and partly cleared; and, in the midst of fallen trees and dead branches, the beautiful leaves of the plantain-trees could be seen, with now and then a field of cassada or manioc, though this latter is getting very scarce. The plantain is almost the only staple of food here. Through the leaves of the plantain-trees peeped out the stem of the sugar-cane, which is here very abundant. I could see large tracts of ground-nuts. When meat is scarce the people pound the seed of the ground-nut trees and cook it in leaves, or simply roast it. Near the village were patches of the tobacco-plant and of the liamba (hemp). In the places where plantain-trees had been newly planted I often saw a kind of squash, the pounded seed of which is considered a great dainty.

I had to-day a serious trouble with two of my

Commi men, Mouitchi and Rapelina, slaves lent me by my friends Djombouai and Sholomba on the Fernand Vaz. They had lately become, I knew not why, discontented and troublesome, and were detected to-day in pilfering powder, bullets, and other articles, with the intention of laying in a store of ammunition before running away. Mouitchi was a lazy fellow, and his loss would not have been a very serious matter to me; but it would not be prudent to lessen the numbers of my small party, and leave these Commi men in the interior. I was obliged to have them both disarmed, and, after considering for some time, decided that it would be best to tell them they might go and find their way back to the coast, if they liked to try. The elders of Niembouai, when they saw I intended to dismiss the two men, treated the matter as a very serious one, and came to me to say that I could not be allowed to leave the men in the country in that way, but that I must name two of the elders of the place to be their protectors or masters. My object, however, was not to get rid of the men, but to show my displeasure at their misconduct; and I thought the best way to do this was to pretend to be utterly indifferent whether they accompanied us any further or not, for this would be likely to make them repent and beg to be taken back again. The event proved that I was not mistaken: they left the village, but came back repentant the next day.

July 12th. We did not leave Niembouai Olomba without trouble. First, my porters of Niembouai West wanted an increase of pay; then the people of Niembouai Olomba wanted them to leave me with them, and to go back to their own country, saying that they could take care of me. Magouga retorted that he also could take care of me. On their referring the matter to me, in order to please both parties, I said I would take half my porters from Niembouai West, and the other half from Niembouai Olomba. I felt very much inclined to take only the men of Niembouai Olomba, as the others had shown signs of fear, having come to me two or three times, saying that they had heard that the people in the villages before us did not wish to see the Oguizi, and had sent word to that effect.

When at length we started, Magouga and the chief of Niembouai Olomba were both with me; and with Rebouka we formed the rear-guard of the caravan. I kept constantly on the alert, and took care always to make one of these two leading men walk before me, for, in so wild a country, one cannot be too careful.

We were now on our march to the country of the Njavi tribe, who live to the east of Ashango-land. My Ashango porters were to convey me to the principal village of the Njavi, and I had hoped that all would go smoothly, now that we had left Niembouai and were again on the road. Unhappily, further troubles were in store for me. Several of the porters—taught, I am afraid, by my own mutinous servants Rapelina and Mouitchi—went on ahead, and, concealing themselves in the forest, let us pass them, and then made off to their own village. When we halted to rest the porters, I discovered that several of them were missing. The absentees all belonged to Niembouai West. We waited for them, but in vain. Both they and their loads were gone.

Being determined to check this new evil at its commencement, I ordered a halt near Mobana, and, seizing Magouga, placed three of my Commi men as guard over him, with orders to shoot him if he attempted to escape; and I told him that I should not release him until the lost property was restored by the Niembouai porters under his leadership. In the meantime the old chief of Niembouai Olomba, with his people, came to me, and said, "I have nothing to do with this—here are all my people, here are all their loads. Why did you not take my people only? We do not steal in my village." Soon the Mobana people, who had heard that we were near, and who are related by marriages to the people of Niembouai Olomba, came out to us, and asked us to come into their village, saying, "Why should the Oguizi remain in the woods, while there is a village near?" I accordingly accepted their invitation, and proceeded to Mobana.

The news of the robbery soon spread to Niembouai, and several of the elders, taking my part, set upon the thieves, who had run back to the village, hacked them with their swords, and sent back to me the three boxes they had carried off. This was not, however, till the following day; meantime, it was a little reign of terror at Mobana, for none of us slept, having to keep watch all night with our loaded muskets over Magouga and the porters, who remained in our hands. On examining next morning the three boxes which had been plundered, I found that none of the articles they contained had been actually stolen; but the contents of several bottles of medicine had been either drunk or poured away, and the empty bottles put back into their places. A quantity of arsenic was amongst the deficiencies, and I heard afterwards that some people of Niembouai had died mysteriously after touching the white man's goods.

I believed, of course, that Magouga and the porters who had not run away were innocent of the theft, having had no connivance with the thieves; but the day after the property had been restored, I found, when I awoke in the morning, two of my boxes missing. They had been taken during the night out of the hut in which I slept, and which was divided into three compartments; the innermost was the room in which I slept, and my stock of goods was put into the other two; wooden doors have now become scarce, and the shutter was hardly good for anything, so that the thieves had come during the night without much difficulty, and had taken two boxes, which, fortunately, contained only salt, shot, some soap, arsenic, and a few beads. I immediately called Rakombo, the chief of Mobana, and accused him and his people of the theft. For three days the palavers lasted; every day they came, saying they had stolen nothing; that the theft had been committed by some one they did not know. For three days palaver after palaver was held—they could not find the thieves. I could see from the sorrowful faces of Rakombo and of his people that they did not know really who had stolen these two boxes; and they said if they only knew the village to which the things had been taken, they would go and seize some of their women. Suddenly I heard a tremendous uproar, and saw the people coming towards the hut where Magouga and some of his people were staying, and brandishing their swords and spears, and shouting, "The Niembouai people have stolen the things." I had great trouble in saving Magouga's life; and my men had to lay hold of one or two of these raging warriors, and threaten to kill them if they injured Magouga. They shouted "Ibamba, we have nothing to do with you or with your people: it is only with these Niembouai people, who have brought shame on our village!"

It was some time before I could quiet the villagers; at length something like peace was restored, and, at night, Magouga and his men left me and returned to their homes, for fear of other palavers.

Mobana is a large place, with houses like those of Niembouai. Numerous bee-hives hang against the houses or are scattered among the plantain-trees. Goats are plentiful; some of them are of great size, and very fat. These generally form part of the dowry given when a woman is married. While at Mobana, I assisted at the departure of a young woman who had been given in marriage to a man of a neighbouring village. Her father was to take her there, with all the marriage outfit (*trousseau de mariage*). It consisted of eight of the plates of the country, such as I have already described; two large baskets for carrying plantains from the plantations, or calabashes full of water from the spring; a great number of calabashes; a large package of ground-nuts; a package of squash seeds; two dried legs of antelope; some fine nchandas (the name given to the denguis here), and her stool. Several members of her family carried this elaborate outfit. The bride-elect was smartly dressed; her chignon had been *built up* most elaborately the day before. As she left the village, the people remarked to each other, "Her husband will see that the Mobana people do not send away their daughters with nothing!"

Her old mother accompanied her to the end of the street, and then returned to her home, looking proud and happy at having seen her daughter go with such an outfit.

July 15th. Mobana is situated on the top of a high hill, at a height of 2369 feet above the level of the sea. The range, at the foot of which Niembouai is situated, is the highest of the four ranges, reckoning from the coast. From Mobana the land slopes down gradually towards the east. I here heard again of a large river further east.

When we entered Mobana, the villagers wanted my men to smear themselves with *ntchingo* or red powder, bringing for this purpose several of their wickerwork dishes, on which was placed a quantity of the pigment. This I found a general custom amongst the Ashangos when a host wishes to welcome a guest; and a visitor to a village or a house is only too happy when the elders or the owner of the house request him to make himself red, for it is a sign of their good will. As we were entering the village we met a Niembouai man coming out quite furious about something or other, and venting threats and curses; on asking him what was the matter, he said that the Mobana people had not offered him the *ntchingo*, and he was going back to the place whence he came. My men did not like this any more than other Ashango customs, and refused to smear themselves.

July 18th. Since I left Mongon I have only been able to take a single meridian altitude, the sky having been constantly clouded. I succeeded in taking one yesterday. I am very glad to find that I am getting a little to the north, while proceeding on my eastward route. At the foot of the hill on which Mobana stands, there is a stream called Bembo, flowing in a north-easterly direction. The natives pointed towards the east when I inquired as to its further course.

I have at last succeeded in hiring porters. Rakombo and his men have sworn to carry me to the Njavi country. The good old chief of Niembouai Olomba took his departure to-day, to return to his own village. I gave a parting present to him and to his men. Before he left me, he consigned me to the hands of Rakombo, charging him in due form with the care of me.

The country, as far as I am able to see eastward and south-eastward, continues hilly, the hills being of moderate elevation. There are three paths from Mobana leading into the Njavi country; one towards the north-east, one nearly due east, and a third south-east. Mobana is in 1° 52′ 56″ S. lat.; I was unable to take observations for longitude, but, by my dead reckoning, I place it in about 12° 27′ E.

July 21*st*. We were not able to resume our march until this morning.* We proceeded in an easterly direction, passing several villages, one of which was called Kombo; and after a march of nearly four hours we reached the village of Mouaou Kombo.

* I took down only a few of the names of our porters, which were as follows:—

Head man, Rakombo, chief of the village.

Nchanga,	Iloko,	Moubon,
Banda,	Matomba,	Moudjo,
Mayombo,	Rembo,	Mboga.
Mohendai,	Nbako,	

CHAPTER XVII.

FATAL DISASTERS AT MOUAOU KOMBO.

Unpromising state of affairs on arriving at Mouaou Kombo—Rakombo is threatened—Obstacles raised by the Villagers—Fair promises of the Chief—A Secret Meeting of the Villagers—Demands of the People—We leave the Village—Night Encampment in the Forest—Threats and Promises from the next Village—Invited to return to Mouaou—Reconciliation—Arrival of a hostile Deputation from the next Village—A man accidentally Shot.

At this fatal village of Mouaou Kombo my eastward journey came to an end, and all my hopes of traversing Equatorial Africa, at least in the present expedition, were dashed to the ground.

The first events on my arrival at the place were not encouraging; but still the difficulties I encountered were only of the ordinary sort which every African traveller meets with, and were nearly overcome, when the event happened which brought my further progress to an end. In the first place, I found that Rakombo and his Mobana porters intended to break through their agreement to take me to the Njavi country. The Mouaou people belonged to a different clan from the Mobanana, and there appeared not to be a cordial understanding although there had been a good many intermarriages between them. We had no sooner arrived at the village—the elders of which at first behaved well, giving me a large house to stay in—than the Mobana porters, having laid down their loads, gave us the slip; one by one, on some pretence or other, they sneaked off amongst the trees which surround the village, and we saw them no more. It was in vain that I threatened Rakombo. I could see nothing to enable me to fix the blame on him; he declared that the Mounou people would not allow him to take me onward. We were now left to the mercy of strangers.

On the second day after my arrival (July 23rd), the head chief, named Kombo, made his appearance, and gave me presents of goats and plantains to indicate that I was welcome; then he called the villagers together and made them a long speech, to the effect that the Niembouai and Mobana people having left the "Spirit" in their hands, it fell to their duty to take me onward to the Njavi country; and that they were not to rob me, for, if they did, they would surely die, as had happened to the Niembouaians. It was then that I learnt that the thieves must have been tasting my arsenic, or had probably mixed it with the salt they had stolen. I soon made friends with the people, engaged porters and paid them, and all seemed to be going on well for a fresh start.

There was an obstacle somewhere, however, for on the day following I found no signs of readiness for departure. The chief came to me, and explained that the men were obliged to go to the forest to cut firewood to leave with their wives. It is true that this is the custom of these people; for, amongst the Ishogo and Ashango, the men on leaving their wives have to gather a sufficient quantity of firewood to last their families during their absence. Kombo, addressing himself to Igala—for, when holding a palaver, these people never address themselves directly to the person for whom the speech is intended—said, "I see by the look of the Oguizi that he thinks I am deceiving him, and that I lie: he must not judge me so harshly. A man may have a fine body, yet, if his heart is bad, he is an ugly man; therefore, if a man's heart is good, people should not look at his body. To-morrow the Oguizi will see whether I have a good heart or a bad heart: Kombo will take him to the Njavi country."

In the afternoon the village street became deserted. I walked down it, but could see no one. I called my men together; Igala shook his head, and said that they were all gone to "mogoua oroungo" (hold a secret meeting), and that it boded no good.

Such was indeed the case. When the meeting broke up all the men of the village assembled before my hut, and the chief began a long rambling speech, the purport of which was that I must give them more goods before I could leave the place. He said the Niembouai and Mobana people had left me because they were unable to take me to the Njavi; that he alone could help me forward, and I must therefore pay him at least as much as I had paid the people at the other places. He asked particularly for the pieces of a large brass kettle which I had broken yesterday, and also for many measures of gunpowder, which, as I have before explained, they wanted to barter for other articles with the Ashangui tribe.

I had intended the precious fragments of my kettle as a parting present to the porters when they should have safely conveyed me to Njavi-land, and, being irritated with the evidently underhand dealings of these fellows, I refused their request. The question of more pay was not, however, what had drawn the people to their secret meeting. The true cause of the meeting was the arrival of a deputation, from some villages further ahead, to threaten the Mouaou people with war if they came with me through their villages. The aim of the embarrassed Kombo was apparently to trifle with me with a view of gaining time, during which he might settle his outstanding palavers with the hostile villagers further on.

The next day (July 25th), on finding there was no chance of our departure, I made up my mind to retire for a time from the village, and show my displeasure in that way; this being an effective mode of bringing them to reason, for I knew they would come and humbly promise everything I wanted to induce me to come back to the village. To spurn the hospitality of a village, and retire offended from it, touches the primitive African in his tenderest feelings and stings him to the quick. I made all the porters return the pay in beads that I had given them, and then with my men transported my baggage to a distance in the woods, on the borders of one of those beautifully clear streams which are so frequent in this mountainous region. The amount and weight of my baggage were still very great, and carrying the boxes was a work of great labour. The path down to the place of our retreat was very steep, and, from what I could gather by a survey of our position, I found we should be on the main eastern road from Mouaou. The villagers looked on at our proceedings in mute amazement.

Before evening the whole of the baggage was removed. My men erected sheds, and collected firewood to cook our supper. The place was a very pleasant one, under the shade of magnificent trees whose closely interwoven crowns would protect us from the night-mist, which dissolves in a soaking drizzle almost every night in this humid country. The path near our encampment was a broad and well-trodden one, showing that it was one of the highways of the district.

As soon as we had finished, I sent Igala and two other men, well-armed, along the path to try to find the next village, and ascertain, if possible, why they did not wish us to pass through. My messengers returned in about two hours, Igala laughing whilst describing to me the ignominious way in which the warriors of the village, armed to resist our progress, ran away at the sight of him and his two companions. The villagers told him that they had no quarrel with me, but had an old feud with the Mouaou people about two slaves that were owing to them, and that they were determined not to let them pass until the debt was paid. "If that is the case," said Igala, "why don't you come and fetch our luggage and take us on yourselves?" To this they returned evasive answers; they would call a council of the people to consider the matter, and give us an answer to-morrow, &c. &c. It was impossible to get at the truth of the case. How I wished I had an armed party, strong enough to force my way through the barriers which the caprice and trickery of these savages opposed to my progress! With twenty men like Igala and Macondai, I would have set all these vapouring fellows at defiance, and have been half-way across the continent by this time. Before we laid down to rest I had branches cut from the trees and strewed all around our encampment, to prevent, by the noise and impediments they would cause, a nocturnal surprise, which I thought very likely to happen, for parties of men from time to time sneaked through the woods, and, after talking to us and taking note of our position, quietly went back again. They were armed with bearded spears similar to those carried by the Fans, and which they get from the Ashangui tribe. I did not sleep all night. My negroes kept watch, taking it in turns, three sleeping and three waking, and I made them tell stories one after the other, speaking loud, so as to show the people we were awake and watchful.

July 26th. Early in the morning, as I had expected, a deputation from Mouaou, consisting of all the elders of the village, came to me, and with sorrowful countenances asked why I had deserted them. They prayed me to come back, and repeated that it was not their fault that my journey had been delayed, but the fault of the next village ahead. They promised earnestly that if I came back they would send me forward in two days, and by another route, to the south-east, so as to avoid the hostile villages, the people of which, they said, had made up their minds now to take me, but had laid a plan to leave me in the middle of the forest and run away with the baggage. They assured me that there were three roads from this place to the Njavi country—one to the north-east, one to the east, and a third to the south-east.

As the promised answer did not come from the other village, and the Mouaou elders seemed to be sincere in their repentance, I agreed to go back. In a few moments all my baggage was shouldered by strong men, and, with shouts of rejoicing, we marched up the hill to the village. All the population was then out to receive us. The chief came in state, with his countenance painted and his royal bell ringing, and, after repeating what the elders had said, made us presents of goats and plantains. Soon after, the *kondé* or head wife of the chief came to tell us that she was cooking a large pot of the koa root for me and my men, and all went pleasantly. The villagers were thoroughly sincere this time, and I felt happy, for there were not likely to be any more obstacles in my way before arriving in the Ashangui country, on the banks of the large river, which every one was now telling me of, and which I supposed to be the Congo. I had heard that in one day we should get through the districts on this side of the Ashangui country; that, in a few hours after leaving Mouaou Kombo we should be among the Njavi tribe; and that we could, in the same day, pass through the country of the Abombos.

Alas! the joy was soon turned into terror! Four

men from the hostile village, arrayed in warrior's attire and brandishing plantain-leaves over their heads, came in. They said they had held their palaver this morning and had decided not to let the Oguizi pass; there would be war if the Mouaou people attempted to bring me.

Kombo, who was seated by my side, told me to hide myself in my hut, so as not to give the strangers the pleasure of seeing me; he then ordered my men to make a demonstration with their guns to intimidate these vapouring warriors. I laughed as I saw the men taking to their heels as soon as Igala advanced towards them, firing his gun in the air. But my men got excited, and hurrying forward into the open space to fire their guns in the air, one of the weapons loaded with ball went off before the muzzle was elevated. I did not see the act; but, immediately after the report of the guns, I was startled to see the Mouaou villagers, with affrighted looks and shouts of alarm, running in all directions. The king and his koudé, who were both near me, fled along with the rest.

"Mamo! Mamo!" (the untranslatable cry of anguish of these poor Africans) was now heard on all sides. I rushed out, and not far from my hut saw, lying on the ground, the lifeless body of a negro; his head shattered and the brains oozing from his broken skull. Igalo ran to me with terrified looks, saying, "Oh, Chaillie, I could not help it; the gun went off!" The infallible consequences of the deed flashed across my mind. The distrust of my motives amongst these people, which had only just been overcome, would now return with redoubled force. They would make common cause with the enraged warriors of the neighbouring villages; hundreds of men armed with poisoned spears and arrows, would soon be upon us. I called to the king to come back and not be afraid; but already the war drums were beating. Kombo shouted: "You say you come here to do no harm and do not kill people; is not this the dead body of a man?" As it was out of the question our trying to make our way eastward, without goods and without escort, there was no help for it but to flee back to the Ishogo country as fast as we could.

I got my men together, seven in number, and gave a few hasty directions about the baggage with which our hut was filled. I did not know what to do. The thought flashed across my mind that it would be best to set fire to the hut and escape in the confusion; but I dreaded the further sacrifice of life that might be caused by the explosion of so much gunpowder. Our main purpose now was to get away on the forest path before the warriors, who would otherwise impede our advance and rouse other villages ahead. Ammunition was what was most necessary to us now; I served out a good supply of bullets and powder to each man; loaded some of them with my most valuable articles, my journals, photographs, natural history specimens, and a few of my lighter goods, and took, for my share of the burdens, five chronometers, a sextant, two revolvers, rifle, with another gun slung at my back, and a heavy load of ammunition. "Now boys," I said, "keep together, do not be afraid, and do not fire until I give the order; if it is God's will that we should die, we must die; but let us try our best, and we may reach the sea in safety!" I was afraid a panic would seize them, and all would be lost; but the brave lads, although struck with horror, and fully comprehending the gravity of the situation, stood their ground.

CHAPTER XVIII.

RETREAT FROM ASHANGO-LAND.

A Palaver proposed to settle the Death of the Man—A Woman killed—The War Cry!—Retreat commenced—Igala and myself wounded with Poisoned Arrows—Narrow Escape of Macondai and Rebouka—We are closely pursued by the Natives—Collections and Note-books thrown into the Bush—We make a Stand—Two Men Shot—Pursuit continued—I am wounded a second time—Igala shoots the Bowman—We make another Stand—Cross the Bembo—Pass Mobana—Still pursued—Make a final Stand—The Pursuers driven off at last—A Halt—The Party all collected together—Sleep in the Forest—Night-March through Niembouai—Friendly Conduct of the Head Chief—We are well received at a Plantation—Arrival of Magouga—We continue the March to Ishogo-land.

FOR a moment there seemed a chance of the affair being patched up. Igala had explained, in shouting to the frightened Kombo and the elders, that it was all an accident, and that I would pay the value of twenty men in goods if they would listen to me. I had hurriedly taken out a quantity of beads and cloth and spread it on the ground in the middle of the street, as the price of the life. One of the head men had even come forward, saying "it is good, let us hold the palaver." The war drums had ceased beating. But it was but a gleam of sunshine in the midst of a storm: at that moment a woman came rushing out of a hut, wailing and tearing her hair—the head wife of the friendly head man had been also killed by the fatal bullet which, after killing the negro, had pierced the thin wall of her hut!

All this occupied only a few moments. A general shout arose of "war!" and every man rushed for his spear or his bow. I gave the order for the retreat; for I saw at once that there was no chance of peace, but that a deadly struggle was about to commence. Away we went; Igala took the best of our remaining dogs, and led the van; I bringing up the rear. It was not an instant too soon; before we were well on the forest path leading from the village, a number of arrows were discharged at us; Igala was hit in the leg, and one of the missiles struck me on the hand, cutting through one of my fingers to the bone. Macondai and Rebouka, in leaving the village, narrowly escaped being transfixed with spears, and only succeeded in repelling their assailants by pointing their guns at them. If I had not stopped them from firing, they would have shot a number of them. Wild shouts, and the tramp of scores of infuriated savages close behind us, put us on our mettle. I shouted to my men not to fire, for we were in the wrong, and I told the villagers that we would not shoot them if they did not pursue us to the forest, but that if they followed us we should certainly kill them. My Commi boys behaved exceedingly well; they were cool and steady, and, keeping a firm line, we marched away through the street of the village.

Our pursuers had the disadvantage that they were obliged to stop every time they wanted to shoot, to adjust the arrow and take aim, and in the forest paths we were often out of sight round turnings in the road before they could deliver their shot. Moreover, their bravest men durst not come up to close quarters with us, although they often came near enough to make us hear their shouts of defiance; they cried out that it was of no use our attempting to escape from them, that we did not know the road through the bush, and should never get out of it alive. They seemed to be most bitter against Igala, whom they called *Malangu*, cursing him and his mother in the most revolting style. "You have tasted blood," they shouted out, "and your own blood must be shed." They dodged about, took short cuts through the jungle, and we were in constant fear lest some spear or arrow should come from behind the trees on our flanks, and finish us for good. Besides it would be impossible long to keep up the pace at which we ran. After behaving so steadily at starting, a sudden and unaccountable panic seized my men when we were some distance on the road, and for about ten minutes no shouts of mine could make them stop. To lighten themselves they threw load after load into the bush, and it filled me with sorrow to see my precious photographs, instruments, stuffed animals, note-books, route-maps, bottles of choice specimens in spirits, and other valuables, such as mementos of friends, scattered about the path, the toil of months irrecoverably lost.

After we had run some four or five miles, finding that our enemies still pursued us, I felt that it was time to make a stand and give them a specimen of our power, for if we allowed them to go on in this way there would be danger of their rousing against us the villagers ahead, and then it would be almost impossible to escape. I ordered a halt. Mouitchi, one of our number, was missing, and we concluded he had fallen a victim; our pursuers, before we left the village, had shouted to us that they had killed him; poor Igala, my best and bravest man, complained sorely of the wound in his leg. He believed the lance was poisoned, and said, "I shall die, Chaillie, and shall never see my daughter again!" There was time only for a few words of encouragement; our pursuers were in sight, and a number of men were threading the jungle apparently with a view of flanking us. I shouldered my long-range rifle, a splendid weapon made by Beckwith, and, as the leader advanced adjusting his bow, I fired. His right arm dropped broken and powerless by his side, and the next man behind fell with a crash amongst a mass of fallen leaves and branches. Rebouka also fired at a man in the bush, who disappeared suddenly, as if shot, down a steep bank. This served as a check for the present, and we jogged on more leisurely.

We had not gone far when a tumultuous shouting was heard behind us and a large number of warriors hove in sight, more furious than ever. The path was most difficult, over one steep hill after another, and the village of Mobana, likely to be hostile to us, was only about a mile from us. We increased our speed, but our pursuers were within range, and a paralysing thud, accompanied by a sharp pain, told me that I had been again struck. This time it was in my side; I had no time to stop to take the arrow out, and the barbed head having gone through the leather belt of my revolvers, the point was working in my flesh every step I took, causing the most acute torture. Had its force not been arrested by the resistance of the leather, it would probably have killed me. After I was struck, Igalo, the unfortunate cause of all our woe, who kept close by me during our flight, turned round and by a quick and well directed shot laid the too-skilful bowman low. The unfeigned sorrow and devotion of my men at this juncture were most gratifying to me. I was getting weak from loss of blood, and a burning thirst was tormenting me. They asked what was to become of them if I should die? I told them to keep together, come what might; and, if they escaped, to deliver all my journals and papers to the white men. Wherever we stopped for a few minutes during this disastrous day, they came round me and asked me how I felt, and what they could do for me.

After I was wounded my strength began to fail me, and I had myself to follow the example of my men in throwing away things to lighten the load I carried. To my great sorrow I had to throw into the bush my beautiful double-barrelled breech-loading rifle, a magnificent weapon, carrying a two and a half ounces steel-pointed ball. My sorrow was the greater inasmuch as it was a present from a dear friend of mine, Mr. G. Bishop of Twickenham.

We were still pursued, and another check was necessary. Igala said, "I know I am going to die, but let me kill a few of these fellows first." He concealed himself behind a tree, whilst we continued forward to draw on the men, for we had found that the tactics of our pursuers was to send to the van their most expert bowmen to get as near to us as they safely could, while the rest of them remained behind, shouting loudly, to make us believe that they were all far off. The foremost was not long in coming within Igala's range, who fired, and the man fell.

At last we crossed the difficult stream near Mobana called the Bembo, and commenced the ascent of the steep hill on which the village is situated. It was a critical stage in our flight. We thought it likely messengers might have gone by other paths to rouse the people against us, as the men who pursued us shouted out, "Men of Mobana, do not let the Ogouizi's people pass! they have killed our people!" As we expected, we found the fighting men all ranged in battle array at the further end of the village. Our road, however, lay a little out of their way; we passed quickly, and were soon again immersed in the shade of the forest path.

So far from being free from our tormentors after this, we were now followed by the Mounou and Mobana warriors united. The path led at first down the hill and we hurried along it at full speed so as not to be caught at a disadvantage. A little further on, halfway up another hill, Igala and Rapelina stayed behind and shot another man, wounding him only, and sending him howling back to his companions.

After this there was a lull for a short time. We stopped and considered what was best to be done.

We were all tired with our long run over the rugged hilly forest road, and irritated besides at the pertinacity of our blood-thirsty pursuers. I had wished to escape without causing any further sacrifice of life if possible, but it was plain that unless we killed more than we had done we should be unable to free ourselves from our enemies before nightfall, and then they might surround us and massacre us all. My men and myself agreed that we should here choose a place to make a last stand, and give them a lesson that should put a stop to them.

We had leisure to look out for a good position, for we knew the district, and remembered every hill. On the slope of one of the hills there was a place where a number of trees grew close together. We stationed ourselves each behind a broad trunk, but all within a short distance from each other, and there waited the arrival of our pursuers. As usual, the bowmen came on first, but we heard the noise of a multitude not far behind them, all bellowing forth curses on our heads. As soon as a good number were visible down the broad and tolerably straight road, Igala and Rapelina both fired. One man fell, evidently dead, and another was wounded in the face, to all appearance his jaw broken. Ngoma then took his aim, but his shot fell wide. The fellows seemed to be cowed at this unexpected onslaught, and when we suddenly emerged from behind the trees and showed ourselves, they all beat a retreat. It was our last combat, and although we heard them for a long time afterwards, it was always at a great distance. The forest in this part was not dense, but open, the ground covered with a few bushes and tall trees, with magnificent crowns of foliage, towering up at intervals of twenty to fifty yards from each other. The open nature of the forest very much improved our chances of escape; for we were enabled to see our enemy at a distance, and were not in danger of being out-flanked. The country was very rugged, hill succeeded hill, and sometimes the slopes were very steep.

We now breathed more freely. We halted, laid down our loads and rested, keeping a sharp look-out at the same time. I examined Igala's wound and my own. The blood had run very copiously from my finger, and my clothes were quite saturated with it; but the flow of blood appeared to have carried off the poison, for I felt no further ill effect from the wound except the pain, and it was healed in about three weeks afterwards. The action of the poison used by the natives is not very rapid; it causes corruption of the flesh around the wound, discharge of matter, and eventually gangrene; when an arrow or spear penetrates into the bowels, death is, of course, certain to ensue, but if the wound is only an external one it is very seldom fatal. The arrow-head which had pierced my side was found, when wrenched from the wound, to have been poisoned; but the coating of poison had been fortunately scraped off it in passing through the leather, and my wound, though extremely painful, was not a dangerous one, Igala's wound was still very painful; indeed towards night it got much worse, and I was afraid he would become lame. I had no medicine to give him, for all had been left behind. I began to fear for the safety of this brave and faithful negro. If he lost his life in this affair, I felt that I should never forgive myself.

As we were again shouldering our *otaitais* (now almost empty) to resume our march, we descried a man a short distance off, walking stealthily through the bushes up the hill and occasionally hiding himself. He was coming towards us, and we were at once on our guard again. Igala volunteered to go down and watch his movements. We waited the result in dead silence, each man gun in hand, and looking round the hill in expectation of seeing that we were surrounded. The man came nearer, and we saw that he had a gun in his hand: it was Mouitchi, whom we had given up for lost! He had escaped without a scratch, by running along by-paths in the forest within sound of the noisy crowd of our pursuers. He told us that both the men we had hit in the last encounter were dead, and that our pursuers had resolved to desist from following us, saying that they should all be killed one by one if they went on. The arrival of Mouitchi put us all in good spirits, for we took it as a good omen. We now saw a chance of the whole party arriving safely on the sea-coast.

The forest after this resumed its accustomed stillness, undisturbed by the savage war-cries and still more savage curses of the infuriated Ashangos. We had another village to pass, Niembouai Olomba, where I thought we might be attacked. Before we reached the place we met two women in the path belonging to Mobana. Igala wanted to shoot them, but I prevented him and gave him a sharp reprimand for thinking of such an act. I had given him an order at starting that if any women, old men, or children should be met with on the road he must let them pass unhurt, but that he was to shoot down armed men without mercy, this being necessary for our safety. Igala did not like this style of making war; he said this was not the white man's country, and we ought not to fight in white man's fashion. If I had not restrained him he would have shot every Ashango we saw, regardless of age or sex.

Thus we went on till sundown. We were then near the village of Niembouni Olomba, and had travelled at least over twenty miles of ground without food since our flight commenced at nine o'clock in the morning. I thought it unsafe in our exhausted state to run the gauntlet of this large and possibly hostile village, through which lay the only path we knew, and my men agreed with me that our best plan would be to retire into the forest, some distance from the main road, and sleep there till midnight. We might then pass through before the fighting men were aroused and seized their weapons, and we should have strength to run, as before, until we had reached a good place for making a stand to defend ourselves.

The plan was carried out. We plunged into a dense part of the forest, and then lay down on the ground to sleep, in a small open space, muzzling our dog that he should not betray our hiding place. Darkness had closed in: silence was broken only by the mournful cry of a solitary owl. My exhausted men thought neither of leopards, nor poisonous snakes, nor hostile savages, but slept soundly; as for myself, I was too anxious to sleep, and Igala distressed me by his moaning from time to time, although he tried all he could to suppress it.

The night air was misty and cold. As I lay awake on the damp ground, I thought of kindred and friends in the far north, of the many happy hours I had spent in happy homes, amidst every luxury of civilized life; and I felt desolate, as though all was now ended. I also thought of those who, in the comfort of their own fire-sides, carp at the narratives of travellers, and begrudge the little honour and fame they may gain. I am sure that if they had only passed through a tithe of the hardships travellers undergo, they would be more indulgent.

At last I thought it must be near midnight, so I awoke my men and sent two of them into the path that leads to the village, telling them to go and see if all was quiet. They returned with a favourable report. Then calling them all close to me, I said, "My boys, I have fought for you as hard as I could, but the time may be at hand when I shall not be able to do so any more. I may be killed to-night, or I may not be strong enough to fight much longer. Whatever happens, remain together; listen to Igala, your chief, and do not throw away my Journals.* Even if you have to throw away everything else, do

* One of the volumes of the Journal, together with my route-maps, numerous notes, and two copies of astronomical and meteorological observations, had already been lost in the retreat.

not throw them away, but deliver them into the hands of the white men on the coast."

My men clung close round me as I spoke, and all, with voices full of love, said, "Chaillie, you are not to die! You are not to die! We will bring you alive to our people! You shall always be with us." I answered, in a laughing tone, in order to cheer them up: "I did not say I am to die to-night; but only that I might die. Don't you know that Chaillie knows how to fight?" They all said, "Yes, yes; and we also know how to fight—we are men!" We then shouldered our bundles and guns, and struggled through the entangled thicket, tearing ourselves with thorns, into the path, and thence to the village street. We here paused, and called each other in a low voice to make sure we were all together; for it was so intensely dark that we could not see a yard before us. It was necessary to guard against a possible ambush, for the villagers must have been aware that we were near their place on the preceding evening, and they knew that we could not venture to travel except along the main road of the country, which passed through their village. We then stepped forward, like desperate men resolved to fight for our lives to the last. We took the middle of the street, which was a very long one, treading cautiously, with our guns cocked, and ready at the slightest warning. At one house we heard people playing the wombi (native harp*) inside; we crossed lightly to the opposite side of the street,

* See, for description of this instrument, 'Adventures in Equatorial Africa.'

and passed without having alarmed the inmates. We then came near the end of the street, and were thinking that all danger was passed, when suddenly a bright fire blazed up right before us! As we stood motionless waiting for the next move, a kind voice spoke out in the darkness—"It is the Oguizi's people; go on! go on! there is no harm to you in my village; pass on! you will find the path smooth; there is no war for you!" It was the voice of the old king, who was thus, with some of his people, waiting our passage, with the good intention of speeding us on with kind words. They had got the materials for the fire ready beforehand to light us on our way. What a load was taken from our minds! We had expected here a deadly struggle, and found instead the road made clear for us. But we were not quite sure that some act of treachery might not be intended; so, instead of stopping to talk, we passed on without saying a word in reply to the kind speech of the chief.

On we went in the darkness of the night; through swamps and water courses, over stony hills and thorny brakes, often losing the path, and wandering about for some time before finding it again. At about three o'clock in the morning we came to a field of cassava. We halted, made a fire, gathered some of the roots, and roasted them to eat, for we had had no food since our flight began the preceding morning, and were quite worn out with fatigue and hunger. This renewed our strength, and I offered up a silent prayer to that gracious Providence who had so marvellously preserved my little band.

July 27th. A little before daylight (as soon as we could see our way through the forest), we resumed our march, Igala limping along with his lame leg, and I marching among the men encouraging them with hopeful words. After going a short distance we came to a place where two paths diverged, and a dispute arose amongst my men as to which was the right way. Rebouka, who was now leading us, fixed upon one way as the right one, and Ngoma declared the other was the proper path; he knew it, he said, by a monkey trap by the side of the road, which we had passed on coming to Niembouai Olomba. The majority declared in favour of Rebouka, and so we took his path.

We continued on this road till midday, when it was necessary to halt and make a search for something to eat, for we were all ravenous with hunger. Some of the men dispersed on foraging expeditions, and two of them soon returned successful, having found a small grove of plantains from which they gathered several bunches nearly ripe. We made a fire on the margins of a pretty rivulet under the shade of trees, cooked and ate our meal. Soon after, having resumed our onward march, we arrived at a small village surrounded by plantations, which we knew at once we had not seen on our outward journey. Ngoma was now triumphant, and Rebouka and his followers discomfited. I was obliged to interfere to put an end to their dispute, and we then boldly walked into the village and spoke to the people.

The place proved to be a plantation of one of the head men of Niembouai Olomba, next in influence to the king. He was a fine old fellow, with snow-white hair, and with that genial expression of features which is often seen in negroes of the better sort. He received us with great kindness, inviting us to stay and eat something; and, on our accepting his offer, ordered his women to cook us a fowl and some plantains. The women gave my men sugar-cane and mpegui nuts, and the old man apologized for not having a goat to offer us.

The people of the village naturally asked us why we had returned so soon. My men were not behind hand in satisfying their curiosity; but they took care to conceal the fact that we were the aggressors, though through no ill intention on our part. They said we had been attacked, and had had to fight our way back. Each of them boasted of his own feats and prowess, saying how many of the warriors of Mouaou Kombo he had beaten off.

Whilst we were thus engaged, our old guide Magouga came in. The arrival of this faithful old man was most fortunate for us. He proved himself to be a real friend in need. He had heard, when he got up in the morning at Niembouai, that we had passed in the middle of the night, and had immediately set off to overtake us. He must have walked very fast. He seemed overjoyed to see us, and said he had returned to Niembouai Olomba from Mobana, intending to remain until he had heard of our safe passage through the Njavi country; for he had anticipated that we should have great difficulties with the people of Upper Ashango-land, who were a bad set. He seemed really grateful for the services

I had rendered him at Mobana, in saving him from the fury of the people when they were excited about the robbery, and he said that, now we had come back, he would see us safe to the Ishogo country. Magouga seemed not to have heard a correct account of the Mouaou affair. All he knew was that the people had driven us away, and that we had killed many of their warriors. He told us that one of the men shot by Igala was the head warrior of Mobana, and that this was likely to be made a *casus belli* between the Mobana villagers and the people of Mouaou Kombo, who were held to be the cause of the death. The Mobanans were already cooking the "war dish"* in order to march against the village of Mouaou Kombo. It was evident from the confused statements of Magouga, that the country was all in a ferment behind us. He said the Mouaou people had abandoned their village and retired to the forest, fearing lest I should return and burn it. They said all the arrows they had shot at me would not pierce me, but had rebounded from my flesh; and they were filled with superstitious fears of the power of so mysterious a being. I must here add that my men and myself kept the fact of my having been wounded a secret from all the negroes on our homeward march; my men knew as well as myself how important it was

* The "war-dish" is the pot of magic herbs and fetiches which is cooked with a great deal of mystery and ceremony on the eve of going to meet an enemy. The mess is cooked in a very large vessel, and the affair is presided over, as a matter of course, by the most renowned fetich doctor of the tribe. So soon as the cooking is completed, the warriors swallow part of the contents of the vessel, and smear their bodies over with the rest; when they have succeeded in exciting themselves to the requisite pitch, they rush forth to attack the village they intend to *panda* (assault).

that I should maintain the reputation of being invulnerable; and it was universally believed that the arrows of the Ashangos glanced from my body without hurting me. Magouga said he had heard that at one time I had turned myself into a leopard, had hid myself in a tree, and had sprung upon the Mouaou people as they came to make war on my men; that at other times I turned myself into a gorilla, or into an elephant, and struck terror and death among the Mouaou and Mobana warriors. Magouga finished his story by asking me for a "war fetich," for he said I must possess the art of making fetiches, or I and my men could not have escaped so miraculously.

After a good rest and a hearty meal, we left the good old chief of the plantation-village, and continued our homeward march, now under the guidance of Magouga. On parting I gave the old chief a quantity of beads out of our remaining stock, and also a red powder flask, which latter present delighted him beyond measure, and he said he would keep it in remembrance of me. We were fortunate after all in taking the wrong path, for besides being led by it to the plantation of the hospitable old chief, we were enabled to avoid the village of Niongo, where, if we did not meet with obstacles, we should at least have been delayed in our journey.

CHAPTER XIX.

JOURNEY TO THE COAST.

Arrival at Mongon—Magouga recounts the Story of our Adventures to the Villagers—Reach Niembouai—Mistrust of the People—Restitution of Stolen Property—Magouga consents to guide us to Mokenga—Reach the last of the Ashango Villages—Passage into Ishogo-land, and out of danger of Pursuit—Magouga's Diplomacy—Arrival at Mokenga—Friendly Reception—Magouga delivers us safely into the hands of the Villagers—My Men exaggerate the Deeds of Valour they had performed—Arrival at Yengué—Project of descending the Ogoulou in a Canoe—Lose our Way—Distant View of the Apono Prairie—Igoumbié—Reach Mokaba—The Ngouyai—March to Nchiengain's—Cross the River—Nchiengain's Village—Reception at Máyolo—Operation of the African Law of Inheritance—March to Ashira-land—Alarm of the Ashira People—Avoid Olenda—Sojourn at Angouka's—Cross the Ofoubou—Quengueza's Encampment—Sorrows of the old King—Devastations of the Plague at Goumbi—Quengueza wants to go to the White Man's Country—Descend the River—Arrival at "Plateau"—Gratitude of the Commi People—Departure for England.

After parting from the Niembouai elder at his plantation-village we continued our journey towards the west, accompanied, as I have said, by Magouga. About half-past three p.m. we reached the village of Mongon, having taken a short cut by one of the numerous by-paths of the country, made by the people from one plantation to another.

On our way to Mongon we were very much amused by a crowd of chimpanzees in a wooded hollow. We were marching along the edge of a deep valley, when we were brought to a stand by the loud jabbering of what we thought was a multitude of people. Magouga was puzzled, for he knew there was no village near; we listened, and found the sounds proceeded from the dense woods in the valley beneath us. Through breaks in the foliage we presently saw the dusky forms of a number of chimpanzees, moving about, swaying the branches, and making the most ludicrous noises. On observing them attentively we found there were two groups, one of them stationed at some distance from the other, and the two appeared to be holding a conversation together, or hurling shouts of defiance backwards and forwards. There must have been thirty or forty of them together in the trees below us. I never before observed so many anthropoid apes together.

It was fortunate that we had Magouga with us, for the villagers of Mongon were thrown into great consternation at our unexpected arrival, and some of them were beginning to run away as we entered the village. I made the old man march at the head of our party, for I did not know what might happen. He shouted to the people to allay their fears, saying, "I am Magouga, do not be afraid, the Oguizi's people are going back." We made halt at the *ouandja* and were soon after surrounded by the people, all asking with looks of astonishment, "What does this mean? Why have you returned?" It appeared that news had arrived here that Magouga had been killed at Mobana, and his people had mourned for him.

Magouga was equal to the occasion. He made a long speech, narrating all the events in which he had performed a part, cursing the Niembouai people for stealing my goods, and describing how the Mobana villagers wanted to kill him. Then with regard to our affair at Mouaou Kombo he gave a most exaggerated account. He said the villagers had attacked us because they did not want us to pass; that we had killed eighteen of them, and that all the arrows shot at me had glanced off without doing me any harm; and then he again related the history of my various transformations. So well did he describe our misfortunes, that the Mongon people all took our part. "What a shame it is," said they, "that war should be made on such men, who do no harm, who take nothing by force, and bring us only good things." They said they would resist the Mouaou warriors if they came near their village. The women after this brought us fowls, eggs, and ripe plantains, which they exchanged with us for a few trinkets. We were pressingly invited to remain for the night in the village; but I thought this would be an imprudent proceeding, so I made an excuse. We left the place towards the evening, and, after marching three or four miles, slept in an abandoned plantation on the road to Niembouai West.

July 28th. We slept very little during the night, for neither myself nor my men considered we were yet quite out of danger of an attack. We lay down with our loaded weapons by our side, three of my men lying in the same hut with myself.

Rising at daylight we resumed our march, walking very rapidly till nearly noon, when we arrived at

Niembouni, where our guide resided. The same mistrust of our proceedings was shown here as at Mongon, but on recognising Magouga the villagers became reassured. Our excellent guide took us down the street to his own house; but we had little peace all the remainder of the day, for the people were eager to learn the particulars of the late events from the lips of the eloquent Magouga. The story as related by him waxed more sensational after each repetition; but what pleased the villagers most was the way in which he described us as saving his life when threatened by the Mobana people. At this there was tumultuous cheering, with shouts of "You are men! you are men! How can people make war on such men?"

July 29th. Notwithstanding the gush of popularity of the preceding evening, the Niembouni villagers have evidently not yet shaken off their distrust of me. Early in the morning I saw people casting furtive glances at me, and little groups of elders were observable at a distance from my hut, engaged in close confabulation. The cause of all this was made apparent shortly afterwards. The people were afraid that I should do something to them in revenge for the articles that had been stolen between Niembouni Olomba and Mobana, when I passed through their territory on the eastward journey. At length one of the negroes, who I suppose had been chosen to carry out the perilous mission, came and handed me a bottle partly filled with arsenic, saying that he was a stranger to the village, and that the bottle having been given to him as my property, he had come to return it. I learnt afterwards that my men had threatened the people with punishment if they did not restore the whole of the stolen property.

I had not intended to pass another night at Niembouai, and this distrust on the part of the people confirmed me in my determination. Magouga had, however, given us a goat, and it was necessary to remain until it was killed and cut up into pieces for convenience of carriage. Rumours of armed men being seen in the bush round the village circulated about in the course of the day, and the villagers pretended to be alarmed lest they should be attacked on account of us. At length we left the place, and after an easy march reached the village, mentioned in the earlier part of this narrative, which the Ashango and Njavi people share together.

We were again accompanied by our steady friend Magouga, who, after putting his house at Niembouai in order, announced his readiness to guide us safely as far as Mokenga. He was the only native who consented to accompany us out of the district belonging to his tribe, during any part of our journey towards the coast. There are very strong reasons why these people of the interior object to going far westward; they are liable to be detained and enslaved, and it never happens that an Ishogo or an Ashango man, who has once left his country for the sea-board tribes, returns to his native land. Perhaps they thought we might kidnap them. Besides, we had lost nearly all our property, and I was no longer the rich Oguizi that dazzled all people with my wealth on my outward march; it was therefore a most disinterested act on the part of Magouga to accompany us; for he could not have been attracted by the prospect of good pay or plunder.

The villagers here were this time exceedingly friendly, bringing us plantains, cooking-pots, calabashes of water, and firewood. However, we did not stay long at their village, but proceeded onward towards the west. About five o'clock we reached Moyego, a large Ashango village which we had passed on our march eastward without stopping at it, in opposition to the entreaties of the inhabitants. Magouga had friends living here, and as the villagers pressed us strongly to stay, and gave us many presents of food, we passed the night here. When they heard our account of the Mouaou affair they said that it was no concern of theirs, that the Mouaou people belonged to a different clan from them, and that they wished we had killed more of them.

July 30th. Continuing our march this morning, we reached before noon Magonga, the last, or most westerly, of the Ashango villages, situated on the banks of the Odigenga. I did not wish to make any stay here, so we marched through the village without stopping, much to the surprise and disappointment of the inhabitants, who were curious to know what had happened to cause our return to the coast. Magouga was very much annoyed because I would not stay, and said he would not go with us any further. I told him I did not want him, for we knew the road as well as he did. We crossed the Odiganga, and fixed our head-quarters on the other side of the stream, so that, in case of attack, we should have the stream between us and the people of Magonga, whom we had left in rather a bad humour. The villagers came to us, and we bought a few plantains and some provisions with the few beads that I had remaining. About two hours afterwards, as we were eating our dinner by the roadside on the path to Mokenga, Magouga made his appearance, making the excuse that he was obliged to pretend to be vexed with me, otherwise the villagers would have laid on him the blame of my not staying in their town; in future I was not to mind what he said when we were in a village; "Recollect," he said, "you go out of the country, but I remain in it, and must take care to keep friends with the people." This little anecdote shows how full of deceit and diplomacy these primitive Africans are, and how difficult it is to know when they are speaking the truth.

Since we had crossed the Odiganga we have been amongst the Ishogo tribe, and I felt for the first time that we were safe from fighting; we had quitted the territory of the tribe with whom we had had so deadly an encounter, and had placed a broad and rapid river with high banks between them and ourselves. The villagers on the western side of the Odiganga brought us a great number of articles for sale, denguis, fowls, bongos, fruit, and nuts, and wished us to stay; but we had resolved not to make any lengthened stay anywhere. We passed several Ishogo villages in succession, and in the evening arrived at a small plantation not far from Ayamba, or Diamba. We slept at the plantation, and on the following morning, after a march through the forest, reached the village.

July 31*st*. The Ishogo chief of Ayamba presented me with a goat. We were conducted by the villagers into the strangers' ouandja, where we cooked our morning meal. As usual we were much pressed by the people to remain a day or two with them, but I was firm in my determination to march on: we did not need porters, and knew the road, so were independent of them all. I had declined to stay at Ayamba on my outward march, and the people recalled this to mind, saying that they believed their place must be bewitched, as I had refused both times to stay in it. Magouga repeated his old game of pretending to be dreadfully angry with me for not staying, but of course I took no notice of him this time, except to laugh at the trick.

In the afternoon we reached the good village of Mokenga. The astonishment of the inhabitants at our return was unbounded. We were soon surrounded by an eager crowd, all asking questions, and Magouga became at once a man of great importance. It filled him with pride to be able to say to the villagers, when order was somewhat restored, and all were ready to listen to his account of our journey, "Here we are, people of Mokenga! Your men gave into my hands the Ibamba and his people at Niembouni, and now I give you them back in safety." In narrating the events of the past few weeks he repeated the little troubles he had had at Niembouni and Mobana, and when he came to the Mouaou Kombo business he got quite eloquent, and made a most exciting story of it. I found that he had gradually increased the number of the people we had killed. . At the last place where he told his tale eighteen was the number; he now stated it was thirty. My Commi men were just the same. Modest and tolerably accurate at first, before we were quit of the Ashango territory, they now began to boast frightfully of the deeds of valour they had enacted. Like Sir John Falstaff, they gradually augmented the number they had slain with their own hand. Each of them declared in turn that he had killed several of the enemy, and Mouitchi, who had sneaked into the forest at the commencement, and had taken no part in the struggle, was more boastful than any of them. He was firm in his statement that he had killed five with his own hand. The further we travelled from the scene of action, the more my valiant Commi boys exaggerated the number they had slain; until at Quengueza's the total had reached the fearful figure of 150.

The sympathy and hospitality shown to us by the Mokenga people, after the speech of Magouga, were quite remarkable. Old Mokounga, our former Ishogo head guide, took me to his own house, saying I was his guest and must stay with him, and the villagers invited my men to stay with them. Sugar-cane, plantains, and ground-nuts were brought to us and given to my people; Mokounga gave me a goat; kettles and firewood were brought to us to cook our food; in short, the kind-hearted people seemed to be sincerely happy to see us back amongst them, and I felt happy myself.

August 1st—3rd. We remained at Mokenga three days, as we all required rest, and I had another motive for staying in the great pleasure which it gave to the villagers who had been so kind to us. Mokounga, I was sorry to find, suffered greatly from sore legs; they were much swollen, and discharged a quantity of watery humour. It was fortunate that the rumour about my causing sickness in every one who came in contact with me had not reached these Ishogo people. Mokounga told us that the disease in his legs made its appearance two or three days after he left me on the outward journey, and he attributed it, as usual, to some one having bewitched him through jealousy of my friendship. On the night of my arrival there was a slow beating of drums and mournful singing in one of the houses of the village—a sign that some one lay dead there. I was told it was a woman who died three days previously: the next morning the corpse was carried away to the cemetery in the woods. I was pleased to find that the people here were not so much afraid of death as the tribes nearer the sea; they do not abandon a village when a death occurs. Indeed, the villages are so large that this custom would be very difficult to keep up. Mokenga is, I think, the most southerly village of the Ishogo tribe, who occupy a narrow territory extending for about 150 miles from the north-west to the south-east, running nearly parallel to the large Ngouyai river. The country of this tribe must begin very near the banks of the Rembo Okanda.

The Ashango occupy about the same *length* of territory, but theirs is a much *broader* tract of land. Both tribes, and the Aponos also, are bordered on the south by the Njavi people; these latter being also found beyond the Ashango.

August 4th. We left the village this morning, followed by the best wishes of the Mokenga people, but none of them accompanied us. As we disappeared in the forest, they shouted after us, "Come again! come again, Oguizi, and bring us trade!" Old Magouga, who, notwithstanding all his tricks and odd ways, had been a faithful friend to us, remained here. I made a parting present both to him and Mokounga. They accompanied us to the woods through which the path led, and in bidding us adieu, shouted "Come again! come again!"

After a short march we arrived at the village of Yengué, charmingly situated on the banks of the beautiful Eckmühl, or Ogoulou River. As soon as we made our appearance, the villagers brought their canoes to ferry us across, and all of them, like the inhabitants of other places we had passed, asked the reasons of our coming back. When we told them our tale, they said they wished we had killed all the Mouaou warriors. "How could such far-away people know the value of the good things you brought them?" said they; "and how could such men of the bush understand your fashions?" We were surrounded by such a crowd of people that we were glad to get out of the village, and cook our morning meal in a retired place on the road-side.

I had some thoughts of purchasing a canoe at Yengué, and travelling down the Eckmühl into the

Ngouyai, and thence to the Apono country; but on stating my intentions to some of the villagers they told me that there was a waterfall a few miles below the village, and that it would be necessary to pass our canoe by land round the obstruction. We could not, however, get any very exact information about the river; and, fearing there might be other difficulties, I gave up the plan, and decided to travel back by the same path by which we had come.

We were now travelling without a guide, for no one was willing to accompany us after Magouga had left us. As a natural consequence, we had not gone far before we lost our way. The path we took led us to an Apono village which we had not seen before; it was beautifully situated on the top of one of the hills which form the last and lowest range of the mountains we had come from. From the village we had a wide prospect over the prairie of the Apono country, the yellow colour of which contrasted strongly with the dark-green hues of the forest that clothed the hilly ranges. The view extended to the other side of the prairie, where we could see the mountain-range which divides the Otando from the Ashira Ngozai territories. A stretch of country, moderately hilly and covered with forest, extended between our position and the yellow prairie.

The villagers fled at our approach, but we luckily found Dibako, a Mokaba man who had been one of our porters in our eastward journey, and he proved a true friend in need to us. After we had rested a while and refreshed ourselves with a drink of limpid water—for we felt the heat severely after descending from the hilly country—he volunteered to guide us to the right road, and a little before sunset we reached with his aid the village of Igoumbié.

August 5th. We left Igoumbié to-day, to the great sorrow of the villagers, who wished me to stay longer with them. Our Apono guide continued in our company.

The Ishogos, notwithstanding their many faults, are the kindest-hearted and the gentlest negroes I ever met with. As soon as my men had shouldered their "otaitais," and the people saw that we were ready to start, the whole population came out. This time we had to pass through the whole length of the village. They followed behind us—the women were the most conspicuous. They all shouted out, "Go on well, go on well; nothing bad shall happen to you!" When we reached the end of the village, and just before turning into the path that would take us out of their sight, I turned round, and, taking off the remnant of what was once a good hat, I waved it in the air. Immediately a dead silence succeeded the noise, and I shouted, "Farewell, good Ishogos!" As I disappeared from their view among the trees of the forest we were entering, suddenly a wild and sorrowful shout of the multitude reached our ears. They all cried out with one voice, "We shall see the good Oguizi no more! We shall see the good Oguizi no more!" Then all became again silent, and once more we trod the path of this gigantic jungle on our way to the sea-shore.

On leaving Igoumbié we took a different road from that which we had followed in our eastward journey. After about three hours' walk, we emerged on the open grassy hills which form the eastern boundary of the Apono country. After marching past numerous Apono villages on the western side of these hills, we reached in the afternoon the village of Mokaba. On the road, in a solitary part of the prairie, we passed by a tall pole with the head of a man stuck at the top, to all appearance quite recently placed there. My men passed the place with a quiver of horror, for they guessed what this ghastly object meant. We were told by our guide that it was the head of one of the chiefs, who had been decapitated on suspicion of being a wizard—another victim to the horrid superstitions of these people. The head had been placed on a pole by the road-side as a warning to all who approached Mokaba.

I was glad to find that the palm-wine season was now over, and the Mokaba villagers constrained to be much more sober than they were on my former visit. The palm-trees had nearly finished blooming, and the ascending sap, which supplies the fermentable liquor, no longer flowed in sufficient quantity. My old friend Kombila was the only one who had liquor enough to get drunk upon, and he was so harmless over his cups that I had no annoyance from him.

Late in the afternoon I took a walk into the prairie, which extends for a long distance in the neighbourhood of Mokaba. I cannot express the pleasure I felt in being once more in open country. I seemed to breathe freer; the eye wandered far away over a vast expanse, and the sensation was delightful after being confined so long in the dark forests of Ishogo and Ashango-land. To feel the wind fanning one's face was a luxury that had long been denied me. As I traversed the paths which led over the grassy expanse, my mind wandered to former scenes, the fields of my native country, and I longed to be back. What dangers had I not passed through since I left England on this mission! Perils by water, fire, pestilence, and war. With a grateful heart I thanked Him who had watched over the lonely traveller who had trusted in Him.

As I wandered along, occupied with these thoughts, the day declined and the sun set. It did not, however, become dark, for a bright moonlight shone over the landscape, and the evening was most enjoyable. Gradually I retraced my steps towards Mokaba.

August 6th. The crowd and noise in the village were so annoying that I was obliged this morning to leave the place and establish myself on the banks of the Ngouyai, which flows about a mile-and-a-half to the west of Mokaba. I did not know, when on our eastward march, that the town was so near to the river. At this time of the year the Ngouyai has but a feeble current; I was told by the Mokaba people, that further up stream, in the Njavi country, the river was narrower and encumbered with rocks and rapids. Although it was now towards the end of the dry season there were no hippopotami to be seen in the river. It appeared to me now that I might save the toilsome walk over the stony prairie by navigating the stream down to Nchiengain's village. I tried therefore to hire a canoe from the Mokaba people, offering a good price for the use of it. The wiseheads of the village took the matter into consideration, but I could not prevail upon them to lend me the canoe. They did not think they should see it again, and they would not accompany me to Nchiengain's and return with the canoe. There was the same disinclination shown here to travelling with me, as I have described before; they were all afraid that I should sell them as slaves when I had got them out of their territory. They were willing to sell me the canoe outright, but I was now too poor to buy it.

Before I left Mokaba, Kombila made me a farewell speech, and entreated me to come back again and bring trade. All the elders, who stood around us, backed up the prayer; "We want trade," they said, "we love the white man's things; oh! why are we so far from the white man's country?"

On our march to Nchiengain's, we passed the village of Dilalo, where, on our eastward march, the inhabitants had set fire to the prairie to oppose our progress. A crowd of women came after us as we took the path leading outside of the place, and besought us to come in and rest ourselves in the village. They wanted beads, they said, like the women of the other towns, and when I persisted in my refusal to enter a place where we had been treated so ill, they set to cursing their own men for being the cause of it all.

We slept at night in a beautiful little wood by the banks of a pleasant stream.

August 7th. We passed several villages early in

the morning, followed by crowds of the inhabitants all begging us to stay with them, and creating a deafening uproar by their shouts. On reaching the banks of the river, we persuaded two Apingi men, who were coming down in a small canoe, to fetch for us Nchiengain's large ferry-boat which lay on the opposite side. When we had crossed the river, my men fired their muskets as a signal of our approach; and we had not marched far, before we saw the old chief advancing to meet us, followed by the greater part of the inhabitants of the village. Nchiengain held a sword in his hand, and his men carried their spears and bows, all to give *éclat* to our reception. One would have thought it was a war party coming out to meet an enemy, and some of my men were at first afraid.

The good old fellow hugged me in his arms and seemed overjoyed to see me. News of what had happened had already reached him, and he had expected soon to see us back. He joyfully told me that he and his people had been all well since my departure, and that he knew now I did not bring disease and death with me. He gave me also the welcome news that Máyolo had recovered from the illness which had seized him when at Mokaba. I was struck by the scantiness and shabbiness of the grass-cloth clothing of the Apono and Apingi people here, after being so long amongst the well-dressed Ishogos and Ashangos, with their fine bongos and ample denguis.

We remained six days enjoying the hospitality of Nchiengain, a delay that was very necessary on account of our exhausted state; I and Igala had suffered the most, and this welcome rest was necessary to us. The climate is much warmer in the valley of the Ngouyai; and during our stay we could see dark clouds gathering over the Ashango Mountains, sure signs that the rainy season was near at hand. The Aponos said that within a month the rains would come.

On the 13th of August, at daylight, we left Nchiengain's village for Máyolo. I am not sure, however, about the day, for I had missed my reckoning. Since my sextant was lost on the first day of the retreat from Mouaou Kombo, I have of course taken no observations, which used to enable me, by the help of the 'Nautical Almanack,' to know the day of the month. No Apono people accompanied us, and we were attended only by two of Máyolo's sons and one of his people, who came to Nchiengain's to meet us. At half-past seven a.m. we reached the river Dooya, which is at this season the only stream on the road that is not dried up; we therefore stopped here for breakfast, although it was so much earlier than the hour at which we usually took that meal. We reached Máyolo in the afternoon. Old Máyolo came to meet us attended by a crowd of villagers; he was looking plump and hearty. Presents were made to me of a native cap and several bongos; this is a custom with this people when they wish to welcome a friend who has returned safe from a long journey. I found that the small-pox had again made its appearance in Máyolo in the height of the dry season; and, as Rapelina, one of my Commi men, had not had the disease, we established our olakos or sheds outside the village.

Old Máyolo was so much impressed with the account of our affray with the Mouaou people and our escape from their poisoned arrows, killing at the same time so many of them—for, as I have said before, my men exaggerated more and more at every place the number we had slain—that he firmly believed some potent talisman had protected us in the fight. The morning after our arrival he came into my shed in a mysterious manner, looking about to see that no one was near us, and said, "Chaillie, you are an Oguizi, and I know you can make mondahs, although you say you do not. How could the arrows of the Ashango glide off your body without hurting you, if you had not a war fetich on you? and how could you kill so many without any of your men being killed? I cannot understand this, for I know that the Ashangos are great warriors. If you love me, make one of these great war mondahs for me, that I and my people may go into the fight without being hurt, and that everybody may be made afraid of Máyolo." The earnestness of manner and excitement of the old man were quite ludicrous. I entirely failed to persuade him that I had no such mondah, and still more incredulous was he when I said that our safety was due to a kind Providence who had watched over us. He left me at last dissatisfied, and questioned my men; Igala was quite ready to make and sell to him any amount of fetiches.

I had an opportunity during my stay in Máyolo of observing how the curious law of inheritance existing amongst these tribes is carried out. Oshoumouna, the nephew and heir of Máyolo, had died of small-pox since my departure from Máyolo for the interior, leaving two wives—one young and good-looking, the other old and ugly. These wives of Oshoumouna I knew very well, for I had given one of them a coat for her husband on my former visit, and had often bought plantains of the other. To my surprise I found one of them now married to Máyolo and looking quite joyous, dressed in her best; the other was married to Ikala, Oshoumouna's younger brother. According to my notions of African law, Ikala ought to have inherited all the property of his deceased brother, including the pick of the wives. I asked why this had not taken place, and was told that it is the older brother who inherits the property of his younger brothers in the event of their decease, and not *vice versâ*. If Ikala had died first, Oshoumouna would have taken his wives and all the rest of his property, but, as the case stood, Oshoumouna having no elder brother, his uncle Máyolo had the right of dividing the property as he thought fit; but with the understanding that some of the wives must be given to the younger brother. My Commi men and several of the Otando people criticised rather sharply old Máyolo's appropriation of the pretty wife; they thought he was greedy in wanting all the best things for himself.

I was much amused one evening at Máyolo, whilst my men and a number of villagers were lying about the fires near our encampment, by a story or parable related by a very talkative old fellow who seemed to be the wag of the village. It was as follows:—

AKENDA MBANI.

Redjioua had a daughter called Arondo, and she was very beautiful. Redjioua said, "A man may give me slaves, goods, or ivory to marry my daughter, but he will not get her; I want only a man that will agree that when Arondo falls ill, he will fall ill also, and that when Arondo dies, he will die also." Time went on; and, as people knew this, no one came to ask Arondo in marriage; but, one day, a man called Akenda Mbani ("never goes twice to the same place") came, and he said to Redjioua, "I come to marry Arondo, your daughter; I come, because I will agree that when Arondo dies, I will die also." So Akenda Mbani married Arondo. Akenda Mbani was a great hunter, and, after he had married Arondo, he went hunting, and killed two wild boars. On his return, he said, "I have killed two boars, and bring you one." Redjioua said, "Go and fetch the other." Akenda Mbani said, "My father gave me a *nconi* (a law) that I must never go twice to the same place." Another day he went hunting again, and killed two antelopes; on his return, he said to Redjioua, "Father, I have killed two kambi (antelopes), I bring you one." The king answered, "Please, my son-in-law, go and fetch the other." He answered, "You know I cannot go twice to the same place."

Another time he went hunting again, and killed

two bongos (a kind of antelope). Then Redjioua, who saw that all the other animals were being lost, said, "Please, my son-in-law, show the people the place where the other bongo is." Akenda Mbani replied, "If I do so I am afraid I shall die."

In the evening of the same day, a canoe from the Oroungou country came with goods, and remained on the river side. Akenda Mbani said to his wife Arondo, "Let us go and meet the Oroungous." They saw them, and then took a box full of goods and then went back to their own house. The people of the village traded with the Oroungous; and, when the Oroungous wanted to go back, they came to Akenda Mbani, and he trusted them ten slaves, and gave them a present of two goats, and many bunches of plantains, mats, and fowls; then the Oroungous left. Months went on; but, one day, Arondo said to her husband, "We have never opened the box that came with the Oroungous. Let us see what there is in it." They opened it, and saw cloth; then Arondo said, "Husband, cut me two fathoms of it, for I like it." Then they left the room; then Arondo seated herself on the bed, and Akenda Mbani on a stool, when suddenly Arondo said, "Husband, I begin to have a headache." Akenda Mbani said, "Ah, ah, Arondo, do you want me to die?" and he looked Arondo steadily in the face. He tied a bandage round her head, and did the same to his own. Arondo began to cry as her headache became worse; and, when the people of the village heard her cry, they came all round her. Redjioua came, and said, "Do not cry my daughter; you will not die." Then

Arondo said, "Father, why do you say I shall not die? for, if you fear death, you may be sure it will come."* She had hardly said these words than she expired. Then all the people mourned, and Redjioua said, "Now my daughter is dead, Akenda Mbani must die also."

The place where people are buried is called Djimai; the villagers went there and dug a place for the two corpses, which were buried together. Redjioua had a slave buried with Arondo, besides a tusk of an elephant, rings, mats, plates, and the bed on which Akenda Mbani and Arondo slept; the cutlass, the hunting bag, and the spear of Akenda Mbani were also buried. The people then said, "Let us cover the things with sand, and make a little mound." When Agambouni (the mouth-piece—the speaker of the village) heard of this, he said to Redjioua, "There are leopards here." Then Redjioua said, "Do not have a mound over my child's burial-place, for fear that the leopards might come and scratch the ground and eat the corpse of my child." Then the people said, "Let us then dig a deeper hole," and they took away Arondo and Akenda Mbani, and placed both on stools, and then dug and dug, and put back the things that were to be buried with Arondo, and then laid her in her place. Then they came to Akenda Mbani, who then awoke and said, "I never go twice to the same place; you put me in the tomb and you took me away from it, though all of you know that I never go to the same place

* When an African is ill, his friends consider it will cause his death to say he will die.

again." When Redjioua heard of this he became very angry, and said, "You knew that Akenda Mbani never goes twice to the same place; why did you remove him?" Then he ordered the people to catch Agambouai, and cut his head off.

MORAL.

Formerly it was the custom with married people that when the woman died the man should die also, and *vice versâ*. But since the time of Akenda Mbani, the custom is altered, and the husband or the wife no longer die with their partners.

We left Máyolo at daylight on the 16th of August, my men being all heavily-laden with plantains, for we could not prevail upon any of the Otando people to accompany us, and help in carrying our loads. I felt quite grieved when even the good Máyolo—to whom I had given so many presents, and with whom I had remained so long—refused to accompany me outside the village. As we left, sheet-lightning was playing through the dark clouds which hung over the mountains of Ashango-land.

On the fourth day of our toilsome march over the rugged hills and through the dark forests of the mountain range which divides Ashira from Otando-land, we arrived in the afternoon at the first plantations of the Ashira Ngozai people. Before we saw the cultivated places we heard the axes ringing through the forests, showing that the natives were hard at work felling trees for new plantations; this being the time of the year—the height of the dry season—when such work is done, the dry weather being favourable to the burning of the felled trees. Planting begins a few days after the trees have been burnt, with the first rains. My men had by this time eaten all their stock of plantains, and we were beginning to suffer from the want of food. We did not know how the Ashira people would receive us, after the very unsatisfactory way in which Mintcho and his party had parted from us at Máyolo. I thought it best therefore to avoid meeting with them if it were possible. We helped ourselves to a few plantains from the trees, sufficient for our present wants, and marched on. Passing the place where we had left Macondai ill of the small-pox, we continued our march, and just before nightfall reached the Olenda slave-village which I described in the account of our eastward journey. This I was determined to pass without stopping or having any dealings with the people; so, ordering my men to have their guns in readiness if any attempt should be made to stop us, we marched on, the people shouting after us as soon as they knew who we were. We got free of the village at last, and pushed on for the banks of the Ovigui. We were all exhausted with fatigue, and some of my men wanted to lie down and sleep by the roadside. I encouraged them, however, to keep up, and at last we reached the river side. It was then quite dark; we made a fire, roasted our plantains for supper, and then lay down to sleep.

Rising at the first peep of day, after a restless night, I was surprised to find the Ovigui quite low, and easily fordable. The stream, which had been so formidable to cross in the rainy season, was now reduced to a mere shallow brook, with water reaching only to the knee. We crossed it, and entered upon the open prairie before it was yet quite light. I had half a mind to proceed straight to Olenda and, taking the inhabitants unawares, to seize some of the principal thieves of my property; but on second thoughts I judged it best to avoid the place altogether, and cross the prairie to the village of my friend Angouka. In our march we passed near to the deserted village of my old enemy Mpoto, who died of the small-pox during those terrible days of February and March. My men looked upon the abandoned cluster of huts as a place accursed, and took care to give it a wide berth in passing.

All the Ashira people whom we had seen since leaving the slave-plantation the previous evening had fled from us at the first sight, so that we held no communication with any one till Angouka's men came to meet us. We had fired guns on approaching the village, and this was answered by a number of the chief's people coming out of the grove which surrounds the place, armed to the teeth, to see who it was that was coming. When they recognised us they could scarcely contain their joy. We were led amid shouts of welcome to the house which Angouka had built for me when he expected me to stay with him on my outward march. Angouka has now a feud with the Ademba clan (Olenda's) of his tribe; he hates them most bitterly; he is a harsh-tempered man, but has acted in the most loyal and friendly way towards me, so that I cannot help liking him.

We remained fourteen days at Angouka's place. The day after my arrival I was laid up with a severe attack of fever, the effect probably of the weeks of toil, anxiety, and privation I had undergone since the disastrous day at Mouaou Kombo. The fever yielded on the fourth day to the frequent and large doses of quinine which I took, but it left me so weak that I was unable to walk far for several days afterwards. The people of Olenda were all this time in great fear lest I should take vengeance on them for their misdeeds; indeed, after my recovery, Angouka made a proposition to me to join my men in burning the village. This I declined, and preferred to lay the whole case before my staunch and powerful old friend Quengueza, who would, I was sure, punish the tricky knaves much more effectually than I should, if he thought it was necessary. In the end, the leading men of Olenda sent to offer to compound for their sins by giving me slaves, and asked how many I should be satisfied with. This offer of course I refused to listen to.

We left Angouka's on the 10th of September, the first hour of our march being through the magnificent groves of plantain-trees, which this industrious and energetic old chief has established near his village. Continuing our journey, we came to a cluster of abandoned olakos which had been tenanted by Bakalai. The place must have been abandoned in hot haste, for mosquito-nets had been left hanging under the sheds, and on raising one of them I was struck with horror to see the skeleton of a man lying under it. On the road, in many places, we saw human skulls and bones, sad evidence of the ravages of the plague, and showing how many had died in the forest on their march from one place to another, their bones gnawed and scattered by prowling hyenas and leopards.

We missed the path during the journey, and were guided only by knowing that we were going in the right direction for the Ofoubou by the compass; finally, we reached the banks of this river, but at a point much lower down than the village of Galipadi. Whilst at Angouka's, we had received a message from Quengueza, saying that, when his people came back from Goumbi, he would send some of them to me. He was staying on the banks of this river cutting ebony and deciding palavers amongst the Bakalai, and we now endeavoured to make our arrival known to him, by marching along the banks and firing our guns. At length our signals were heard: we saw a canoe approach the place where we stood, and on its approach recognised Nchéyouélai, one of the king's principal slaves. The water of this river was very low; we had to go some distance before arriving at Quengueza's encampment. On reaching it we were received with a most hearty welcome; the loyal old chief hugged me to his breast, and I am sure I reciprocated the joy he felt at our meeting. He beat his *kendo*, and, in a kind of solemn chant, thanked the spirits of his ancestors for my safe arrival.

Sholomba of my own village was here, and some other negroes whom I knew. Nothing could be done until they had heard the story of our adventures. My men did not wait for me to tell the tale; but began their own story. As they proceeded, they waxed warmer and warmer, rising and gesticulating to show how they surrounded the enemy, and how they slew them all, one after another. The more the narrators exaggerated, the more they were applauded by the other men, until all with one accord shouted, "We have slain 150 of our enemies!" This story Quengueza would not believe, and said he would not be satisfied until he had heard the whole account from my own mouth; "for," added he, "I have heard from the Ashira the tale of the 150 dead men, and I did not believe them." So all of them assembled round me, and I gave them a faithful account of the whole affair. They all listened very attentively, and at the most stirring parts of the narrative, when I described our turning in the forest path and facing the crowd of enraged warriors, they clasped their hands and cried out, "You are men! you are men!"

In return, Quengueza narrated to me the events that had happened since his parting from me at Olenda. It was a most sorrowful story. The *evira*, or small-pox, broke out at Goumbi whilst Quengueza was still at Olenda, and his departure was hastened by the news brought to him of the plague. It had caused fearful havoc; relatives, wives, slaves, all had caught the infection and nearly all had died. Goumbi was obliged to be forsaken. For many weeks the old chief, with the relics of his clan, lived in temporary abodes or olakos on the opposite side of the river. Quengueza believed that if he had not returned home at the time he did, his beloved son Kombé would also have died. The old man was greatly affected at the remembrance of his losses and the death of so many that were dear to him; and I could not help feeling sympathy for him. "The Bakalai," said he, "are all gone; the Rembo people are all gone; my beloved Monbon (his head slave) is dead; I am alone in the world." It appeared that he had not even entered Goumbi since he left me at Olenda; but, finding the plague raging there on his return, he had established his home on the opposite bank of the river, and his nephews, who had accompanied him and me to Ashira-land, together with most of his men, had died. I looked with sadness on his noble figure, with his hoary head whitened by years and bowed down with the remembrance of his troubles, and I grieved for him from the bottom of my heart. He was like an old oak of the forest left standing alone, after all its companions had been overthrown by the storm. We spent the evening by the side of the fires of our encampment, Quengueza and myself side by side, talking over our troubles, and my men telling the story of their adventures to their Rembo comrades, this time in more moderate terms.

We spent several days at Quengueza's encampment. I had great difficulty during this time in combating a tendency to sleepiness and lethargy, which had come over me since we had arrived safely amongst our friends. We all suffered much from hunger in the encampment, as food was scarce in this depopulated country. At length, news came that a vessel had arrived off the mouth of the Fernand Vaz, and I was seized with an uncontrollable desire to get away at once to the sea-shore.

The canoes were not able to take the whole of our party at once, including Quengueza's wives, ebony, and slaves; so we agreed that I should go first and wait for him at Goumbi. When we departed, the old chief told me to call at Obindji's town to bid good bye to Njambai, the present chief; Obindji being no more, for he was one of the victims of the plague.

We glided down the now placid waters of the Ovenga, passing the many Bakalai villages; the numerous abandoned houses bore sorrowful witness of the devastations of the fearful scourge that had swept over this part of the country. We slept at night on the banks of the river, and the next morning passed by the ruins of Goumbi; no longer the flourishing well-peopled village it used to be, but a mere crowd of half-ruined, burnt, and deserted houses. Quengueza's new settlement was a little further down the river, and the place was called Sangatanga. Almost every one we met bore traces on his or her face of the ravages of the small-pox; and there was not one who had not lost a near relative during these unhappy times. In fact, the Abouya clan of the Commi is almost destroyed; in a few years there will be nothing left of this people, once the most important clan of the Rembo.

I visited Goumbi after my arrival at Sangatanga. The aspect of the place filled my heart with sadness; even the gentle breeze whispering through the plantain groves seemed to me a mournful sound. I looked for the house of my good old friend Adouma, who on my former journey took me to the Apingi country;

nothing was left of it but a few poles, and it was the same with the habitations of many other negroes who had formerly been good friends to me; the owners were dead, and their houses were in ruins. The little fetich-houses in their neighbourhood remained standing, with their talismanic creepers growing round them, but there was no one to take care of them; I took the opportunity to lecture the negroes who were with me, on the folly of believing in these fetiches, which they might see had no power to avert the calamity that had overtaken their owners.

Soon after this, Quengueza himself arrived with all his followers, in their canoes. Many of the survivors of his clan had been trying to make him suspect witchcraft as being at the bottom of the misfortunes that had befallen him, and were crying out for the pona ogangn to sacrifice more victims and still further reduce the numbers of the people. But the old man would not listen to these miserable croakers. I was glad to see him resist all their appeals; he said there was no witchcraft in this plague, but it was a "wind sent by Aniambié (God)." "Enough people had died," he continued, "and we must not kill any more."

The old chief seemed to have lost heart completely, and was thinking of leaving his country for good. "If I was a young man," he said, "I would go with you to the white man's country; and even old as I am, if your country was not so far off, I would go with you. If it was no further than the Mpongwé country (the Gaboon), or Fernando Po"—for he had heard of this place, although he had a very indistinct notion where it was—"I would leave the Rembo and go and live with you. You have escaped the plague and the arrows of the Ashangos; you will reach your land, but remember that your old friend will always think of you." When I finally bade him adieu, he tried to make me promise to come back and stay with him. "Come again," he said, "and go no more into the bush; and when you come bring me a big bell, a sword with a silver handle that will not rust, and two chests, one of brass and another of ebony, for I want to see how you work the wood that we send to you."

We arrived at my own place, "Plateau," on the 21st of September. It is impossible to describe the joy which the people showed on seeing us all come back in safety, for, with the exception of Igala's wound in the leg which was still inflamed, discharging sometimes a good deal of matter, none of my Commi boys was the worse for the journey they had accomplished.

In the evening of the day of our arrival, as I was taking a solitary walk over the open prairie towards the sea, the sister of Igala came to speak to me. With tears coursing down her cheeks, she said, "White man! with a good heart you have taken care of our people. You did not let them die of the plague. On the day of fight you stood by them. No wonder that we love you; you are as one of ourselves; you do not drive us away from you." This unaffected demonstration of gratitude, I must say, made me feel well rewarded for all the care I had taken of my loyal Commi boys. With the exception of the little outburst at Niembouai of Mouitchi and Rapelina—whom we must excuse as having been slaves all their lives and knowing no better, indeed they were afterwards ashamed of their misconduct—I am proud and grateful to think of the fidelity, honesty, steadiness, and pluck displayed throughout the journey, by these sharers of my labours. I need scarcely say that I felt also proud and glad that I was able to bring back all my men, with the exception of Retonda, who died of disease, safe and sound to their families and friends. They had shown so much confidence in me, in volunteering to accompany me on the expedition, which they were told would be likely to occupy two or three years, that it was a source of pride to me to be able to show the Commi people that their confidence had not been misplaced.

The vessel at the mouth of the river was the Maranee, Captain Pitts, and was loading for London. I had lost nearly all my property in the disastrous flight from Ashango-land, and the house and store which I had built at "Plateau" I had made a present of to the American missionaries of the Gaboon, who wished to establish there a native Christian teacher. I had, therefore, neither money nor property; but Captain Pitts kindly consented to take me as passenger. We set sail six days after my arrival.

And thus I quitted the shores of Western Equatorial Africa with the blessings and good wishes of its inhabitants, whose character displays so curious a mixture of evil qualities and virtues of no mean order. Whether I shall ever return to the land where I have laboured so hard in endeavouring to extend the bounds of our knowledge, is doubtful; but I shall bear a kindly remembrance of the country and its inhabitants as long as I live.

CHAPTER XX.

PHYSICAL GEOGRAPHY AND CLIMATE.

Great Forest of Equatorial Africa—Scanty population—Scarcity or absence of large African animals—Hilly ranges—River systems—The Ogobai—French exploring expeditions—Amount of rain—Seasons—Rainy climate of Central Equatorial Africa—Temperature—Heat of the sun's rays—Coolness of the forest shades.

EQUATORIAL Africa from the western coast, as far as I have been, is covered with an almost impenetrable jungle. This jungle begins where the sea ceases to beat its continual waves, and how much further this woody belt extends, further explorations alone will be able to show. From my furthest point it extended eastward as far as my eyes could reach; I may, however, say that, near the banks of a large river running from a north-east direction towards the south-west, prairie lands were to be seen, according to the accounts the Ashangos had received.

This gigantic forest extends north and south of the Equator, varying in breadth from two to three degrees on each side of it.* South of the Equator, it ex-

* All the living plants collected on my return to the coast, I presented to Dr. J. D. Hooker, for the Royal Botanic Gardens at Kew, of which he is the able Director. I am very glad to find that one of the orchids I collected near Goumbi proved a new species of *Angræcum*; and Dr. Hooker has done me the honour to name it after me. Orchidaceous plants are abundant in the tracts of woodland near the sea; but they were less plentiful in the interior.

tended much further southerly than I have been, and on the north it reached further than I travelled in my former journey. Now and then prairies looking like islands, resembling so many gems, are found in the midst of this dark sea of everlasting foliage, and how grateful my eyes met them no one can conceive, unless he has lived in such a solitude.

Now and then prairies are seen from the sea-shore; but they do not extend far inland, and are merely sandy patches left by the sea in the progress of time.

In this great woody wilderness man is scattered and divided into a great number of tribes. The forest, thinly inhabited by man, was still more scantily inhabited by beasts. There were no beasts of burden—neither horse, camel, donkey, nor cattle. Men and women were the only carriers of burden. Beasts of burden could not live, for the country was not well adapted for them. The only truly domesticated animals were goats and fowls—the goats increasing in number as I advanced into the interior, and the fowls decreasing.

I was struck by the absence of those species of animals always found in great number in almost every other part of Africa. Neither lions, rhinoceroses, zebras, giraffes, nor ostriches were found, and the great variety of elands and gazelles (although found almost everywhere else in Africa) were not to be seen there. Travellers in my locality would never dream that such vast herds of game could be found on the same continent as those described by different travellers. Hence large carnivorous animals are scarce; leopards and two or three species of hyenas and jackals only being found. Little nocturnal animals are more common, but they are very difficult to get at. Reptiles abound in the forest. There are a great many species of snakes, the greater part of which are very poisonous. Some are ground-snakes, others spend part of their lives upon trees, while some are water-snakes. Among the ground-snakes one of the most to be dreaded is the *Clotho nasicornis*. There are several species of *Echis* and of *Atheris*; these are generally found upon trees; they are small and very venomous. A very dangerous snake is the black variety of the cobra (*Dendraspis angusticeps*). This snake is much dreaded, for, when surprised or attacked, it rises up as if ready to spring upon you. There is also a large water-snake found often in the beautiful clear water of the streams of the interior, described by Dr. Gunther under the name of *Siturophaga grayii*. I have often seen this snake coiled up and resting on the branches of trees under water.

Lizards are also abundant in some districts, and it is amusing to watch how they prey on the insect world. Among them I noticed a night species, that lives in the houses, and which is the great enemy of cockroaches. They are continually moving from one place to another during the night in search of their prey. During the day they remain perfectly still, and hide themselves between the bark of trees forming the walls of the huts.

The country is also very rich in spiders; they are of wonderful diversity of form. Some of them are so large, and their webs so strong, that birds are said to be caught in them. There are house-spiders, tree-spiders, and ground-spiders. These spiders are exceedingly useful, and rid the country of many unpleasant flies. How many times I have seen them overpower prey which seemed much stronger than themselves! The web-spiders seemed to have but a few enemies, but the house and wall-spiders, which make no web, have most inveterate enemies in the shape of two or three kinds of wasps. During the day I have seen these wasps travelling along the walls with a rapidity that astonished me, and, finally, when coming to a spider, immediately pounce upon the unfortunate insect and overpower it by the quickness of the movements of their legs, and succeed in cutting one after the other the legs of the spider close to the body, and then suck it, or fly away with it to devour it somewhere else.

I consider some species of ants, snakes, lizards, and spiders as most useful, for they destroy a great quantity of insect and other vermin. The great moisture of the country I have visited, with its immense jungle, is well adapted for the insect world, and would prove a very rich field to a naturalist and collector who would make it his special study and business. I was surprised how closely several of them mimicked or imitated other objects; some looked exactly like the leaves on which they most generally remain; others are exactly of the colour of the bark of trees on which they crawl; while others looked exactly like dead leaves, and one or two like pieces of dead branches of trees. Dragon-flies of beautiful colour were met near the pools.

Bats are very abundant, and I had succeeded in making a fine collection of them. They sometimes came by hundreds and spent the whole of the night flying round a tree which bore fruits they liked, and the noise made by their wings sounded strangely amid the stillness which surrounded them.

Squirrels are rather numerous, and there are a good number of species. Birds of prey and snakes are their great enemies. In 'Equatorial Africa' I described how I saw a snake charming a squirrel, and made the little creature come to him.

There are eight species of monkeys, but they are not all found in every district. They live in troops, but when old they live generally by themselves or in pairs. Of all the Mammalian animals inhabiting the forest the monkey tribe is the most numerous; but the poor monkey is surrounded by enemies, the greatest being man, who sets traps everywhere to catch him; then he is continually hunted by the negroes with guns or arrows; the guanonien, an eagle, is also his inveterate enemy.

The guanonien is a most formidable eagle, and, in spite of all my endeavours, during my former and this last journey, I have been unable to kill one; but several times I have been startled in the forest by the sudden cry of anguish of a monkey who had been seized by this "leopard of the air," as the natives often call it, and then saw the bird with its prey disappear out of sight.

One day, hunting through the thick jungle, I came to a spot covered with more than one hundred skulls of monkeys of different sizes. Some of these skulls must have been those of formidable animals, and these now and then succeeded, it appears, in giving such bites to this eagle that they disabled him. For a while I thought myself in the Valley of Golgotha. Then I saw at the top of a gigantic tree, at the foot of which were the skulls, the nest of the bird, but the young had flown away. I was told by the natives that the guanonien comes and lays in the same nest year after year. When an adult specimen will be procured, it may be found to rival in size the condor of America.

By the side of wild men roamed the apes, the chimpanzee forming several varieties. These are called by the negroes the Nschiego, Nschiego Nkengo, Nschiego Mbouvé, and Kooloo Kamba, all closely allied, and I think hardly distinguishable from each other by their bony structure. Then came the largest of all, the gorilla, which might be truly called the king of the forest. They all roamed in this great jungle, which seems so well adapted to be their homes, for they live on the nuts, berries, and fruits of the forest, found in more or less number throughout the year; but they eat such a quantity of food that they are obliged to roam from place to place, and are found periodically in the same district.

The elephant has become scarce, and recedes farther and farther every year into the fastnesses of the interior.

Miles after miles were travelled over without hearing the sound of a bird, the chatter of a monkey, or the footstep of a gazelle, the humming of insects, the falling of a leaf; the gentle murmur of some hidden stream only came upon our ears to break the deadness of this awing silence, and disturb the grandest solitude man can ever behold—a solitude which often chilled me, but which was well adapted for the study of Nature.

I was surprised at the small number of new birds I found. I did not find more than ten species different from those of my former collections.

At a certain distance from the coast hills commence, which gradually increase in elevation, and form mountain ranges, running parallel to each other in a south-east and north-west direction. They range along the whole of the western coast, and seem to bear themselves towards the southern part of Africa.

Between these mountains and the sea the country I have explored is generally low and marshy. Several rivers rising on the western slope of the first range flow through these lands and discharge themselves into the sea.* Consequently these rivers are short, and being so near together, the quantity of water they throw into the sea is not great. The most important commercially being the Gaboon, on account of its port.

I mentioned, in 'Equatorial Africa,' that I had been surprised by the enormous quantity of water discharged into the sea by the rivers forming the delta of the Ogobai. I further said that the Ogobai was formed by two rivers, the Rembo (river) Okanda and the Rembo Ngouyai; the former I had not seen,

* Names of rivers—Benito, Muni, Mondah, the delta of the Ogobai, Nazareth, Mexias, Fernand Vaz, and the Commi river.

but it runs, according to what I heard, from a north-east direction; the latter from a south-east direction. The Ngouyai I had seen and crossed in my journey to the Apingi country. My further explorations this time have led me higher up the stream, and proved that my former conclusions were correct.

These two rivers are the only ones that break through the coast chains of mountains, and thus we must not wonder at the tremendous amount of water they throw into the sea, in despite of the enormous absorption by radiation, when we consider the very great amount of rain falling in the interior.

Between the Niger and the Congo there is no river that brings down such a quantity of water as the Ogobai. The enormous amount of rain that falls in these equatorial regions will account at once for the greater volume of water of this river, which has a far greater basin than all the other rivers between the Congo and the Niger.

The first table-lands of the interior gradually sloping down eastward, form a valley. In this valley from the north-east the Rembo Okanda glides gradually southward, increasing by numerous streams until it unites with the Rembo Ngouyai. I have heard that the Okanda has several rapids.

The Rembo Ngouyai comes from the south-east, and flows northward, gradually increasing by its tributaries; it breaks through the range of mountains, forms a series of falls and rapids, unites with the Okanda, and then the two rivers take the name of Ogobai.

Going eastward in my present journey the land rose higher and higher until we reached Niembouai

Olomba; it then sloped gradually towards the east, with small streams running in that direction, and flowing no doubt towards the large river mentioned by the natives—a river that may be the Congo, or one of its large tributaries. I should think that it was about two degrees further eastward, somewhere about 15° or 16° east longitude.

After I had drawn attention to the great basin of the Ogobai, the attention of the French Government was attracted towards it, and two expeditions have been made; one in the year 1862, and the other in 1864.

Unfortunately the two expeditions chose the worst time of the year for their errand, the dry season, when the rivers are shallow and full of banks.

The first expedition did not reach the junction of the Okanda and the Ngouyai; but afterwards, M. Serval, whose enterprise is an honour to the French navy, from the Upper Gaboon crossed by land to the Ogobai, and reached a point not far from the junction.*

* The map made by M. Serval appeared after I had started a second time for Africa, and was sent to me by my friend M. V. A. Malte-Brun, with a kind letter saying how glad he was that I was vindicated; for some people had said in England that I had gone nowhere, and Dr. Barth had done me the honour to map the furthest parts of my exploration as only a few miles into the interior.

I have not seen Eliva Olanga, called by Serval, Eliva Jonanga. When at the Falls of Ngouyai, I heard that it was on the other side of the Ashankolo mountains. With regard to latitude, its position would agree with my map, but my astronomical observations for longitude put it more to the westward than M. Serval does. I should not trust, perhaps, entirely to my observations while at Olenda; but at Máyolo I took a great number of observations of lunar distances, and the longitude of this place may therefore be considered as well determined.

An *eliva* is not properly a lake, but really a broad extension of a river between ranges of hills.

The second expedition was a like failure; it commenced exploring in July instead of waiting until November. Nevertheless it had a great advantage over the first; for it had a small steam tender besides a larger steamer. The expedition went as far as the junction of the Okanda and Ngouyai. Unfortunately, I have never seen any published record of this interesting exploration, which went a little further than the first. The exploration of the Okanda will be a great service rendered to geographical science. The French having possession of the Gaboon, no one could do it better than they.

Climate.—Now that I have given a general view of the configuration of this part of Africa, I will speak of the climate.

Unfortunately the book in which was recorded all my observations concerning the amount of rain falling, the duration of the showers or storms, the heat of the sun and of the atmosphere, has been lost; now and then I recorded in my journal a few observations, so I shall not be able to give to the reader in this chapter a general *résumé* of the daily record.

The Ashango mountains seem to be, if I may use the negro expression, the home of the rain. I doubt very much whether in any other country in the world it rains more than in the mountainous regions of the interior. On the western coast, near the equator, there are only two seasons, the rainy and the dry, as described in 'Equatorial Africa.'

The rain begins in September and ends in May. In 1864 a long dry season took place, as I have said in the course of this narrative, called *enomo onguero*;

this is an exception to the rule. The dry season lasts from June to August.

As far eastward as Máyolo, or rather, I may say, as far as the mountains inhabited by the Ishogos, the seasons keep themselves pretty distinct; but as the reader may see on perusing my book, the further I went eastward, the less distinct became the dry season.

The dry season came from the west and the rain from the east. North of the equator the rain seemed to come from the north-east. South of the equator it seemed to come almost direct from the east. The more I advanced in the Ashango country the higher the land became, and also the more moist; but there was no thunder or lightning or heavy rain. At that time the state of the Eckmühl river, of the Ngouyai, and of its affluents showed, as the reader will see, that they were far below their height of the wet season. It is a remarkable fact that the higher I went up these streams, the more they had fallen.

It is clear that it rains more or less in the mountainous regions of the interior throughout the year, and if it rains there when it is the height of what is called by them the dry season, what must it be in their rainy season? The amount of rain must be far more than in the countries near the sea-shore. I noticed in my former journey, while among the cannibals (chap. xviii. page 320), the cloudy and rainy state of the atmosphere in August.

The highest fall of rain I noticed before my rain-gauge disappeared, was 7½ in. in twenty-four hours, and, as far as I can remember, more than 200 inches fell near the sea-shore during the year.

I have given so lengthy an account of the seasons in 'Equatorial Africa' that I need not here enlarge upon this subject.

As I advanced into the interior the prospect became apparent of a continuous rainy season, for the books of Burton, Speke and Grant, showed me that I had probably nothing other to expect. The distinguished discoverer of Lake Tanganyika says in his 'Lake Regions of Central Africa,' page 287:—"As it will appear, the downfalls of rain begin earlier in Central Africa than upon the Eastern Coast."

It has been seen that I made the same observation in the West. In page 286 of the same volume, this accurate observer says:—"The *Masika* or rains commence, throughout, in Eastern Unyamwezi, the 14th of November. In the north and western provinces the wet monsoon begins earlier and lasts longer. At Msene it precedes Unyanyembe a month; in Ujiji two months. Thus the latter countries have rainy seasons which last from the middle of September to the middle of May."

It will be seen by this, that the rainy season on the eastern shores of Lake Tanganyika, falls at the same time as in Western Equatorial Africa, although the two countries are separated by about twenty degrees of longitude.

The lamented Speke says:—"While on the equator, or rather a trifle north of it, it rains more or less all the year round. In the dry season it blows so cold, that the heat is not distressing."

My observations agree with those of Burton in this, that although we are on the two extreme sides, east and west, we observe that the rains come from the interior.

The observations of Speke agree entirely with mine concerning the weather under the equator. We must therefore come to the conclusion that the rains proceed from some central woody and mountainous district somewhere between the east and west coasts, where, no doubt, exist several lakes not yet discovered.

In reading the account of the ill-fated expedition of Tuckey on the Congo, we read, page 200 and 201:—

"*September* 1. The rains commence the latter end of September, and continue to March.

"This day we observed, for the first time, a rise in the river.

"*September* 4. Rain falling."

This sudden rise of the Congo will, no doubt, occur owing to the rains coming from the northward—that is, from towards the equator. I must remind the reader of the cloudy and misty state of the atmosphere, which I have described in the mountains of the interior; there were showers, which were becoming heavier every day, in July, and I learned from the natives that about a month afterwards the heavy rains would begin. This would account for the rise of the Congo.

What struck me was, while at Máyolo, the great perturbation of the magnetic needle during tornadoes. As the tornado rose above the horizon there seemed to be a dip of the magnetic needle; then, as it rose higher, the needle took its natural position, and then vibrated sometimes for thirty seconds. This I observed in the prismatic compass, the only instrument I had.

The temperature of the countries I have explored, though situated near or under the equator, is not so high as that of several countries further removed from it, but I must say beforehand that I am unable to judge of the temperature of the furthest countries that I visited, for I was not there in the hot season; and I have no doubt that the heat is sometimes still greater there than what I have observed, as it was greater at Máyolo than on the seashore. It has been noticed long ago that the temperature of countries situated under the same degree of latitude varies considerably. The extent of the sea, deserts, the prevailing winds, the gulf stream, the elevation of continents, &c., have a powerful influence. So Africa, under the equator from west to east, may have different temperatures, according to its physical features.

In Western Equatorial Africa, the great moisture of the country and the vast forests are, no doubt, the causes of the heat not being so great, the immense jungle absorbing the heat radiated by the sun. The hottest months of the year are December, January, February, March, and April. In May, the temperature begins to decrease; in June it begins to be cool, and July and August are the coldest. Then as the rains commence to make their appearance, the heat begins to increase.

The same periodical changes of temperature, as far as I have been able to judge, apply to the coast and to the countries of the interior. On the sea-shore the maximum of heat is from 86° to 88°, very seldom rising higher. In the interior, at Máyolo, the maximum, I remember, was 98°; no sea-breeze was felt there.*

In the interior, the maximum of heat in February, March and April was at about three o'clock p.m., the minimum between four and half-past five a.m.; but after midnight, the thermometer fell very little.

The coldest days experienced on the sea-shore, as observed by others, have been 64° and 65°; I myself never saw it lower than 68°. During the dry season in July and August the maximum is generally between 75° and 80°. I must here say that near the shore I took but very little notice of my observations, besides noting them down; but in the interior it was different. While in the Ashango country, the temperature for a few days never rose

* The following is a copy of a portion of my register of temperature at Máyolo, which was preserved in my Journal. The degrees are of the centigrade scale.

	In the Village of Máyolo.									In the Forest.					
	A.M.		P.M.							Noon.	P.M.				
	10.	12.	1.	2.	3.	4.	5.	6.	7.	12.	1.	2.	3.	4.	5.
April															
1	..	..	..	33	[illegible]	[illegible]	..	[illegible]	29	..	..	..	..	..	..
8	..	..	..	33	33½	[illegible]	..	..	[illegible]	..	..	..	..	..	..
14	..	[illegible]	..	..	..	..	..	..	..	29	30	..	..	..	..
20	[illegible]	..	..	..	..	[illegible]	..	..	..	..	30	[illegible]	30	[illegible]	..
23	..	[illegible]	..	..	..	[illegible]	[illegible]	..	..	30	..	30	..	[illegible]	..
25	..	..	..	[illegible]	..	..	..	..	..	..	[illegible]	[illegible]	..	..	[illegible]
28	..	..	..	[illegible]	..	..	[illegible]	..	..	[illegible]	31	31	31	[illegible]	..
May															
6	..	..	..	[illegible]	..	[illegible]	33	..	..	..	..	30	[illegible]	[illegible]	..
8	..	..	[illegible]	..	..	[illegible]	..	..	..	..	..	29	..	..	..
10	..	..	..	..	..	[illegible]	27	..	..	..	..	..	..	..	..
14	..	..	..	[illegible]	..	..	31	..	..	..	..	[illegible]	[illegible]	[illegible]	..

higher than 72°, but I saw it as low as 64° at six o'clock a.m. The sky was constantly cloudy. But it does not follow that, though the heat of the atmosphere is less than in some other countries—the reasons of which I have given—that the heat of the sun would be less also; at any rate, I hope that my few observations may awaken the spirit of inquiry on the subject, and that simultaneous observations of the heat of the sun and of the atmosphere may hereafter be made in different countries.

But it will be necessary first to adopt a uniform system for ascertaining the power of the sun, and I will raise my humble voice in favour of the subject being discussed. Unfortunately, there being no general system for ascertaining the heat of the sun, I used the one that appeared to me the most correct; so I am afraid I cannot compare my observations with those of others.

I had two thermometers, which I placed at some distance from each other, sometimes fifty or one hundred yards apart, sometimes nearer, and I was surprised at the closeness of their results; a degree was generally the maximum of difference.

My thermometers were laid on a white board, in order to avoid the moisture rising from the earth, which was very great. I began these observations only in the Ashira country, and was not able to carry them further, for my sun thermometers were stolen on my journey between Ashira and Otando-land. The weather being warmer at Máyolo, I should have found the thermometer marking higher still than I had at Olenda. The maximum, at Olenda, I found was 148¾, temperature of the air 92° and 94°. The rays of the sun were of the same power at ten a.m. and five p.m., varying generally from 118° to 125°; at noon, from 130° to 135°.

These observations were taken in February and March. Towards one o'clock, the maximum of heat of the sun was attained. So it will be seen that the sun had passed its maximum at one, while the maximum of the heat of the atmosphere occurred at three o'clock. The greatest heat in the shade this year at Mr. Bishop's observatory at Twickenham was 89°, whilst the heat of the sun was 106° only; this shows the much less power of the sun in these latitudes than in Equatorial Africa.

Making these observations in the heat of the sun were exceedingly exhausting, for I had to go near my thermometer with only a cap on, so that no shadow could fall upon it, and I could only carry them on after intervals of two or three days, for they generally produced a headache the next day.

I remarked that sometimes a single cloud passing over the sun, at the time of observation, would send the thermometer down, in a few seconds, 8° or 10°, and sometimes more. While at Máyolo, I carried on my observations, almost at the same time, in an airy verandah in the village and in the forest. I found the temperature in the forest not varying more than 1° (cent.) from one to three o'clock, while sometimes it had increased in an open space in the verandah to 7° or 8°; the temperature of the forest never reaching more than 31° centigrade, and then it is found rather pleasant. And well may the traveller thank Providence that with such a powerful sun he can travel under the protection of leafy forests, and be protected from its rays.

CHAPTER XXI.

ETHNOLOGY.

Isolation of the tribes in the interior of Western Equatorial Africa—Scantiness of the population—Divisions of tribes and clans—Patriarchal form of Government—Comparison of customs between Western Equatorial tribes and Eastern—Laws of inheritance—Cannibalism—Migrations always towards the West—Decrease of population—Its Causes—The African race doomed to extinction.

Now I must give a general outline of the numerous tribes of men that inhabit this vast jungle.

In these mountainous recesses man is what we may call primitive; he is surrounded by dense forests; no trading caravan from the east or from the west, from the north or from the south, has penetrated to him; he has been shut up from the world around him, and in the course of his slow migration he has taken the place of others who had disappeared before him. The individuals who leave the interior country for the sea-shore never come back, to tell their countrymen of the white man or of the sea. The path is closed to them, there is a gulf between the sea and the interior, but not between the interior and the sea.

What struck me in travelling through this great wooded wilderness was the scantiness of the population, and the great number of tribes speaking different languages and dialects. Tribes bearing different names considering themselves different nations, though

FAN WARRIORS. FROM A FRENCH PHOTOGRAPH

BIBLIOTECA NAZIONALE NAPOLI

speaking the same language, and tribes speaking the same language divided from each other by intervening tribes speaking another language. These tribes were divided into a great number of clans, each clan independent of the others, and often at war with one or other of them; in some tribes villages of the same clan were at war with each other.

Part of one tribe in some cases have no knowledge whatever of the other part; the further I went towards the east the less the people travelled, the less they knew of what surrounded them, for they had no trade to incite them to travel. I was nevertheless struck by the great affinities these tribes presented to each other. The patriarchal form of government was the only one known; each village had its chief, and further in the interior the villages seemed to be governed by elders, each elder, with his people, having a separate portion of the village to themselves. There was in each clan the ifoumou, foumou, or acknowledged head of the clan (*ifoumou* meaning the "source," the "father").

I have never been able to obtain from the natives a knowledge concerning the splitting of their tribes into clans: they seemed not to know how it happened, but the formation of new clans does not take place now among them.

Kings never obtain power over large tracts of country, as we see in Eastern Africa; the house of a chief or elder is not better than those of his neighbours.

The despotic form of government is unknown; no one can be put to death at the will of the chief, and a council of elders is necessary before one is put to death. In such cases the palavers are long, and there must be a good majority for the sentence to be carried out. The intricacies of the law are unknown to them. A tooth for a tooth is their maxim. Wounding and killing by accident are not recognised as extenuating circumstances. If any one, by accident, kills another, by the falling of a tree which he cuts down being the cause of the person's death, he is killed. If a gun goes off by mishap and kills any one, the man who held the gun is put to death. According to their theory, the person causing such accident has an *aniemba* (witchcraft), and must be got rid of. But, though no one has a right to put to death any *free* man (for every one may kill his own slaves), woe to the man or woman who has incurred the displeasure or hatred of the head of the family, for the latter is sure to bring, at some future time, some witchcraft palaver, and then oblige him or her to drink the much-dreaded *mboundou*, or, by his influence, excite the superstitious fears of his people, and get rid of them, either by selling them into slavery, or by having them killed. Very few cases occur in which the father of the family is made to drink the *mboundou*, for he may compel any of his people to drink it. Every one is under the protection of some one. If, by death, a negro is suddenly left alone, he runs great risk of being sold into slavery. Pretexts for such a deed are not found wanting. Every one must have an elder to speak his palavers for him, hence the young and the friendless cling to the elder, who is like a father to them all; thus they do not become scattered, and the more people an elder has, the more potent his voice becomes in the councils of the village; besides, any free man, by a singular custom, called *bola banda*, which consists in placing the hands on the head of an elder, can place himself under the protection of the patriarch who is thus chosen, and henceforward become one of his people. Of course, the man under whose protection another places himself belongs to a different clan. South of the equator the tribes were milder than those I had seen in my former journey north of the equator. I found no tribes where the villages were continually fighting with each other, as among the Bakalai, Shekiani, Mbondemos, Mbisho, and the Fans. The law of the strongest did not prevail; no raid for the sake of plunder was committed by one village upon another; one of the reasons being that no village was strong enough to do so—besides, the people of neighbouring villages intermarry much with each other, for polygamy, with its many drawbacks, had in some respects its advantages.

Tribes and clans intermarry with each other, and this brings about a friendly feeling among the people. People of the same clan cannot marry with each other. The least consanguinity is considered an abomination; nevertheless, the nephew has not the slightest objection to take his uncle's wives, and, as among the Bakalai, the son to take his father's wives, except his own mother.

The reader will at once see the striking difference there is between the tribes of East Africa and those which I have visited. When we read Burton, Speke,

Grant, and Livingstone, we see that in the East the chiefs are powerful, often cruel, putting their subjects to death; villages of neighbouring tribes are continually sacked, the cattle plundered, and the people killed or carried into slavery. Property seems to be secure nowhere.

Polygamy and slavery exist everywhere among the tribes I have visited; the wealth of a man consisting first of wives, next of slaves; the slaves always belonging to a different tribe from that of their owner.

Their religion, if it may be called so, is the same in all tribes. They all believe in the power of their gods (idols), in charms, fetiches or mondahs, and in evil and good spirits. Mahommedanism has not penetrated into this vast jungle. They all believe in witchcraft—which I think is more prevalent in the West than in the East—causing an untold amount of slaughter. Travellers in the East have not noticed it as prevailing so much as I have done. They behold with superstitious fear the appearance of the new moon.

Their laws of inheritance are alike, except among the Bakalai.

The Western tribes believe in the *alumbi*, a custom which Eastern travellers have not described, but they speak of chalk, and of little houses containing jaws or bones of men.

The Western custom of the *djembai* (see 'Equatorial Africa'), is known under another name in the East.

The doctors of both East and West have the same powers and functions, and are called by nearly the same name, in both regions—Ouganga, Uganga, Mganga, or Nganga.

The law of inheritance among these Western tribes is, that the next brother inherits the wealth of the eldest (women, slaves, &c.), but that if the youngest dies the eldest inherits his property, and if there are no brothers, that the nephew inherits it. The headship of the clan or family is hereditary, following the same law as that of the inheritance of property. In the case of all the brothers having died, the eldest son of the eldest sister inherits, and it goes on thus until the branch is extinguished, for all clans are considered as descended from the female side.

What struck me also was that at each step occasioned by death the heir changes his name. The chief of the Abouya clan of the Commi was formerly called Oganda, then his next brother was called Quengueza, and another Kombé-Niavi, names which my friend Quengueza has successively borne, being now called Oganda, and no one would dare to call him by the name of Quengueza. The title is generally assumed after the bola ivoga has taken place.

On my second journey, Obindji, the Bakalai chief, was called Ratenou, having taken the name of his father—the Bakalai, as far as I know, being the only tribe among which the son inherits his father's property.

The only custom I have not found prevalent among them all was cannibalism, the traces of which and records of which I have not found amongst any of the tribes inhabiting south of the equator which I have visited. In my former work on Equatorial Africa, after the many inquiries I made among the Fans of the interior, I learned that they and the people in the north-east direction were the only ones who ate human flesh, and that they did not know where cannibalism stopped. Hence I mentioned that cannibalism had migrated from north-east to south-west, and not from south to north; my last journey has entirely demonstrated to me the truth of that hypothesis; and it shows how little they travelled, that no one has ever heard of the Fans in the Southern country I have visited.

The fables of all the tribes were nearly alike, and it is wonderful how they are handed down from generation to generation.

Their languages, though not the same, have great affinities to one another, but they seem to have been derived from two distinct sources, namely from tribes of the north and north-east, and from tribes of the south-east and east. On this subject I must refer the reader to the Comparative Vocabulary given in the Appendix (III.) to this volume.

The question naturally arises, how such a state of political disintegration as I have described has taken place.

We must come to the conclusion that Africa has not escaped many political convulsions followed by great wars and migrations; that the same natural laws which govern our race have prevailed in Africa, and that migration has taken place from east to west.

I could learn nothing from them on these subjects, the past being a dark sea of which they knew nothing and about which they did not care. Some of their

FAN WOMAN AND CHILD. FROM A FRENCH PHOTOGRAPH.

legends seem to imply that there had been great wars; old men of the Commi tribe even remember when their clans were continually at war with each other.

The migration of the tribes, as I have already observed, seems to have followed the same laws as migrations among ourselves; I did not meet with a single tribe or clan who said they came from the west; they all pointed towards the east as the place they came from.

The migration of the Fans (people of which I have given an account in 'Equatorial Africa') has suddenly burst westward, and I believe that there has never been a migration with which we are acquainted in Western Africa, which has made so quick a descent on the sea-board. Fifteen or twenty years ago the Fans were only heard of by the sea-shore tribes, a few villages were said to be found in the mountains at the head water of the Gaboon; now the people have come down from their mountains and have settled everywhere on the banks of the Gaboon; their villages are numerous between the Moonda and the Gaboon, and are distant only a few miles from the sea; indeed, the Fans are now seen often among the settlements of the traders. I give a representation of a Fan woman, from a French photograph, which will give the reader a fair idea of a cannibal *belle*. I have also given a sketch of a group of Fan warriors, taken from a French photograph.

These warlike people have swept everything before them. The Bakalai and Shekiani villages have not been able to withstand their onset; and now Bakalai,

Shekiani and Fan villages are intermingled with each other and often fighting with each other, for these three tribes are the most warlike in this part of Africa. The Bakalai and Shekiani are decreasing very fast, and the Fans in the course of time will take their place, and also that of the Mpongwé.

What the cause may be of the sudden migration of these cannibals, I have not been able to discover.

The migration of the Fans towards the western board is but a repetition of the former migrations of other tribes, the remnants of which we now see on or near the sea-shore.

From the Gaboon to Cape St. Catherine the tribes bearing different names, and the tribes inhabiting the Ogolai as far as the Okanda, speak the same language, with the exception of the Aviia, who are said to speak the same language as the Loango people down the coast. The Mpongwé, Oroungou and Commi were once interior tribes.

Quengueza pointed out to me the place where the people of Goumbi had their village, and where he lived when a young man; it was about forty miles higher up the stream. The Abogo clan of the Commi of the Fernaud Vaz supply the hereditary chief of the sea-coast tribe, on account of their having settled there first.

The Bakalai themselves were strangers on the banks of the River Ovenga, and it is only of late years (about twenty years) that they have settled there by permission of the predecessor of Quengueza. The Bakalai have only of late migrated from the north to the Ashankolo, and hence to the banks of the Ovenga; they have also migrated to the banks of the Ngouyai, and have scattered themselves further east than the Ovigui river.

Old Remandji, the king of the Apingi, whom I visited in my first journey, remembered well the time when he could go with the Apingi to the Anenga tribe. Since then the road has been stopped, the Bakalai having made their appearance on the way there.

The Shekiani have come and settled themselves on the sea-shore from inland, between the Mpongwé and Cape Lopez people. Three Ishogo villages have settled among the Apono, about two years before my arrival; Ishogo and Ashango live in one village, and Ashango and Njavi do the same in another, the Njavi having migrated towards the west. All these are instances of what I advance, namely, that the tribes are always moving, and that the movement is towards the west.

There are tribes that have remained a long time at the same place, such as the Ashira Ngozai, on account of the beautiful country in which they live: but lately many have expressed the desire to come and settle on the banks of the Ovenga, and would do so if it were not for the warlike Bakalai, who, since the plague, have dwindled down, and will disappear soon unless strengthened by migration from the Bakalai of the north, who may be driven southward by the cannibals.

The reader will be able at once to see, by the description I have just given, how such political disintegration has taken place, and how people speaking the same language have in the course of time been separated from one another, and finally come to consider themselves as different nations. We must conclude that Africa has never been very thickly inhabited; hence the villages on migrating have settled where they chose.

I have been struck with the steady decrease of the population, even during the short time I have been in Africa, on the coast and in the interior; but before I account for it, let me raise my voice in defence of the white man, who is accused of being the cause of it. Wherever he settles the aborigines are said to disappear. I admit that such is the case; but the decrease of the population had already taken place before the white man came, the white man noticed it but could not stop it. Populous tribes whom I saw for a second time, and who had seen no white man and his fiery water, have decreased, and this decrease took place before the terrible plague that desolated the land had made its appearance. The negroes themselves acknowledge the decrease. Clans, in the lifetime of old men, have entirely disappeared; in others, only a few individuals remain.

Where the Slave Trade exists the population must certainly decrease in a greater ratio; and where the fiery water is sold to the natives in great quantity, it must also affect their health. Happily the Slave Trade will never flourish as it did in times past, and it may be said now to be almost entirely done away with. In the country of my late exploration, the only people who continue the traffic in slaves are negro agents, from the two Portuguese islands St.

Thomas and Prince's, who purchase people for their masters, who are also negroes. They cross to and from the mainland in small canoes, and thus avoid the cruisers.

The decrease of the African population is owing to several causes :—The Slave Trade, polygamy, barrenness of women, death among children, plagues, and witchcraft; the latter taking away more lives than any Slave Trade ever did. The negro does not seem to diminish only in the region I have visited; but in every other part of Africa, travellers, who after the lapse of a few years have returned a second time in the same country, have noticed a decrease of population.

Tuckey, in exploring the Congo, noticed it, and expressed his astonishment at seeing the country so little inhabited, compared to what he expected from the accounts he had read of that river in the works of the Catholic missionaries.

The women of the interior are prolific, and in despite of it shall we assume that the negro race has run its course, and that in due course of time it will disappear, like many races of mankind have done before him? The Southern States of America were, I believe, the only country in which the negro is known to have increased.

The reader who has followed me through the volume of my former exploration and the present book, will have been able to gather an idea of the general character and disposition of the negro of this part of Africa, as he now stands. I have made researches to ascertain if his race had formerly left remains, showing that he had once attained a tolerably high state of civilization; my researches have proved vain, I have found no vestige whatever of ancient civilization. Other travellers in different parts of Africa have not been more successful than I have.

How they came to invent looms to work their grass cloth, no one could tell. Their loom has been used from generation to generation without its being improved. To my question—"Who taught them to smelt and work iron?" their answer was that as long ago as they knew, the people had worked in the same way. I think everything tends to show that the negro is of great antiquity, and has always remained stationary. The working of iron, considering the very primitive way they work it, and how easy it is to find the ore, must have been known to them from the remotest time, and to them the age of stone and bronze must have been unknown.

As to his future capabilities, I think extreme views have prevailed among us. Some hold the opinion that the negro will never rise higher than he is; others think that he is capable of reaching the highest state of civilization. For my own part, I do not agree with either of these opinions.

I believe that the negro may become a more useful member of mankind than he is at present, that he may be raised to a higher standard; but that, if left to himself, he will soon fall back into barbarism, for we have no example to the contrary. In his own country the efforts of the missionaries for hundreds of years have had no effect: the missionary goes away and the people relapse into barbarism. Though a people may be taught the arts and sciences known by more gifted nations, unless they have the power of progression in themselves, they must inevitably relapse in the course of time into their former state.

Of all the uncivilized races of men, the negro has been found to be the most tractable and the most docile, and he possesses excellent qualities that compensate in great measure for his bad ones. We ought therefore to be kind to him and try to elevate him.

That he will disappear in time from his land I have very little doubt; and that he will follow in the course of time the inferior races who have preceded him. So let us write his history.

APPENDIX I.

Descriptions of Three Skulls of Western Equatorial Africans—Fan, Ashira, and Fernand Vaz—with some Admeasurements of the rest of the Collection of Skulls, transmitted to the British Museum from the Fernand Vaz, by P. B. Du Chaillu. By Professor Owen, F.R.S., &c.

The pains and skill which M. Du Chaillu has devoted, under most difficult and trying circumstances, to obtain from the scenes of his explorations in Western Equatorial Africa materials for the advancement of natural history, have earned for him the respect and gratitude of every genuine lover and student of the science for its own sake.

Amongst those specimens which he succeeded in sending down to the coast for embarkation, before his furthest expedition into the interior, which ended, unfortunately for geography, so disastrously, was a collection of upwards of one hundred skulls of natives of Western Equatorial Africa, to which class of objects I had particularly requested his attention before his departure from England on his second journey to the gorilla-country.

Of this collection, the chief part of which is now in the British Museum, I have taken admeasurements of ninety-three skulls, four of the chief of these admeasurements being given in a subjoined table. Of these skulls I have also profile views and outlines of the greatest horizontal circumference of the cranium; and from the monograph in preparation I have selected three specimens for more particular description, from photographs of which the accompanying woodcuts have been taken.

Figures 1, 2, and 3 are of the skull (No. 24) of a male native of Fernand Vaz between twenty and thirty years of age.

The cranium is narrow, and so is proportionally long; the occiput is convex or hemispheroid; the forehead low and narrow; the parietal bosses scarcely marked; the frontal sinuses are slightly protuberant, the right more so than the left. Viewing, with one eye, the upper surface of the cranium, held at arm's length, with the foremost part of the face just hidden by the frontal or supraciliary border of the cranium, the outer border of the hind half of the zygomata is visible. Viewed from the base, as in fig. 3, the intervals between the arches and the alisphenoid walls of the cranium appear of the greater width commonly characterizing the skulls of low races as compared with more advanced and bigger-brained people.

The usual sutures of the adult are present, together with the outer half of that between the ex- and super-occipital (on the outside of the skull); the frontal suture is obliterated, as in most adult skulls. The lambdoid, or occipito-parietal suture, is moderately broad and crenulate, with a small "wormian" ossicle on the left side. The mastoid suture is narrow and crenate where it joins the ex-occipital, but becomes a linear "harmonia" as it extends to the jugular foramen. The masto-parietal is crenate but

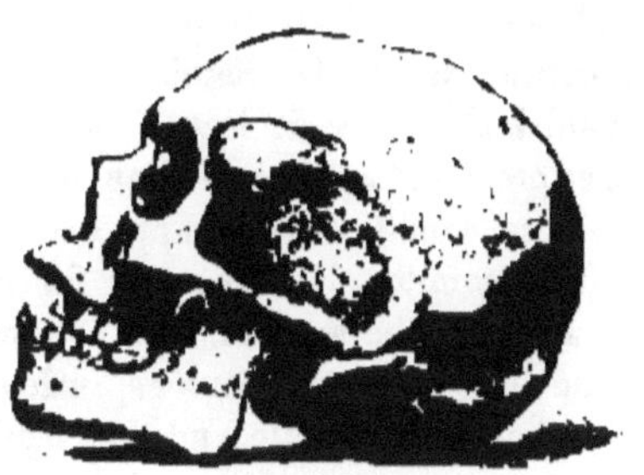

Fig. 1.

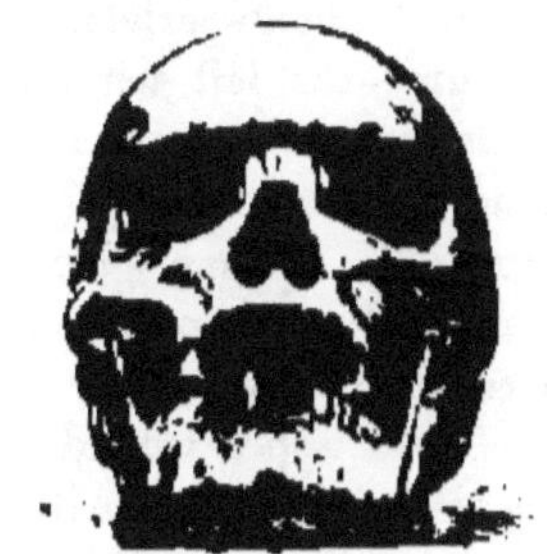

Fig. 2.

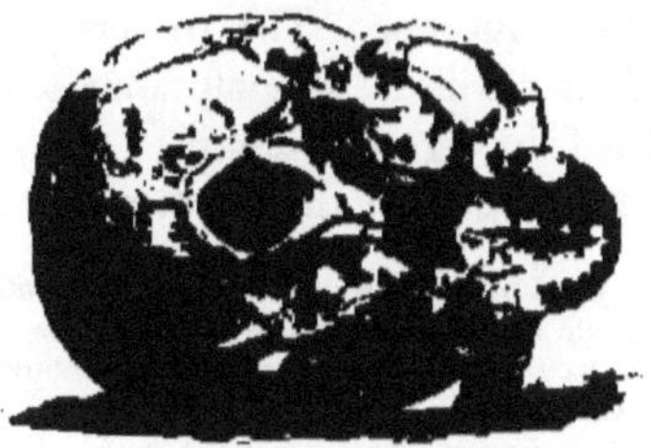

Fig. 3.

Skull, Male—Fernand Vaz

1. Side View. 2. Front View. 3. Rear View.

narrow, and sinks anteriorly into a post-squamosal pit. The sagittal suture is crenulate, but narrower than the lambdoid, where it leaves that suture; it then becomes crenate,* again crenulate, but contracts to a wavy linear condition as it approaches the coronal. This is a minutely wavy line for about an inch and a half from the sagittal, then becomes finely crenulate and broader until about an inch from the alisphenoid, where it is crenate, and then again linear and wavy. A mere point of the upper and hinder angle of the alisphenoid joins the parietal, consequently there is no "spheno-parietal" suture. The spheno-frontal suture—the left ten lines, the right eleven lines in length—is linear, almost straight, slightly squamous. The squamo-parietal suture is, as usual, squamous; the squamo-sphenoid is a linear harmonia, such also is the spheno-malar suture. The fronto-malar is continued forward from the spheno-frontal suture. The "upper curved ridge" of the super-occipital is well defined, but without a median occipital prominence; the more feeble lower curved ridge terminates above the persistent parts of the super-ex-occipital sutures. The par-occipital ridges are moderately developed. The supra-mastoid ridges† are well defined through the depth of the supra-mastoid groove running from the supra-mastoid or post-

* By "crenate" I mean where the waves, or angles, or "denticulations" of the sutural margin do not send off secondary waves or angles; in which case I use the term "crenulate." The breadth of the suture is the extent across which the waves or angles interlock.

† 'Descriptive Catalogue of the Osteological Series, Museum, Royal College of Surgeons,' 4to., 1853, p. 825, *et seq.* Syn: "backward extension of the posterior root of the zygomatic process" in anthropotomy; Sharpey's 'Quain's Anatomy,' ed. 1864, vol. i., p. 36.

squamosal fossa towards the meatus auditorius externus. Above this the upper and outer border of the tympanic projects as a "super-auditory ridge." Stylohyals, one inch in length, are anchylozed to the petrosal. The frontal is slightly protuberant above the spheno-frontal suture, between it and the beginning or fore-part of the temporal ridge.

The nasals are short, narrow, concave lengthwise, convex transversely, but with little prominence.

The malars slope outward to their lower margin, near which they are tuberous lengthwise. The anterior alveolar part of the upper jaw slopes forward, as in fig. 1. The contour of the bony palate (fig. 3), is that of a full ellipse. The molars (*m* 1, *m* 2) are smaller than in Australians.

The angle of the mandible is well-marked; the ascending ramus is subquadrate; the incisive alveoli bend a little forward to their outlets; a mere roughness takes the place of the "spinæ mentales," on the inner or back part of the symphysis.

The three true molars are present in each side of the lower jaw; those of the left side, especially the first and second, are more worn than those of the right; the third is on the grinding level on the left side, but has risen only half toward it on the right side. The age of the individual, as at the prime of life, may be inferred from this state of dentition; it is also plain that the left side, or half, of the jaw had chiefly been used in mastication. The size of the three molars is inferior to that in Australian jaws, but superior to that in most Europeans.

The cranium of this skull, in comparison with that

of an European of similar general proportions, as to length and breadth, shows more of the elliptical, less of the oval, character of horizontal contour; the European skull being wider, as usual, at the parietal bosses. The larger brain of the European has been accompanied also with greater height and breadth and forward convexity of the forehead, more protuberant sides of the cranium below the temporal ridge, and a nearer approach to the horizontal plane of the part of the occiput between the great foramen and the upper curved ridge. The more produced and longer nasals, the less produced and more vertical incisive alveoli, the less prominent malars, also distinguish the skull compared, as they do the majority of modern European skulls, from those of Africans.

The next skull which I have selected for the photographer is that (No. 57) of a male of the Fan, or cannibal race of Western Equatorial Africa, figs. 4, 5, and 6. It has belonged to a larger and more powerful individual than the former skull. The forehead rises higher, the parietal protuberances are more prominent, as is the sagittal region from which the parietals more decidedly slope towards the temporal ridges. The lambdoid, mast-occipital, masto-parietal, squamous, squamo-sphenoid, spheno-frontal, and spheno-malar sutures remain; the sagittal, coronal and frontal, are obliterated; the horizontal contour of the cranium is more oval than in the average European skull compared with the one from Fernand Vaz, owing to the more lateral contraction of the forehead in the Fan.

The super-occipital is pretty regularly convex, as

Fig. 4.

Fig. 5.

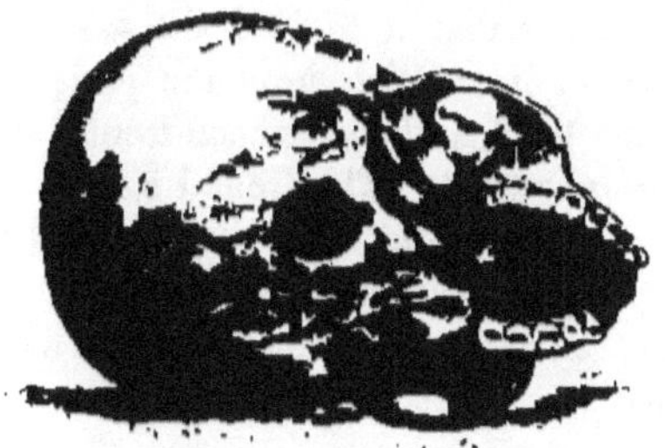

Fig. 6.

SKULL, MALE—FAN.

4. Front View. 5. Side View. 6. Base View.

in the former skull; the surface—chiefly ex-occipital—extending from the foramen magnum to the occipital protuberance, as in the former skull, forms with the plane of that foramen a less open angle than in most European skulls; the vertical extent of brain there is less, and the occipital surface in question is not pushed down so nearly to the level of the plane of the foramen magnum. The occipital protuberance is stronger in the present skull than in the former, but the upper curved ridge extended from it sooner subsides, and the lower curved line is less marked. The foramen magnum is rather smaller; the right par-occipital tuber is more produced. The mastoid processes are larger; the supra-mastoid ridge is more curved, and extended upwards; there is no post-squamosal pit; the super-auditory ridges* are more obtuse than in figs. 1—3.

The lambdoid suture is feebly and irregularly crenate along its upper or medial half, and becomes crenulate at the lower half, resuming a linear simplicity near its junction with the mastoid. A forward extension of the fore and upper angle of the squamosal shows plainly that it divided the part of the alisphenoid, which it overlies, from the parietal, on both sides of the head, and the spheno-frontal suture is shorter than in No. 24. The frontal sinuses make no outward prominence, and the glabella is continued by a gentle concave curve into the nasal part of the skull's profile. The nasals are broader, shorter, and less prominent than in No. 24. The malars are

* These are seldom wanting, and are not to be confounded with the supra-mastoid ridges.

deeper, more uniformly convex, and have not the lower border turned outward. The forward direction of the upper incisive alveoli is the same in degree as in No. 24, but they are rather longer. The bony palate is more contracted anteriorly. The external pterygoid plates are broader, shorter, and more everted than in No. 24. The cranial walls are thicker and denser; they are 4½ lines thick in the parietal and frontal bones, along a section taken half an inch from the medial line of the calvarium; the parietal is a little thinner at the boss, and thins as it descends; but near the squamosal suture it retains a thickness of three lines. The diploë is scanty and feebly marked, and owing to the general density of the cranial walls the weight of the skull is considerable, being, without the lower jaw, 2 lbs. 2¾ oz. avoird.

The molars, as in No. 24, are intermediate in size between those of Australians and the generality of those of Europeans.

The third skull (No. 96, figs. 7, 8, and 9) is of an aged female, also of the Fan tribe, retaining only the two canines and one molar of the left side of the upper jaw, and with an edentulous mandible of a peculiar form, combining, with the usual characteristics of that condition in aged individuals, an upward production of the fore-part, through the "stimulus of necessity" of a biting proximity of the lower to the upper incisive alveoli between the retained upper canines, as shown in fig. 7. The alveoli of the lost molars are absorbed in both jaws, but those of the lost incisors, though obliterated, have been maintained in much of their pristine length, and have

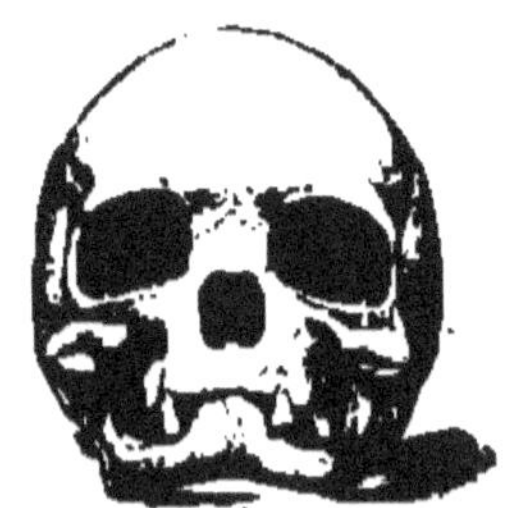

Fig. 7.

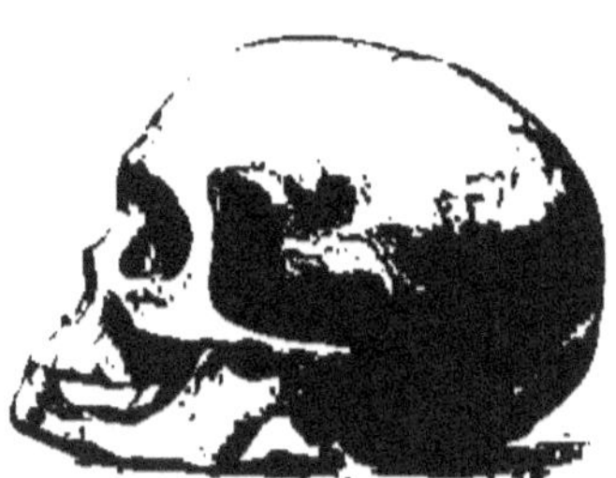

Fig. 8.

Fig. 9.

Skull, Aged Female—Fan Tribe.

7. Front View. 8. Side View. 9. Base View.

become bevelled off to an edge, after the fashion of the scalpriform incisors of Rodents.

The cranium, though smaller, resembles in general form and proportions that of the male Fan. The usual sutures, however, remain.

The lambdoid is narrow, and the crenation hardly grows to crenulation toward the lower and outer end of the suture, where a small "wormian" is wedged between the mastoid and super-occipital on the left side. The occipital condyles are less convex, more worn down, than in the male skulls, as if from the practice of carrying weight on the head. The lower curved ridge of the occiput is well defined, and the surface between it and the foramen magnum shows the usual characters of muscular attachment, but there is neither an upper curved ridge nor occipital spine, and the surface above the lower ridge is convex, and smooth like the rest of the outer part of the super-occipital. The mastoid processes are small; the supra-mastoid ridges low and smooth; the super-auditory ridges very short. The parietal protuberances are as little defined as in No. 24. The sagittal suture is "crenate;" the coronal suture is linear at both ends, crenulate but narrow at the mid-part. The apex of each alisphenoid joins the parietal; the extent of the spheno-parietal suture not exceeding three lines, that of the spheno-frontal suture is ten lines. The malars are not protuberant; on the contrary, the outer surface of each is concave—a rare variety.*

The deficiency of masticating machinery has pre-

* This character is less truly shown in fig. 7 than in fig. 8.

vailed long enough to affect the base of the zygomatic process; the chief part of the articular surface for the mandible is formed by the anterior, slight convexity (eminentia articularis), the smaller depression behind being unusually shallow. This approach to the character of the same articular surface in "edentate" mammals is not without interest.

The bony palate is oblong and subquadrate: it is shallow, through absorption of its lateral walls: its surface is more than usually hard and irregular, through pressure against it, probably by tongue and mandible, of unchewed alimentary subtances, and the palato-maxillary and intermaxillary * sutures remain: the maxillo-premaxillary suture is obliterated on the palate as elsewhere. The internasal suture is partly obliterated at its upper half: the naso-maxillary sutures remain; both are linear.

The frontal sinuses are slightly prominent, and are accordingly more marked, in this old negress's skull (fig. 8) than in the strong man's of the warlike and cannibal tribe of Fans (fig. 5).

The mandible shows strikingly the senile characters due to absorption of alveoli; the forward slope of the rami from the condyles; the reduction of the coronoid processes to a slender pointed form. The anterior outlets of the dental canals open upon the fore part of the broad shallow superior border of the horizontal ramus, which is left by the absorption of the sockets: anterior to each orifice the border shows a slight protuberance of ivory hardness against which the obtusely worn crowns of the upper canines

* The median palatal suture between the two maxillaries is here meant.

had their appulse. The trenchant, or transversely wedge-like, growth of the socketless incisive border of the mandible, rising between the upper canines, when the mouth is shut, has been already noticed as the peculiar feature of the present mandible.

MEASUREMENTS OF THE THREE SKULLS.

	Nos.					
	24.		37.		98.	
	in.	lines.	in.	lines.	in.	lines.
Horizontal circumference of cranium...	19	4	22	0	18	5
From one auditory meatus to the other over vertex...	12	8	13	0	12	9
Long diameter of cranium, outside	7	8	7	8	6	1
Greatest transverse diameter, outside	5	3	5	6	5	0
From anterior edge of foramen magnum to that of the premaxillary alveolar border	4	3	4	2	4	1
From anterior edge of foramen magnum to hindmost part of occiput	3	5	4	1	3	2
Length of skull, from premaxillary alveolar border to line dropped from hindmost part of occiput	7	9	8	3	7	3
Breadth of lower jaw, through angles	3	10	...		3	2
Longitudinal diameter of cranium, inside	...		6	8	5	9
Transverse diameter of cranium, inside	4	10	5	0	4	8
Height of cranium, inside	5	8	5	5	4	10
Length of foramen magnum...	1	4½	1	4½	1	4½
Breadth of foramen magnum	1	2½	1	2½	1	0
Height of alisphenoid in a straight line from foramen ovale	1	11	2	0	1	11
Breadth of alisphenoid, upper border...	0	11	0	10	0	10½
Breadth across zygomatic arches	5	3	4	10	4	7
Transverse diameter of orbit	1	8	1	7	1	6
Vertical diameter of orbit	1	5	1	4	1	3
Inter-orbital space...	0	11	0	11	0	11
Length of nasal bones, in a straight line	0	10	0	0	0	10
Transverse diameter, middle	0	3½	0	5	0	3
Transverse diameter, lower portion	0	5½	0	7	0	0
Height of the symphysis of the lower jaw, exclusive of teeth	1	8	...		0	11

The following are three of the dimensions of ninety-three skulls from Fernand Vaz and the Interior :—

No.	Length of Skull.		Length of Cranium.		Breadth of Cranium.		Circumference of Cranium.		No.	Length of Skull.		Length of Cranium.		Breadth of Cranium.		Circumference of Cranium.	
	in.	lines.	in.	lines.	in.	lines.	in.	lines.		in.	lines.	in.	lines.	in.	lines.	in.	lines.
1	7	9	7	0	5	0	19	6	34	8	0	6	9	5	6	18	0
2	7	10	7	3	5	0	20	0	35	8	0	7	0	5	3	19	0
3	8	0	7	8	5	3	19	6	36	7	7	6	6	5	3	18	3
4	8	4	6	0	5	3	18	8	37	8	0	7	3	5	3	19	9
5	7	10	6	8	5	3	18	9	38	7	4	6	9	5	3	18	6
6	7	10	6	0	5	3	18	9	39	7	1	6	8½	5	0	17	8½
7	7	10	6	6	5	4	18	8	40	7	7	6	0	5	3	18	6
8	8	0	7	0	5	0	18	6	41	7	10	7	0	5	0	18	9
9	7	10	6	7	5	0	18	0	42	8	0	7	0	5	3	19	4
10	8	5	7	6	5	6	20	3	43	7	7	6	9	4	9	17	9
11	7	6	6	8	5	8	18	0	44	7	7½	6	8	5	0	17	8
12	7	7	6	7	5	8	18	9	45	7	10	6	7	5	8	18	8
13	8	0	6	7	5	0	17	10	46	7	9	6	9	5	6	18	8
14	8	1	7	2	5	6	19	6	47	8	0	7	1	5	9	19	3
15	8	0	6	9	5	0	18	0	48	8	8	7	3	5	9	20	0
16	8	5	7	3	5	0	19	6	49	8	2	7	0	5	6	19	0
17	7	10	7	0	5	4	18	9	50	8	1	6	9	5	3	18	6
18	7	0	6	6	5	2	17	9	51	8	0	6	9	5	3	18	0
19	8	0	7	1	5	6	19	8	52	8	2	7	8	5	3	19	8
20	7	10	6	9	5	3	18	9	53	7	10	6	9	5	3	18	0
21	8	0	7	8	5	3	19	0	54	8	8	7	3	5	3	19	3
22	7	4	6	7	5	4	18	6	55	7	11	7	0	5	3	18	0
23	8	0	7	9	5	0	18	0	56	7	8	6	0	5	3	18	8
24	7	10	7	3	5	3	19	4	57	8	9	7	6	5	6	22	0
25	7	10	6	9	5	3	19	6	58	8	0	7	0	5	3	19	8
26	8	0	7	1	5	2	19	6	59	7	10	6	9	5	0	18	8
27	7	5	6	3	5	0	17	0	60	7	7	6	6	5	3	18	0
28	8	0	7	0	5	8	18	9	61	8	2	6	9	5	3	18	9
29	8	0	7	0	5	6	19	0	62	8	5	7	8	5	6	19	9
30	7	10	7	0	5	8	18	9	63	7	7	6	9	5	0	18	3
31	8	0	7	0	5	8	19	0	64	8	2	6	9	5	3	18	6
32	8	0	6	0	5	6	18	9	65	8	6	7	0	5	6	19	8
33	8	1½	6	9	5	6	18	6	66	7	10	6	9	5	6	18	9

No.	Length of Skull.		Length of Cranium.		Breadth of Cranium.		Circumference of Cranium.		No.	Length of Skull.		Length of Cranium.		Breadth of Cranium.		Circumference of Cranium.	
	in.	lines.	in.	lines.	in.	lines.	in.	lines.		in.	lines.	in.	lines.	in.	lines.	in.	lines.
67	7	10	6	6	5	0	18	6	81	8	2	7	0	5	6	19	0
68	7	7	6	6	5	3	17	9	82	8	0	7	0	5	3	19	3
69	8	0	7	0	5	3	19	0	83	8	0	7	0	5	0	19	0
70	8	0	7	0	5	3	18	9	84	8	0	6	9	5	3	18	9
71	7	10	7	0	5	3	18	9	85	7	0	6	0	5	0	17	3
72	8	0	7	3	5	6	19	6	86	7	10	7	0	5	0	19	8
73	7	10	7	0	5	3	18	9	87	8	3	7	3	5	3	19	3
74	8	0	7	0	5	3	19	0	88	8	2	7	0	5	8	18	9
75	7	7	6	6	5	0	18	0	89	8	2½	7	0	5	0	19	0
76	8	3	7	3	5	0	19	6	90	7	10	6	6	5	0	17	6
77	7	10	6	6	5	0	18	9	91	7	10	6	6	5	3	18	3
78	8	0	6	9	5	0	18	0	92	7	10	7	0	5	6	19	0
79	7	4	6	9	5	3	17	9	93	7	3	6	1	5	0	18	3
80	8	0	7	0	5	3	18	0									

Making allowance for difference of sex—the skulls not exceeding seven inches eight lines in length, being most of them plainly female—the range of diversity is here much less than would be found in the same number of European skulls from a locality of the same extent as the ground from which M. Du Chaillu gathered the above collection.

And this comparative conformity appears to depend on a corresponding uniformity in the manner of life, in the fewer wants, the less diversified pursuits, of the Equatorial Africans. Their food, the mode of obtaining it, the bodily actions, muscular exertions, and mental efforts stimulating and governing such acts, vary comparatively little in the people visited by M. Du Chaillu. The cannibal habits of the Fans offer the main difference, and with them are associated the larger cranial dimensions, as a general rule. But, in all, the prevalent low social status, the concomitant sameness, and contracted range, of ideas—the comparatively limited variety in the whole series of living phenomena, from childhood to old age, of human communities of the grade of the Ashiras and Fans—govern the conformity of their low cranial organisation.

In my work on the Archetype skeleton I note, among other characters of the general homology of bones of the human head, the degrees of variability to which the several vertebral elements were respectively subject.*

The centrums and neurapophyses of the cranial vertebræ maintain the greatest constancy, the neural spines the least, in the vertebral column of mammals, as in the cranial region thereof in the vast series of the varieties and races of mankind: the hæmal arches and their diverging appendages are the seats of intermediate degrees of variation.

Accordingly, between the lowest forms of African and Australian skulls and the highest forms of European skulls, the difference in size and shape is least in the basi-occipito-sphenoids, in the ex-occipitals, alisphenoids, and orbitosphenoids: it is greatest in the super-occipital, parietals, frontals, and nasals. The maxillary and mandible are next in degree of variability, especially at the terminal anterior part which represents the hæmal spine, and is the seat of the characters which Ethnology terms "prognathism,"

* 'On the Archetype and Homologies of the Vertebrate Skeleton.' 8vo. 1848, p. 137.

"orthognathism," "opisthognathism." As in the neural, so in the hæmal arches, the parts become subject to variety as they recede from the centrum. The palatal bones (pleurapophyses) show most constancy, the maxillaries (hæmapophyses) the next degree, the pre-maxillaries (hæmal spines) the least constancy.*

So, likewise, with regard to the centrums themselves, the terminal one or "vomer" is more variable than those behind it.

The tympanic (pleurapophysis) offers as few characteristics to the ethnologist, as does the palatine. The malar bones and zygomatic arches—diverging, as appendages, from the maxillary arch—are seats of variety only inferior to the neural spines. The pterygoid processes are almost, if not quite, as variable as the malar bones.

Accordingly, the variability or value of ethnological admeasurements depends on the vertebral elements, or general homology, of the parts they may happen to include. The length of the skull is more constant than that of the cranium, in the entire series of human races, because it includes the vertebral centrums, whilst the other includes only neural spines. Moreover, the parts that chiefly vary the length of the skull are those behind the foramen magnum, and those before the palatine bones.

The dimension from the anterior border of the foramen magnum to the fore part of the pre-sphe-

* The range of variety in this vertebral element may be estimated by the fact that all the ordinal characters of the class of birds derived from the "rostrum" are furnished by modifications of the premaxillary and premandibular bones.

noid, or to the palato-maxillary suture, is, perhaps, regard being had to sex, as constant as any. The part behind the cranial centrums is chiefly affected by the super-occipital; the part in front by the pre-maxillary. The extreme height, breadth, and length of the cranium, with the curves and contours of the dome, help the ethnologist with the range of differences which it has pleased him to express by the terms: brachycephalic, brassocephalic, brachistocephalic, subbrachycephalic, mesocephalic, mecocephalic, mecistocephalic, dolichocephalic, dolichistocephalic, pyramidocephalic, ōoidocephalic, cymbocephalic, stenocephalic, eurycephalic, cylindrocephalic, hypsicephalic, orthocephalic, phoxocephalic, sphenocephalic, platycephalic, sphærocephalic, cubicephalic, &c., with the terminal varieties, as in brachycephalous and brachycephaly, played upon each compound; to which add "phænozygous," "cryptozygous," as the cranial dome may give or hide a view of the zygomatic arches; also dolichorhinous, brachyrhinous, platyrhinous, or platyrhinal, &c., &c., for all the gradations of diversity of the neural spines of the foremost vertebra.

There is no particular harm in such army or display of terms of art—save where they are extended from signifying a gradation or variety of cranial form to the constant character of a race, a nation, a family, or a period—in the absence of that extent and amount of observation which is absolutely requisite to prove or disprove such constancy. In the extensive series of skulls of the natives of a limited tract of the northern part of the peninsula of Hindustan, varieties of shape of the cranium were observed which might be expressed by at least half a dozen of the above-cited Greek polysyllabics, and even of opposite extremes, and this, not only in the general series of Nepalese skulls, but sometimes in the minor series of a tribe or village.* Very analogous are the results as affecting "brachycephalic," dolicocephalic," &c., "families," "varieties," or "races," to which a correspondingly expanded survey of the skulls of the aboriginal Indians of America has led the accurate and painstaking ethnologist, Dr. Aitken Meigs.†

In the first place he finds that, in the general series of aboriginal American crania, there is a range of diversity of proportions of the cranial cavity, which would give the ethnologist grounds for distributing them into three groups: 1, *Dolichocephali*; 2, *Mesocephali*; 3, *Brachycephali*; but these are not coincident with areas or periods. Not any of them is distinctive of a particular family, or race, or nation, or other group, either according to time or to space. Thus the skulls of the Creek Indians may be, in a general way 'eurycephalic,' *i.e.* shorter and more broadly oval than those of the Assinaboins, and these, in like manner, than the crania of the Ottawas. But among the Creeks is a specimen (No. 441) which is "brachycephalic," and a skull of one of the Dacota Indians "stands between the Assinaboin's and the Creek's" (p. 37). Among the Osages of the Upper

* "Report on a series of Skulls of various Tribes of Mankind inhabiting Nepal," in 'Reports of the British Association for the Advancement of Science,' for 1850.

† 'Proceedings of the Academy of Natural Sciences of Philadelphia, May, 1860.

Missouri is a "longish head, inclining to the Swedish form, occupying a position intermediate between the long and short heads" (p. 20); a third (No. 54) has "the coronal region almost round, like that of the true Germanic head" (p. 19). Another specimen (No. 54) "belongs to the angularly round or square-headed Gothic type" (p. 19). Others, again, are "brachycephalic." Among the Blackfoot Indians are some skulls "decidedly dolichocephalic" (p. 17); but in No. 1227, of a Chief (and probably, therefore, with a more laterally expanded brain) the skull "occupies an intermediate place between the long and short heads" (p. 17). The skull of a Mohican also occupies "a position intermediate between the long and short heads, and approaches the Mongol form" (p. 20). "The Ottawas of Michigan may be partly referred to the arched type" (p. 22). But "No. 1007 is brachycephalic" (*ib.*). Others of this tribe, Nos. 1006, 1008, 1009, "depart from this type and approach the Swedish form. I have consequently placed them in the "dolichocephalic" division" (p. 22). The State of Michigan, however, was once occupied or hunted over by other aboriginal tribes, the Menominées, *e. g.*, "the cranial specimens of which differ from each other not a little" (p. 22).

The details of these differences are very instructive as to the degree of value of the terms of cranial shapes as denoting ethnological groups. Thus, after pointing out those approaching or attaining the "Brachycephali," Dr. Meigs writes:—"Among the Miamis of Indiana we again encounter the dolichocephalic type" (p. 22). But here also it is added that the skull of a Chief, No. 542, "is in many respects like the German heads in the collection, especially those from Tübingen, Frankfort, Berlin: it has the Swedish occiput" (*ib.*). "No. 1055 approaches the angular Gothic form" (*ib.*). In others "the outline of the crown forms a more or less rounded oval" (*ib.*). "No. 106 approaches the arched type." "The specimens in the collection constituting the Seminole group vary not a little from each other" (p. 25). After descriptive details, Dr. Meigs proceeds: "It will thus be seen that in this group there are at least two, if not three, distinct types" (p. 26).

How often one feels the desire to ask an author the meaning in which he uses the word "type"! As applied to cranial configuration, the grades or shades of transition are such that the choice of any one step in the series for a term of comparison must be arbitrary.

With regard to the aborigines of America, the ethnologist may classify them according to their tribes, family names, or autonomy, or according to the districts inhabited by them, or according to their cranial characters. But, it is abundantly shown by Dr. Meigs, as, indeed, was to be inferred from the 'Crania Americana' of Moreton, that, with the arbitrary assumption of certain proportions, dimensions, &c., as "type-characters," the cranial classification would differ from the tribal or national, geographical or epochal one.

What constitutes the prevalent "dolichocephalic type," ethnologically speaking, among the African skulls which have called forth the present remarks, is not, as the term would imply, a greater length of cranium than in Indian and European skulls which would be called "brachycephalic," or "hypsicephalic," but merely a want of filling out of the brain-case by lateral or vertical expansion. The dimension of "length" is more constant than that of "breadth" or "depth" in the cerebral hemispheres of the human brain.

Were the natives of Western Equatorial Africa, discovered or visited by M. Du Chaillu and represented by the skulls which he collected and transmitted, as constant, keen, and clever hunters as the North American Indians, there might then be expected to rise among them here or there an individual with qualities making him superior in his craft, and enabling him to direct and dominate over the more common sort. And in proportion as the brain might have a concomitant increase of size in such "Chief," we should expect the long ("dolichocephalic type") to merge into the broad ("brachycephalic"), or lofty ("hypsicephalic), or globular (sphærocephalic) modifications of cranial configuration.

In all the Negro skulls in the present collection, as in those of Boschismen, Mincopies, Australians, and every other variety that has come under my observation, the essential characters of the archencephalous subclass and of its sole genus and species are as definitely marked as in the skulls of the highest white races.

APPENDIX II.

INSTRUMENTS USED IN THE EXPEDITION TO ASHANGO-LAND.

First Supply. (From Mr. Potter, successor to Cary.)

1 Aneroid, brass, in morocco case, 2 inches in diameter, registering from 15 to 31 inches.

2 Compasses, prismatic, with stand, shades, and reflector, 3 inches diameter (Singer's patent).

2 Compasses, pocket (Singer's patent), 1½ inches diameter.

Drawing instruments, one set in German silver, in case, 6 inches by 9½ inches.

Drawing pins, 2 dozen.

2 Horizons Artificial, folding roof, improved iron trough and bottle, in sling case.

Hypsometrical Apparatus, viz.:—

- Bull's-eye lantern, copper boiler, 3 reservoirs for spirits, oil, or candle.
- 3 Thermometers for heights by boiling water, marked to 215°, in brass case.
- 2 Thermometers, thermal or sun, marked to 230°, in brass case.
- 2 Thermometers, graduated for Fahrenheit and Centigrade.
- 1 Thermometer, graduated for Centigrade and Reaumur.

Magnetic-electro machine, with 90 feet of cord or conducting wire.

2 Magnifiers, or reading glasses, large size.

Mercury, 7 lbs. in stone bottle, as reserve supply.

Parallel-ruler, Acland's pattern, 18 inches.

Protractor, circular, with compass rectifier, in mahogany box.
Protractor, circular, in brass.
Rain gauge and spare glasses (Livingstone's pattern).
Scale, 18 inches metal, graduated to inches, and subdivided to tenths and hundredths, in box.
Sextant, 4 inches radius, silver arc, cut to 20".
Tape, 100 feet.

Extras.

Spare glass for rain gauge; spare compass cards; leather skins to clean glasses; tin foil, &c.

Most of the above instruments were damaged by the canoe being upset, in attempting to land through the surf.

Second Supply.

2 Aneroids, brass, 2 inches diameter, registering from 15 to 31 inches.
2 Compasses, prismatic, 3 inches diameter, shades and reflector.
1 Compass, pocket.
1 Sextant, 6 inches radius, silver arc, cut to 10".
4 Watches, by Mr. J. Brock (George Street, Portman Square).
1 Watch, by Frodsham (Strand).

BOOKS, &c.

Nautical Almanacks, 1863-4-5-6.
Work books, ruled to form.
Skeleton Map, ruled in squares, 75 sheets.
Memorandum books.

EXTRA INSTRUMENTS.

1 Sextant, 6 inches radius, presented by G. Bishop, Esq., Twickenham; cut to 10".
1 Binocular, presented by the Directors of the Night Asylum, Glasgow, after the lecture I delivered for that institution.
1 Telescope, presented by the same.
Universal Sun Dial, presented by the Royal Geographical Society.

Remarks on the Instruments used in taking the Astronomical Observations.

No. 1 Sextant, 4 inches radius, by Cary, was used for the altitude of the stars and planets in connection with a lunar.

No. 2 Sextant, 6 inches radius, by Cary (the best instrument), always used for time, and in taking the distance in a lunar and meridian altitude.

No. 3 Sextant, used for altitude of the moon under 120° (art. horiz.), and when more than that quantity one of the other sextants was used.

All the above were lost in my retreat, except the watches and two aneroids.

All the instruments above enumerated were carefully tested before leaving England. The aneroids brought back were again tested after my arrival.

My watches proved to have kept very good time; and I ought to express here my thanks to Mr. Brock, of George Street, Portman Square, for the care he took in supplying me with the best watches. They are still in good order; and I am greatly indebted to Sir George Back for recommending Mr. Brock to me. The instruments by Mr. Potter, successor of Mr. Cary, of 181, Strand, proved to be excellent, and stood well the rough travelling they had to go through.

OBSERVATIONS FOR LATITUDE.

Date.	Place.	Object.	Meridian Alt. Artificial Horizon.			In. Error.		Temp.	Latitude S.			Remarks.
			°	′	″	′	″	Fahr.	°	′	″	
1864 Oct. 21	Gogndi	Mars	131	08	40	− 2	20	75	1	33	16	
22	..	α Cygni	87	14	00	− 2	20	78	1	36	46	
24	..	Fomalhaut ...	123	36	10	− 2	20	78	1	36	37	
26	Junction of Niombal with Ovenga	Fomalhaut ...	122	30	10	+ 1	10	78	1	38	23	
Nov. 6	Junction of Ofoubou with Ovenga	Fomalhaut ...	122	83	10	− 0	10	...	1	36	14	
22	Olenda	Fomalhaut ...	122	48	20	+ 1	10	80·0	1	41	31	
29	..	Fomalhaut ...	122	48	30	− 1	10	81·5	1	48	28	
29	..	α Eridani ...	67	41	00	+ 1	00	80·0	1	43	18	
29	..	α Arietis	130	53	00	− 1	00	80·0	1	44	58	
29	..	Mars	129	8	20	− 1	20	79·7	1	44	55	
Dec. 11	Mandji, above Nagoshi Falls........	α Eridani ...	60	49	00	− 4	40	77·9	1	16	28	
14	Dibuan	Capella	85	38	20	− 1	20	74·3	1	21	10	
14	..	Mars	130	06	20	− 1	20	74·3	1	20	53	
14	..	α Eridani ...	67	04	00	− 1	40	80·6	1	24	38	Rejected.
27	Olenda	α Eridani ...	67	40	20	− 2	20	80·6	1	43	20	
27	..	Capella	84	51	30	− 1	50	78·4	1	44	49	
30	..	Mars	130	29	40	− 1	00	76·1	1	41	12	
30	..	Capella	64	32	00	− 0	20	76·1	1	43	48	
1865 Mar. 30	Máyolo	β U. Majoris	63	09	10	− 1	30	79·7	1	51	22	
30	..	α U. Majoris	31	24	30	− 1	20	79·7	1	51	29	

Apr. 2	..	Pollux	119	37	36	− 1	30	68·0	1	51	42
2	..	α Crucis	59	04	20	− 1	00	77·0	1	51	17
6	..	α U. Majoris	51	25	50	− 0	50	75·2	1	50	44
May 1	..	α Crucis	59	03	20	− 1	10	77·0	1	51	05
5	..	η U. Majoris	76	22	20	− 0	30	77·9	1	51	02
6	..	α Crucis	59	04	00	− 1	20	78·4	1	51	06
12	..	α Centauri	63	13	40	− 1	00	77·0	1	51	25
14	..	β U. Majoris	62	09	40	− 1	30	78·8	1	51	05
15	..	α Centauri	63	13	50	− 1	00	77·8	1	51	31
15	..	β Centauri	64	19	50	− 1	00	77·0	1	51	25
15	..	Arcturus	130	33	50	− 1	00	77·0	1	50	37
16	..	α Crucis	59	4	10	− 1	00	75·0	1	51	22
16	..	α Crucis	59	04	10	− 1	00	75·0	1	51	23
18	..	β U. Majoris	62	10	00	− 1	00	75·0	1	50	41
18	..	γ U. Majoris	67	27	20	− 1	10	78·8	1	51	33
18	..	α Crucis	59	04	30	− 1	30	78·8	1	51	13
18	..	ε U. Majoris	62	59	00	− 1	10	78·8	1	50	59
30	Nehlengain's	α Crucis	59	04	00	− 1	10	78·8	1	51	15
30	..	Arcturus	136	33	40	− 1	40	77·0	1	51	14
31	..	β Centauri	64	21	50	− 3	20	77·0	1	51	10
June 2	..	η U. Majoris	76	25	20	− 4	00	73·0	1	51	10
2	..	Antares	131	30	40	− 3	20	70·7	1	51	1
5	Mokala	α Crucis	59	21	40	− 3	30	77·6	1	38	47
5	..	η U. Majoris	70	10	10	− 3	40	76·1	1	38	30
6	..	α Crucis	59	20	00	− 2	30	78·8	1	38	37
6	..	ζ U. Majoris	64	33	00	− 2	40	77·0	1	38	19
6	..	η U. Majoris	70	09	30	− 3	00	77·0	1	38	00

OBSERVATIONS FOR LATITUDE.

Date.	Place.	Object.	Meridian Alt. Artificial Horizon.			In. Error.		Temp.	Latitude S.			Remarks.
			°	′	″	′	″	Fahr.	°	′	″	
1863 June 6	Mohaba	α Centauri ...	63	29	40	− 3	00	76·1	1	58	32	
8	..	α Crucis	59	20	00	− 2	50	73·2	1	58	28	
10	Igoumbié	α Crucis	59	22	40	− 3	30	76·1	1	59	28	
10	..	β Centauri ...	64	37	30	− 3	30	75·2	1	59	00	
10	..	α Centauri ...	63	32	00	− 3	20	73·2	1	59	33	
11	..	α Crucis	59	22	40	− 3	30	77·0	1	59	28	
11	..	ψ U. Majoris	76	09	10	− 3	30	75·8	1	58	57	
11	..	Arcturus	130	18	40	− 3	20	73·8	1	59	39	
11	..	α Centauri ...	63	31	30	− 3	00	73·2	1	59	28	
14	Yengué	β Centauri ...	64	40	40	− 3	20	71·8	2	0	40	
14	..	α Centauri ...	63	23	20	− 2	00	74·2	2	0	52	
15	Mokenga	β Centauri ...	64	41	00	− 3	40	77·0	2	0	47	
15	..	Arcturus	130	16	00	− 3	40	70·6	2	1	2	
16	..	Arcturus	136	16	00	− 3	20	77·0	2	0	52	
10	..	α Centauri ...	63	35	20	− 3	40	76·0	2	1	04	
17	..	β Centauri ...	64	41	40	− 3	30	73·4	2	1	11	
17	..	ψ U. Majoris	76	14	20	−17	30	71·6	2	3	23	Hazy atmosphere.
17	..	ε Boötis	120	43	40	− 3	30	72·5	2	1	42	
17	..	α Coronæ ...	121	42	50	− 3	40	70·7	2	0	36	
28	Niembouai	Antares	131	45	50	− 3	00	70·7	1	58	47	
28	..	Arcturus	130	19	20	− 3	00	72·5	1	50	00	
July 3	Mongon	α Centauri ...	63	26	80	− 3	80	71·2	1	56	45	
17	Molana	α Centauri ...	63	19	10	− 3	50	72·0	1	52	56	

OBSERVATIONS FOR LUNAR DISTANCES.

Date.	Place.	Time by Watch.	Object.	Alt. and Distance.	Index Error.	Temp.	Resulting Longitude, E.
1863		h m s		° ′ ″	′ ″	Fahr.	° ′ ″
Jan. 6 ...	Oleuda	3 47 10	☉ Alt.	48 37 0	on 6 40		
		3 50 20	☾ Alt.	81 46 20	off 0 20		
		3 54 0	Distance	115 48 10	on 1 40		10 10 0
		3 55 15	.. .. ..	115 51 0			
		3 56 45	.. .. ..	115 49 0			
		3 59 15	☾ Alt.	85 47 10			
		4 1 30	☉ Alt.	42 1 20	...	87·8	Sun W. of Moon.
..		4 4 15	☾	88 1 20	off 0 30		
		4 5 45	☉ Alt.	46 29 20	on 6 40		
		4 8 20	Distance	115 54 50	on 1 40		10 17 45
		4 9 35	.. .. ..	115 54 0			
		4 13 10	.. .. ..	115 56 20			
		4 14 30	☉ Alt.	34 5 0			
		4 16 0	☾ Alt.	93 23 30	...	87·8	Sun W. of Moon.
Jan. 17 ..		7 37 55	☾ Alt.	79 29 20	on 5 20		
		7 40 15	☉ Alt.	32 19 10	on 3 10		
		7 42 51	Distance	109 41 10	on 0 30		10 43 30
		7 44 30	.. ..	109 41 30			
		7 48 13	.. ..	109 41 30			
		7 51 31	☉ Alt.	66 37 50			
		7 53 10	☾ Alt.	73 10 20	...	81·5	Sun E. of Moon.

OBSERVATIONS FOR LUNAR DISTANCES.

Date.	Place.	Time by Watch.	Object.	Alt. and Distance.	Index Error.	Temp.	Resulting Longitude, E.
		h m s		° ′ ″	′ ″	Fahr.	° ′ ″
1865 Jan. 17...	Okeda (contd.)	7 39 50	☾ Alt.	63 11 10	on 5 40		
		8 0 42	☾ Alt.	62 2 20	on 2 10		
		8 7 0	Distance	109 33 20			
		8 9 30	,, ...	109 33 20	on 1 0		10 33 0
		8 12 30	,, ...	109 32 30			
		8 13 0	⊙ Alt.	68 30 0			
		8 21 10	☾ Alt.	58 22 20	...	80·6	Sun E. of Moon.
Feb. 3 ...		8 41 22	Pollux Alt. ...	108 29 10	on 1 40		
		8 45 32	☾ Alt.	68 33 30	on 5 30		
		8 49 53	Distance, farthest limb	57 19 0			
		8 51 13		57 17 10	on 0 50		10 48 43
		8 56 7		57 17 0			
		8 50 40	☾ Alt.	62 21 50			
		9 2 20	Pollux Alt. ...	112 13 20	...	81·5	Star E. of Moon.
		9 4 43	☾ Alt.	80 6 40	on 5 10		
		9 6 35	Pollux Alt. ...	114 0 40	on 5 20		
		9 9 52	Distance, farthest limb	57 10 50			
		9 12 40		57 10 0	on 0 30		10 44 0
		9 14 33		57 9 40			
		9 16 52	Pollux Alt. ...	116 20 0			
		9 21 10	☾ Alt.	72 50 0	...	80·6	Star E. of Moon.

Place	Time h m s	Object	Observed ° ′ ″	Index error	Therm.	Result	Remarks
	9 27 20	Pollux Alt. ...	117 28 0	on 5 40		11 5 15	
	9 29 33	☾ Alt.	69 1 50	on 5 30			
	9 34 20	Distance, farthest limb	57 1 50	on 0 30			
	9 40 35		56 56 30				
	9 44 10		56 56 0				
	9 46 45	☾ Alt.	61 18 30				
	9 51 03	Pollux Alt. ...	119 23 10	...	80·6		Star E. of Moon.
	9 57 0	Canopus Alt. ...	74 12 20	on 0 30	80·6		For time.
	9 59 45	.. ..	73 53 0				
April 1... Mayolo	2 19 55	☾ Alt.	95 30 0	on 0 20		10 43 0	
	2 23 0	⊙ Alt.	108 34 30	on 17 20			
	2 24 53	Distance	72 11 30	on 0 40			
	2 26 15	.. ..	72 11 10				
	2 27 15	.. ..	72 11 40				
	2 28 13	.. ..	72 12 20				
	2 29 42	⊙ Alt.	103 37 20				
	2 31 52	☾ Alt.	100 29 0	...	91·4		Sun W. of Moon.
	2 51 0	☾ Alt.	108 8 20	on 0 10		10 18 30	
	2 53 14	⊙ Alt.	92 4 10	on 17 0			
	2 56 51	Distance	72 20 0	on 1 0			
	3 3 24	.. ..	72 24 10				
	3 4 7	.. ..	72 23 30				
	3 5 11	.. ..	72 23 10				
	3 6 40	⊙ Alt.	89 21 30				
	3 21 11	☽ Alt.	119 17 40	...	92·3		Sun W. of Moon.

OBSERVATIONS FOR LUNAR DISTANCES.

Date.	Place.	Time.	Object.	Alt. and Distance.	Index Error.	Temp.	Resulting Longitude, E.
		h m s		° ′ ″	′ ″	Fahr.	° ′ ″
1865 April 1...	Maiyolo (cont.)	6 17 30	Venus Alt. ...	56 2 20	6 10		
		6 20 14	☾ Alt.	119 37 40	17 20		
		6 23 10	Distance, nearest limb	35 3 40			
		6 25 32		35 6 0	on 0 40		11 5 15
		6 26 42		35 7 0			
		6 28 12	Venus Alt. ...	51 21 0			
		6 30 25	☾ Alt.	116 24 0	...	84·2	Planet W. of Moon.
		6 33 33	☾ Alt.	115 12 0	on 17 20		
		6 35 30	Alt. of Venus...	18 3 20	on 6 10		
		6 37 25	Distance, nearest limb	35 11 0			
		6 39 36		35 10 50	on 0 40		10 53 45
		6 41 30		35 12 50			
		6 47 24	Venus Alt. ...	42 48 20			
		6 54 22	☾ Alt.	107 32 20	...	84·2	Planet W. of Moon.
April 2...		6 0 30	☾ Alt.	139 10 0	on 1 20		
		6 4 17	Alt. of Venus...	60 19 10	on 1 30		
		6 6 50	Distance, nearest limb	47 38 40			
		6 8 35		47 38 40	on 1 30		10 48 15
		6 10 0		47 38 0			
		6 11 42	Alt. of Venus...	57 0 10			
		6 18 25	☾ Alt.	137 36 10	...	86·9	Planet W. of Moon.

6 14 50	☾ Alt.	137 28 40	on 1 40		
6 17 13	Alt. of Venus ..	54 87 0	on 1 30		
6 20 12	Distance, nearest limb	47 40 0			
6 22 27		47 40 20	on 1 30		10 50 30
6 24 2		47 41 20			
6 26 7	Alt. of Venus ...	50 42 10			
6 28 25	☾ Alt.	134 56 30			Planet W. of Moon.
7 10 30	Capella Alt.	57 11 10	on 1 20	...	For time.
7 12 18	"	50 46 20	...	80·0	
9 5 20	Alt. of Spica ...	79 8 40	on 3 0		
9 6 58	☾ Alt.	74 9 20	on 14 20		
9 11 31	Distance, farthest limb	101 57 20			
9 13 50		101 50 50	on 0 40		11 34 45
9 15 3		101 50 20			
9 17 4	☾ Alt.	70 30 0			
9 18 50	Spica Alt. ...	85 50 40	...	78·8	Star E. of Moon.
9 20 31	Spica Alt. ...	66 20 0	on 3 10		
9 21 41	☾ Alt.	68 23 20	on 14 0		
9 25 2	Distance, farthest limb	101 51 30			
9 26 10		101 49 10	on 0 30		11 4 30
9 27 52		101 50 20			
9 30 35	☾ Alt.	64 27 20			
9 32 20	Spica Alt. ...	92 13 40	...	78·8	Star E. of Moon.

OBSERVATIONS FOR LUNAR DISTANCES.

Date.	Place.	Time.	Object.	Alt. and Distance.	Index Error.	Temp.	Resulting Longitude, E.
1863		h m s		° ′ ″	′ ″	Fahr.	° ′ ″
April 2...	Mayolo (cont^d.)	9 34 21	Spica Alt. ...	80 20 0	on 3 40		
		9 36 9	☾ Alt.	82 1 30	on 14 0		
		9 38 6	Distance, farthest limb	101 47 0	1 0		11 31 30
		9 39 29		101 46 10			
		9 41 25		101 45 50			
		9 43 7	☾ Alt.	58 52 10			
		9 45 0	Spica Alt. ...	98 15 20	...	78·8	Star E. of Moon.
		10 11 8	☾ Alt.	106 49 20	on 4 0		
		10 13 10	Saturn Alt. ...	85 12 10	on 13 10		
		10 15 22	Distance, farthest limb	108 0 0	on 0 40		11 37 0
		10 16 22		107 59 10			
		10 17 42		107 57 40			
		10 19 10		107 58 30			
		10 20 41	☾ Alt.	41 49 30			
		10 21 15	Saturn Alt. ...	113 29 20			
		11 33 43	Antares Alt. ...	57 24 20	on 1 0	...	For time.
		11 36 43	,, ...	58 30 0	...	77·0	
April 3...		4 22 10	⊙ Alt.	46 44 40	on 5 30		
		4 26 15	☾ Alt.	107 25 20	on 14 0		

h	m	s	Observation	°	′	″	Index error	Therm.	Longitude
4	28	6	Distance	96	38	0	on 0 30		10 38 ·15
4	29	32	,, ...	96	39	50			
4	30	31	,, ...	96	38	10			
4	31	45	,, ...	96	39	10			
4	33	1	☾ Alt.	110	14	0			
4	35	22	☉ Alt.	40	26	30	...	92·8	Sun. W. of Moon.
7	20	30	Aldebaran Alt.	61	35	0	on 5 0		10 35 45
7	24	23	☾ Alt.	131	42	20	on 5 0		
7	27	56	Distance, nearest limb	43	38	0	on 0 30		
7	29	33		43	38	30			
7	31	10		43	39	0			
7	33	52	☾ Alt.	133	18	30			
7	36	40	Aldebaran Alt.	54	8	0	...	85·1	Star W. of Moon.
9	37	40	☾ Alt.	100	30	40	on 17 0		10 36 30
9	40	30	Pollux Alt. ...	58	2	20	on 6 40		
9	43	0	Distance, farthest limb	99	1	10	on 0 40		
9	45	17		99	1	20			
9	47	35		99	2	20			
9	51	0	Pollux Alt. ...	58	44	20			
9	52	43	☾ Alt.	107	49	40			Star W. of Moon.

April 11

OBSERVATIONS FOR LUNAR DISTANCES.

Date.	Place.	Time. h	m	s	Object.	Alt. and Distance. °	'	"	Index Error. ' "	Temp.	Resulting Longitude, E. ° ' "
1875 April 11	Máyolo (contd.)	10	6	12	☾ Alt.	114	5	0	on 16 0	Fahr.	
		10	9	14	Regulus Alt. ...	120	1	0	on 6 0		
		10	14	31	Distance, farthest limb	62	41	0	on 0 40		10 28 0
		10	16	6		62	40	30			
		10	17	37		62	41	10			
		10	19	4		62	41	30			
		10	22	5	Regulus Alt. ...	114	18	0			
		10	23	22	☾ Alt.	122	12	40			Star W. of Moon.
April 13		8	32	40	Sirius Alt. ...	68	9	0	on 0 40		
		8	34	44	„	67	8	30			
		8	37	25	„	65	53	0			
		8	39	36	„	61	51	20	...	77·4	For time.
		9	8	22	Saturn Alt. ...	61	22	20	on 6 0		
		9	15	13	☾ Alt.	44	43	30	on 12 10		
		9	18	43	Distance, farthest limb	27	22	20	on 0 40		10 33 30
		9	22	56		27	24	10			
		9	25	6		27	24	50			
		9	20	42	☾ Alt.	50	2	30			
		9	30	16	Saturn Alt. ...	105	12	0	...	76·4	Planet W. of Moon.

Date	h	m	s	Observation	°	'	"	Index error		Result	Remarks
April 20	9	33	11	Saturn Alt. ...	106	36	0	on 6 0		10 33 0	Planet W. of Moon.
	9	34	33	☾ Alt.	53	41	30	on 2 40			
	9	36	11	Distance	27	30	30	on 0 40			
	9	41	37	.. ..	27	33	10				
	9	44	42	.. ..	27	34	0				
	9	46	2	.. ..	27	34	30				
	9	48	3	☾ Alt.	59	50	0				
	9	50*	4	Saturn Alt. ...	114	38	0	...	76·4		
	21	17	55	☉ Alt.	105	35	30	on 0 40	...		For time.
	21	19	31	☉ Alt.	106	18	20				
	21	39	55	☾ Alt.	129	47	0	on 0 40		11 36 15	Sun E. of Moon.
	21	35	35	☉ Alt.	113	34	20	6 0			
	21	38	40	Distance	58	29	10	on 0 40			
	21	39	32	.. ..	58	29	0				
	21	40	25	.. ..	58	28	20				
	21	41	21	.. ..	58	29	0				
	21	43	3	☉ Alt.	117	0	0				
	21	46	10	☾ Alt.	123	30	0				
May 1 ...	7	22	45	Sirius Alt. ...	74	34	10	on 0 30			For time.
	7	24	35	.. ..	73	42	20				
	7	26	22	.. ..	72	50	0				
	7	31	38	Spica Alt. ...	86	59	10				
	7	35	0	.. ..	88	44	30	...	78·8		

OBSERVATIONS FOR LUNAR DISTANCES.

Date.	Place.	Time.	Object.	Alt. and Distance.	Index Error.	Temp.	Resulting Longitude, E.
		h m s		° ′ ″	′ ″	Fahr.	° ′ ″
1865 May 1...	Maiyolo (contd.)	7 42 14	☾ Alt.	103 52 10	on 12 0		
		7 44 46	Spica Alt. ...	93 34 20	on 6 20		
		7 46 44	Distance, farthest limb	81 20 0			
		7 48 22		81 19 20	on 0 30		11 37 0
		7 49 30		81 19 20			
		7 51 20		81 18 40			
		7 53 58	Spica Alt. ...	98 2 20			
		7 56 28	☾ Alt.	97 38 0	...	77·0	Star E. of Moon.
"		7 59 18	☾ Alt.	96 26 0	on 12 0		
		8 1 53	Spica Alt. ...	101 53 20	on 6 0		
		8 3 28	Distance	81 13 0			
		8 5 8	"	81 13 30	on 0 30		11 20 0
		8 6 19	"	81 12 30			
		8 7 35	"	81 12 30			
		8 9 30	Spica Alt. ...	105 34 40			
		8 11 32	☾ Alt.	91 2 10	...	77·9	Star E. of Moon.
		8 19 12	Spica Alt. ...	110 19 20	on 6 0		
		8 21 15	☾ Alt.	86 40 0	on 11 50		
		8 22 58	Distance	81 6 20			
		8 25 2	"	81 6 0	on 0 40		11 17 30
		8 26 15	"	81 5 30			
		8 28 0	"	81 5 0			

..	8 29 35	☾ Alt.	82 51 30			
	8 32 35	Spica Alt. ...	116 42 0	..	77·4	
	8 47 17	Saturn Alt. ...	114 20 0	on 6 0		
	8 49 60	☾ Alt.	73 40 0	on 11 30		
	8 52 5	Distance	85 16 50	on 0 50		11 19 45
	8 54 17	.. ..	85 13 30			
	8 56 30	.. ..	85 15 20			
	8 57 38	.. ..	85 11 50			
	8 59 43	☾ Alt.	69 6 10			
	9 1 45	Saturn Alt. ...	121 26 0	..	77·0	Planet E. of Moon.
	9 4 55	Saturn Alt. ...	125 2 20	on 6 0		
	9 6 28	☾ Alt.	66 8 0	on 11 30		
	9 7 56	Distance	85 10 0	on 1 0		11 19 15
	9 9 2	.. ..	85 10 20			
	9 10 45	.. ..	85 9 40			
	9 13 30	.. ..	85 9 0			
	9 14 03	♃ Alt.	62 31 10			
		Saturn—too high			77·0	Planet E. of Moon.
May 4...	12 10 30	Jupiter Alt. ...	68 10 0	on 0 40		For time.
	12 12 33	.. ..	88 56 10			
	12 14 3	.. ..	89 39 40		77.0	

OBSERVATIONS FOR LUNAR DISTANCES.

Date.	Place.	Time.	Object.	Alt. and Distance.	Index Error.	Temp.	Resulting Longitude, E.
1865		h m s		° ′ ″	′ ″	Fahr.	° ′ ″
May 4 ...	Máyolo (contd.)	12 22 30	Spica Alt. ...	118 42 40	on 0 40		For time.
		12 24 31	.. ..	117 44 30			
		11 6 5	☾ Alt.	77 21 0	on 6 50		
		11 8 26	Jupiter Alt. ...	60 47 40	on 8 0		
		11 9 57	Distance, farthest limb	109 40 30	on 0 30		10 58 15
		11 12 10		109 40 0			
		11 14 15		109 40 0			
		11 15 42		100 39 40			
		11 17 23	Jupiter Alt. ...	64 51 0			
		11 19 43	☾ Alt.	70 20 0	...	77·0	Planet E. of Moon.
		11 22 35	☾ Alt.	68 35 20	on 7 0		
		11 24 27	Jupiter Alt. ...	68 4 0	on 9 0		
		11 26 36	Distance, farthest limb	109 35 0	on 0 30		11 10 30
		11 27 58		109 34 40			
		11 29 15		100 34 30			
		11 30 30		109 31 10			
		11 32 0	Jupiter Alt. ...	71 21 0			
		11 33 29	☾ Alt.	63 40 0	...	77·0	Planet E. of Moon.
		11 35 30	☾ Alt.	62 30 40	on 7 0		
		[illegible]	[illegible]	[illegible]	[illegible]		

	11 39 44	Distance, farthest limb	100 29 50	on 0 40		10 50 0
	11 41 31		109 29 0			
	11 43 11		109 28 40			
	11 44 22		109 28 0			
	11 45 58	Jupiter Alt. ...	77 32 20			
	11 47 42	☾ Alt.	50 40 20	...	77·0	Planet E. of Moon.
	11 53 19	Jupiter Alt. ...	80 45 20	on 7 0		
	11 51 59	☾ Alt.	53 15 30	on 9 0		
	11 57 50	Distance, farthest limb	109 23 0	on 0 40		11 18 15
	11 59 25		109 23 0			
	12 0 35		109 22 0			
	12 2 4		109 21 30			
	12 1 9	☾ Alt.	48 46 10			
	12 7 11	Jupiter Alt. ...	80 50 40	...	77·0	Planet E. of Moon.
May 6 ...	10 36 30	Jupiter Alt. ...	49 59 30	on 1 40		For time.
	10 37 58	"	50 36 30			
	10 40 15	"	51 39 40			
	10 44 14	Antares Alt. ...	91 3 30	on 1 30		
	10 46 13	"	91 50 0			
	10 47 30	"	92 21 10		77·9	

OBSERVATIONS FOR LUNAR DISTANCES.

Date.	Place.	Time.	Object.	Alt. and Distance.	Index Error.	Temp.	Resulting Longitude, E.
		h m s		° ′ ″	′ ″	Fahr.	° ′ ″
1865 May 6 ...	Maiyalo (contd.)	11 1 30	☾ Alt.	121 12 40	on 6 30		
		11 4 30	Jupiter Alt. ...	62 44 20	on 5 20		
		11 7 25	Distance	85 43 40			
		11 9 42	"	85 42 50	on 0 40		11 7 15
		11 11 53	"	85 42 20			
		11 13 27	"	85 42 20			
		11 15 10	Jupiter Alt. ...	67 31 0			
		11 18 2	☾ Alt.	113 5 10	...	77·0	Planet E. of Moon.
		11 19 44	☾ Alt.	112 16 0	on 6 50		
		11 22 7	Jupiter Alt. ...	70 37 40	on 5 20		
		11 24 24	Distance	85 38 0			
		11 26 18	"	85 37 30	on 0 40		11 11 15
		11 31 43	"	85 37 0			
		11 33 10	"	85 30 0			
		11 35 8	Jupiter Alt. ...	76 22 0			
		11 38 40	☾ Alt.	103 59 30	...	77·0	Planet E. of Moon.
"		11 48 25	☾ Alt.	98 13 20	on 7 0		
		11 51 8	Jupiter Alt. ...	83 26 0	on 5 0		
		11 53 50	Distance	85 28 40			
		11 54 44	"	85 29 30	on 0 50		11 1 0
		11 56 9	"	85 27 50			
		11 58 48	"	85 27 40			

		12 1 43	Jupiter Alt. ...	87 59 0			Planet E. of Moon.
		12 4 22	☾ Alt.	90 24 30	...	77·0	
		12 9 30	☾ Alt.	87 32 20	on 7 0		
		12 11 12	Jupiter Alt. ...	92 2 20	on 5 0		
		12 14 6	Distance	85 22 30			
		12 15 30	,, ...	85 21 30	on 1 10		10 33 0
		12 16 35	,, ...	83 21 10			
		12 19 0	,, ...	83 20 30			
		12 21 34	Jupiter Alt. ...	96 27 20			
		12 28 5	☾ Alt.	61 17 20	...	77·0	Planet E. of Moon.
June 1 ...	Mouendi	10 40 33	Jupiter Alt. ...	95 26 0			For time.
		10 42 7	,, ...	96 5 50	on 4 0		
		10 43 45	,, ...	96 45 40			
,,		10 46 15	Arcturus Alt. ...	123 44 30	on 3 30		For time.
		10 48 22	,, ...	123 3 50			
		10 50 18	,, ...	124 31 0	...	72·2	
,,		9 33 3	☾ Alt.	90 3 0	on 6 0		
		9 35 42	Jupiter Alt. ...	67 10 6	on 5 0		
		9 37 0	Distance	99 46 40			
		9 38 45	,, ...	99 40 50	on 8 20		11 10 15
		9 39 30	,, ...	99 47 0			
		9 42 32	,, ...	99 43 10			
		9 43 30	Jupiter Alt. ...	71 34 20			
		9 47 10	☾ Alt.	83 13 40	...	72·5	Planet E. of Moon.

OBSERVATIONS FOR LUNAR DISTANCES.

Date.	Place.	Time.	Object.	Alt. and Distance.	Index Error.	Temp.	Resulting Longitude, E.
		h m s		° ′ ″	′ ″	Fahr.	° ′ ″
1863 April 1...	Majolo (contd.)	6 17 30	Venus Alt. ...	50 2 20	6 10		
		6 20 14	☾ Alt.	119 57 40	17 20		
		6 23 10	Distance, nearest limb	35 5 40	on 0 40		11 5 15
		0 25 32		35 6 0			
		6 26 42		35 7 0			
		0 28 12	Venus Alt. ...	31 21 0			
		6 30 25	☾ Alt.	116 24 0	...	84·2	Planet W. of Moon.
		6 33 53	☾ Alt.	115 12 0	on 17 20		
		6 35 30	Alt. of Venus ...	18 8 20	on 6 10		
		6 37 25	Distance, nearest limb	35 11 0	on 0 40		10 53 45
		6 39 30		35 10 50			
		6 44 30		35 12 50			
		6 47 24	Venus Alt. ...	12 48 20			
		6 31 22	☾ Alt.	107 32 20	...	84·2	Planet W. of Moon.
April 2...		6 0 30	☾ Alt.	130 10 0	on 1 20		
		6 4 17	Alt. of Venus ...	60 19 10	on 1 30		
		6 6 30	Distance, nearest limb	47 30 40	on 1 30		10 48 15
		6 8 35		47 36 40			
		6 10 0		47 38 0			
		6 11 12	Alt. of Venus ...	57 6 10			
		6 13 25	☾ Alt.	157 30 10	...	88·9	Planet W. of Moon.

6	14	50	☾ Alt.	137	28	40	on	1	40			
6	17	13	Alt. of Venus ..	34	37	0	on	1	30			
6	20	12	Distance, nearest limb	47	40	0	on	1	30		10 56 30	
6	22	27		47	40	20						
6	24	2		47	41	20						
6	26	7	Alt. of Venus ...	50	42	10						
6	28	20	☾ Alt.	134	56	30						Planet W. of Moon.
7	10	36	Capella Alt.	57	14	10	on	1	20	...		For time.
7	12	18	,,	50	40	20		...		80·0		
9	5	20	Alt. of Spica ...	79	8	40	on	3	0			
9	8	58	☾ Alt.	74	9	20	on	14	20			
9	11	31	Distance, farthest limb	101	57	20	on	0	40		11 34 45	
9	13	30		101	30	50						
9	15	3		101	56	20						
9	17	4	☾ Alt.	70	30	0						
9	18	50	Spica Alt. ...	85	30	40		...		78·6		Star E. of Moon.
9	20	31	Spica Alt. ...	86	20	0	on	3	10			
9	21	41	☾ Alt.	68	29	20	on	14	0			
9	25	2	Distance, farthest limb	101	51	30	on	0	30		11 4 30	
9	26	10		101	48	10						
9	27	52		101	50	20						
9	30	35	☾ Alt.	64	27	20						
9	32	20	Spica Alt. ...	92	13	40		...		78·8		Star E. of Moon.

OBSERVATIONS FOR LUNAR DISTANCES.

Date.	Place.	Time.	Object.	Alt. and Distance.	Index Error.	Temp.	Resulting Longitude, E.
1863		h m s		° ′ ″	′ ″	Fahr.	° ′ ″
April 2...	Máyolo (cont^d.)	9 34 24	Spica Alt. ...	66 20 0	on 3 40		
		9 36 9	☾ Alt.	62 1 30	on 14 0		
		9 38 8	Distance, farthest limb	101 47 0	1 0		11 31 30
		9 39 29		101 46 10			
		9 41 25		101 45 30			
		9 43 7	☾ Alt.	58 52 10			
		9 45 0	Spica Alt. ...	98 15 20	...	78·8	Star E. of Moon.
		10 11 8	☾ Alt.	106 49 20	on 4 0		
		10 13 16	Saturn Alt. ...	35 12 10	on 18 10		
		10 15 22	Distance, farthest limb	108 0 0	on 0 40		11 37 0
		10 16 22		107 59 10			
		10 17 42		107 57 40			
		10 19 10		107 58 30			
		10 20 44	☾ Alt.	41 49 30			
		10 24 15	Saturn Alt. ...	113 29 20			
		11 33 43	Antares Alt. ...	37 24 20	on 1 0	...	For time.
		11 36 43	.. ..	38 50 0	...	77·0	
April 3...		4 22 40	☉ Alt.	46 44 40	on 5 30		
		4 26 15	☾ Alt.	107 25 20	on 14 0		

4	28	0	Distance	96	58	0	on	0	30		10 36 ·15
4	29	32	,, ...	96	59	30					
4	30	31	,, ...	96	58	10					
4	31	45	,, ...	96	59	10					
4	33	1	☾ Alt.	110	14	0					
4	35	22	⊙ Alt.	40	20	30	...			92·3	Sun. W. of Moon.
7	20	50	Aldebaran Alt.	61	35	0	on	5	0		
7	24	25	☾ Alt.	134	42	20	on	5	0		
7	27	36	Distance, nearest limb	43	58	0	on	0	30		10 55 45
7	28	33		43	58	30					
7	31	10		43	59	0					
7	33	32	☾ Alt.	133	13	30					
7	30	40	Aldebaran Alt.	54	8	0	...			85·1	Star W. of Moon.
9	37	40	☾ Alt.	100	50	40	on	17	0		
9	40	30	Pollux Alt. ...	58	2	20	on	6	40		
9	43	0	Distance, farthest limb	99	1	10	on	0	40		10 58 50
9	45	17		99	1	20					
9	47	55		99	2	20					
9	51	0	Pollux Alt. ...	53	44	20					
9	52	45	☾ Alt.	107	40	40					Star W. of Moon.

April 11

OBSERVATIONS FOR LUNAR DISTANCES.

Date.	Place.	Time.	Object.	Alt. and Distance.	Index Error.	Temp.	Resulting Longitude, E.
1875		h. m. s.		° ' "	' "	Fahr.	° ' "
April 11	Máyolo (contd.)	10 6 12	☾ Alt.	114 5 0	on 16 0		
		10 9 14	Regulus Alt. ...	120 1 0	on 6 0		
		10 14 34	Distance, farthest limb	62 41 0	on 0 40		10 28 0
		10 16 0		62 40 30			
		10 17 37		62 41 10			
		10 19 4		62 41 30			
		10 22 5	Regulus Alt. ...	114 18 0			
		10 23 22	☾ Alt.	122 12 40			Star W. of Moon.
April 13		8 32 40	Sirius Alt. ...	68 9 0	on 0 40		
		8 34 44	„	67 8 30			
		8 37 23	„	65 53 0			
		8 39 36	„	61 31 20	...	77·4	For time.
		9 8 22	Saturn Alt. ...	94 22 20	on 6 0		
		9 15 13	☾ Alt.	44 43 30	on 12 10		
		9 18 43	Distance, farthest limb	27 22 20	on 0 40		10 35 30
		9 22 36		27 24 10			
		9 25 8		27 21 50			
		9 29 42	☾ Alt.	50 2 30			
		9 30 16	Saturn Alt. ...	105 12 0	...	76·4	Planet W. of Moon.

Date		Time	Observed	Reading	Index error		Result	Remarks
..	..	9 33 14	Saturn Alt. ...	100 36 0	on 6 0			
		9 34 33	☾ Alt.	53 41 30	on 2 40			
		9 36 41	Distance	27 30 30	on 0 40		10 33 0	
		9 41 37	.. ..	27 38 10				
		9 44 42	.. ..	27 34 0				
		9 40 2	.. ..	27 34 30				
		9 48 3	☾ Alt.	39 50 0				
		9 50° 4	Saturn Alt. ...	114 58 0	...	70·4		Planet W. of Moon.
April 29		21 17 35	☉ Alt.	105 33 30	on 0 40	...		For time.
		21 19 31	☉ Alt.	106 18 20				
..		21 32 33	☾ Alt.	129 47 0	on 0 40			
		21 35 35	☉ Alt.	116 34 20	6 0			
		21 38 40	Distance	58 29 10	on 0 40		11 36 15	
		21 39 32	.. ..	58 29 0				
		21 40 25	.. ..	58 28 20				
		21 41 21	.. ..	58 29 0				
		21 43 3	☉ Alt.	117 0 0				
		21 46 19	☾ Alt.	123 30 0				Sun E. of Moon.
May 1 ...		7 22 45	Sirius Alt. ...	74 34 10	on 0 30			For time.
		7 24 35	.. ..	73 42 30				
		7 26 22	.. ..	72 50 0				
		7 31 38	Spica Alt. ...	86 50 10				
		7 35 0	.. ..	88 44 30	...	78·8		

OBSERVATIONS FOR LUNAR DISTANCES.

Date.	Place.	Time.	Object.	Alt. and Distance	Index Error.	Temp.	Resulting Longitude, E.
		h m s		° ′ ″	′ ″	Fahr.	° ′ ″
1865 May 1...	Maipula (contd.)	7 42 14	☾ Alt.	103 32 10	on 12 0		
		7 44 46	Spica Alt. ...	88 34 20	on 6 20		
		7 40 44	Distance, farthest limb	81 20 0	on 0 30		11 37 0
		7 48 22		81 10 20			
		7 49 30		81 19 20			
		7 51 20		81 18 40			
		7 53 58	Spica Alt. ...	99 2 20			Star E. of Moon.
		7 56 28	☾ Alt.	97 38 0	...	77·9	
..		7 38 18	☾ Alt.	98 26 0	on 12 0		
		8 1 53	Spica Alt. ...	101 33 20	on 6 0		
		8 3 28	Distance	81 13 0	on 0 30		11 20 0
		8 5 8	.. .. ..	81 13 30			
		8 6 19	.. .. ..	81 12 30			
		8 7 35	.. .. ..	81 12 30			
		8 9 30	Spica Alt. ...	103 34 40			Star E. of Moon.
		8 11 32	☾ Alt.	91 2 10	...	77·9	
		8 19 12	Spica Alt. ...	110 10 20	on 6 0		
		8 21 15	☾ Alt.	88 40 0	on 11 50		
		8 22 58	Distance	81 6 20	on 0 40		11 17 30
		8 23 2	.. ..	81 6 0			
		8 26 15	.. ..	81 5 30			
		8 28 0	.. ..	81 5 0			

Date	Time	Object	Observed	Index error	Barometer	Result	Remarks
	8 29 35	☾ Alt.	62 51 30				
	8 32 33	Spica Alt. ...	116 42 0	..	77·4		
..	8 47 17	Saturn Alt. ...	114 20 0	on 6 0			
	8 49 30	☾ Alt.	73 49 0	on 11 30			
	8 52 5	Distance	83 16 30	on 0 50		11 19 45	
	8 54 17	,, ...	83 15 30				
	8 56 30	,, ...	83 13 20				
	8 57 38	,, ...	83 14 50				
	8 59 43	☾ Alt.	69 6 10				
	9 1 43	Saturn Alt. ...	121 20 0	..	77·0		Planet E. of Moon.
..	9 4 55	Saturn Alt. ...	123 2 20	on 6 0			
	9 6 28	☾ Alt.	60 3 0	on 11 50			
	9 7 56	Distance	83 10 0	on 1 0		11 19 15	
	9 9 2	,, ...	83 10 20				
	9 10 43	,, ...	83 9 40				
	9 12 30	,, ...	83 9 0				
	9 14 09	♃ Alt.	62 31 10				
		Saturn—too high			77·0		Planet E. of Moon.
May 4...	12 10 30	Jupiter Alt. ...	88 10 0	on 0 40			For time.
	12 12 31	,, ...	88 56 10				
	12 14 9	,, ...	89 39 10		77.0		

OBSERVATIONS FOR LUNAR DISTANCES.

Date.	Place.	Time.	Object.	Alt and Distance.	Index Error.	Temp.	Resulting Longitude, E.
1865		h m s		° ′ ″	′ ″	Fahr.	° ′ ″
May 4 ...	Mayolo (contd.)	12 22 30	Spica Alt. ...	118 42 40	on 0 40		For time.
		12 24 31	,, ...	117 44 30			
		11 6 3	☾ Alt.	77 24 0	on 6 50		
		11 8 28	Jupiter Alt. ...	60 47 40	on 8 0		
		11 0 57	Distance, farthest limb	109 40 30	on 0 30		10 38 15
		11 12 10		109 40 0			
		11 14 15		109 40 0			
		11 15 42		109 30 40			
		11 17 23	Jupiter Alt. ...	64 51 0			
		11 19 43	☾ Alt.	70 20 0	...	77·0	Planet E. of Moon.
		11 22 35	☾ Alt.	68 35 20	on 7 0		
		11 24 27	Jupiter Alt. ...	68 4 0	on 9 0		
		11 26 58	Distance, farthest limb	109 35 0	on 0 30		11 10 30
		11 27 38		109 34 40			
		11 29 15		109 34 30			
		11 30 30		109 34 10			
		11 31 0	Jupiter Alt. ...	71 21 0			
		11 33 29	☾ Alt.	63 40 0	...	77·0	Planet E. of Moon.
		11 35 30	☾ Alt.	62 39 40	on 7 0		

	11 39 44	Distance, farthest limb	109 29 30	on 0 40		10 50 0
	11 41 31		109 29 0			
	11 43 11		109 28 40			
	11 44 22		109 28 0			
	11 45 58	Jupiter Alt. ...	77 39 20			
	11 47 42	☾ Alt.	56 40 20	...	77·0	Planet E. of Moon.
	11 53 19	Jupiter Alt. ...	80 45 20	on 7 0		
	11 54 59	☾ Alt.	53 15 30	on 9 0		
	11 57 50	Distance, farthest limb	109 23 0	on 0 40		11 18 15
	11 59 23		109 23 0			
	12 0 35		109 22 0			
	12 2 4		109 21 30			
	12 4 9	☾ Alt.	48 46 10			
	12 7 11	Jupiter Alt. ...	86 50 40	...	77·0	Planet E. of Moon.
May 6 ...	10 36 30	Jupiter Alt. ...	49 59 30	on 1 40		For time.
	10 37 38	,, ...	50 30 30			
	10 40 15	,, ...	51 39 40			
	10 44 14	Antares Alt. ...	91 3 30	on 1 30		
	10 46 13	,, ...	91 50 0			
	10 47 30	,, ...	92 21 10		77·9	

OBSERVATIONS FOR LUNAR DISTANCES.

Date.	Place.	Time.	Object.	Alt. and Distance.	Index Error.	Temp.	Resulting Longitude, E.
		h m s		° ′ ″	′ ″	Fahr.	h m s
1865 May 6 ...	Máyolo (contd.)	11 1 30	☾ Alt.	121 12 40	on 6 30		
		11 4 30	Jupiter Alt. ...	62 44 20	on 5 20		
		11 7 25	Distance	85 43 40			
		11 9 42	.. ..	85 42 50	on 0 40		11 7 15
		11 11 53	.. ..	85 42 20			
		11 13 27	.. ..	85 42 20			
		11 15 10	Jupiter Alt. ...	67 31 0			
		11 18 2	☾ Alt.	113 5 10	...	77·0	Planet E. of Moon.
..		11 19 44	☾ Alt.	112 16 0	on 6 50		
		11 22 7	Jupiter Alt. ...	70 37 40	on 5 20		
		11 24 24	Distance	85 38 0			
		11 26 18	.. ..	85 37 50	on 0 40		11 11 15
		11 31 49	.. ..	85 37 0			
		11 33 10	.. ..	85 36 0			
		11 35 8	Jupiter Alt. ...	76 22 0			
		11 38 40	☾ Alt.	100 59 30	...	77·0	Planet E. of Moon.
..		11 48 25	☾ Alt.	98 19 20	on 7 0		
		11 51 8	Jupiter Alt. ...	69 28 0	on 5 0		
		11 53 30	Distance	85 28 40			
		11 54 44	.. ..	85 29 30	on 0 30		11 1 0
		11 56 0	.. ..	83 27 30			
		11 58 49	.. ..	85 27 40			

Date	Place	h	m	s	Object	°	'	"	Index error	Temp.	Remarks
		12	1	45	Jupiter Alt. ...	67	59	0			
		12	4	22	☾ Alt.	90	24	30	...	77·0	Planet E. of Moon.
		12	0	30	☾ Alt.	67	52	20	on 7 0		
		12	11	12	Jupiter Alt. ...	92	2	20	on 5 0		
		12	14	0	Distance	85	22	30			
		12	15	30	,, ...	85	21	30	on 1 10		10 53 0
		12	16	55	,, ...	85	21	10			
		12	19	0	,, ...	85	20	30			
		12	21	34	Jupiter Alt. ...	90	27	20			
		12	23	5	☾ Alt.	91	17	20	...	77·0	Planet E. of Moon.
June 1 ...	Mouendi	10	40	33	Jupiter Alt. ...	93	28	0			For time.
		10	42	7	,, ...	90	3	50	on 4 0		
		10	43	45	,, ...	96	45	40			
,,		10	46	15	Arcturus Alt. ...	125	44	30	on 2 50		For time.
		10	48	22	,, ...	125	3	50			
		10	50	18	,, ...	124	31	0	...	72·2	
,,		9	33	9	☾ Alt.	90	8	0	on 6 0		
		9	35	42	Jupiter Alt. ...	67	10	0	on 5 0		
		9	37	0	Distance	99	46	40			
		9	38	45	,, ...	99	46	50	on 2 20		11 16 15
		9	39	56	,, ...	99	47	0			
		9	42	38	,, ...	99	45	10			
		9	45	30	Jupiter Alt. ...	71	31	20			
		9	47	10	☾ Alt.	83	13	40	...	72·5	Planet E. of Moon.

OBSERVATIONS FOR LUNAR DISTANCES.

Date.	Place.	Time.	Object.	Alt. and Distance.	Index Error.	Temp.	Resulting Longitude, E.
1865		h m s		° ′ ″	′ ″	Fahr.	° ′ ″
June 1 ...	Mourendi (contd.)	9 43 46	☾ Alt.	82 26 30	on 6 10		
		9 51 0	Jupiter Alt. ...	73 59 20	on 5 20		
		9 52 40	Distance	99 42 10			
		9 54 2	"	99 41 50	on 3 30		11 19 0
		9 55 29	"	99 40 30			
		9 56 35	"	99 40 30			
		9 58 41	Jupiter Alt. ...	77 18 20			
		10 0 0	☾ Alt.	76 56 20	...	72·5	Planet E. of Moon.
		10 7 21	☾ Alt.	73 16 10	on 6 0		
		10 10 12	Jupiter Alt. ...	82 16 20	on 5 0		
		10 12 11	Distance	99 34 10			
		10 13 18	"	99 34 30	on 3 50		10 58 45
		10 14 30	"	99 33 30			
		10 15 52	"	99 32 40			
		10 17 46	Jupiter Alt. ...	65 42 20			
		10 19 31	☾ Alt.	67 11 20	...	72·5	Planet E. of Moon.
		10 24 52	Jupiter Alt. ...	68 46 40	on 5 40		
		10 26 22	☾ Alt.	64 1 20	on 4 40		
		10 29 0	Distance	99 27 0			
		10 30 45	"	99 20 40	on 3 50		10 57 45
		10 32 7	"	99 26 40			
		10 33 45	"	99 20 40			

Date	Place	h	m	s	Observation	°	′	″	Index error	Therm.	h m s	Remarks
		10	35	34	☾ Alt.	50	32	10				
		10	37	4	Jupiter Alt. ...	93	59	20	...	72·2		Planet E. of Moon.
		10	57	30	Jupiter Alt. ...	102	28	20	on 6 0		11 8 30	
		10	59	5	☾ Alt.	48	5	20	on 5 0			
		11	1	0	Distance	90	15	10	on 3 10			
		11	2	26	,, ...	90	14	30				
		11	3	22	,, ...	90	14	20				
		11	4	33	,, ...	89	13	40				
		11	7	2	☾ Alt.	44	9	10				
		11	9	37	Jupiter Alt. ...	107	20	0	...	72·0		Planet E. of Moon.
June 7 ...	Mokaba	7	56	20	Regulus Alt. ...	92	7	20	on 3 40		11 34 45	
		7	59	25	☾ Alt.	88	46	20	on 17 20			
		8	0	48	Distance, nearest limb	90	30	0	on 2 30			
		8	4	13		90	32	10				
		8	6	41		90	32	20				
		8	7	5		90	32	30				
		8	8	58	☾ Alt.	92	29	30				
		8	11	52	Regulus Alt. ...	81	47	0	...	70·1		Star W. of Moon.
		8	15	0	Regulus Alt. ...	83	19	0	on 3 40		11 22 45	
		8	16	37	☾ Alt.	90	24	0	on 17 40			
		8	18	32	Distance, nearest limb	90	37	0	on 2 40			
		8	20	5		90	37	30				
		8	21	26		90	37	50				
		8	22	37		90	38	20				
		8	24	8	☾ Alt.	90	12	10				
		8	26	52	Jupiter Alt. ...	77	45	40	...	73·0		Star W. of Moon.

OBSERVATIONS FOR LUNAR DISTANCES.

Date.	Place.	Time.	Object.	Alt. and Distance.	Index Error.	Temp.	Resulting Longitude E.
1863		h m s		° ′ ″	′ ″	Fahr.	° ′ ″
June 7 ...	Mukaha (cont^{d}.)	8 29 0	Regulus Alt. ...	71 44 20	on 5 40		
		8 30 20	☾ Alt.	102 28 30	on 17 20		
		8 32 54	Distance	90 41 0			
		8 34 32	,, ...	90 42 0	on 2 30		11 59 0
		8 36 9	,, ...	90 42 10			
		8 37 21	,, ...	90 43 20			
		8 39 12	☾ Alt.	106 10 30			
		8 41 40	Regulus Alt. ...	70 35 0	...	74·3	Star W. of Moon.
		8 44 20	Regulus Alt. ...	63 24 40	on 8 0		
		8 46 8	☾ Alt.	100 19 40	on 17 40		
		8 47 40	Distance	90 46 40			
		8 49 58	,, ...	90 47 20	on 2 30		11 23 45
		8 51 30	,, ...	90 48 0			
		8 53 18	,, ...	90 48 50			
		8 55 14	☾ Alt.	113 14 20			
		9 0 32	Regulus Alt. ...	61 57 40	...	73·4	Star W. of Moon.
		9 13 30	☾ Alt.	120 40 0	on 9 0		
		9 15 0	Jupiter Alt. ...	63 43 0	on 17 30		
		9 16 32	Distance, farthest limb	30 36 0			
		9 18 13		28 16 10	on 3 30		11 20 15
		9 19 30		28 16 10			
		9 20 45		26 15 20			
		9 22 50	Jupiter Alt. ...	73 13 20			
		9 24 40	☾ Alt.	125 9 0	...	72·5	Planet E. of Moon.

Date	Place	h	m	s	Object	°	′	″	Index error	Temp.	Result
..		9	27	5	☾ Alt.	126	8	40	on 0 40		
		9	28	48	Jupiter Alt. ...	75	53	50	on 17 40		
		9	30	11	Distance, farthest limb	26	12	0	on 8 30		11 10 15
		9	31	41		26	12	0			
		9	33	20		26	10	40			
		9	36	10		26	10	0			
		9	37	51	Jupiter Alt. ...	79	52	30			
		9	43	5	☾ Alt.	132	8	40	...		Planet E. of Moon.
June 11 ...	Igoumbié	9	54	28	Jupiter Alt. ...	86	54	20	on 8 0	...	For time.
		9	56	40	.. ..	87	50	40			
		9	58	21	.. ..	88	34	30			
		10	4	15	Arcturus Alt...	130	40	0	on 8 0		
		10	6	43	.. ..	130	2	30			
		10	8	50	.. ..	129	32	20	...	71·6	
		11	25	8	Arcturus Alt...	97	23	50	on 8 30		
		11	26	34	.. ...	96	41	20			
		11	28	22	.. ...	90	2	50		73·4	
..		10	12	5	Jupiter Alt. ...	101	38	40	on 5 20		
		10	14	8	☾ Alt.	33	2	40	on 17 30		
		10	15	45	Distance, farthest limb	28	12	50	on 8 0		11 8 30
		10	17	27		28	13	10			
		10	18	38		28	14	10			
		10	19	50		28	15	10			
		10	21	35	☾ Alt.	36	35	20			
		10	43	20	Jupiter Alt. ...	118	38	20	...	73·4	Planet W. of Moon.

OBSERVATIONS FOR LUNAR DISTANCES.

Date.	Place.	Time.	Object.	Alt. and Distance.	Index Error.	Temp.	Remaining Longitude, E.
1865		h m s		° ′ ″	′ ″	Fahr.	° ′ ″
June 11...	Igoumbié (cont^d.)	10 43 11	Jupiter Alt. ...	114 42 0	on 6 0		
		10 51 10	☾ Alt.	70 9 30	on 17 10		
		10 52 35		28 29 0			
		10 54 30	Distance, farthest limb	28 29 10	on 8 30		11 28 30
		11 4 0		28 32 40			
		11 5 57		28 33 50			
		11 7 12	☾ Alt.	77 28 20			
		11 10 0	Jupiter Alt. ...	123 25 20	...	73·4	Planet W. of Moon.
„		11 11 48	Jupiter Alt. ...	124 0 0	on 6 0		
		11 13 25	☾ Alt.	80 20 0	on 17 40		
		11 14 47		28 38 0			
		11 15 54	Distance, farthest limb	28 37 30	on 3 40		11 23 45
		11 16 55		28 38 40			
		11 17 46		28 30 10			
		11 18 53	☾ Alt.	82 51 20			
		11 20 30	Jupiter Alt. ...	128 45 0	...	73·4	Planet W. of Moon.
		11 31 10	Jupiter Alt. ...	129 45 40	on 6 20		
		11 38 32	☾ Alt.	89 0 0	on 17 30		
		11 33 57		28 45 0			
		11 35 15	Distance, farthest limb	28 46 0	on 3 30		11 8 15
		11 30 20		28 46 30			
		11 37 5		28 47 10			

h	m	s	Object	°	′	″	Index error	Therm.	Result	Remarks
11	38	10	☾ Alt.	91	25	50				
11	41	53	Jupiter Alt. ...	132	27	0	...	73·0		Planet W. of Moon.
11	43	43	Jupiter Alt. ...	132	51	20	on 5 40			
11	45	13	☾ Alt.	94	43	20	on 17 20			
11	47	30	Distance, farthest limb	28	30	0	on 3 20		11 14 30	
11	49	11		28	51	10				
11	50	16		28	51	10				
11	51	15		28	52	10				
11	52	25	☾ Alt.	97	39	10				
11	54	47	Jupiter Alt. ...	135	10	20	...			Planet W. of Moon.
11	56	39	Jupiter Alt. ...	133	29	40	on 5 40			
11	58	17	☾ Alt.	100	30	10	on 17 30			
11	59	39	Distance, farthest limb	28	54	50	on 3 20		11 9 15	
12	1	2		28	55	30				
12	1	53		28	53	50				
12	2	47		28	56	0				
12	4	2	☾ Alt.	109	8	30				
12	6	16	Jupiter Alt. ...	133	52	0	...	72·8		Planet W. of Moon.
12	11	7	Jupiter Alt. ...	137	23	20	on 5 40			
12	12	40	☾ Alt.	106	37	30	on 17 40			
12	15	15	Distance, farthest limb	29	0	0	on 3 10		11 23 0	
12	16	20		29	0	20				
12	17	3		29	0	30				
12	18	4		29	1	10				
12	19	12	☾ Alt.	109	47	0	...	72·5		Planet W. of Moon.
			Jupiter Cloudy.							

OBSERVATIONS FOR LUNAR DISTANCES.

Date.	Place.	Time.	Object.	Alt. and Distance.	Index Error.	Temp.	Resulting Longitude, E.
1865		h m s		° ′ ″	′ ″	Fahr.	° ′ ″
June 30...	Nictubroad ...	10 51 20	Antares Alt. ...	120 13 20			
		10 53 38	,, ...	123 43 10	on 3 30		For time.
		10 55 10	,, ...	125 21 30			
		10 59 4	Vega Alt. ...	91 56 30			
		11 2 18	,, ...	92 29 40	on 3 20		
		11 3 30	,, ...	92 42 30			
		11 5 44	,, ...	93 4 20	...	67·6	
		8 56 9	Jupiter Alt. ...	104 0 0	on 7 20		
		8 58 2	☾ Alt.	90 18 0	on 17 40		
		8 59 40	Distance... ...	76 43 20			
		9 2 0	,, ...	76 43 10	on 3 30		11 23 0
		9 2 40	,, ...	76 42 30			
		9 3 40	,, ...	76 42 10			
		9 4 35	☾ Alt.	86 53 20			
		9 7 23	Jupiter Alt. ...	108 44 20	...	69·2	Planet E. of Moon.
		9 9 0	Jupiter Alt. ...	109 15 40	on 7 0		
		9 10 15	☾ Alt.	84 17 30	on 17 40		
		9 11 40	Distance... ...	76 40 0			
		9 13 20	,, ...	76 39 40	on 3 40		11 44 45
		9 14 24	,, ...	76 39 40			
		9 15 34	,, ...	76 39 0			
		9 17 1	☾ Alt.	81 0 0			
		9 18 44	Jupiter Alt. ...	113 3 40	...	69·6	Planet E. of Moon.

9	28	44	Jupiter Alt. ...	110	47	20	on 6	30				
9	30	23	☾ Alt.	74	25	10	on 18	0				
9	32	0	Distance	76	33	20						
9	33	9	,, ...	76	32	10	on 8	30		11	42	15
9	34	8	,, ...	76	31	40						
9	35	10	,, ...	76	31	30						
9	36	16	☾ Alt.	71	30	0						
9	37	56	Jupiter Alt. ...	120	6	40	...		68·4	Planet E. of Moon.		
9	40	23	Jupiter Alt. ...	120	57	40	on 6	0				
9	41	48	☾ Alt.	68	40	40	on 18	0				
9	43	29	Distance	76	28	40						
9	44	44	,, ...	76	28	10	on 8	30		11	57	15
9	46	9	,, ...	76	28	10						
9	47	4	,, ...	76	27	40						
0	48	24	☾ Alt.	65	31	20						
9	51	0	Jupiter Alt. ...	121	27	20	...		68·0	Planet E. of Moon.		
9	58	8	☾ Alt.	60	30	0	on 6	40				
10	0	12	Jupiter Alt. ...	127	20	0	on 18	0				
10	2	39	Distance	76	22	20						
10	4	5	,, ...	76	19	50						
10	6	5	,, ...	76	20	20	on 3	30		12	4	0
10	6	56	,, ...	76	20	0						
10	7	32	,, ...	76	19	40						
10	9	20	Jupiter Alt. ...	129	36	20						
10	11	27	☾ Alt.	54	22	20	...		68·0	Planet E. of Moon.		

OBSERVATIONS FOR LUNAR DISTANCES.

Date.	Place.	Time.	Object.	Alt. and Distance.	Index Error.	Temp.	Resulting Longitude, E.
1863		h m s		° ′ ″	′ ″	Fahr.	° ′ ″
July 5 ...	Mongon	9 21 20	Jupiter Alt. ...	121 27 10			
		9 23 30	.. ...	122 12 30	on 8 30		
		9 24 47	.. ...	122 38 20			
		9 29 45	α Centauri Alt.	62 30 20			
		9 31 38	.. ...	62 27 0	on 8 30		For time.
		9 33 49	.. ...	62 10 0			
..		8 10 25	Spica Alt. 7 ...	132 10 40	on 10 0		
		8 13 13	☾ Alt.	125 9 0	on 10 0		
		8 14 31	Distance	47 48 20			
		8 16 0	.. ..	44 49 50	on 8 50		12 24 0
		8 17 35	.. ..	44 49 0			
		8 18 28	.. ..	44 50 0			
		8 20 56	☾ Alt.	128 5 20			
		8 23 40	Spica Alt. ...	126 20 0	...	71·6	Star W. of Moon.
		8 27 32	Spica Alt. ...	124 28 40	on 9 40		
		8 30 18	☾ Alt.	131 25 20	on 9 40		
		8 32 25	Distance	44 51 0			
		8 33 41	.. ..	44 53 30	on 8 30		12 7 30
		8 34 47	.. ..	44 53 40			
		8 35 40	.. ..	44 56 40			

8	37	26	☾ Alt.	133	36	20					
8	40	52	Spica Alt. ...	122	9	20	...			71·6	Star W. of Moon.
8	44	22	Spica Alt. ...	125	23	40	on	0	10		
8	47	10	☾ Alt.	187	0	20	on	0	10		
8	48	32	Distance	45	10	0					
8	50	4	,, ...	45	0	10	on	3	40		12 7 30
8	51	7	,, ...	45	0	10					
8	52	25	,, ...	45	0	40					
8	54	32	☾ Alt.	139	18	40					
8	57	17	Spica Alt. ...	110	14	20	...			71·2	Star W. of Moon

Note.—There is an error in the third observation of Spica Altitude.

The resulting latitudes, longitudes, and heights have been all calculated by Edwin Dunkin, Esq., of Greenwich Observatory.

HEIGHTS OF STATIONS.

Date.		Stations.	Aneroid. No. 1.		Aneroid. No. 2.		Boiling Point. No. 71.	Boiling Point. No. 72.	Temp.	Remarks.
1864							°	°	Fahr.	
Sept.	28	At sea-level	29	0[illegible]	30	0[illegible]	212[illegible]	212[illegible]	80	
Oct.	26	Goumbi hill (place of observation)	29	5	29	9	211[illegible]	211[illegible]	79	
	26	Goumbi (back hill-top)	29	4	29	8	..	..	79	
	28	River-level, Niembai (junction with Ovenga)	29	5	29	9	..	..	83	
	31	River-level, Ovenga (junction with Ofoubou)	29	5[illegible]	30	0	211[illegible]	212	85	
Nov.	1	.. ..	29	0[illegible]	30	0[illegible]	212	211[illegible]	73	
	4	.. ..	29	4[illegible]	29	9	..	..	86	
	12	.. ..	29	7	30	1[illegible]	..	..	82	
	12	Hill-top, back of Obindji	29	4[illegible]	29	8[illegible]	211[illegible]	211?	82	Lid shut 211[illegible], 211[illegible].
	12	River-level, Obindji (observation)	29	5[illegible]	30	0	..	..	77	The observation on Nov. 12, of the boiling-point thermometer No. 72, has not been used.
	18	Hill-top, back of Obindji	29	8	29	7[illegible]	..	..	67	
	19	River-bank, Obindji	29	5[illegible]	30	0[illegible]	..	..	81	
	17	Nomba Rigoubou	29	2[illegible]	29	0[illegible]	..	..	80	
	20	Olenda	29	1	29	5	..	..	78	
	24	Nchounda	29	0	29	4	..	..	62	
	24	.. ..	28	0[illegible]	29	3[illegible]	..	..	78	
	26	Olenda	28	0[illegible]	29	3[illegible]	210[illegible]*	210[illegible]*	82	
Dec.	1	On the road	29	2	29	6	..	..	77	
	2	Opangano	29	0[illegible]	29	4[illegible]	..	..	83	
	2	Lambengué	29	1[illegible]	29	5[illegible]	..	..	79	

	3	Louvendji	29 1½	29 5½	..	..	81
	7	Laba	29 1½	29 8½	..	..	82
	8	"	29 3½	29 7½	..	..	78
	9	Nagoshi	29 3	29 7½	..	..	82
	9	Fougamou	29 2¾	29 7	..	..	83
	13	Dihaou village	29 3¾	29 7¾	..	..	79
	13	"	29 3¾	29 7¾	211½*	211¾*	80
	15	"	29 1½	29 6½	..	..	83
1865							
April	2	Máyolo	29 1½	29 0½	..	..	77
May	31	Nchiengain...	29 4¾	29 8¾	..	..	73
June	3	Rembo, Nchiengain	29 2¼	29 8½	..	..	80
	7	Mokaba	29 2¼	29 7¼	..	..	82
	10	Njavi plantation	29 0½	29 8½	..	..	70
	10	Dogoundou	29 1¾	29 0¾	..	..	70
	11	Igoumbié	29 2½	29 7½	..	..	73
	12	On the road	29 3½	29 8½	..	..	80
	13	Yengué	29 3	29 8	..	..	75
	15	"	29 2½	29 6	..	..	84
	17	Mokenga	28 8¾	29 3¾	211$\frac{1}{12}$	..	80
	22	On the road	28 9	29 4	..	..	77

* This may be 211¾ and 211½ : Aneroids will show which are the right ones.

HEIGHTS OF STATIONS.

Date.	Stations.	Aneroid. No. I.		Aneroid. No. II.		Boiling Point. No. 11.	Boiling Point. No. 12.	Temp.	Remarks.
		″	‴	″	‴	°	°	Fahr.	
1863 June 21	Madombo	28 28	3 5	28 29	8 0	211 1/16	211¼	75	
24	On the road	28 28	2 0¾	28 28	7 3¼	..	..	...	
25	Olako	28	1⅛	28	6¼	..	..	72	
26	Njavi and Ashango village	28	1½	28	6¼	..	..	73	
27	Niembouai	27	7¼	28	1¼	208¾	..	69	
July 5	Ouano river	28	3¾	28	8	..	..	73	
5	On the road, top of hill	27	7¼	28	2	..	..	73	
5	Mogiama	27	3¾	27	8¼	..	..	73	
5	Mongon	27	1¼	27	6⅛	..	..	71	
8	Birogou Bouanga	27	0⅛	27	5⅛	207½	..	69	
13	Mobana	27	2⅛	27	7⅛	..	..	69	
21	Mouaou Kombo	27	5¼	28	0	..	..	69	

SYNOPSIS OF RESULTS.

By Edwin Dunkin, Esq., F.R.A.S., *Superintendent of the Altazimuth Department, Royal Observatory, Greenwich.*

After discussing the foregoing observations, and taking into consideration that there is always a considerable difference between the results determined from East stars and those determined from West stars, I have concluded that the final results are as under :—

Name of Station.	Adopted Latitude, South.			Adopted Longitude, East.			Height above Sea-level by	
							Barometer.	Boiling Water.
	°	′	″	°	′	″	Feet.	Feet.
Goumbi, about 40 ft. above river	1	35	34		...		143	179
,, (back hill-top)		...			...		238	...
Junction of Niembai with Ovenga	1	38	23		...		143	...
Junction of Ofoubou with Ovenga	1	36	14		...		39	55
Hill-top, back of Obindji ...		...			...		258	208
River-level, Obindji		...			...		54	...
Nomba, Rigoumbou		...			...		369	...
Olenda	1	44	22	10	30	34	520	...
Nchonda		...			...		613	...
"On the road"		...			...		429	...
Ojanganoo...		...			...		553	...
Lambengué		...			...		478	...
Louvendji		...			...		490	...
Lulu		...			...		383	...
Mandji	1	16	26		...		...	...
Nagoshi		...			...		322	...
Fougamou		...			...		347	...
Dibaou (Ofogal)	1	21	3		...		323	326
Máyolo	1	51	14	11	0	37	493	...
Nchiengain	1	51	10	11	14	35	325	...
Mokaba	1	58	20	11	21	51	414	...
Njavi plantation		...			...		610	...
Dogoundou		...			...		473	...

Name of Station.	Adopted Latitude, North.			Adopted Longitude, East.			Height above Sea-level by	
	°	′	″	°	′	″	Barometer.	Boiling Water.
							Feet.	Feet.
Igoumbié	1	59	22	11	25	0	410	...
"On the road"		...			...		305	...
Yengué	2	0	49		...		369	...
Mokenga	2	1	9		...		530	508
"On the road"		...			...		738	...
Mulombo		...			...		1220	...
"On the road"		...			...		1186	...
Olako		...			...		1480	...
Njavi and Ashango village ...		...			...		1481	...
Niembouai	1	58	54	11	50	38	1883	1910
Ouano river		...			...		1283	...
"On the road"		...			...		1908	...
Mogiama		...			...		2204	...
Mongon	1	56	45	12	9	57	2488*	...
Birogou-Bouanga		...			...		2571	...
Mobana	1	52	50		...		2309	...
Mouaon Kombo		...			...		2074	...

* By my own calculation of the boiling-point of water observation, the altitude is 3433 feet.

NOTE.—The apparent discrepancy in the relative height of places near the sea-level arises principally from the fact that the method of observation usually adopted is not sufficiently accurate for the determination of low elevations. The variation in the pressure of the atmosphere during the interval between the observations made on different days at two or more stations, may cause a discordance of several hundred feet, unless a correction be applied for the amount of the variation. The only way to obtain this correction is to have corresponding barometric observations statedly made near the sea, or at a station of known altitude. By this means we obtain materials for correcting the observed barometric readings, or of those deduced from the boiling-point thermometer. In practice, however, it has been found impossible for travellers in the interior of a continent to be assisted in this manner; consequently all heights of African stations lately published, determined from similar observations, are liable to an uncertainty ranging from ± 200 feet, on account of this constant varying pressure of the atmosphere. From this it can be easily seen that the absolute and relative heights of stations on a river near the sea-level, must be subject to apparent inconsistencies, or at least to irregularities, if the observations be faithfully made and computed.

Edwin Dunkin.

APPENDIX

COMPARATIVE TABLE OF WORDS IN SEVERAL

English.	*Commi.*	*Bakalai, or Bakèlè.*	*Apono, Ashira, Ashango.*
sun	kombé	diobo	dioumbi
moon	ogouailli	gondai	soungui
star	igaigaini	yiatéli	bouailoli
clouds	pindi	diti	dimangou
water	aningo	madiba	mamba
rain	...	mbouio	founa
river	mbéné	abouion	rombo
fire	ogoni	yéijo	rôhi
prairie	olobi	soungou	kvamou
firewood	coni	yéijo	maisandjou
warm	topiou	mbédjé	hagama
cold	ifou	diyebé	yiole
I eat	mi uia	...	...
face	ouma jiou	braba	ozo
nose	mjoumbo	diolo	mbaalo
mouth	ogouaua	gomano	moun
ears	arouille	baolé	maro
head	ounajiou	moolé	morou
hair	étoué	longo	manga
body	onnova	nlolo	niona
arm	ogogo	mbo	miogo
leg	ngolo	nkodo	quero
hand	ago	dikoundjou, bongo	difaho
wife	ouinto	...	...
finger	nlongou	ino	milembo
nail	...	nialo	niala
foot	nchoujou	dibo	ditambi
eyes	intobo	miabi	disho
beard	etoué	dilédou	miniomi
chin	...	nkéhé	gandou
woman	ouinto	mouniadi	mogauto
man	olome	molomo	dibagala
teeth	ano	masbrongou	bei
mother	ngouai	miaouon	ngouya
fowls	njogoni	coaha	makobo
goat	mboni	ambodo	étava

III.

LANGUAGES OF WESTERN EQUATORIAL AFRICA.

Mpovi.	*Njavi.*	*Ishogo.*	*Obongo.*
akombé	ditati	kombé	dioumbi.
nshoungui	esungui	gondai	soungui.
milanga	fouelila	motanga	nèchi.
epindi	...	oba.	
manba	manba	mamba	manba.
boula	foula	bosa.	
mbono	mbali	bei.	
iko	...	shoto	rouai.
...	...	motobé.	
koni	biandjou	ezako	biandjou.
pion	lvionvion	edionkou.	
esholi	moshou	sholi.	
nai nia	mésouchu.		
oso	mbousbou	ozô.	
pambo	mbashou	opambo	djiou.
moula	mounou	moula	mogma.
metro	itougué	lato, or éato	diarou.
mosbo	monshoué	moshé	mourou.
shogué	shougui	shogué	uchoasie.
djiolo	niolo	mokoula.	
mogo	igogo	ogogo.	
makodo	igolo	okolo.	
mizavi	lokaka	dikaka	miemba, or miemba.
...	...	...	moumito.
niougo	moshèvi	mizavi.	
diata	niadia, niadi	diata.	
ékaka	mutambi	etambé	itambi.
misho	misho	misho	mishou.
yiéiou	daidou	kaidou.	
...	...	édèko.	
moguelo	mogashou	moguelo	mokasho.
moboune	moumogo	mómógô	bagala.
...	...	mino.	
agia	mamo	mohota.	
shoan	mekoko.		
étava	lava	étava	étava.

English.	*Commi.*	*Bakalai, or Bakele.*	*Apono, Ashira, Aisingo.*
plantain	orondo	ako	dicondai, or digondai
father	rirlo, tata	ahouro	tata
one	mori	lévoto	moshi
two	mbani	bêba	bëi
three	raro	bilali	irero
four	nai	benaï	irano
five	tani	bitani	samano
six	rona	na kuoto	irana
seven	roigenum	bitani nabiba	kumbo moshi
eight	ananaï	bitani nabilali	kumbo bëi
nine	enougoume	bitani na benaï	...
ten	igoume	dioum	igoum
oil	agali	...	maali
house	nago	alaouen	...
dog	mboa	...	bouandi
tobacco	tako	talaco	...
lamp	ilambe	...	...
pipe	ozo	...	...
palm wine	mimbo	madouma - mbila	malamou - samba
plantain wine	...	madouma - mooo	malamou-maishi
girl	omana nento	mngaito	mouana
boy	omana olome	mosengo.	
king, chief	oga	mpounou	madomba
antelope	kambi	kambi	kambi
parrot	nguzo	coche	cosso
fish	...	basho	niama
fowl	njogoni	couba	coco
eggs	aqué	magne	maqué
iron	obo, mianga	doubandja	doubandja
slave	shaka	shako	movega
freeman	nchié	nahé	foumou
sugar-cane	esuu	counqui	...
ground-nut	bénda	bénda	fenda
cassada	ogouasiga	mondo	digongo
bullock	niaré	niaché	pagasa.
honey	olembai	bio	bouya
I go	mikenda	mako-mo	magnonendo
morning	ibanga	macoumdiché	ngouali makali
evening	nombo	angolomé	nalishiga
night	ogonaibe	rabouai	dibéti

Mpovi.	*Njavi.*	*Ishogo.*	*Obongo.*
makondo	mako	ocondou	diondi.
... ...	tato	teta.	
... ...	mo	mpoco	mou.
... ...	bioli	mbani	bei.
... ...	bitato	tebaro	metato.
... ...	bina	loaï	djimabougo.
... ...	bitano	itani	djio.
... ...	mamouna	morobu	samouna.
... ...	mabo	... ...	nobima.
... ...	pombo	... ...	misamouno.
... ...	ona	... ...	nchouma.
... ...	goumi	... ...	mbò-ta.
... ...	medi	miandé.	
... ...	nobo	afba	aboubou.
... ...	... ...	... ...	bouendi.
... ...	... ...	... ...	mbolo.
... ...	... ...	... ...	ilamba.
... ...	... ...	... ...	moho.
... ...	... ...	maguembadi - madonou.	
...	...	madoucou-macondo.	
...	...	mouanengué.	
... ...	... ...	pai.	
... ...	... ...	molanga.	
... ...	... ...	ngosho.	
... ...	... ...	niama miagombei.	
... ...	... ...	nchóaho.	
... ...	... ...	magué.	
... ...	... ...	merago.	
... ...	... ...	movéga.	
kounwa	... ...	koumou.	
... ...	... ...	momoo.	
... ...	... ...	benda.	
... ...	... ...	ndjoume.	
... ...	... ...	oubou.	
... ...	... ...	...	mia kaij.
makiakia	maguelo	diko.	
... ...	... ...	shiti.	

LONDON: PRINTED BY W. CLOWES AND SONS, STAMFORD STREET,
AND CHARING CROSS.

www.ingramcontent.com/pod-product-compliance
Lightning Source LLC
Chambersburg PA
CBHW031938290426
44108CB00011B/598
* 9 7 8 3 7 4 1 1 2 7 6 6 3 *